CITIZENSHIP IN
QUESTION

WITHDRAWN
FROM
COLLECTION

WITHDRAWN
FROM
COLLECTION

CITIZENSHIP IN QUESTION

EVIDENTIARY BIRTHRIGHT AND STATELESSNESS

BENJAMIN N. LAWRANCE &
JACQUELINE STEVENS, EDITORS

Duke University Press • Durham and London • 2017

© 2017 Duke University Press
All rights reserved
Printed and bound by CPI Group (UK) Ltd, Croydon, CR0 4YY
Interior design by Courtney Leigh Baker
Typeset in Garamond Premier Pro and Scala Sans

Library of Congress Cataloging-in-Publication Data
Names: Lawrance, Benjamin N. (Benjamin Nicholas), editor. |
Stevens, Jacqueline, [date] editor.
Title: Citizenship in question : evidentiary birthright and statelessness /
Benjamin N. Lawrance and Jacqueline Stevens, editors.
Description: Durham : Duke University Press, 2016. |
Includes bibliographical references and index.
Identifiers:
LCCN 2016026992 (print)
LCCN 2016028137 (ebook)
ISBN 9780822362807 (hardcover : alk. paper)
ISBN 9780822362913 (pbk. : alk. paper)
ISBN 9780822373483 (e-book)
Subjects: LCSH: Citizenship. | Statelessness. | Asylum, Right of. |
Belonging (Social psychology)—Political aspects.
Classification: LCC JF801.C573525 2016 (print) | LCC JF801 (ebook) |
DDC 323.6—dc23
LC record available at https://lccn.loc.gov/2016026992

COVER ART: Documents from the files of the Deportation Research Clinic,
Northwestern University. Published with permission.

Dedicated to the memory of
JOHANN "ACE" FRANCIS, 1979–2013,
and to the millions of people struggling to prove
who they are and questioning the law
for its betrayed promises of peace, dignity, and justice.

CONTENTS

PREFACE: ACE'S STORY

The following is a keynote address by Johann "Ace" Francis, a U.S. citizen wrongfully deported for ten years to Jamaica, delivered at the "Citizenship-in-Question" symposium, Boston College Law School, April 19, 2012. Explanatory remarks in square brackets were inserted from Skype interviews with Mr. Francis by Jacqueline Stevens on December 21, 2009.

Just being here, in something like this, is huge. I wrote a speech, but it's hard to capture ten years of one's life. You might be asking yourself, how could someone get in a situation like this? I was born in Jamaica, but I grew up in Washington State. My stepfather was in the military so I was in a military family. And we moved all over the country. I moved there [to Washington] when I was seven. When you grow up and you think of yourself as an American, you really don't think otherwise, or to go to immigration when you are fourteen years old [the year his mother naturalized, thus automatically conferring on Ace his U.S. citizenship]. I bought a car when I was sixteen. And then when I was eighteen, I got in trouble. It was spring break and we went to Oregon.

I was in high school, ready to graduate, and my mother moved to Georgia. I said, okay, I'll move down with her when I graduate. But, I lost her phone number. We didn't have cell phones then. And I lost my pager. I was on a trip to Oregon, [to] a town called Seaside. A lot of people [were there] on spring break. Two girls in a convertible (two white females) were in this parking lot. My friends started talking to them. Their boyfriends were pulling in. They were drinking on the back of a pick-up and came up hostile. Everybody got in the fight. The police came up and everyone was trying to leave. When they came around, there were four of them on top of me in the corner.

I'm in an area where the police know the families of the kids. They [the district attorney] came to me and said, "Thirty-six months. This is the best we can do." I have no family. Hey, thirty-six months, are you crazy? This was a fight, but "if you go to trial and you lose you're going to get five to seven years," they told me. I served time in a boot camp program. I was proud that I graduated. On graduation day, I was told that I couldn't leave because I have this INS hold. I said, "I thought I was a U.S. citizen." They said, "Can you prove it?" To tell you honestly, I didn't know if I was a U.S. citizen. I told them how I came [to the United States], with my mother. But when they said, "When did she get her U.S. citizenship?" I couldn't answer. They shipped me to Arizona. To Eloy. They flew me to Las Vegas and from there drove me to Eloy [Detention Center].

So my mother's looking for me in Washington State. By the time she found out that I was in jail, I'm in [an immigration jail in] Arizona. She was looking for me in Oregon, but by the time she found out I was in Arizona, I'm already in Jamaica.

At Eloy Detention Center

I didn't know I was supposed to see a judge. I waited three months. I never actually saw the judge until I was deported. To tell you the truth, when I went in front of the judge he didn't ask me any questions. When I spoke with the judge, as a matter of fact, there was no question and answer, so I didn't talk to the judge. "You're deported forever," he said. That was really tragic. I talked to the guy there who handed me the papers and I spoke with the guards on numerous occasions and tried to get in contact with my mother. And the system is kinda set up to the fact that you don't really get to explain things. I'm eighteen and I work at Taco Bell. You have no money for a lawyer. I was waiting to try to prove I was a U.S. citizen and I was waiting to get in touch with my family. There were people waiting there [at Eloy] two years. I decided I was going to go along with it. What they do is if you can't prove you're right [that you are a citizen], you're deported. The demand is on you to prove your current situation. And really at that point in time, I was just a scared child who really didn't know where to go or where to turn.

[Seeing the judge] was like an aftermath thing. I [had] already signed everything. It was more [like] him telling me what I did, and [then] based on what you did, you are deportable and you know that. It wasn't an investigative conversation to understand who is in front of him. More of a telling you that, "Okay, we know what you did, and you did wrong, and you're not a U.S. citizen, and you're going to be deported, and you signed this sheet of paper [agreeing to deportation]."

So I got to Jamaica [redacted], 1999. On my birthday. That was so bittersweet. I'm released there. I slept on the bench at Kingston International Airport. They had a little police department, and I went there and said I got deported and they said, "What?!" Really, what they did was kicked me out the door. I spent that night on the bench, with the mosquitoes biting me. I was happy that I was out of the facility [Eloy].

My mother didn't know I was in Jamaica. I spent one year [in Jamaica] when I was fifteen and my mother brought me to my father [who never had custody and is not listed on Ace's birth certificate], and that's how I knew how to get in contact with him. My father has thirteen kids, and I'm the only one that is in the U.S. That was so lucky. My father got in contact with my mother. "Wow, we've been looking for you!" It was a sigh of relief that I wasn't dead or hurt somewhere. That's the first time hearing my mother's voice again. . . . It was almost painful. I didn't cry but I was alone. I'm from Jamaica but there are no Jamaicans in Washington State. I didn't have any family, no auntie or uncle. All I knew were my mother and sister, and moving to Jamaica, there wasn't even that.

I was living in the house where my father grew up, a rural area near the airport. It's really the woods, where people still have outside bathrooms. For breakfast I'd get up and go in the bush and drink coconuts. It's so amazing what you can do with a coconut. You can make oil, there's fresh meat, milk. You drink two, you'll be filled up. Before it's a coconut it's called jelly. It's actually soft in the middle. I lived off of jelly coconuts. The land also had sugarcane. That's not really a well-balanced diet. The house had holes in the floor and ceiling. When it rained too much you've got to set up buckets. It's the most primitive living you can think about.

In high school I had a personality. I was the [TV] anchor. I was the guy who ran for president. Moving [with my mother to Georgia] was not an option for me. I was very popular. I had that spark, always trying to make something out of nothing. I'm five foot seven and played basketball. I started my own basketball clinic in the local area. I don't have any work so I would go to whatever shops and ask them to sponsor my team, and really that was mostly for uniforms and the rest of the money was for dinner.

The worst thing about it [being in Jamaica] was I couldn't say my name is Johann and I've been deported from the U.S. and I'm a citizen. Those people who are deported, [they] are outcasts. They are looked down upon. You had your chance and you blew it. Why should I help you now? The first couple of years were really hard because I still had an American accent. I had to come up with a story about how I went to school there but I'm back here. I'm still going with that story up to this day.

That was a mental drain. Those first four years were very difficult for me because I had an accent and I was unable to speak Jamaican without the accent. I've been constantly somebody else. I think three people knew my true story. I don't know if you know psychology, but when you hear a foreign person that speaks another language and when they get upset they start speaking that language; it's an expression of themselves and who they are, and they relate better speaking the language they know, and feel frustrated speaking a language they don't know. That's me for ten years. In the seventh or eighth year I started associating myself with other deportees for the sake of being home in America. That was so weird. I could relate to them whether I was a citizen or not. I could relate to them. I told one or two of them the truth because you wanted to talk to somebody. You want to tell your story.

I figured it out about my seventh or eighth year. My mother told me. She was under the assumption that I was unnaturalized and then deported. Up to last night I had to explain it to her. No, I didn't get unnaturalized. They made a huge mistake. She was under the impression that there was nothing that could be done. And I didn't know. I only listened to what the judge told me. And the judge told me never to return.

I didn't know or understand the whole law. I knew they weren't supposed to, but they did. I signed the papers. It's my fault and the judge said never to return [Ace starts crying]. I have nightmares. I could have stayed in there. . . .

The system down there [in Jamaica] is so bad. They're just putting medical and birth certificates on computer records. Everything before was manual. They're checking records thirty years back. I filed on three different occasions to get [my birth certificate, the first document in the U.S. government file for Ace from when he entered as a child]. I needed a birth certificate number. [In 2009 the Jamaican government] started an online program where they'll look for your number for you, and somebody called me and provided a number. I was so happy. I really didn't have any identification. I had to be very creative just getting a tax number so I can work [in Jamaica]. All my IDs are from my work IDs.

[Until obtaining the birth certificate] I was unable to prove who I was. I could prove who my mother was, but I couldn't prove who I was. This was the first valid identification I've had in ten years. When I got it, I told myself, this is the prettiest piece of paper I've seen.

Back in the United States

[After I arrived at the Miami airport, on December 24, 2009], Homeland [Security] stopped me. You go through the checkpoint, and they asked me how I am, and I said I was good and gave them my passport. He was looking at the computer, staring with a confused look, like he didn't know what to think or do. "What kind of trouble have you been in?" I said, "I got something better for you." I pulled out the papers [the consular officer in Jamaica gave him in a sealed envelope, in case there was a problem]. I said, "They deported a citizen." He said, "They can't do that."

I'm scared, really. I'm keeping notes, and I kid you not, the simplest thing stirs so much emotion. You hear the buzz from the hot water, coming back home, my first hot shower. The water smells different. I've been away for so long. It's like if you haven't eaten salt for ten years and someone gives you, like, a chimichanga.

Mr. Francis lived in the Atlanta area and worked at Atlanta's Hartsfield-Jackson Airport as a manager for a company that sells credit cards on behalf of an airline. He was heartbroken about the ten years he felt he lost, from nineteen to twenty-nine, especially for the missed educational opportunities: "maybe not a Boston College education, but an education somewhere," he told the audience. Mr. Francis died of cancer in early 2013.

ACKNOWLEDGMENTS

This volume reflects important collaborations beyond those of the coeditors, Benjamin Lawrance and Jacqueline Stevens, who first conceived of the project at a dinner party in Berkeley, California, in 2009. Comparing experiences outside academia, Lawrance as an expert witness and Stevens as an investigative journalist, they noted similarities in their encounters with people struggling to prove their identity and citizenship. Conversations with Dan Kanstroom, Rachel Rosenbloom, and Rogers Smith, all of whom have expertise at different edges of the overlap between citizenship law and theory, ultimately led to the five of us convening a symposium.

The chapters in this volume came out of "Citizenship-in-Question: Evidentiary Challenges to *Jus Soli* and Autochthony from *Authenticité* to 'Birtherism,'" an event hosted by Dan Kanstroom at Boston College Law School and the Boston College Center for Human Rights and International Justice in April 2012. The symposium and publication of this volume were made possible with generous support from the Conable Endowment in International Studies, the Program in International and Global Studies, and the Department of Sociology and Anthropology, in the College of Liberal Arts, at the Rochester Institute of Technology (RIT); the Boston College Center for Human Rights and International Justice, of Boston College Law School; the University of Pennsylvania Program on Democracy, Citizenship, and Constitutionalism; and Northeastern Law School.

We would like to thank many individuals who were involved at various stages in the collaborative process leading to the publication of this book, including (alphabetically), Peter Agree, Aaron Belkin, Rebecca Biron, Israel Brown, Barbara Buckinx, Charlie Bush, Jennifer Chacón, Elizabeth Cohen, Dalton Conley, Beverly Crawford, Roberto Dominguez, Alexandra Filindra, Mark Fleming, Jeremy Haefner, Jacqueline Hagan, David Hollenbach, Ann Howard, Dan Kowalski,

Dani Kranz, Christine Kray, David Leal, Uli Linke, Haiming Lui, Mark Lyttle, Alexandra Margalith, James Martel, Siobhán Mullally, Erik Owens, Rhacel Parreñas, Gerald Phelps, Andres and Maria Robles, Nestor Rodriguez, Vincent Rougeau, Andrea Saenz, Rogers Smith, Peter Spiro, Debbie Steene, Esteban Tiznado, Robert Ulin, Darshan Vigneswaran, Rose Cuison Villazor, Brian Watts, Mark C. Weber, and James Winebrake. We would particularly like to thank our friends and families for their patience, generosity of spirit, and limitless encouragement. Lawrance thanks the invaluable support of his invincible assistant, Cassandra Shellman. Stevens thanks attorney Andrew Free for his brilliant work litigating on behalf of detained and deported U.S. citizens encountered through her research and for procuring documents responsive to her requests under the Freedom of Information Act. She also thanks research assistants Charles Clarke, Horia Dijmarescu, and Hayley Hopkins. Manuscript preparation was supported by Weinberg College at Northwestern University.

We deeply appreciate the remarkable talents of Duke University Press, particularly Courtney Berger, Sandra Korn, and Liz Smith, as well as Rebecca Musselman for her index, and the insights of the readers, especially those of the final reviewer, whose attention to the manuscript initially and after its revisions significantly improved the final version.

We are indebted to Johann "Ace" Francis, who contacted Stevens by e-mail shortly before his return to the United States from ten years of wrongful exile. Though he did not live to see this volume's publication, he inspired us and lives in every page and every story.

INTRODUCTION

JACQUELINE STEVENS

Citizenship Studies and Ambiguities of the Ascriptive Citizen

Experiences such as those of Ace, a U.S. citizen deported from his own country at age nineteen, rarely receive public attention (see the preface to this volume). Ad hoc reporting by the news media tends to cover such incidents as idiosyncratic horrors inflicted by an inept officialdom on an unwitting, unlucky individual lacking the wherewithal to set the record straight. Readers or television viewers are led to believe that the events are anomalous errors amenable to correction. Stories such as ones titled "Wrongfully Deported American Home after 3 Month Fight" (Huus 2010) or "Texas Runaway Found Pregnant in Colombia after She Was Mistakenly Deported" (Dillon 2012) imply that if the individuals were more wealthy, or older, or just more articulate, or if the bureaucrat put some thought into her work, then such oddities would vanish altogether. The government would be using the legal definition of citizenship correctly, deporting only identifiable foreigners, and we would find our taxonomy of citizens, on one hand, and aliens, on the other, perfectly adequate for describing different populations.

One reason that these cases are not widely reported is that it is just as difficult for journalists to produce evidence of a subject's U.S. citizenship as it is for the citizens themselves. The putative citizen was not conscious at the moment of her citizenship's instantiation, and DNA databases are neither widespread nor transparent repositories of the truth. Testimony by mothers may not be available or may be dismissed as biased. In short, for its verification the status of citizenship has no independent eyewitnesses, just state documents and their government curators. The government can simply insist that the documents and databases it creates and controls prove a citizen's "alienage." Citizens thus are at the mercy of information the agency opposing them is creating, maintaining, and hiding from them (Stevens 2011a). This makes challenges to government classifications difficult or impossible. Moreover, earlier errors may render their discovery as such impossible. Differences between spellings or dates on a birth certificate and in a database may create a permanent problem for someone who is a legal citizen. Or the government simply may lie about, conceal, or fail to produce evidence that might vindicate an individual's claim to citizenship, such as when Thai officials assert DNA results disproving citizenship but do not share the medical report with the individuals affected, who in turn cannot challenge the foreign status the government assigns them (Flaim, chapter 8 of this volume). Thus, largely for reasons of practical obscurity, the conundrums of those denied citizenship have been marginal to prevailing theoretical and policy debates about citizenship and immigration.

The essays collected here take up the challenges posed by "citizenship in question," a phrase coined by coeditor Benjamin Lawrance. We use the term in two different senses. First, the chapters describe how states question the citizenship status of their own citizens. Second, as editors and contributors, we reflect on how the state renders its own citizens stateless to raise our own questions about citizenship as it is presently practiced. The following chapters describe and theorize the significance and meanings of governments mistaking their own citizens for foreigners. The authors also provide insights into the psychological causes and consequences of these systemic practices. Invisible to many scholars of migration and citizenship, these often liminal actions and possibilities illuminate concepts at the heart of citizenship.

Citizenship in Question: Evidentiary Birthright and Statelessness focuses attention on how states create and interrogate individuals' evidence of citizenship and considers the implications of the state's micro-level authorizations and revocations of this status for the concept of citizenship more generally. Some chapters focus on policies and data that reveal citizenship in question, for instance, Polly Price's review of the statistics on birthright citizenship policies and migration and birth patterns in South America that produce de jure citizenship and effective statelessness (chapter 1), or Jacqueline Bhabha's cross-country analysis of challenges facing the contemporary Roma (chapter 2). Others focus on the nuances of individual-level experiences in court cases or at the border. For instance, Benjamin Lawrance describes his experiences giving testimony on a possibly Portuguese asylum seeker in England via Togo (chapter 3). And Rachel Rosenbloom writes about U.S. children delivered by midwives in Texas and denied U.S. passports who then encounter internal border patrols in their own neighborhoods (chapter 7). The specific demands birthright citizenship may incite for evidence of ancestry or other *documentary* proof of birthright citizenship provoke reconsidering the concept of citizenship as presently understood. The chapters provide new and important descriptive contributions to citizenship studies and encourage retheorizing citizenship's core meanings.

In addition to exploring evidentiary challenges to proving citizenship, the essays in this collection describe effective statelessness and its consequences. This occurs when courts, relying on regional and international law, make documentary requirements so demanding that respondents cannot possibly meet them and are rendered stateless, bereft of their attendant rights under international law. As refugees from civil and regional wars in the Middle East and Africa seek asylum on a scale previously not contemplated, immigration offices and courts adjudicating their cases in Europe and North America will have their hands full deliberating forensic questions whose proper scrutiny would require teams of investigators spanning continents. Absent funds for such work, and amid episodic panics over terrorist infiltrators, inferences will be made based on quite literally flimsy evidence and guesswork. Crucially for this volume, such ordeals invite close attention to those features of citizenship that appear as a series of significations that begin with a registry and an identity card and end with people sorted into states staged as quasi-random boxes for the storage of those inspected. Often the documents send people to the locations that they prefer to inhabit, but sometimes they may be sent elsewhere because of confusions about their documented status, not their having the wrong one. Or documents may scatter people in the infinitely vast legal space that lies between these boxlike states. Even developments in international law responsive to the plight of the stateless (Szreter 2007) cannot rescue those who cannot prove what they are not, that is, not a citizen of any state or "stateless," any more than they can prove who they are.

The debate over whether to extend citizenship to undocumented residents or to further enhance barriers at the borders rages worldwide. This volume's contribution to such debates is to raise fundamental questions about whether the citizenship they are discussing actually exists. The ideology of citizenship assumes a stability not only of personal identity via documents and laws that assign citizenship but also of borders, as well as the coincidence of genetic, legal, and de facto families. Yet the authors here observe how personal identities are rendered indeterminate because of changes in documentation regimes, laws denoting citizenship, and a country's borders themselves. These studies of what might be called "administrative citizenship," that is, citizenship and alienage performed by officialdom, reveal instructive tensions between citizenship as an abstract concept and citizenship as operationalized. From Argentina to Australia, Togo to Thailand, regimes cannot reliably distinguish citizens from noncitizens. Such a discovery suggests the need to revisit attitudes and policies premised on viewing citizenship as categorical and easily observed.

The striking similarities in citizenship's (mis)recognitions across countries, the brutal consequences, and the high rate at which they are occurring suggest symptoms of underexplored qualities of the concept of citizenship. These events are symptomatic of key facts and meanings of citizenship and not merely aberrations of normal citizenship conventions. Moreover, the scope of such infelicities is much larger than usually recognized. In chapter 1, Polly Price points out that in Mexico alone, forty million births are not registered, causing problems for those who, through their parents' citizenship, automatically acquire U.S. citizenship at birth when born in Mexico but lack official paperwork and face questions about their legal identities. Kamal Sadiq describes the administrative processes that produce widespread effective statelessness in India and Malaysia (chapter 9). He and Amanda Flaim, in her work on Thailand (chapter 8), reveal that the very administrative regimes implemented to integrate unenumerated individuals into the state bureaucracy are actually removing them from political society and the welfare state altogether. Only after one is expected to have a piece of paper can one be judged for not having it.

The disparity between the rituals of administration and the facts of habituation—that people struggle to prove through and to a bureaucracy who they are in everyday life—invites reflection on the paradoxes of an identity that seems at once given and scripted, qualities captured by the concept of "ascriptive." According to the *Merriam-Webster* dictionary, "ascriptive" refers to "arbitrary placement (as at birth) in a particular social status."[1] The sense here is that ascription is something that is not chosen but happens to one because of social or political structures. In contrast, the etymology of "ascriptive" takes us to the ritual for individuals deliberately joining a political community. During the Roman Empire, cognates of *ascribere* referred to the first step of submitting one's name for the purpose of enrolling in a Roman colony, a process Latins could use to become Roman citizens (Smith 1954, 18).[2] The act of securing and performing their membership was their ascription to a particular group.

Ascriptive citizenship can be defined as an identity that can occur through writing. Or it can be defined as ontological, that is, given at birth, *as if* biologically.[3] These possibilities and their relation invite analyzing citizenship through tropes of deconstruction. The metonymic relation among citizenship's qualities as natural (from the Latin *nasci*, meaning "birth"), a legal identity, and an identity ascertained by writing suggests opportunities for reflecting on the meanings of their disruptions, paradoxes, and chaotic confusions. What if the events bringing citizenship's failures to the fore are not just burdens on the individual but revelations of how written ascription materializes, more or less completely, into that ascription experienced as given, as at birth? Susan Coutin, a scholar who has for years grappled at close range with documentary regimes and thus is familiar with the elusive and illusory truths of "real citizenship," writes: "Of course, 'real' [citizenship] is a problematic term, a point that suggests that distinctions between 'reality' and 'fiction' may be difficult to sustain. This difficulty arises not because law 'in action' differs from law 'on the books' but rather because by creating the domain of the undocumented, the unauthorized, and the 'as if,' law itself gives rise to its own violation, creating worlds that are governed both by law and by something else that is not law" (Coutin 2013, 112). Another way to represent citizenship's paper-thin and thick realities is as the materialization of legal words into things, along the lines celebrated by G. W. F. Hegel and complicated by Friedrich Nietzsche (see esp. Hegel 1967 [1821], §167, remark, and Nietzsche 1974 [1882, 1887], §58). Citizenship's propensity to include and exclude members, that is, national protagonists and antagonists, arbitrarily and the location of these modern operations in written, civil law are strong inducements to mobilize for citizenship's interpretation insights of deconstruction. The content as well suits the form, a method that emerged out of questioning deportations based on citizenship being stripped or denied by laws instantiating seemingly biological distinctions the laws themselves created.[4] Citizenship law lends itself to such interventions—to wit, Annette Appell's observation that "the birth certificate is proof of these facts [of age, sex, gender, nationality, race, and parents] (even when it is counterfactual)" (2014, 9). Citizenship's forensic (i.e., legal and public) evidence may be counterfactual to other records and testimonies, and the court findings using these incoherent documents for performing our citizenship are alerting us to something important about the construction of citizenship's contradictions and ambiguities.

By revealing the contingent, questionable documentary evidence constituting citizenship, these chapters convey the literary quality of legal membership. Drawing on insights from Derrida, they help us reflect on how citizens are textual creations materialized by the force of law (Derrida 1989–90). Perhaps the clearest evidence of the force of identity documents and their dangers is concern about fraud. Defenses against documents misconstrued as deceptive suggest an autoimmune response. To keep out unwanted invaders, the sovereign attacks its own community, more or less indiscriminately. Benjamin Lawrance (chapter 3), Beatrice McKenzie (chapter 6), Rachel Rosenbloom (chapter 7), and Kamal Sadiq (chapter 9) reveal hardships entailed by vigilance about fraud that is overzealous or animated by prejudice. Crucially, this collection problematizes Hannah Arendt's famous assertion about the protections citizenship affords us that humanity does not (Arendt 2007b [1943], 273) and suggests qualities of citizenship akin to Plato's *pharmakon* (Derrida 1981b [1968], esp. 100–101). Just as writing more generally is a pharmakon that has qualities of a cure and poison, citizenship, meaning citizenship as certified, may be beneficial and also itself harmful.

Ace's U.S. citizenship—a source of protection and of danger—derived from his mother's naturalization and is an arbitrary placement (as at birth). This would be true as well were he a U.S. citizen by birth in the United States. This also would bestow citizenship on him by means of an "arbitrary placement (as at birth)" through jus soli (law of soil). And the same holds were he to have become a U.S. citizen at birth outside the United States to parents who were U.S. citizens, through jus sanguinis (law of blood).[5] These legal terms of art used throughout this collection convey the ambiguities of citizenship as inherently legal and scripted—on and from a map or a family tree, paradigmatically of children born in the legally fashioned relation of wedlock—and also as signifying the phenomenology of preliterate, material facts of soil and blood.[6]

In modernity, citizenship is the cornerstone of any political society as a membership organization, and it is the quintessential ascriptive form of being, an identity "as at birth," to recall the dictionary's ambiguous definition. "As" could convey that this identity occurs at birth. Or, "as" might mean that an ascriptive status is created *as if* at birth. With the ascription of one's citizenship and other hereditary status identities, including race, it is *as if* we were born with certain prepolitical characteristics. Writing that uses the alphabet, not hieroglyphics, effects the signified as a word and not a thing, materializing, in this context as an identity card as citizenship, and not just evidence thereof (Derrida 1988 [1972]). Citizenship's registration system also creates a state archive with implications for state power: "The power of the archive and of the historico-political order always maintains, within the broadest structures of the apparatus of writing, an irreducible adherence to power that is properly epistemic" (Derrida 1979, 143). Through sheer repetition, the hypothetical condition of a written status "as at birth" comes to define the significance of *what might be* (a merely written entry) as *what is* (the state's knowledge and power) "as at birth." This significance of birth, the meaning of qualities we imagine we acquire ambiguously "as at birth," as opposed to those developed *as if at birth* (as recognizable copies) or later (as recognizable self-craftings or social-craftings—both of which affirm the authority of the written original) (Butler 1991, esp. 22)—and the significance of a national identity, are so central to who we are that we come to believe we are ontologically as the government interpellates us at birth. Our citizenship rules convey who we are as if we were born this way, and this hypothetical condition materializes us into these actual state facts.

Nonetheless, the nonfictionalization of ascription, an inherently literary process, has failed millions of us. It is tempting to imagine these failures result from a combination of deficits of resources and goodwill. But the chapters here, reiterating the same state-led patterns of exclusions, do not suggest there is an underlying truth of birthright citizenship states are not recognizing. Rather, they reveal that we are not citizens in the ways we often imagine we are, as if we were born this way without the state, as though being born Portuguese or Pakistani is the same as being born with brown or green eyes. But of course this is not exactly right, and we need to think further on how birth does and does not create a citizen. The dictionary's parenthetical reference to ascription "as at birth" is precisely what the politics of citizenship's geographic (not geologic) and kinship (not genetic) rules contravene. This is an observation one might make simply on the basis of observed laws, but the sorts of observed disruptions that are occurring in practice between the signifier (i.e., facts and records about birth and other biographical events) and the signified (i.e., state-recognized citizenship) further yield important insights about the sign "citizen."[7]

The preceding discussion, alluding to the events and ambiguities noted in this volume, plays virtually no role in dominant political theories of citizenship, which tend to cluster among three different positions. The first recognizes and endorses clear demarcations between citizens and aliens, and the prerogatives of the nation-state to carefully control and monitor entry of the latter.[8] A second portion of this literature questions the legitimacy of the nation-state's exclusions and proposes a range of legal responses in support of free movement or routes to citizenship other than birth (e.g., Carens 1987, 2013; Shachar 2009; Stevens 2009b) or, in the case of Engin Isin (2012), calls attention to the immanence of existing citizens in motion. A third camp proposes or recognizes substantial shifts of citizenship rights in domestic and international law.[9]

The chapters are gathered here as a response to this first and most widespread intuition about the idealized benefits of preserving the nation-state's conventional boundaries between insiders and outsiders. Rather than challenge views at the level of abstract arguments mobilized by political theory, or economic analyses on the costs and benefits of free movement versus strict border controls, the essays herein provide representations and analyses of what citizenship looks like at a granular level, including the disputes over the very grains and colors of the paper and ink of which it is constructed.

These analyses of citizenship in practice require questioning key assumptions informing our more general theories of citizenship. For instance, many believe citizenship using laws of descent excludes racialized others and that citizenship through the rights conveyed by jus soli would include them. But lacunae in the archives of descent in the United States result in the deportation of more U.S. citizens, largely those of Mexican descent, than failures of laws effecting citizenship through jus soli (Stevens 2011a). In other words, people born in Mexico whose parent or parents are U.S. citizens may acquire U.S. citizenship at birth automatically by operation of law but then fail to have this recognized by the U.S. government. None of this is official policy, but effective statelessness results nonetheless. Thus, citizenship's enforcement occurs in places and through discourses that are largely invisible to the broader public and even to those with expertise on citizenship.

Kristin Collins (2014), in her work on citizenship by descent in the United States, notes the break between law and practice. Describing the inconsistency between the citizenship *policy objective* of avoiding statelessness and the *implementation* of citizenship laws in the context of countries that reciprocally followed patrilineal rules for citizenship, she writes: "In the many hundreds of pre-1940 administrative memos I have read that defend or explain recognition of the nonmarital foreign-born children of American mothers as citizens, I have identified exactly one memo by a U.S. official that mentions the risk of statelessness for the foreign-born nonmarital children of American mothers as a concern" (Collins 2014, 2205n283). Collins recognizes that even though government is creating a method that will systematically render stateless children of U.S. citizens, this operation invites no systematic caution, much less antidote.

As is the case for much work in the field of population production, it is tempting to turn to Michel Foucault's theories of biopower and governmentality. But the persistence of scenarios such as the preceding one revealing citizenship's certifiable failures of signification are those of a randomly acting pharmakon, and not a systemic toxin used in a uniform fashion against a persistent other. These government transcriptions pose a problem for the prevailing Foucauldian disciplinary critique of power and may be one reason these rereadings and rewritings elude theoretical scrutiny: the government's power is being exercised incoherently, by local decree, and largely independent of any standardizing, normalizing discourse. The forces of power and knowledge responding to citizens as aliens, or treating citizens of one country as though they were not citizens of that country, or treating those who are stateless as though they were citizens of a country, are not being implemented through professional or government networks whose concepts might be organized and mobilized in any recognizable pattern, even one that is subtle and diffuse.[10]

The lessons from this collection might be situated alongside the research on inequalities of ethnicity, race, sex, and sexuality that eventually was superseded by questions about whether one could meaningfully discuss these categories as self-evident to anyone save the naive observer. These essays examine the frays at the boundaries of citizenship's legal recognition. As opposed to debates premised on certainty as to shared knowledge of who is and who is not a citizen, this project focuses on the uncertainty of these boundaries and their political, psychological, and personal meanings. The studies in this collection extend inquiry into the theoretical claims about citizenship's contingencies to observations about its individual-level assignations. Just as studies of the discourse of the hermaphrodite called into question intuitions assuming two discrete sexes (Barbin 1980; Fausto-Sterling 1992), and the nonprocreative unions of early Christians troubled claims about the traditional reproductive, heterosexual family (Boswell 1994), and new findings and then discourses on genetic variation undermined ontological taxonomies of race (Hey 2001), the essays in this collection, by revealing micro-level, even molecular-level, confusions about citizenship, challenge the assumption that citizenship is the sort of self-evident characteristic that one either has or lacks.[11] The discrepancies between our ideologies of citizenship and its daily operations raise questions about the meaning of these disparities on which these chapters reflect.

If citizenship is the state's certifications of citizenship, and if these are not self-evident but a legal gray zone (Morawetz 2007a), then citizenship suggests a different morphology (of existence and research) than heretofore understood. Just as insights about the politics of taxonomies and heuristics have reshaped discussions of equality among putatively natural groups, knowledge about the operational details of assigning citizenship has the potential to profoundly affect understandings of this identity as well. To many, it may seem that the phenomenology of citizenship already encompasses practices that are legal, and not biological. Unlike the one-drop rule embraced in the Supreme Court decision *Plessy v. Ferguson* (1896), for instance, the taxonomies of citizenship seem transparently administrative, and not biological. Even those who perceive *nationality* as a natural, material, inherited fact might be sympathetic to problematizing laws on birthright *citizenship*, understood as acts of government, not nature.[12] But this does not occur.

Long-standing and widely shared, though inaccurate, intuitions about identities wrought through birth explain why the concept of citizenship based on birth in a geopolitical territory still incites some of those along the southern border of the United States to fight as Minutemen, and Minutewomen, on behalf of identities created by state cartographers. Even for those who are politically active, the phenomenology of birth inspires a defense of a citizenship that is purely nominal, and not incitements to voter turnout drives, regardless of whether the citizen's identity as such emerges through the state's sacralization of lineages of family or lines on maps.[13]

Likewise, families take shape and change in all sorts of ways inconsistent with the expectations of citizenship laws, both through the creation of new laws for marriage and legitimacy and within specific families, pursuant to changes of marriage, divorce, adoption, and remarriage. Amid the legal flux, citizenship's categorization remains rigid, discrete, and largely exclusionary. Importantly, earlier European governments seemed more interested in accommodating these ambiguities in the laws regulating the civil registers through including uncertain cases. The postrevolutionary French Civil Code of 1792 "did not require mayors to declare the truth of an individual's 'real' or 'natural' identity.... It was not by chance that the Civil Code prescribed the sex of an infant should be 'stated' and not 'verified'" (Noiriel 2001, 44). Gérard Noiriel describes the tribune Simeón disparaging authorities during the Revolution demanding proofs and "treating as an inquisition" reviews of marriage and legitimacy: "It was thus explicitly to protect individuals against arbitrary treatment and to ensure 'family harmony' that the Civil Code defined civil identification as the certification of statements and not research into the truth of an individual's identity" (Noiriel 2001, 44). If the truth of the family were easily discerned, there could be no inquisition. If family facts are potentially ambiguous, due to any of a number of factors—from changes in boundaries to laws that might eliminate a parent's identity at birth, to the vagaries of the sex of the parent or the child—then citizenship is inherently in question and thus at odds with the prevailing ideology that it is self-evident.

Chapter Overviews

The chapters herein reveal what it looks like when citizenship in practice today bumps into the contingencies of borders, laws, and (family) life. To supplement the meanings of "de jure" or "legal" as adjectives denoting the state's recognition of citizenship, these chapters reference "effective" citizenship and also statelessness. Legal citizenship or statelessness may be irrelevant to ensuring the rights associated with either status. *Effective citizenship* is citizenship that would be recognized as such save for quasi-legal, often pseudo-legal challenges by government agents, be they border agents or federal judges. Evidentiary questions may arise because of ambiguities in documents, databases, borders, or laws. The venues where these disputes occur may be at the border, or in homes, workplaces, administrative offices, mail, civil hearings, prisons or immigration jails, or court proceedings. Indeed, in many cases questions about citizenship crosscut several of these dimensions and locations. The cases discussed here also bring into play jurisdictional and evidentiary standards for two or more countries that implicate problems of what Polly Price calls "effective statelessness," when people cannot prove citizenship and are effectively stateless even though the country of their residence does not recognize this statelessness at law. In other words, by operation of law, as the cases in the chapters by Jacqueline Bhabha and Benjamin Lawrance highlight, the government may refuse to recognize people either as citizens or as stateless, leaving them outside the protections of international law designed precisely to address the vulnerability of those Hannah Arendt singled out as the most politically fragile group that exists (those without a state) (2007a [1944]).

These contributions are amenable to several possible groupings. The ones chosen for this volume emphasize, in part I, how global politics of sovereign borders, as well as interpretations of international and regional law, manifest in citizenship determinations. These first chapters introduce readers to how civil authorities respond to dyadic, regional, or global treaties and institutions, including those developing legal definitions of statelessness. The scenarios exemplifying government decisions framed by international and regional law occur in administrative venues and also courts.

The second and third sets of chapters are organized by venue. Chapters in part II describe determinations and exclusions imposed by frontline officials or administrators, that is, those who are directly operationalizing citizenship challenges and denials. Chapters in part III exemplify how national, electoral politics and campaigns may throw the citizenship of leaders and then of the populace into question; they also theorize what it means when people create these distinctions, and thus define one portion of themselves as aliens.

In chapter 1, "Jus Soli and Statelessness: A Comparative Perspective from the Americas," Polly Price explains the global fissures, as well as the treaties and institutions, that instantiate citizenship's as well as statelessness's rules, hurdles, and inadequate protocols for redress. By focusing on how movement among jus soli regimes may produce statelessness, Price alerts readers to how rules that appear inclusive may in practice be exclusive. Price reviews how twenty countries, from Canada in the North to Chile in the South, constitute populations of citizens effectively stateless. Quoting from a U.S. State Department report, Price describes children born to the Ngobe-Bugle, a group that migrates from Panama to Costa Rica for plantation work: "'In these cases the children were not registered as Costa Rican citizens because the families did not think it necessary to register the births, but when the families returned to Panama, the children were not registered there, either'" (U.S. Department of State 2011e). Price highlights the hypocrisy of such infelicities in citizenship's recognition as she explores how international law and treaties acknowledge both the possibility of statelessness and their own massive failure to address it, as well as the consequences for subsequent generations also rendered stateless.

In chapter 2, "The Politics of Evidence: Roma Citizenship Deficits in Europe," Jacqueline Bhabha uses the concept of "legalized illegality" (Çağlar and Mehling 2013) to explore what happens in the absence of documentary evidence for Roma citizens of several European countries. Paying special attention to the European Union and drawing on insights from her earlier work on how evidentiary challenges produce statelessness (Bhabha 2009, 2011), Bhabha draws our attention to failures of regional and global institutions that portend to extend citizenship and also to protect the stateless. Despite regional and international laws demanding otherwise, gaps in civil registries, as well as inconsistencies between those entries and the papers in possession of the Roma (e.g., different spellings or dates of birth), result in substantial deprivations of health care, education, employment, and housing.

Chapter 3, "Statelessness-in-Question: Expert Testimony and the Evidentiary Burden of Statelessness," draws on Lawrance's experiences as an expert witness for asylum seekers in the United Kingdom, analyzing the specific operations in individual cases that produce statelessness. For instance, one account reveals how a woman walked into a government office as a Portuguese national and left effectively stateless. In this and the legal decisions made by officials in Togo, Portugal, and France affecting outcomes in the United Kingdom, Lawrance details how citizenship is waylaid by decisionism, with bureaucrats and judges substituting their own guesswork for the legitimate narratives of those before them. Lawrance provides an insightful discussion of the paradoxical significance of legal practices creating effective statelessness based on government misreadings of their own documents.

In chapter 4, "Reproducing Uncertainty: Documenting Contested Sovereignty and Citizenship across the Taiwan Strait," Sara Friedman situates the production of documentary ambiguities in the context of the fraught relations between the governments of Taiwan and the People's Republic of China. Drawing on extensive interviews with border-crossing spouses and the government officials issuing identity papers, Friedman uses her close readings of their statements to question Derrida's effort to separate the role of intention from the force of documentary identities. Friedman, an anthropologist, offers an ethnography of a Taiwanese government official's anxiety about forged documents being used by mainland Chinese to enter Singapore (for work) and not Taiwan, and the elaborate system in place to authenticate the copy. Her chapter creatively draws on work by Yael Navaro-Yashin (2007, 86) to interpret the nuances in a range of contexts producing and interrogating documentary identification and theorizing how geopolitical structures mobilize "emotional investment for their bearers . . . intertwined with the material form of the documents themselves" for the bureaucrats and supplicants alike.

Again engaging the implications of sovereign decisions on the world stage for the quotidian level of an individual's identity, in chapter 5, Kim Rubenstein explores the impact of colonization on the nation-state's understanding of citizenship. In "What Is a 'Real' Australian Citizen? Insights from Papua New Guinea and Mr. Amos Ame," Rubenstein (with Jacqueline Field) draws on information she encountered through her legal representation of Amos Ame in his effort to have the Australian High Court persist in recognizing him as an Australian citizen, a claim the court rejected on the grounds that the population of Papua New Guinea became part of Australia through what one commentator calls an "accident of European history" (Waiko 1993, 26). The High Court affirmed the removal from Mr. Ame of his Australian citizenship on the grounds that he was not a "real" Australian. The judge ruled that following Papua New Guinea's independence, its new borders ex post facto correctly defined Mr. Ame's Australian citizenship.

In sum, the chapters in part I reveal how fluid boundary formations, crossings, and transformations in the context of global and regional laws of the post-Westphalian international system, as well as the quandaries raised because of colonialism and its aftermath, put citizenship in question.

The chapters in part II focus in more depth on how administrative judgments produce ineffective citizenship. From bureaucrats employed by the United States in the late nineteenth century to Indian government workers today, these chapters document the technical operations that produce ineffective citizenship and effective statelessness. In chapter 6, "To Know a Citizen: Birthright Citizenship Documents Regimes in U.S. History," Beatrice McKenzie, former vice-consul in the U.S. embassy in Kampala, Uganda, offers close readings of several U.S. court cases in which judges evaluated the sufficiency of individuals' facts and documents proving citizenship. The trajectory of the decisions she selects, focused on Chinese exclusion cases in the United States, suggests changing standards of scrutiny over time for verbal and written statements about facts. Attention to these cases highlights both the discretionary character of citizenship findings and their reliance on subjective, nonwritten criteria that are systematically racist.

Rachel Rosenbloom, a former supervising attorney for the Post-Deportation Human Rights Project at Boston College Law School, testified before Congress on the unlawful detention and deportation of U.S. citizens (U.S. House of Representatives 2008). Rosenbloom's chapter 7, "From the Outside Looking In: U.S. Passports in the Borderlands," presents original research on recent policy directives, as well as the new internal border policing and harassment of U.S. citizens behind the uptick in U.S. passport denials in south Texas. Rosenbloom also reveals how transborder lives prompt parents to register as born in Mexico children who were in fact born in territory under U.S. sovereignty (an unidiomatic way to state "the U.S." in order to reiterate the artifice and contingency of nonfraudulent U.S. birth certificates, insofar as Texas was until 1848 the sovereign territory of Mexico). Rosenbloom points out that despite this ruse being well known to Texas county clerks, State Department adjudicators ignore the accurate Texas birth certificates and, after locating fraudulent Mexican birth registration, defer to narratives of fraud against the U.S. government and reject U.S. citizens' passport applications. Her research indicates the precariousness, unreliability, and centrality of government papers for assigning citizenship and highlights the importance of these evidentiary reviews to determinations of U.S. citizenship.

In chapter 8, "Problems of Evidence, Evidence of Problems: Expanding Citizenship and Reproducing Statelessness among Highlanders in Northern Thailand," Amanda Flaim draws on the field research she obtained from a 2009–11 United Nations study she designed and supervised. Flaim surveyed 292 villages with more than 700,000 people and found a civil registration system that on the basis of putative DNA tests and other seemingly arbitrary or pseudoscientific findings produced statelessness incommensurate with underlying biographies. One statement from a stateless villager is especially revealing: "I was working in the fields when a man . . . interviewed my young daughter and my elderly mother-in-law about everyone in the house. When I came home from the field, I saw a piece of paper, but I couldn't read it and I didn't know what it was. My mother-in-law and my child did not understand what it was either. Then I let my children play with the paper, but they tore it up." This individual's statelessness thus was produced by the state's tracking of her, as well as her location and illiteracy, not her legal status.

In chapter 9, "Limits of Legal Citizenship: Narratives from South and Southeast Asia," Kamal Sadiq extends his research into "paper citizens" (Sadiq 2008) by describing more recent field research in India and Malaysia on how the enormous expansion of the twentieth-century state is paradoxically producing statelessness. Sadiq's work conveys a point that emerges from Flaim's research as well. As Sadiq puts it, the state's requirement of identity papers to keep its machines humming means an incessant demand for "information that the poor, the homeless, and the mobile do not emit." Sadiq thus alerts us to how the Indian welfare state, like many others described in this collection, fails the very people on whose behalf it was seemingly designed.

This view of the modern state provides a new context for considering Jane Caplan and John Torpey's claim in their important 2001 collection that Weberian equality before the law "tends to raise up persons and groups who had previously been thought not worthy of notice, yet it simultaneously reduces those subordinated to the state's governance to a status as subjects of direct administration and surveillance" (5). An examination of the micropractices of modern states, perhaps especially in postcolonial, developing countries, suggests that the infrastructures established for equality before the law are actually removing the poor from government social welfare programs rather than enhancing access to them. Such patterns contradict T. H. Marshall's (1992 [1949]) theory that enlarging citizenship increases the availability of access to new material rights. Again, these insights are available only by aggregating the individual-level analyses of what Sadiq calls "state artifacts" of identity documents and their specific function in producing class-based internal civic banishment, because of and not despite protocols of modern citizenship. Together the chapters in part II reveal how the hurdles of documentation, reflecting more and less overt and targeted commitments to national purity, deprive millions of their citizenship rights.

For the most part, evidentiary challenges to citizenship occur in dark corners of bureaucracies, their details only vaguely articulable even by those directly affected. But on occasion disputes erupt not only in courts but also in public discourse during political campaigns or over local cases. Although the forensics of citizenship generally receive little public attention, national elections may trigger attention to the citizenship bona fides of political candidates and thus also make salient citizenship's delineations among the population more generally. Both Margaret Stock and Alfred Babo explore how strategic questioning of the citizenship status of presidential candidates and presidents occurs in tandem with broader legal changes and public conversations about these. Margaret Stock, a practicing immigration attorney, professor, and retired U.S. Army colonel who crafted citizenship policies to allow U.S. military personnel to naturalize, reviews how certain campaigns in the United States have questioned the citizenship of presidential candidates and sitting presidents, and how a proposed change to U.S. citizenship law would have made it impossible for past presidents to have assumed office. Chapter 10, "American Birthright Citizenship Rules and the Exclusion of 'Outsiders' from the Political Community," historicizes the attacks of "birthers" on the credibility of President Barack Obama's Hawaiian birth records, reviews the origins and meaning of the Fourteenth Amendment's references to a "natural born citizen," and explains the implications of more restrictive rules for U.S. citizenship for past presidents and what this might mean going forward.

In chapter 11, Alfred Babo describes the strategic questioning of presidential candidate Alassane Ouattara's nationality as Ivorian, or *ivoirité*, a term employed by a previous president, Henri Konan Bédié. Babo's chapter, "*Ivoirité* and Citizenship in Ivory Coast: The Controversial Policy of Authenticity," documents how candidates used ivoirité, an autochthonous authenticity rhetoric, to "eliminate political rivals." Babo takes readers back to the origins of authenticity and its aftermath. He documents how its implementation has resulted in discrimination against "hundreds of thousands of Ivoirian nationals" and "permitted government agents, particularly the military and police," to challenge the authenticity of identity documents and thereby strip citizens of their rights. Stock and Babo describe the intersection of national elections with broader policy debates. Stock focuses on the ambiguity of laws and unintended consequences of nativist interpretations, while Babo attends closely to the evidentiary reviews that occur more frequently in the wake of disputes over presidential qualifications.

Babo explicitly highlights the episodic character of these questions, which arose in 1993 and resulted in the defeat of presidential candidate Ouattara, even though in 2010 Bédié "reversed himself and appealed to his supporters to vote for Alassane Ouattara, who was henceforth permitted to run for election after a long battle over his nationality and citizenship issues," a turnaround revealing the situational if not arbitrary or even random timing of these challenges. Likewise, Stock points out how similar citizenship challenges could have been but were not posed of presidential candidates at different periods in U.S. history.

In chapter 12, "The Alien Who Is a Citizen," I reflect on the meaning of the U.S. government detaining and deporting its own citizens. Drawing on insights from Franz Kafka and Derrida, the chapter explores how these episodes might best be understood as apologues, that is, morality stories told to enhance the government's authority, and not as rational efforts to make individualized determinations of citizenship. The chapter explores the meaning of these cases through deconstructions of illustrative court decisions and a regulation explaining how "aliens" may prove they are "U.S. citizens" in an immigration court, a paradoxical protocol, since by definition aliens are not U.S. citizens. The scenarios in law and practice highlight Kafka's depiction of harms inflicted by bureaucracies in liberal democracies as a form of self-oppression characteristic of modernity.

Finally, Daniel Kanstroom's afterword draws on insights gleaned from his own pathbreaking scholarship and litigation as the founding director of the Boston College Law School Post-Deportation Human Rights Project. Kanstroom has been developing protocols for a Declaration on the Rights of Expelled and Deported Persons. His afterword opens with a tantalizing thought experiment on the proof that might be demanded of someone claiming to be a citizen of the world, reflects on the problems for those claiming citizenship in one nation-state, and explains the importance of expanding human rights protections to all people, regardless of recognized citizenship.

Bias, Affect, Money

Many other themes crosscut the material in these three parts, including the distinction between deserving and accidental or strategic citizens; decisionism at all levels of government review; the affect elicited by identity papers; and monetary barriers to effecting recognition of one's citizenship. These themes do not intersect in any obvious way but emerge as key factors that shape the possibilities of achieving effective citizenship. The idea of deserving citizens appears in McKenzie's chapter. McKenzie's recollections of her consular work recalls as well Bhabha's epigraph quoting French president Nicolas Sarkozy on the difference between immigrants who are "worthy" of French nationality and those who are not. McKenzie's point about people who can tell a recognizable story about their citizenship captures a recurring pattern of official decisions based on biases and traits that are extralegal but have important consequences for supplicants seeking official status. For instance, Babo points out the encounter of a woman whose application for a national identity card was rejected in the Ivory Coast because of a patronymic name associated with Burkina Faso. After fluently speaking to the agent in the local dialect, the officer "insulted her mother and asserted that such women sold their Ivoirian nationality to foreigners by marriage." Similarly, Friedman, Flaim, Lawrance, and Rosenbloom emphasize the role of snap judgments by border agents or low-level office clerks—the absence of evidence or reason leading Flaim to describe the contingency of agents' mere "beliefs," and Lawrance, the specious "assumptions" absent evidence driving these official, life-altering determinations.

Relatedly, several chapters point out the role of affect in these seemingly formal engagements. Friedman describes the "affective states" of desire, anxiety, humiliation, lack, and pride that are "intertwined with the material form of the documents themselves" (chapter 4; and see Stoler 2004) and also register in the encounters between the officials and the applicants. Lawrance describes the inquisitorial atmosphere incited by paper documents whose information comes largely from what one's parents provide to authorities for birth registries and certificates, and about which the individual possessing an identity card would have no firsthand knowledge.

Sadiq describes how the state artifact of citizenship documentation has "affective attributes . . . of loyalty, belonging, membership, and identity." Document fees pose more prosaic monetary hurdles to obtaining identity documents, a tax not only on the right to vote but also on the right to have any legal recognition whatsoever. Such impediments are important to debates in citizenship studies about the relevance of citizenship to welfare and other civil and political rights (Soysal 1994, 2012).

In addition to citizenship and migration studies, these chapters raise questions about newly emerging research questions at the intersection of political theory and administrative law. The investigations that follow, in conversation with the research agendas of Giorgio Agamben and Foucault, as well as left and right critiques of liberal democracies by Walter Benjamin and Carl Schmitt, respectively, invite us to reflect on the significance of civil and not criminal legal institutions as the sites of these encounters. There are crucial differences among the discourses, institutions, and sovereignty noted by these theorists and the paradoxes of citizenship's (mis)recognitions. Whereas Foucault and Agamben stress biopower that is producing its own subjects and narrating its own authority, the legal dilemmas for citizenship in question lack a coherent epistemic or political logic and do not even tell a good story. One might fail at being Thai because a child throws away a piece of paper, or because a government official requires a DNA report and then sits on the results. Second, the sovereign decisionism that pervades all of these encounters advances its authority through civil and not the criminal or national security laws discussed by Benjamin and Schmitt. At the same time, such laws allow and incentivize physical violence, often commingled with rhetoric of criminality and illegality that is largely not triggered by other encounters with civil authority. And third, the subversions of citizenship from within its own practices reflect neither the racist logics described in critiques of failed liberalism, nor the coherent subject positions of most Foucauldian discourse and analysis. These chapters are about the ascribed performances of the inherently ambiguous statuses of the citizen and the alien and also their remarkable persistence as such across time and space, unlike the abstractions of the Foucauldian sodomite and homosexual, for instance, which have specific meanings based on patterns inferred from reading a cross section of materials produced in a specific time and place (Foucault 1978).

Citizenship as Arbitrary

In conclusion, I want to say a few words about characterizing the decisions that make and unmake citizens as "arbitrary," a concept that appears throughout these chapters. What does "arbitrary" mean? Are inconsistencies among cases and between oral histories and official edicts symptoms of bureaucratic randomness, or are intuitively unfair outcomes evidence of systemic biases, and thus not at all arbitrary in the sense of the first meaning? This question might be posed of many other disparities in group treatments, including the distribution of wealth, employment, and educational resources across a range of peoples and not just citizenship papers. The dual meanings of (mis)recognitions return us to the question of whether the cases described in these chapters can be remediated by better bureaucracies, or whether birthright citizenship inherently entails systemic absurdities and injustice. Can we fix the pharmakon of citizenship so that its effects are under the control of knowledgeable authorities wielding power appropriately? Or does the very nature of citizenship pose a systemic risk of serious haphazard, harmful outcomes not worth the potential pragmatic benefits?[14]

Mariane Ferme, pointing out the challenges faced by deterritorialized citizens of Sierra Leone, represents these features of "arbitrariness and the law" as (1) a "well-guarded secret that exists to serve the interests of particular categories of people"; (2) "arbitrariness in the way laws are applied"; and

(3) situations in which the state obscures the "threshold between legality and illegality" (2004, 83). This theme is pursued as well in the astute analysis of "capricious citizenship" put forward by Sujata Ramachandran (2015) in her study of Bengali-speaking Indian citizens. Contrariwise, Barbara Yngvesson and Susan Bibler Coutin, in their study of adoptees, emphasize the possible truth of identity's significations: "Paper trails, which ought to substantiate truth, sometimes plunge their referents into a reality that is incommensurable with their sense of self" (2006, 84). Apparently, a certificate can be arbitrary because it is embedded in a system of outcomes that systematically serve powerful interests, as nonsense, or because it does not give us the truth.

Not everyone who finds citizenship's pattern of recognitions and mistaken revocations unfair sees these actions as "arbitrary." In chapter 6, McKenzie argues: "Citizenship is not an arbitrary status bestowed upon individuals in government offices stateside or abroad. . . . It is, however, more easily defended by some individuals than others." Peter Nyers (2006) also takes this perspective, focusing on "accidental citizens" as a phrase used to impugn the status of those born in the United States to parents who are not white and were foreign-born. McKenzie finds these variations in citizenship determinations a logical consequence of appeals from differently situated supplicants, while Nyers, a critic of birthright citizenship, sees the pejoratively labeled accidental citizen a necessary outcome of sovereignty, and also a symptom of sovereignty's illegitimacy (2006, esp. 35–37).

Those who represent citizenship and national identity as created through the random self-divisions of what could be called the "Human Being Project"—an ongoing practice whereby people are constantly (re)producing and attacking themselves represented as others, the view of this introduction—are using an analytic framework at odds with those who represent the cases in these chapters as exemplifying errors citizenship done right would not incur. Returning to a point made earlier, it might appear that this view of citizenship and foreignness as emerging from legal texts and practices and not prepolitical groups or attachments should be self-evident. Citizenship per se seems to emerge from law, and its signs are entirely written. Nyers argues that the concept of the "accidental citizen" makes this especially clear. This figure "breaks the bond between nativity and nationality, creates a potential catastrophe for birthright conceptions of citizenship," and thus reveals the "bond forged between sovereign and subject at birth [is] arbitrary" (2006, 35). Nyers's critique of the concept of the accidental citizenship is apt. Yet, as Derrida helps us to understand, the logical contradictions implicit in the accidental citizen do not express their potential to undo and thus destroy belief in birthright citizenship. Citizenship's written documents are the state's references through letters, not a less real realm of mere symbols. The writing in the state archive has the force of state truth, a force, as Hegel points out, more robust than any biological or other prepolitical, unascriptive fact.

Reflecting on J. L. Austin's characterization of performatives onstage or uttered in "special circumstances" as abnormal or parasitic of ordinary contexts, Derrida asks, "Is the risk [of a statement spoken in a staged or abnormal context being taken for a felicitous performative] a failure or trap into which language may *fall* or lose itself . . . or, on the contrary, is this risk rather its internal and positive condition of possibility? Is that outside its inside, the very force and law of its emergence?" (1988 [1972], 17). These interpretative questions help explain why the citizen who is effectively stateless, as well as the so-called accidental citizen, whether or not later officially expatriated, do not inherently unveil a true citizenship untroubled by confusions. The utterance "I promise . . . to pay you a million dollars" announced in a play, that is, an easily staged performance outside the original context where it might effect actual results, does not, in fact, problematize or undo the exemplary force of the performative "I promise" in ordinary speech and contexts. Likewise, citizenship's legal performances, and others J. L. Austin (1962) finds "felicitous," such as marriage's "I do," occur under conditions that also are staged, that is, in a courtroom before a judge. It is a testament to the power of writing and state rituals that at any point words and signs are so easily taken as original, authentic, or real, as at birth (!), that generally only Brechtians and devotees of Kafka perceive the judge's courtroom and its proceedings a form of theater.

Consider Nyers's point that the enemy combatant and U.S. citizen "Yaser Hamdi" is "actually spelled 'Himdy,' " attributing the error in U.S. references to an "improper translation from the Arabic to English on his Saudi passport and then on his American birth certificate" (2006, 39n5). This narrative suggests the authority of some putatively original document to signify a correct "Himdy." But of course the name and spelling are never other than copies, of a phonetic name either created or uttered by an ancestral relative or scribe, perhaps one from which "Himdy" was an inaccurate copy of a previous name that could have been transcribed as "Hamdi." Presumably Nyers would agree that the difference between a transliteration of the letter *i* or *y* from the Arab to the English alphabet is strictly arbitrary.

Contemplating these contexts, that is, signifiers of signifiers, Derrida writes, "Rather than oppose citation or iteration," including its copies (e.g., "Hamdi" to "Himdy"), "one ought to construct a differentiated typology of forms of iteration" (1988 [1972], 18). One example of this typology might be the intergenerational (re)production or iteration of a name. Derrida continues, "In such a typology, the category of intention will not disappear," that is, for this example, the current experience or phenomenology of the family name inscribing membership will remain important, but these politics "will no longer be able to govern the entire scene" (18). The string of family names can be understood as iterations of a family romance and not apolitical truisms that compel obedience or rebellion. Via deconstruction, knowledge of the arbitrary iteration of "Himdy" as a name and as a citizen with a specific nationality emerges from such encounters with its ambiguities and contradictions and those of larger psychic and political structures specific to its possibility made explicit.

The tension between a critical understanding of the accidental citizen's logical flaws, on the one hand, and a deconstructive view, on the other, is symptomatic of what might very well be the signature paradigm of legality's paradoxes, figured by Walter Benjamin as the "subordination of citizens to laws" (1986 [1921], 284), insofar as these laws exist only through these citizens. The ambiguities and contradictions of citizenship are all seemingly "arbitrary." Consider the third definition of "arbitrary" in the *American Heritage Dictionary*: "*Law* relating to a decision made by a court or legislature that lacks grounding in law or fact . . ." Birthright citizenship as law depends on signs that are closer to literary tautologies materializing as facts than an ostensive representation, and thus any decisions on this basis are always arbitrary.

Perhaps it is this tension between the legality associated with most of the sovereign's prerogative when they are rational and evenhanded, and the sovereign's decisions on citizenship as those of caprice that mobilizes the spirit of critique scholars in this collection bring to their endeavors. When circulated through the legal system of law review articles and courts, forums where some of our authors appear regularly, their responses may prove more immediately effective than other scholarly critiques. Lawrance agitates over the conundrum posed when judges or lower-level government personnel produce decisions that are paradoxically legal de facto but not de jure, observing the increasing deployment of "*de facto* statelessness," a vague term of art mobilized inconsistently in the international legal community (Harvey 2010, 261). Lawrance highlights the importance of scholars marshalling their expertise in history, anthropology, literature, and the law for leveraging the epistemological privilege of academic inquiry to question and destabilize concepts whose force of law is not weakened by their incoherence alone. Regardless of their specific politics or theories, the chapters individually, and especially cumulatively, orient the audience to underexamined intuitions about citizenship and statelessness, provoking further queries about not only the magnitude of harms of birthright citizenship but also their meanings iterated through operations that exclude ourselves under the pretense we are excluding others.

NOTES

Thanks to Laura Green for comments on an earlier draft, as well as to the co-conveners of the conference from which these chapters were drawn: Dan Kanstroom, Rachel Rosenbloom, and Rogers Smith. I also want to acknowledge the insights shared by those who have resisted government misconduct, available at http://deportationresearchclinic.org. And for his invaluable support and feedback, a special thanks to my partner in organizing the conference and this collection, Benjamin Lawrance. Many thanks as well to the anonymous reviewer for enormously helpful comments responsive to an earlier draft.

1. On the difference between words and concepts, see Pitkin 1973 and Ziff 1967.

2. "I suppose that the process of 'ascriptio' consisted, in this case, of dividing the names handed in among the different colonies; very probably these lists would be publicly exhibited, and we need not doubt the sincerity of those who had been thus 'assigned.' Professor Daube has written to me on this point as follows: 'One small matter of interest is that apparently 'ascribi' has several senses. It signifies primarily 'to be enrolled.' But since in the vast majority of cases one who is enrolled for a colony subsequently becomes a member—namely, by his inclusion in the first census—the verb is often used as denoting 'to become a member'" (Smith 1954, 19).

3. For more on how practices that instantiate identities at birth come to be favored as ontological and essential, as opposed to those identities that are understood as developing through our own decisions or actions, see Stevens 1999, 2009b. These texts and Stevens 2011a inform the analysis here.

4. Deconstruction arose "as an attempt to come to terms with the Holocaust as a radical disruption produced as a logical extension of Western thinking" (Johnson 1987, xviii).

5. As a purely bureaucratic question, it would have been much easier for deportation agents to affirm his U.S. citizenship than that of someone who obtained this through jus soli, simply because the same federal agency that would deport Ace possessed the documents confirming his U.S. citizenship, whereas the Department of Homeland Security does not have direct access to the birth certificates maintained by state agencies. Ace's inability to procure his own birth certificate in Jamaica, a copy of which his mother had turned over to the U.S. government when he was six, meant his effective citizenship status was one of statelessness.

6. There is a rich literature on the role of miscegenation and marriage law in various city-states and nation-states, and in colonial and postcolonial contexts, all highlighting the discrepancies between biological ("blood") and legal families, and their implications for citizenship. See Domínguez 1986; Haney-Lopez 2006; Lape 2004, Loraux 1993, 2000; Stoler 2002.

7. The meanings of the terms as used here are from Ferdinand de Saussure's *Course in General Linguistics* (1986 [1916]).

8. Middle to late twentieth-century examples of the first include most famously Michael Walzer's (1983, chap. 9) defense of using kinship rules for determining membership in the modern state; Peter Schuck and Rogers Smith's (1985) argument that the Fourteenth Amendment should not be interpreted to apply to children of parents who reside in the United States without legal authority; and John Rawls's (1999) idea that citizenship rights derive from intergenerational communities based on racial and ethnic descent. All these authors, and many others, argue at some point that the sorts of expansive rights to social welfare that T. H. Marshall (1992) locates in the development of the modern state require a range of prudential cultural and economic closures to ensure a feeling of national cohesion and preclude economic collapse.

9. For instance, Yasmin Soysal (1994) has argued that the benefits of the European Union's social welfare state are available on the basis of residence and not citizenship; Aihwa Ong (1999) has argued that people are more frequently strategizing to acquire the economic benefits from acquiring new citizenships; and Ayhan Kaya (1999) has shown how German political institutions have established autonomous cultural communities for enclaves of Turkish residents in Germany, despite their lacking rights of citizenship, developments embraced by Seyla Benhabib (2007) in her arguments, contra Walzer, that states should extend and protect residents regardless of their citizenship status but still maintain this distinction and its basis in current paradigms of birth.

10. Foucault's description of Ubu-esque or bumbling yet brutal, clownlike state authority in *Abnormal* (2003a [1974–75] , esp. 34–54) is much more fitting and also largely ignored by Foucauldian critics.

11. For a study of citizenship as a legal "gray area" in U.S. courts, see Morawetz 2007a.

12. For an explanation of why nationality also is best understood through law and politics, not biology, see, e.g., Durkheim 1915; Lévi-Strauss 1969; Stevens 1999.

13. U.S. Americans bemoan low rates of voter participation but then fiercely attack the credentials of putative foreigners.

14. For a lengthy literature review and analysis of the utilitarian and so-called liberal arguments for citizenship based on the nation-state, see Stevens 2009b, especially the introduction and chapter 1.

PART I. INTERNATIONAL AND REGIONAL PROTOCOLS

CITIZENSHIP AND STATELESSNESS PROTOCOLS

1. JUS SOLI AND STATELESSNESS

A COMPARATIVE PERSPECTIVE FROM THE AMERICAS

POLLY J. PRICE

The New World is comparatively generous in the law's provision of citizenship to all persons born within national boundaries, including the children of undocumented persons and temporary visitors. A striking feature of citizenship practices in the Americas is the near uniformity of reliance on jus soli. Indeed, the jus soli principle "has primarily become a Western Hemisphere tradition" (Etzioni 2007, 353). The predominance of jus soli is said to account for the relatively low rate of statelessness in the Americas compared with other parts of the world.[1] Some experts claim the Western Hemisphere is "indisputably the region with the fewest people affected by statelessness" (Institute on Statelessness and Inclusion 2014, 8). But the definitions of "stateless" in international law instruments and in practice lack precision and thus confound easy measurements of political, civic, and economic status. As the introduction to this volume notes, merely possessing citizenship as a formal matter conceals the problem of governments treating their own citizens as foreigners, both deliberately and because of indifferent or incompetent administration.

As a result of decisions on the ground, even the most expansive laws mandating citizenship at birth fail to alleviate fundamental deprivations of human rights. As many chapters in this book discuss, authorities may withhold recognition and thus produce an "ineffective citizenship." Relatedly, international human rights laws on statelessness fail to address this problem. In this chapter,

I explore the limitations of the international legal definition of statelessness in order to illustrate two points. First, as explained later, what should be termed "effective statelessness" is a necessary adjunct to the concept of de jure statelessness. Without this conceptual pairing, we cannot judge the actual relationship between a state and those who belong to it. In the Americas, as I will show, a substantial number of persons entitled to citizenship cannot prove it, or such proof is disregarded by government officials. At the same time, these persons do not qualify for protection under international law because they are not legally "stateless."

Second, without some measure of "effective statelessness," claims that the Americas should be viewed as a relative success story because of the jus soli norm are questionable. Jus soli prevents statelessness only where it is accompanied by meticulous and generally recognized documentation. Effective statelessness can exist in any nation, and it is a hidden problem in the Americas, jus soli notwithstanding.

Effective statelessness occurs due to poor documentation of births and administrative ineptitude, as well as intentional discrimination. In the Americas, including the United States, the predominant reasons for effective statelessness include inability to prove nationality, as well as the failure of countries to document or recognize their own citizens. International treaties on statelessness fail to provide a sufficient safety net and thus offer no meaningful remedy to the problems of ineffective citizenship addressed here and in this book more generally (see esp. Lawrance, chapter 3, this volume).

Statelessness and Belonging: A Problem of Definition

Two international conventions constitute the primary framework for definitions of and responses to statelessness: the Convention Relating to the Status of Stateless Persons (1954) and the Convention on the Reduction of Statelessness (1961).[2] In international legal instruments, the term "stateless" refers to "a person who is not considered as a national by any State under the operation of its law" (UNHCR 2014b, 9). States are the final arbiters of whether an individual or a group under any definition is statelessness (Harvey 2010, 257).[3]

Article I of the 1954 convention defines a stateless person as one "who is not considered as a national by any State under the operation of its law." Among other obligations under that convention, contracting states must treat stateless persons the same as lawful aliens in that country, including granting access to wage-earning employment, housing, public education, and public relief. Upon request, states are also obligated to issue travel and identity documents to stateless persons within their territory. Further, stateless persons are not to be expelled except on "grounds of national security or public order."

The Convention on the Reduction of Statelessness (1961) attempted to strengthen international intervention by specifying the circumstances in which states should award legal status to stateless persons, including citizenship to persons born within their borders who would otherwise be stateless. The 1961 convention favors jus soli by stipulating that an important measure to avoid statelessness at birth is to provide nationality to children born in the territory who would otherwise be stateless. The Office of the United Nations High Commissioner for Refugees (UNHCR) is the designated organization to investigate the status of persons who may be stateless, and to assist such persons in making claims to the relevant government authorities.

Statelessness is also linked to the Convention Relating to the Status of Refugees (1951). Designed to protect persons fleeing persecution in their own countries, the convention defines persons needing protection, as well as the responsibilities of the states to which they have fled. The convention recognizes that while some refugees may have a nationality, asylum seekers are effectively stateless if they cannot return to the country of their nationality. The legal status of stateless persons, including its ambiguities, thus has important implications for refugees (Bradley 2014, 102–3).[4]

Operationalizing definitions of "statelessness" has proved difficult. Adjudicators and scholars sometimes refer to those who fall under the definition of a "stateless person" in the 1954 convention as " de jure" stateless persons, even though that term does not appear in the convention itself. Confusingly, the 1961 convention references "de facto" stateless persons, but without a definition. Nor does one exist in any other international instrument. The ambiguity matters. The UNHCR maintains that persons who are de facto stateless lack the protections guaranteed those otherwise recognized as stateless under the 1954 convention (UNHCR 2014b, 5). The 1961 convention on the Reduction of Statelessness references protection for de jure stateless persons, but it also recommends that persons who are de facto stateless should be protected as well, to enable them to acquire an effective nationality. Thus, statelessness exists as a matter of international law but still does not provide human rights protections to those who are effectively stateless and cannot prove it because of obstructions by officials in states from which they seek proof of either citizenship or lack thereof (a problem Lawrance pursues in detail in chapter 3 of this volume).

Attempts to define de facto statelessness have not solved the problem. For instance, one definition includes persons "outside the country of their nationality who are denied diplomatic protection or assistance by that country" (Blitz and Lynch 2009, 5). Another references those who are unable to document or prove nationality, and those whom a government does not recognize as citizens despite a colorable claim to that status (Southwick and Lynch 2009). The Expert Meeting on the Concept of Stateless Persons (2010) at Prato, Italy, proposed that an individual is stateless "if all states to which he or she has a factual link fail to consider the person as a national" (Bingham, Reddy, and Köhn 2011). Unlike de jure statelessness, no formal process determines whether an individual is "de facto" stateless. Rather, it is an ad hoc classification applicable when either an individual is unable to prove his citizenship, or when his country of origin refuses to recognize his citizenship.

The definitions of stateless persons in the two international conventions have been widely recognized as deficient in recognizing the full scope of the problem for those affected (Van Waas 2008, 19–27). From the perspective of a person who cannot prove citizenship, de jure statelessness and de facto statelessness are one and the same. This chapter shows how this produces a possible "statelessness in waiting," or, as noted in the introduction, a "statelessness in question" that bears many of the hallmarks of "citizenship in question." Many of the contributing factors leading to a formal determination of statelessness emerge from a precarious existence, including the inability of vulnerable populations to register births and problems in acquiring documents (Fullerton 2014, 148; Sadiq 2008). The term "effective statelessness" aptly describes the political, social, and even geographic exclusions experienced by those whose own country fails to recognize them as such. My hope for the following discussion is that careful use of concepts specific to the operations of citizenship in question and statelessness in question may better inform ongoing debates about statelessness and the politics of ineffective citizenship.

Effective Statelessness: Examples in Latin America

Academic inquiry with respect to citizenship in Latin America has tended to focus on equality, participatory democracy, and access to government services rather than acquisition of citizenship status or proof thereof. As a result, statelessness in the Western Hemisphere has drawn little attention, necessitating reliance on reports by government and human rights groups.

As a general rule, de jure statelessness in the Western Hemisphere is thought to be uncommon, in large part because predominant migration patterns are into jus soli regimes from countries that also recognize citizenship status for most births occurring outside the nation. In theory, at least, a claim of citizenship as a matter of law would normally exist for the vast majority of the population.

The notable exception is the Dominican Republic, which recently changed from a jus soli regime to jus sanguinis, creating an estimated 200,000 stateless persons of Haitian descent (Fullerton 2014, 148). From 1929 until 2010, the Dominican Republic awarded citizenship to those born on its territory, with the exception of children of diplomats and those "in transit" through the country. But Dominican government officials routinely refused to register births of persons of Haitian descent on the ground that Haitian migrants in the country were "in transit," even if they were long-term residents. The Inter-American Court of Human Rights ruled in 2005 that the Dominican Republic's denial of nationality through its refusal to issue birth certificates violated that country's own constitution (*Yean and Bosico v. Dominican Republic* 2005). The Senate of the Dominican Republic rejected the judgment, followed shortly by a decision of that country's Constitutional Court upholding the previous interpretation that undocumented migrants should be considered as being "in transit."

Two later developments in the Dominican Republic greatly exacerbated the problem of de jure statelessness. In 2010, the amended Dominican Constitution denied citizenship to children born in the Dominican Republic to parents in the country illegally (U.S. Department of State 2012a). In 2013, the Constitutional Court ruled that this new provision could be applied retroactively. According to human rights groups, more than 200,000 persons of Haitian descent are now stateless; the government insists that this number is less than 25,000. The Inter-American Commission on Human Rights issued a strongly worded press release expressing its "deep concern" over the court's ruling (Organization of American States 2013). In October 2014, the Inter-American Court of Human Rights called for the Dominican Republic to provide redress for human rights abuses, illegal deportations, denial of identity documents, and arbitrary deprivation of nationality, a ruling the Dominican Republic formally rejected.

The Dominican government continues to assert that even children born of Haitian parents who were legal permanent residents cannot be registered as Dominican nationals. Government officials have taken strong measures against providing citizenship to persons of Haitian descent born in the country whose parents were unable to document their legal stay in the country. These measures included refusals to renew Dominican birth and identity documents. The government stated that such refusals were based on evidence of fraudulent documentation, but advocacy groups alleged that the moves targeted persons whose parents were Haitian or whose names sounded Haitian and constituted acts of denationalization. Thousands of Dominican-born persons of Haitian descent lack citizenship or identity documents. The U.S. Department of State characterizes these persons as "effectively stateless," adopting the favored modern terminology while avoiding the de facto and de jure categorizations from the earlier round of conventions related to nationality (Fullerton 2014; U.S. Department of State 2012a).

Elsewhere in the Americas, examples of "effective statelessness" include individuals who lack any documentation to prove the location of their birth, and those who migrate to or seek refuge in another country that does not recognize them. Indigenous populations within Latin America are particularly susceptible to these problems. Civil conflicts exacerbate such problems, with large numbers of persons displaced by civil conflicts facing effective statelessness, despite eligibility for protection as refugees (see Lawrance, chapter 3, this volume).[5] Several nations in Latin America have encountered significant numbers of refugees fleeing civil conflicts in Colombia and elsewhere. Some of these displaced persons seek regularization of their status by refugee applications in host countries, but many do not. In Brazil, for example, 17,500 unregistered Colombian refugees were thought to be living in the country's Amazon region (U.S. Department of State 2008b). An estimated 4,000 Haitian immigrants entered the country, making their way through Peru, Colombia, and Bolivia via the Dominican Republic and Panama in hope of securing employment in one of the large infrastructure projects (U.S. Department of State 2011c).

Effective statelessness can occur when displaced persons are neither recognized as refugees nor assisted by their home country's consulates where they are located. The number of asylum and refugee claims recognized by Brazil and other countries lags behind the number of applicants, sometimes substantially. In Bolivia, for example, UNHCR reported in 2008 a recognized refugee population of more than six hundred persons that was "steadily increasing." But in that year the government completed processing and agreed to provide refugee protection in only thirty cases, with older cases still under review and new applications yet to be considered (U.S. Department of State 2008a). While these persons wait, many of them have no proof of citizenship from their country of origin and no formal status where they are.

Ecuador and Costa Rica present starker numbers. The Ecuadorian government received nearly eight thousand applications for refugee status in the first nine months of 2008 alone, adding to a backlog of several thousand pending cases. Both UNHCR and the Ecuadorian government reported difficulty in dealing with the number of applications. In 2011, UNHCR estimated that there were more than 55,000 recognized refugees in Ecuador. An additional 133,000 persons were "in need of international protection," 92 percent of whom were thought to be Colombians. Various nongovernmental organizations reported that the Civil Registry did not always cooperate in registering refugee children or registering children of refugees born in the country, despite legal requirements to do so (U.S. Department of State 2008a, 2011f). Many of these persons fled their homes without proof of nationality, if they had such documents at all.

As of 2009, UNHCR also reported 12,298 recognized refugees in Costa Rica, the majority of whom were from Colombia. The large influx led to a significant backlog of refugee applications, many from individuals who will wait years for a determination of status. Of those claims that have been considered, a high percentage have been rejected while refugees have used the asylum request process to obtain documentation to allow them to transit through a country to the United States (e.g., U.S. Department of State 2010a, 2011e).

Internal displacement presents similar problems. For several decades Colombia has faced a guerrilla uprising, which has resulted in more than 300,000 deaths (Mapping Militant Organizations 2012). The turmoil in Colombia has displaced more than 5 million people within that nation's borders since 1985. The estimate greatly exceeds the government's registered number of 3.9 million due to the high number of indigenous and Afro-Colombian groups affected by displacement (U.S. Department of State 2011d). These groups disproportionately lack access to citizenship documents.

Even where civil strife is not an issue, widespread failure to register births poses a significant problem of effective statelessness. For example, several hundred thousand persons in Bolivia lack citizenship documents, preventing them from obtaining international travel documents and accessing other government services (U.S. Department of State 2011b). Persons who were born in Nicaragua also have difficulty obtaining documentation of that fact, especially in rural areas. The local civil registries should register births within twelve months, upon the presentation of either a medical or a baptismal certificate. But many persons lack such certificates, and one estimate indicates that 250,000 children and adolescents still in Nicaragua lacked legal documentation (U.S. Department of State 2012b).

Persons without a registered birth are unable to obtain a *cedula* (national identity card) in Nicaragua. As the report explains, these persons had difficulty participating in the legal economy, conducting bank transactions, and voting. Persons who lacked a cedula also were subject to other restrictions in employment, access to courts, and land ownership. Women and children lacking citizenship documents were reportedly more vulnerable to sexual exploitation by traffickers. The government did not effectively implement laws and policies to provide persons the opportunity to obtain nationality documents on a nondiscriminatory basis. Apart from equality of treatment and access to citizenship rights within Nicaragua, migrants outside of the country face problems proving that they are Nicaraguan citizens (U.S. Department of State 2012b).

Recent data suggest the registration problem may grow worse. In 2012, approximately 12.5 percent of the eligible population was thought to lack proof of citizenship. The government also raised the cost of a *cedula* (including renewal of an expired card) to approximately fourteen dollars, when almost half of all citizens live on less than one dollar per day (U.S. Department of State 2011g).

Migration is also a cause of failure to register a birth. The U.S. Department of State has identified problems of statelessness in the border areas Costa Rica shares with Panama and Nicaragua, including this example: "Members of the Ngobe-Bugle indigenous group from Panama came to work on Costa Rican plantations, and sometimes their children were born in rudimentary structures on the plantations. In these cases the children were not registered as Costa Rican citizens because the families did not think it necessary to register the births, but when the families returned to Panama, the children were not registered there either" (U.S. Department of State 2011e). A similar problem occurred with other Nicaraguan families who migrated to work on Costa Rican coffee plantations (U.S. Department of State 2010a). There is no indication that these births have since been registered in either Costa Rica or Nicaragua.

Peru has also experienced problems documenting births. In 2008, more than 1 million citizens lacked identity documents and thus could not fully exercise their civil, political, and economic rights as citizens. An estimated 15 percent of births were unregistered. As of 2011, that number had grown to an estimated 4.7 million Peruvians. Without documents, these individuals are profoundly marginalized both economically and politically. A recent report states that "poor and indigenous women and children in rural areas were disproportionately represented among those lacking identity documents" due to the absence of a birth certificate (U.S. Department of State 2011h).

In Mexico, although there are no official governmental statistics, nongovernmental organizations estimate that up to 30 percent of the children in Mexico are unregistered (Asencio 2012), with one group estimating the total number of unregistered persons at more than ten million (Center for Migration Studies 2012). Street children, children from single-parent homes in rural areas, indigenous children, and children of internally displaced person or refugees are often unregistered. Unauthorized migrants and minorities tend to have the highest percentages of unregistered children. When the children grow up, the lack of citizenship or identity documents prevents them from entering the formal labor market, obtaining a driver's license or voter registration documents, opening bank accounts, marrying legally, or even registering the birth of their own children. This problem becomes compounded when the unregistered travel to the United States and become "doubly undocumented." Once in the United States, they are ineligible for a Mexican *marticula consular* or U.S. identification. In effect, they are invisible to both the United States and Mexico (Asencio 2012).

The citizenship documentation problems identified by the U.S. Department of State likely underreport the scope of the problem throughout the region. Worldwide, an estimated forty million births go unregistered each year (UNICEF 1998, 662). Furthermore, these instances of effective statelessness are problematic beyond the borders of any single nation. Interregional migration within Latin America, apart from migration provoked by civil disorder or natural disaster, is a significant phenomenon (Durand and Massey 2010, 27).

In sum, for a variety of reasons, a significant but unknown number of persons residing in Latin America possess uncertain nationality. These reasons include widespread failures to register existing citizens at birth, migrants who have difficulty obtaining proof of citizenship, and civil disorders that overwhelm another country's ability to process claims for asylum and refugee status.

Effective Statelessness: Examples in the United States

In the United States, as well, it is sometimes difficult to prove one's citizenship or the location of one's birth. Such instances illustrate the many evidentiary problems associated with proof of citizenship, even with comparatively well-organized systems for recording births, as Rachel Rosenbloom shows is the case for births in Texas adjudicated in recent years (chapter 7, this volume).

Another problem occurs when parents fail to register their children's birth at all. Although this is uncommon in the United States, it does happen. In 2011, for example, two sisters in Kentucky sued in federal court over eligibility for Social Security, resulting in a settlement in which the sisters were issued documentation by the State Department to establish their citizenship. One sister was born at a home in Kentucky, and the other was delivered in the back of a van in Alabama. The births were recorded in a family Bible but were otherwise not documented (Barrouquere 2011). Proof of citizenship for Social Security benefits, in fact, is a fertile area of litigation, with these two Kentucky sisters serving as just one example.

Another example of the problems that can result from a missing or nonexistent birth certificate is the case of Sazar Dent, who was nearly deported to Honduras in 2010 because he could not prove the citizenship of his U.S.-born adoptive mother, a key fact for establishing his own U.S. citizenship. Dent's statement to the immigration judge noted the absence of his mother's birth certificate: "I believe I inherited U.S. citizenship through this adoption, now I seem to meet all of the I.N.S. requirements for qualifying for it, except . . . for her birth certificate, because she was born in 1904 and records started being kept on files only since 1911." The immigration judge ruled against Dent, and in Dent's first appeal to the Board of Immigration Appeals, he asked for assistance obtaining government records related to his mother's citizenship "because he was in jail and his adoptive mother was dead." Based on his mother's earlier application for a Social Security number, in which she provided the date and place of her birth, and the intervention of pro bono counsel, Dent was ultimately successful in his claim to have derived citizenship (*Dent v. Holder* 2010).

Birth certificates, however, are susceptible to fraud, and a black market in birth documents exists in the United States.[6] We know about fraudulent birth documents most commonly through cases of passport fraud, in which a false birth record is used in an attempt to acquire U.S. citizenship. In 2001, Usama S. Abdel Whab, a citizen of Egypt, applied for a U.S. passport, stating that he was born in Brooklyn. In support of this claim, Whab submitted false affidavits from persons supposedly with knowledge of his birth in Brooklyn. When asked for additional supporting documents, Whab submitted a forged baptismal certificate. Whab was convicted of making a false statement in an application for a U.S. passport and deported (*Abdel-Whab v. Orthopedic Association of Duchess* 2006).

A passport applicant must establish both personal identity and U.S. citizenship. As Whab's case indicates, the absence of a birth certificate is not necessarily fatal to obtaining a U.S. passport, as one can submit other (nonfraudulent) proof of birth in the United States. If an individual is unable to produce a birth certificate, he or she must produce, among other things, proof that no official birth certificate exists. The applicant may also submit "birth affidavits" from persons with knowledge of the birth, such as the doctor who performed the delivery or a relative who personally witnessed the birth. But as Sazar Dent's case makes clear, the passage of time can make such proof extremely difficult— either to produce or to verify. Indeed, lack of proof of citizenship is the key factor in some mistaken deportations by the U.S. government of its own citizens (da Silva 2008). In 2010, as many as four thousand U.S. citizens were detained or deported as aliens. The total since 2003 is estimated to be more than twenty thousand (Stevens 2011a).

Another manifestation of effective statelessness is the existence of a U.S. population of migrants whom the United States is unable to deport. Deportation from the United States requires the agreement of the recipient country to accept the person, along with issuance of travel documents by that country prior to deportation. International law and numerous treaties, including the Pan-American Treaty (1928), require countries to accept return of their nationals.

But in recent years, the United States has been confronted by upward of hundreds, possibly thousands, of cases of aliens with final orders of removal for whom deportation is not possible due to failure to obtain agreement with a recipient country. In some instances, it may be that repatriation is refused on a specious ground of lack of nationality because the deportee is deemed undesirable by that nation. An unknown but likely substantial percentage is due to disputed nationality.[7]

Other sources shed light on the scope of the problem. From 2001 to 2004, the Department of Homeland Security (DHS) Office of the Inspector General reported that nearly 134,000 immigrants with final orders of removal instead had been released because of the inability of the U.S. government to repatriate them to their alleged countries of origin (*Hearing before the House Committee on the Judiciary* 2011). Congressional testimony by a former Justice Department official, Thomas H. Dupree Jr., indicates one cause is that "his country of origin may simply be unknown" (Dupree 2011).

Failing resolution at the diplomatic level, an investigation abroad becomes necessary to determine the validity of the claim that a deportee is not a citizen of that country. In jus soli regimes, a birth record will suffice. In jus sanguinis regimes, the inquiry is more complicated, as proof of location of birth in that country is generally insufficient to establish citizenship. Furthermore, the deportee may not have lived in his alleged country of citizenship for many years, making it less likely that that country would have evidence of citizenship such as a passport application. All these investigations, moreover, require the cooperation of foreign government officials.

Another difficulty in establishing nationality may be that the country from which the alien arrived and the country of his or her citizenship are different. This is an issue particularly with persons crossing without documentation at Mexico's southern border, the major conduit through which undocumented migrants flow from Central America into Mexico and eventually the United States (Castillo 2006).

Recently, the United States has used access to temporary worker visas as a mechanism to ensure cooperation for the repatriation of deportees. Under DHS regulations, H-2A and H-2B nonimmigrant visas may be issued only to persons from countries designated by the DHS secretary. Countries included on the list are those that have cooperated with U.S. deportations. Interestingly, participating countries must accept deportation orders against "residents" of a sending nation, in addition to those it would claim as citizens. The sending countries in the program, therefore, have an incentive to receive noncitizen migrants who had been living there, including unauthorized migrants (Price 2013).

But even in those cases in which the United States is unable to deport a person for reasons other than disputed nationality, U.S. law does not require the award of U.S. or any other nationality. These persons have no clear immigration status in the United States. Thus, the 134,000 persons whom the United States allegedly could not deport between 2001 and 2004—and the unknown number before and after them—are effectively stateless. No nation will take them, and they have no immigration status in the United States.[8]

The Generational Promise of Jus Soli: A Perilous Reliance

Given that potentially large populations in the Americas have a precarious citizenship, what is the significance of a shared jus soli in the Western Hemisphere? Jus soli is often held up as the preferred regime for ascriptive citizenship because statelessness does not extend beyond one generation. But as we have seen, poor documentation and related issues can negate formal legal status within one's own country. There are two other ways that nationality laws in the region contribute to effective statelessness, by complicating documentation efforts even when the home country cooperates in the repatriation process.

First, with restrictions on jus sanguinis in many countries in the region, it is possible for second-generation emigrants to lack citizenship in the parents' country, even if the parents' citizenship status there is secure. Thus, the issue of statelessness concerns not only parents who would have difficulty proving their own nationality but also the laws of other nations with respect to awarding citizenship to children born abroad.

This path to effective statelessness is in consequence of jus sanguinis rules of other nations that already fail to provide a fallback nationality at birth. All states incorporate at least some form of jus sanguinis into their citizenship rules (Spiro 2008, 10–11). Most nations have generational limits and registration requirements for the transmission of nationality by descent to persons born outside of that country. In Peru, for example, children born to Peruvian parents outside of the country must be registered by their parents by age eighteen in order for the child to obtain citizenship (U.S. Department of State 2011h). While some of these registration requirements direct the parents to the nearest consulate or embassy for the citizenship to be recognized (e.g., Haiti), others are a form of residency requirement, requiring travel to the home country in order to register the birth. Uruguay, for example, awards citizenship for children born abroad to a Uruguayan parent only if the child is registered in person at that country's Civic Register for Vital Records (U.S. Office of Personnel Management 2001, 90, 210).

In some countries, a child born abroad must return in order to maintain citizenship. In Chile, a child born abroad to at least one parent who is a citizen of Chile must establish a residence in that country before the age of twenty-one. Similarly, Colombia requires that a child born abroad must establish residency in Colombia for citizenship by descent. Ecuador allows a child born abroad to a native-born Ecuadorian father or mother to become a citizen only if the child becomes a resident of that country. Panama limits citizenship by descent from a naturalized Panamanian parent to children who declare their intention to elect Panamanian nationality no later than one year after reaching the age of eighteen. In Venezuela, the parents must return with the child to reside in that country before the child reaches the age of eighteen. Further, the child born abroad must declare Venezuelan nationality before reaching the age of twenty-five (U.S. Office of Personnel Management 2001, 50, 53, 68, 155, 213).

Most nations also have complicated rules to determine nationality for out-of-wedlock births abroad, particularly to establish paternity. Some nations even require "legitimate" births in order to transmit citizenship abroad. In the Bahamas, a child born abroad legitimately to a father who is a citizen becomes a citizen by descent. Registration is required for any person (eighteen years or older) born in wedlock outside the Bahamas to a Bahamian mother. The Bahamas appears to have no process at all for an unwed father to establish paternity (U.S. Office of Personnel Management 2001, 26). The U.S. State Department asserts that this citizenship policy, together with the fact that Bahamas is one of the rare Western Hemisphere nations without jus soli, has resulted in "several generations" of stateless persons living in that country and elsewhere (U.S. Department of State 2011a). Like the Bahamas, Barbados allows fathers to pass their citizenship by descent only if married to the mother. Children born out of wedlock to a Barbadian mother may inherit her citizenship. In both instances the child must be registered with the nearest diplomatic representative. In Argentina, *both* parents must be Argentine citizens in order for a child born abroad to be a citizen of Argentina (U.S. Office of Personnel Management 2001, 19, 29).

Several nations in the Western Hemisphere—including Mexico and Canada—have tightened jus sanguinis rules for children born outside of those nations. By constitutional amendment in 1997, Mexico limited the award of its nationality to the first generation born abroad (Fitzgerald 2005, 176). Similarly, Canada amended its citizenship laws to limit citizenship by descent to one generation born outside Canada. For Canada, this change was said to "protect the value of citizenship" (Citizenship and Immigration Canada 2013). For both Canada and Mexico, the result would be statelessness for the second generation born in the United States, even though the parents would remain Canadian and Mexican citizens.

Mexico is of special interest because its nationals are thought to constitute the highest percentage of the undocumented population in the United States. While Mexico has generational limits on citizenship, it is otherwise relatively generous with respect to awarding Mexican citizenship to the first generation born abroad. A parent who is a native-born or naturalized Mexican is required to register the child at the nearest Mexican consulate, followed by a birth registration in Mexico (U.S. Office of Personnel Management 2001, 133). Proving paternity to satisfy Mexican nationality law, however, remains complicated, both legally and because of the relative scarcity of genetic tests for paternity. It is also unclear how many parents can themselves prove their own Mexican nationality. De jure Mexican nationals may arrive in the United States without proof of *any* nationality.

In the United States, extended residence abroad can mean the inability to pass on U.S. citizenship to children. These children could be stateless at birth if born in a country that relies upon jus sanguinis for citizenship. Under U.S. law, in order for the child to acquire citizenship, the citizen parent must have been physically present in the United States for a specified period prior to the child's birth (United States Code 8, §§ 1401, 1409). The aim of the physical presence requirement is to prevent the transmission of citizenship by descent through generations of expatriates who have had no connection to the United States, but for U.S. citizens born abroad, proving this may require proving the residency of their parents, or even their own parents' U.S. citizenship, which itself may require proving U.S. residency of a respondent's grandparents, thus posing evidentiary hurdles that are impossible to overcome for those unable to pay fees for attorneys, much less investigators (Stevens 2011a).

In sum, effectively stateless migrants or undocumented citizens, even in jus soli regions, can become parents of a new class of stateless children outside of their countries as well as inside. An unauthorized migrant with a clear nationality can return to his country of origin and pursue life where political, economic, and social participation is possible. Stateless people cannot. Illegal immigrants with a firm nationality can also receive consular assistance in matters including protection, travel documents, and judicial proceedings. A stateless immigrant cannot. Absent political action, children could live their entire lives in a country without the possibility of full membership in the polity. They would have no other home and would indeed become a permanent underclass.

Conclusion

Jus soli is endorsed in international agreements as the preferred mechanism to avoid de jure statelessness. But a nearly universal jus soli in the Americas fails to resolve nationality in significant instances. When those numbers are large, disruptions to social and political cohesion cannot be ignored. In this chapter, I described the existence of what I term "effective" statelessness in the Americas as one way to illustrate deficiencies in international treaties designed to protect rights of citizenship. A narrow understanding of statelessness leaves the concept of citizenship largely meaningless.

While jus soli can avoid creating statelessness at birth, government policy and practice can create a permanent underclass of noncitizens—a moral wrong in any democratic nation. These children will not have chosen their situation. As such, they have a special claim in a liberal society (Bosniak 2007, 394). Jus soli is democratically superior because it creates the presumption that populations living within a nation's borders are members of the political community, absent proof of nonmembership by birth elsewhere. Place of birth is a burden of proof issue that should be relatively easy to resolve. Yet it is not, and the blame lies with poor government structures, political inattention, and, all too often, intentional discrimination against vulnerable groups.

In areas where migration is common, the prevention of statelessness relies on careful recording of births and easy access to those records, as well as the commitment of the country of origin to accept return of or render aid to its emigrants. Migration, displacement, and poor administrative reach in rural areas and indigenous communities in the Americas counter much of the benefit of a common reliance on jus soli to assign nationality at birth. As this chapter has portrayed, movement among jus soli regimes may produce statelessness even where law would dictate otherwise. "Effective statelessness" is a hidden problem that the shared tradition of jus soli in the region does not prevent.

NOTES

1. In late 2014, the Institute on Statelessness and Inclusion compared regional differences in stateless populations in its report, *The World's Stateless*. The report credits the prevalence of the jus soli form of ascriptive citizenship as the preferred practice to prevent statelessness: "The Americas currently reports the lowest number of stateless persons. . . . This demonstrates the advantages of a jus soli approach to nationality (i.e., conferral of

nationality at birth to all children born in the territory), the norm in the Americas" (Institute on Statelessness and Inclusion 2014, 58).

2. There are a number of related conventions. The Convention on the Rights of the Child (1989) obligates signatory states to ensure that every child acquires a nationality. Several regional human rights treaties also address statelessness, including the American Convention on Human Rights. The American Convention states: "Every person has the right to the nationality of the state in whose territory he was born if he does not have the right to any other nationality" (Organization of American States 1969). Article 26 of the International Covenant on Civil and Political Rights (1966) also sets out a nondiscrimination clause that applies very broadly, including to nationality legislation and how it is implemented.

3. At least ten million persons are believed to be stateless throughout the world, but it is impossible to know whether this number is accurate or underlying trends (Institute on Statelessness 2014, 7).

4. Megan Bradley explores the "persistent and un-nuanced conflation of refugeehood and statelessness," in part by examining Hannah Arendt's view that "the core of statelessness . . . is identical with the refugee question" (Bradley 2014, 102, 105).

5. The link between refugees and the problem of statelessness has long been recognized in the Americas. The Brazil Declaration and Plan of Action, adopted by twenty-eight Latin American and Caribbean countries in December 2014, is an agreement "to work together to uphold the highest international and regional protection standards, implement innovative solutions for refugees and displaced persons and end the plight of stateless persons in the region" (UNHCR 2014a). The Brazil Declaration builds on the Cartagena Declaration on Refugees (1984), which broadened the refugee definition to encompass displaced and stateless persons.

6. The unique form of federalism in the United States complicates determination of place of birth because no national birth registry exists. The individual states issue birth certificates in a variety of forms, with no agreed upon standard for these documents.

7. The Department of Homeland Security does not provide data on deportees who are released or continued in detention while immigration officers seek a recipient country. We know these situations occur, however, through reported decisions following *Zadvydas v. Davis* (2001) and *Clark v. Martinez* (2005). These cases established that aliens who have been ordered removed from the United States may not be detained indefinitely once removal is no longer foreseeable or when there is no reasonable likelihood of their being deported (Canty 2004; Martin 2001). Such cases provide at least limited data about the existence of persons with no effective nationality.

8. The United States maintains a paradoxical and complex stance with respect to statelessness. The nation is not a signatory to either the 1954 or the 1961 conventions on statelessness. The United States nonetheless agrees that statelessness is undesirable, and it pursues diplomatic efforts around the globe to remedy statelessness. It is also the single largest donor to the United Nations agency tasked with protecting stateless individuals, UNHCR (Price 2013). The United States also defines "refugee" more expansively than is required by the Convention Relating to the Status of Refugees (1951), including deprivation of nationality as persecution (Fullerton 2014).

2. THE POLITICS OF EVIDENCE

ROMA CITIZENSHIP DEFICITS IN EUROPE

JACQUELINE BHABHA

> Roma integration is not only a moral duty, but in the interest of Member States,
> especially for those with a large Roma minority. —European Council
> Recommendation for Roma Inclusion

> One must deserve French nationality and be able to
> demonstrate one's worthiness [of being a French national].
> —Nicholas Sarkozy, then French president

In principle, citizens occupy a privileged space within their state. They enjoy political, legal, and fiscal advantages denied to noncitizens, even long-standing, lawfully resident ones. In contemporary democracies, discrimination in the attribution of these advantages among members of the national citizenry is, in theory, permissible only in limited contexts and when justified by age or other legally sanctioned criteria. Citizenship, then, is intended as an inclusive membership club, one that (unlike most clubs) benefits a majority of the proximate population. Racial, religious, class, gender, and ethnic minority status, it is generally claimed, do not function as legitimate disqualifying factors. As the introduction to this volume makes clear, however, there is a yawning gap between the purported inclusiveness and uniform applicability of the citizenship construct across formally eligible populations, and the arbitrary, ad hoc, and flawed reach of citizenship taxonomies in practice. Careful deconstruction of the mapping of citizenship onto population, such as that carried out by the authors in this volume, makes it clear this status or category is neither categorical nor easily observed. Nevertheless, the notion of an effortless mapping of citizenship onto an entitled population is pervasive and, for all practical political purposes, unchallenged. Citizens benefit from a privileged status that accords them important rights (and only a few duties).

This privileged status does not apply only to citizens of nation-states. Over the past decades, the diffusion of globalization and the growth of post-Westphalian models of political, economic, and legal governance make possible sources of citizenship beyond those of national citizenship. In this chapter, I shall refer to "regional citizenship" and what I will call "global citizenship." Like national citizenship, both types confer a formal entitlement to particular rights and benefits to those who qualify. Regional citizenship is a relatively new phenomenon, one that postdates the establishment of global citizenship that followed the end of World War II. With the growth of regional forms of intergovernmental association in many parts of the world, from North America to Asia and Africa, new regional unions have in some instances generated a distinctive type of citizenship model, with enhanced benefits for in-group members or regional citizens.

The European Union is an important case in point. Citizens of the EU are supposed to enjoy political and legal privileges that non-EU citizens, even long-time resident third-country nationals, lack. It is claimed that EU citizenship automatically vests in each individual citizen of a member state, by virtue of his or her national state citizenship. Eligibility for this regional citizenship is determined by eligibility for individual member state citizenship (according to the criteria established by the relevant member state). The rights and benefits of EU citizenship are distinct from those that flow from citizenship of the member state (Maas 2008–9, 267). These privileges reflect the core of EU citizenship and can be reduced to two fundamental categories: mobility privileges and nondiscrimination privileges. However, a critical difficulty arises with this model as a reliable protector of citizenship rights and benefits: effective implementation of these citizenship privileges generally depends, in practice, on member state willingness to apply or enforce the relevant rights. This introduces a further layer of uncertainty into the notion of regional citizenship, over and above the arbitrariness and complexity inherent in enforcement of claims to national citizenship. Maas warns, "The most important and fundamental challenge faced by EU citizenship is the prospect of Member States or other authorities not respecting the rights it confers" (2008–9, 267).

An additional type of citizenship, global citizenship, vests in those individuals or populations who can qualify for the protective embrace and associated status benefits of international refugee law. For these people, international law has long guaranteed protection from serious threats to life or freedom—a limited form of quasi citizenship available to eligible applicants seeking asylum from persecution outside their own country. For the many who are stateless and therefore lack their own country, international refugee law provides the same guaranteed protection from persecution within the place of their habitual residence as it does for refugees with a citizenship. But again, the realization of benefits guaranteed by global citizenship depends significantly on national state willingness to implement its legal obligations. All the types of citizenship just identified therefore are beset by categorical indeterminacies of evidentiary criteria.

Citizenship and the Politics of Evidence

Forensic evidence, both documentary and circumstantial, is central to operationalizing the exclusionary process of sifting through eligibility for protection. As with many administrative techniques, it performs in a manner that is facially "procedural"—contingent and "merely" operational—but actually deeply substantive. Where eligibility for citizenship privileges is challenged, documents are critical tools for governments and individuals alike. Evidentiary challenges highlight the tension between the supposed self-evidence of citizenship and its actual phenomenology, as the introduction to this volume rightly notes. Access to the enabling documents, which majority communities generally secure through streamlined and simple procedures enacted routinely by courteous and efficient official agencies, can present insuperable barriers for others. Complex and ill-defined laws and regulations—about nationality claims, residence rights, public security or public health threats, bilateral readmission agreements— emerge when these simple procedures fail and attempts to exclude individuals from sought-after benefits have to be challenged. Navigating and asserting the path to citizenship entitlement requires much more than personal narratives consistent with legal criteria put forward by regional or global institutions. It also requires skilled and time-consuming legal representation, an impartial and effective forum for staking claims, the political will underpinning competent public service provision, substantial financial resources, and administrative savvy to painstakingly comply with the reality of bureaucratic "decisionism" in regard to the interpretation of official rules, regulations, and procedures.

Access to critical evidence is a deeply political process. Technical flaws in documentary endowment are not randomly distributed across citizen populations, as, for instance, dates of birth. Rather, they reflect deep-seated exclusions from the presumed level playing field of a right to rights, exclusions that extend from the moment of entry into a registrar's office, social security benefits center, or public hospital to the feeling of security and automatic access to basic sanitation and other services in one's home. Destitution, illiteracy, and pervasive stigma militate against the organizational and institutional clout needed to navigate intricate bureaucratic procedures. This is especially the case when these procedures operate in a highly racialized (or otherwise stratified) social context, where decisional arbitrariness is actually not so much a product of inconsistency as it is a consequence of systemic bias. Problems are compounded when the procedures are embedded in complex, even arcane areas of international law such as eligibility for citizenship by descent, or naturalization following conflict, statelessness, new state formation, expulsion, or eviction.

The ten to twelve million Roma community in Europe provides a compelling case study of the politics of citizenship evidence (Council of Europe 2013, 3). It is widely acknowledged that the legacy of pervasive social and political exclusion of this community in Europe over generations has manifested itself in visible markers of deprivation and rights violations—substandard and impermanent housing, poor health, low life expectancy and high morbidity, extensive exposure to social violence, and discriminatory educational access and provision (European Union Agency for Fundamental Rights, UNDP, and European Commission 2012, 8). As devastating, but less widely acknowledged, is the radical Roma citizenship deficit that presents in tandem with this pervasive exclusion. A dramatic dearth of Roma documentary evidence underpins this deficit—many Roma simply do not have birth certificates, citizenship or other identity certificates, residence certificates, bank accounts, rent books, school attendance documents, marriage certificates, death certificates, or proof of disability, to name just some of the critical elements demanded by the citizenship tool kit. This deficit justifies the routine official exercise of "legalized illegality" in the form of widespread exclusion from core benefits of national, European, or global citizenship (Çağlar and Mehling 2013, 172). This chapter explores the politics of evidence as they impinge on the European Roma community in the context of the three categories of citizenship outlined earlier, and it brings to light the paradoxical situation of this population: a people that have for centuries been *in* Europe but are still widely not considered to be *of* Europe.

A Synoptic Roma History

Though the Roma have been European residents for at least six centuries, large numbers among their community have only tortuous and unreliable access to the privileges that can flow from the citizenship categories mentioned above

(Liégeois 2008, 105). This is not a new phenomenon. Historically the Roma community has been the target of extreme discrimination and exclusion in Europe, raising recurring questions about their entitlement to the benefits of citizenship. Challenges to the Roma's legitimacy as a European population date back centuries, though experts agree that the ancestors of today's Roma population arrived in what is now the European Union as long ago as the fourteenth century. Their status as putative outsiders is one justification for discrimination, while their reputation as supposedly restless itinerants is another. This archetype prevails despite the fact that only small sections of today's Roma community consider themselves travelers or transient, with the vast majority aspiring to the sedentary, secure, and predictable lifestyle of their non-Roma counterparts (Guild and Carrera 2013, 8). Indeed, despite the Roma majority's explicit rejection of an itinerant lifestyle and persistent attempts to secure permanent housing and long-term residence rights, the whole community continues to be stereotyped as erstwhile Indian "nomads" with a transient presence and no legitimate claim to long-term European residence (Warnke 1999, 357–58). The social construction of the community as "nomadic," itinerant, or temporary is used to justify discrimination and marginalization with respect to the putatively more settled or sedentary majority. Take the case of Torino, an industrial city in northern Italy with a long-settled Roma community, many of them second and third generation born in Italy, and a progressive city administration with a commendable history of well-meaning involvement in Roma social service provision (Associazione per gli studi giuridici sull'immigrazione and Rozzi 2013).[1] Despite the Roma's generation-long history in the city, the municipal office responsible for Roma social service provision is still called Ufficio Nomadi (Nomads Office). As Jaroka Livia, a Roma elected representative from Hungary to the European Parliament, has observed: "[The Roma] don't want to be nomads. They want dignity. They want opportunity" (Cohen 2011).

Pervasive stigma and hostility toward the Roma community have, with some geographic variations, existed throughout European history. They peaked with the brutal and widespread persecution inflicted on large numbers during the Nazi period. A report commissioned by the Organization for Security and Cooperation in Europe (OSCE) notes that "most autochthonous Austrian, German and Czech Roma were killed in the Holocaust" (Cahn and Guild 2008, 35). According to some estimates, up to 1.5 million Roma were killed by the Nazis.[2] Although the Weimar Constitution provided for equal rights for all citizens, the Roma in Germany were subject to increasingly discriminatory laws and directives over time: exclusion from public places (1920), mandatory registration (1925) and identification cards (1927), restrictions on movement and required proof of employment (1929), bans on mixed marriages (1933), revocation of naturalization (1933), forced sterilization (1933), withdrawal of civil liberties (1937), racial evaluation (1938), and internment and deportation to concentration camps (1936 onward) (Hancock 2002, 37–42). The Nuremburg Laws were amended to include the Roma and extended beyond Nazi Germany to incorporated and occupied territories of the Third Reich. Even before this extension, many European countries had already enacted discriminatory measures targeting the Roma. In 1912, France required "nomads" to register with the authorities upon entering and leaving the country. In 1927, the former Czechoslovakia's "Law on the Wandering Gypsies" required the Roma to obtain permission to stay overnight in an area (Peschanski 2002, 50–55). In Hungary, a 1928 decree prohibited the Roma from entering cities (Lucero and Collum 2006, 98), and in 1933, Austrian government officials called for the Roma to be stripped of their civil rights (Hancock 2002, 37).

Following World War II, repressive communist policies of cultural restriction, forcible assimilation, resettlement, and coercive sterilization continued to reflect the ongoing belief throughout Europe that the Roma were not citizens of the countries in which they resided (Marushiakova and Popov 2008). As Europe moved out of the Cold War and its Communist-governed federations (in former Yugoslavia, Czechoslovakia, and the Soviet Union) to an expanded European Union of individual nation-states, citizenship was redefined. In the process, many of the traditional exclusions, papered over by Communist regimes, reappeared, including the belief that Roma minorities were foreigners. Responding to a resurgence of acute racism against them, many Roma communities from central and southeastern Europe voted with their feet, fleeing discrimination in their home countries, including the Czech Republic, Poland, Hungary, Slovakia, Serbia, Kosovo, Romania, and Slovenia. Their attempts to secure new rights in Western Europe were met with mixed reactions.

In some cases, the Roma migrants managed to secure refugee status or some form of more limited temporary or subsidiary protection under international law (Cour Nationale du Droit d'Asile 2011); this was particularly the case during the Balkan conflicts.[3] New EU citizenship did not thwart discrimination against Roma migrants, whose rights were affirmed only after protracted court proceedings.[4] Even when Roma secured entry to west European territories, Roma Europeans often encountered hostility and outbursts of hysteria and violence. The European Court of Human Rights (ECHR) has over the past decade held on several occasions that European states have violated nondiscrimination provisions in the European Convention. Their findings have included cases concerning illegal expulsion of aliens, racially biased police investigations and abuse (*Bekos and Koutropoulos v. Greece, Cobzaru v. Romania*), and vigilante "skinhead" anti-Roma violence.[5] Litigation brought before the ECHR by Roma who are de jure EU citizens has also addressed other human rights issues such as race discrimination in education, race discrimination in housing allocation, and forced sterilization of Roma women.[6]

Present-Day Evidentiary Barriers for Roma

Stereotypes continue to color access to citizenship and the delivery of public services to the Roma community today. During the 1990s, Roma asylum seekers fleeing persecution in the Czech Republic and Slovakia began arriving in the United Kingdom, prompting outcry in the British media that they were "gold-diggers searching for an easy life" who should be "kicked out of Britain" (Clark and Campbell 2000, 23, 27). While open borders in the East have facilitated free movement for Roma families seeking to escape endemic unemployment and poverty in post-Communist countries, populist xenophobia in the West combined with the recent economic downturn have fueled an increase in anti-Roma policies and practices. French and Italian hysteria centers on supposedly criminal activities by Roma, including baby snatching (Owen 2008) and one or two cases of murder blamed on the entire Roma community (Faiola 2010). Despite Roma migrants' right to enjoy free movement in France as EU citizens, the country's interior minister has claimed that the population poses "a social difficulty," and therefore "the majority must be returned to the borders" (Rubin 2013). In 2010, then French president Sarkozy promised to investigate "the problems created by the behavior of certain travelers and Roma" living in settlements and to deport them. A government spokesman clarified Sarkozy's remarks: "You can very well be Roma, a traveler, even, at times, French within these communities, but you'll have to respect the law of the republic" (Crumley 2010). Though France's current president, François Hollande, promised to "break the strict policies of his predecessor" in 2012, Roma have only experienced increased marginalization and escalated eviction rates (Sayare 2014); eviction rates in 2013 were double those of 2012 (Human Rights Watch 2014).

These racist attitudes are also prevalent in Italy. In 2011, Italian prime minister Silvio Berlusconi warned of the alleged political threat posed by the Roma, stating, "Milan cannot turn into an Islamic city, a 'gypsyopolis' full of Roma camps besieged by foreigners to whom the left wants to give the right to vote" (*Telegraph* 2011). Pervasive anti-Roma rhetoric has encouraged mob violence and vigilante attacks against Roma individuals and communities (Human Rights First 2008), as well as discriminatory measures such as compulsory fingerprinting, mass expulsions, home demolitions, and deportations (Bryant 2010; Hammarberg 2011; Kostlán 2012).

This long-standing hostility and exclusionary stance have their material correlate. The Roma population continues to experience some of the most difficult and harsh living conditions in Europe. While the situation varies by country, the general picture is bleak: between one-quarter and two-thirds of Roma live in poverty or extreme poverty, often in segregated, substandard settlements (UNICEF 2007, 20–23, 27) without access to adequate housing, water, sanitation, and public utilities (European Union Agency for Fundamental Rights Agency 2009). Life expectancy is ten years shorter for Roma individuals than for their non-Roma counterparts, and a sample of five countries has documented Roma child mortality rates two to six times higher than those of the majority population. The Roma also face disproportionately poor health outcomes due both to lack of access to preventive care and to discrimination when seeking treatment (Council of Europe 2013, 7).

Without assets or proof of formal employment, many Roma community members are unable to register their residences and access the social services to which they are entitled (European Union Agency for Fundamental Rights 2009). As a result, Roma are often forced to take jobs in the unregulated economy, where they are vulnerable to further marginalization, exploitation, and coercion. Securing the benefits of citizenship could radically improve these difficult circumstances. However, as the following sections illustrate, citizenship remains an elusive chimera for a majority of the Roma population in need.

Exclusion from National Citizenship

Though citizenship is most commonly acquired by birth on the national territory (jus soli) or through parentage (jus sanguinis), eligibility in the last analysis follows from overcoming evidentiary hurdles specific to different administrative or judicial venues. These eligibility requirements vary greatly; they typically include proof of a minimum period of continuous residence within the state and/or a certain level of national language and/or cultural proficiency. Production of a record of birth registration is also a normal precondition of citizenship acquisition. People with no claim to citizenship of a country by any of these routes are considered *de jure stateless*—defined in Article 1 of the 1954 UN Convention on the Status of Stateless Persons as someone who "is not considered as a national by any state under the operation of its law."

Effective statelessness (see Price and Lawrance, this volume) can arise in various ways, including birth to stateless parents, regime succession, and state dissolution as new states define citizenship eligibility in such a way as to exclude some members—typically members of marginalized or stigmatized minorities—of the former citizenry. (For instance, in the aftermath of the dissolution of the Soviet Union, Baltic countries imposed language requirements that rendered large numbers of Russian-speaking residents stateless.) Many members of the Roma population living in the former Czechoslovakia lost their national citizenship overnight in just these circumstances. These contexts may pose insurmountable evidentiary hurdles as well. The new Czech Republic purposefully defined citizenship through eligibility requirements set out in a 1993 citizenship law: all individuals had to prove they had maintained permanent residency for five continuous years and that they were fluent in Czech. Among the 150,000 to 300,000 Roma living in the Czech Republic (European Roma Rights Center 2013a, 6), many families were forcibly moved from Slovakia to work in Czech factories during the period of state socialism, but then, denied access to permanent accommodation for decades and ghettoized in non-Czech-speaking communities, found themselves unable to fulfill either of these requirements (Warnke 1999, 357, 358). From citizens they became stateless aliens without leaving their long-term places of residence.

Praxis, a nonprofit organization of legal experts, has worked with the Roma community in Serbia for years and has documented a range of obstacles to securing Serbian citizenship. To obtain Serbian citizenship, an applicant has the burden of proving his or her birth by presentation of a birth registration document, as well as proving registration of a temporary or permanent residence (*Praxis* 2008). But both these sets of documents may be unavailable, and the result is effective statelessness (*Praxis* 2010). With an estimated 250,000 to 500,000 Roma currently living in Serbia (European Roma Rights Center 2013b, 3), a significant proportion of this population consists of erstwhile refugees who fled the country of their birth (e.g., Bosnia, Croatia, Macedonia) during the Yugoslav war. For this reason, many records are unavailable, nonexistent, missing, or destroyed. Stateless mothers giving birth in Serbia often fail to register their children because they are "legally invisible" themselves and therefore fear any contact with officialdom. This defensive strategy merely perpetuates the cycle of intergenerational statelessness, as children born in Serbia inherit the outsider status of their refugee parents. Birth registration deficits are not the only problem. Many destitute Roma families in Serbia are homeless or live in informal settlements (referred to as "illegal camps"). Though Serbian law allows such homeless residents to register with the government to prove their Serbian residency, in practice the process for doing this is unknown by most Roma and beset with administrative complexities (*Praxis* 2008). In addition to evidentiary problems, Roma Serbs have been denied their national citizenship because they cannot afford the financial costs of compliance with cumbersome legal procedures, which may include onerous legal fees. The nuts and bolts of citizenship at work, as described in the introduction, here produce statelessness rather than citizenship.

Approximately 110,000 to 180,000 Roma currently live in Italy (European Roma Rights Center 2013b, 6), distributed largely among three main cities—Rome, Naples, and Torino. Italian citizenship is transmitted by descent, so children born in Italy to nonnational parents do not generally acquire Italian citizenship at birth (Rozzi 2013). There is, however, an important qualification to this rule: where a child is born to parents who are recognized as stateless, by virtue of the 1961 UN Convention on the Reduction of Statelessness (UN General Assembly 1961, 175), the child can legally acquire Italian citizenship at birth. In practice, however, restrictive interpretations of citizenship and immigration laws render such registration as a stateless person elusive. The Associazione per gli studi giuridici sull'immigrazione (ASGI), a nongovernmental organization with a robust staff of highly qualified lawyers that has worked with the Roma community in Italy for years, notes: "Restrictive legislation, policies and practices, concerning citizenship, statelessness and immigration, by both Italy and the States stemming from the breakup of Yugoslavia, . . . produce particularly harsh consequences on the most marginalized and discriminated groups such as Roma people" (Associazione per gli studi giuridici sull'immigrazione 2013, 14). Thus, second- and third-generation Roma born in Italy lack citizenship because they cannot prove their residence or that of their parents. They are trapped in a vicious "catch-22" of decisionism manifested as bureaucratic intransigence. Without citizenship proof, they are ineligible for residence permits, and therefore ineligible for access to state housing and a range of other benefits. Without access to residence permits, they cannot claim citizenship and, with it, the benefits of EU nationality, including freedom of movement, educational subsidies, and access to work training and scholarship schemes. The European Commission against Racism and Intolerance noted in a report on Italy filed in 2005 that "decisions on applications for naturalization, notably on the basis of residence, are excessively restrictive and discretionary, and often characterized by a lack of transparency as to the reasons for rejection." The commission also noted the protracted process for decision making and expressed particular concern that "applications concerning minors over 14 years of age, who have reached adulthood before their application has been processed," have "been required to re-apply according to more stringent naturalisation procedures" (Cahn and

Guild 2010, 37). Indeed adolescents encounter multiple difficulties in establishing effective citizenship and the benefits that flow from it.

As a result of these varied practices, Roma populations in Europe have been excluded from the benefits of their national citizenship. Despite valid claims to that citizenship, state authorities persist in not crediting their documents or narratives as bona fide evidence of citizenship entitlement. A range of evidentiary obstacles can lead to this situation (UNHCR 2010). They include the situation (common among severely marginalized and disadvantaged groups) in which an individual has never been registered in the civil registration system of the country where he or she is born (either because of birth through home delivery or because of fear or ignorance about the necessary procedures). Even where registration in the country's civil registration system has taken place, the registry may be missing, or it may have been destroyed as a result of conflict, or the administrative authority may be unwilling to cooperate with the identification of particular individuals or groups. As the introduction notes, the fact of birth itself does not create automatic allocation of citizenship; it requires "ascription" in the sense of enrollment, a process of writing oneself into the community. Moreover, despite possessing civil registration information, some individuals have had difficulty proving their identity (e.g., that they are indeed the person indicated in the civil registry) due to the fact that data are vague or inaccurate (names misspelled, parents' identifying details missing), the individual in question is separated from family support or networks (because he or she is an unaccompanied child or a survivor of trafficking), or the relevant official entities are unwilling to cooperate by authenticating the civil registry documents or responding to requests for supplementary documents. Long-resident populations, generation by generation, may thus be excluded from access to the citizenship of their country of birth.

Exclusion from Regional Citizenship

European Union citizenship poses a second set of evidentiary problems for the Roma community's access to rights of free movement and nondiscrimination. It confers upon individuals the "right to move and reside freely within the territory of the Member States" (Guild and Carrera 2013, 8) and the right to equal treatment. The EU established the right to free movement of workers as one of the founding principles of the EU, a right enshrined in EU citizenship in 1993 (Atger 2013, 181). Directive 2004/38 describes the right of EU citizens to move freely between states. This freedom of movement facilitates open border crossing;

it also permits an EU citizen to live in a member state other than his or her own for three months without proof of means of support. After three months, the state of residence can require the nonnational EU citizen to provide proof of adequate health insurance and means of support. After five years of residence, the EU citizen may apply for permanent residence. Free movement rights of EU nationals can be restricted only on grounds of public policy, public security, and public health. An EU member state cannot expel an individual because he or she is unemployed or claiming benefits. The EU Charter of Fundamental Rights prohibits collective expulsions from a country (Atger 2013, 181).

Despite this robust edifice of free movement and residence rights for EU citizens, Roma European citizens are routinely disadvantaged. For example, in 2010, the French government ordered a targeted campaign to dismantle Roma settlements and deport EU Roma citizens back to their countries of nationality. Within months, France, with little or no due process, had deported more than a thousand persons and demolished more than a hundred camps. France declared that the removals were "voluntary," but the actions were coercive. Targeted Roma families were told that "individuals who did not accept the offer would have risked losing the 'stipends' and having forcible deportation actions filed against them." In practice, many of the concerned Roma residents "expressed openly their intention to accept 'voluntary deportation' and then come back." Çağlar and Mehling write that "the authorities in France . . . knew very well that they could not legally deport EU Roma citizens . . . [so they developed] a series of laws . . . such that the 'illegality' of state acts was in a way 'legalised' " (2013, 160). No international or European court has punished the French government for this en masse, forced removal. These policies have had serious implications for school-age children, including dwindling school attendance caused by the widespread use of such evictions. In the Lyon metropolitan school area, sixty-four Roma children from informal settlements attending school in "mobile classrooms" had their education interrupted during the 2012–13 school year (Amnesty International 2013). Eviction has a recursive effect and can interfere with access to documentation required for school registration. A teacher in Lille confirmed that lack of documents had led to "a six- to nine-month gap between requesting enrolment and actually going to school" (Amnesty International 2013).

A recent European Agenda for the Integration of Third-Country Nationals defines third-country nationals as including "persons born in the EU but not holding the citizenship of a Member State" (European Commission 2011, 3). Many Roma fall into this category, for reasons that are either de jure or de facto. Unable to establish citizenship in EU member states, the Roma are considered as third-country nationals, thus subject to the integration plan. Carrera argues that "(re)integration has been presented and framed as the solution to prevent mobile Roma from exercising their European citizenship mobility freedoms and being treated as foreigners subject to eviction and return to their home country." He suggests: "Integration has been designed as a policy mechanism for passing the buck over to the Roma themselves as regards the reasons for and consequences stemming from their discrimination, exclusion and negation of EU citizenship rights and freedoms" (Carrera 2013, 6). This analysis is particularly relevant in light of the recent deportations of Roma from EU member states.

Exclusion from Global Citizenship

Refugee status is a powerful form of surrogate global citizenship established and widely recognized after the devastating infliction of persecution by European states on their own citizens during the 1930s and 1940s. Few if any human rights protections have been as effective in protecting populations from harm and redistributing access to the benefits of national membership as this form of global citizenship. Yet here too Roma populations in Europe have found themselves excluded from protection, unable to take advantage of benefits that other populations fleeing persecution have availed themselves of. A case in point are Kosovar Roma, an embattled population that has witnessed multiple persecutions over the last century and that is still struggling to establish a secure and rights-respecting life in Europe.

In October 2013, a fifteen-year-old girl of Roma descent, Leonarda Dibrani, was forced off a school bus by French police officers and deported, with her family, to Kosovo. While Dibrani's father is Kosovar, Dibrani and her siblings were born in Italy. Prior to being deported, the family had spent four years in France applying for asylum because of persecution they had faced in Kosovo. The family alleged a well-founded fear of persecution in Kosovo and a risk of serious social isolation if returned. Despite these claims, Dibrani and her family were deported to Kosovo; as expected, they were attacked a few days after arriving in Kosovo, prompting one police official to state, "[The beating] shows that the Dibranis are not safe here" (*Al Jazeera* 2013). Unfamiliar with the local language and without any social connections, the family found itself isolated, and the children were unable to attend school.

Roma populations fleeing persecution in the former Yugoslavia and now in Kosovo have faced exclusion from the protection of asylum in EU member states because they are considered ineligible to file such claims. There is a paradoxical aspect to such exclusion. Whereas, as the previous section notes,

Roma frequently encounter difficulties in asserting their EU citizenship when it comes to exercising their free movement rights as EU citizens, they have nevertheless found their connection to the EU may be invoked to justify exclusion from international protection as refugees. Romanian, Hungarian, and Czech Roma are often the target of severe discrimination in access to state services (such as the notorious placement of Roma children in schools for the disabled and learning-impaired irrespective of their own abilities) and state protection. (Romanian politicians have repeatedly sought to distance their national identity from that of the Roma, urging that the latter be known as "Gypsies" rather than Roma and that they be considered the responsibility of the EU rather than of the national state.) But as EU citizens they are ineligible to file an asylum claim within the EU.

Roma asylum applicants from Kosovo are disqualified from access to asylum in the EU because Kosovo is seeking EU membership. Rather than the evidentiary challenge to legal sanctuary being documents, the changing status of Kosovo itself interpellates the Roma into a new legal identity they are powerless to mobilize in their quest for legal status. Thus, Roma citizens facing deportation from EU member states to countries of origin where they also lack legal status and access to basic minimum social and economic rights (education, housing, emergency health care, protection from violence) have attempted to secure protection as refugees, on the basis of persecution faced because of their nationality or membership of a particular social group. But they have been unsuccessful, a different aspect of the politics of evidence. To illustrate this aspect of the Roma citizenship deficit, consider the circumstances of Kosovar asylum-seeking families long settled and integrated in Germany or France, who find themselves destitute and disoriented once deported from those countries and forced into informal camps in Kosovo. The exclusion from access to asylum in these cases stems from bilateral agreements signed between states such as Kosovo seeking entry to the EU and EU member states themselves. In return for EU reform packages and a gradual path to EU accession, associated states promise to receive and reintegrate those of their nationals whom EU member states decide to deport. The readmission promise operates as a deportation facilitation tool rather than a reintegration support. For the families returned to Serbia and Kosovo, conditions are extremely bleak. Finally, there are Roma individuals residing in EU member states who are denied asylum claims but do not have a nationality, because they are either de jure or de facto stateless refugees (UNHCR 2010).

In 2010, Germany began to deport Kosovar Roma who had sought refuge in Germany from the Kosovo War in 1999 (Çağlar and Mehling 2013, 169).

When Kosovar Roma fled to Germany during the 1999 war, they were granted "tolerated status," which is a temporary right of residence that is provided for short periods but can be extended (UNICEF 2007, 164). Many refugees from the Kosovo War were given this status in the absence of asylum (UNICEF 2007, 164). However, in preparation for EU membership, Kosovo had agreed to implement a program for reintegration of ethnic minorities (European Union Agency for Fundamental Rights 2009, 158, 165) and subsequently signed a bilateral agreement with Germany in April 2010. This macro-level agreement provided the legal structure permitting Germany to deport Kosovar Roma back to Kosovo (UNICEF 2007, 158). Çağlar and Mehling write that many of the Romanian Roma in Germany who were "voluntarily deported" in 2010 met the refugee convention criteria for asylum but were considered ineligible nonetheless because they were members of the EU (2013, 169). Of course, asylum would have been a more valuable status for them than EU citizenship was, given that their freedom of movement as EU citizens was denied (UNICEF 2007, 164). Çağlar and Mehling conclude: "EU space, no matter how differentiated and stratified . . . , had to be free from the conditions that would necessitate asylum from within" (2013, 170).

According to UNICEF, an estimated 38 percent of Roma returned from Germany to Kosovo were considered de facto stateless (2007, 166). But Kosovo did not have the capacity to provide adequate reception conditions for the Kosovar Roma who were deported from Germany to Kosovo (after living in Germany for eleven years) (UNICEF 2007, 165). Many of them immediately left Kosovo.

Roma: In *Europe,* Not *of Europe*

All three categories of citizenship exclusion (national, regional, and global)[7] highlight the paradoxical situation of the Roma community—what Sardelic usefully refers to as the "nested model of citizenship constellations" that concretizes a sharp hierarchy of rights among nationalities (2015, 165–67). The Roma are *in* Europe but not *of* Europe. More than sixty years after Europe committed itself to establishing a continent free of discrimination, and of inhuman or degrading treatment, many Roma experience life as outsiders and outliers to the increasingly integrated and prosperous European population. One is forced to ask, from this vantage point, does citizenship in Europe really exist when all else fails?

What solutions are available, and what strategies are indicated in the face of these inherited and persistent rights deficits? Legal strategies including litigation and law reform have long played a part in the process of securing protection, and in some limited cases they have produced positive results. However, one of the distinctive aspects about Roma exclusion in Europe today is the plethora of legal provisions, recommendations, resolutions, and regulations that have been enacted and promulgated to outlaw discrimination and encourage integration and assimilation, while the problems remain intransigent, and the affected populations experience their exclusion and marginalization as acutely as ever.[8]

Top-down strategies of litigation and law reform seem to have reached their reformative limit. New approaches are essential to break the current logjam to allow the Roma to develop their own voices. Participation of members of the Roma community themselves—in crafting policies and strategies that generate a voice, a sense of agency and inclusion—seems to be a necessary condition of progress. Supporting a stigmatized and multiply disadvantaged community to take steps that reflect their interests, their priorities, and their strategies for securing change is a complicated and challenging process that displaces the leadership and directive role of traditional reforming organizations in favor of a more democratic, collaborative, and decentralized organizational structure. Yet this seems the most hopeful strategy and one that has the best chance of securing enduring reforms and change. Only in this way are citizens likely to become real citizens, securing a status they have claimed for themselves in the face of exclusion and rejection.

The Spanish Center for Research in Theories and Practices that Overcome Inequality (CREA) has been successful in using a "communicative methodology" that emphasizes collaboration and dialogue with various Roma and non-Roma stakeholders to develop a form of inclusive citizenship. Decades of anti-discrimination legislation and pronouncement have not succeeded in creating a form of inclusive citizenship at the national, regional, or global level. Breaking the cycle of exclusion is a pressing, challenging, and unfinished obligation for the multiple constituencies concerned to reverse the divisive impact of citizenship and transform it into a source of rights and benefits, especially for those minorities who stand to gain most.

NOTES

Epigraph: Sarkozy quoted in Cames 2013, 18.

1. This observation is based on the author's experience over the past five years. The Harvard FXB Center is engaged in an action-research project with Roma adolescents and other local partners in Torino.

2. Exact figures are unavailable, but estimates range from 200,000 to 1.5 million killed, which the Roma call the Samudaripen or Porajmos (Barany 1998, 11).

3. Some favorable decisions have quashed deportation orders. See, e.g., *D [a minor] v. Refugee Appeals Tribunal Anor* [2011] IEHC 431, and *K.H. v. Office of Immigration and Nationality* (OIN) 6.K. 34.440/2010/20. Note that the Irish case is an exception to the general policy that EU citizens may not be granted asylum in other member states on the grounds that they are all "safe countries of origin." Other favorable decisions have reviewed rejection of refugee status by immigration boards or held that deportation would be violative of international law. See, e.g., *Bors v. Canada (Minister of Citizenship and Immigration)*, 2010 FC 1004; *Mohacsi v. Canada (Minister of Citizenship and Immigration) (T.D.)*, 2003 FCT 429; *Balogh v. Canada (Minister of Citizenship and Immigration)*, 2002 FCT 809; *Case of N.A. v. United Kingdom*, no. 25904/07, ECHR August 6, 2008.

4. See *Regina v. Immigration Officer at Prague Airport and another (Respondents) ex parte European Roma Rights Centre and others (Appellants)*, UKHL 56, December 9, 2004.

5. Illegal expulsion of aliens: *Conka v. Belgium*, no. 51564/99, ECHR February 5, 2002; *Connors v. UK* (2005) 40 EHRR 9; and *Hamidovic v. Italy*, no. 31956/05 (pending). Racially biased police investigations and abuse: *Bekos and Koutropoulos v. Greece*, no. 15250/02, ECHR December 13, 2005, and *Cobzaru v. Romania*, no. 48254/99, ECHR July 26, 2007, cited in Cahn and Guild 2008, 31. See also *Angelova and Iliev v. Bulgarian*, no. 55523/00, ECHR July 26, 2007; *Nachova and Others v. Bulgaria*, no. 43577/98, ECHR July 6, 2005; *Stoica v. Romania*, no. 42722/02, ECHR March 4, 2008; *Beganović v. Croatia*, no. 46423/06, ECHR 2009; *Vasil Sashov Petrov v. Bulgaria*, no. 63106/00, ECHR June 10, 2010; *Stefanou v. Greece*, no. 2954/07, ECHR October 4, 2010; *Carabulea v. Romania*, no. 45661/99, ECHR October 13, 2010; and *Dimitrova and Others v. Bulgaria*, no. 44862/04, ECHR April 27, 2011. Vigilante "skinhead" anti-Roma violence: *Šečić v. Croatia*, no. 40116/02, ECHR May 31, 2007, cited in Cahn and Guild, 2008, 31. See also *Case of Moldovan and Others v. Romania* (no. 2), nos. 41138/98 and 64320/01, ECHR November 30, 2005.

6. Race discrimination in education: *D.H. and Others v. The Czech Republic*, no. 57325/00, ECHR November 13, 2005; *Sampanis and Others v. Greece*, no. 32526/05, ECHR June 5, 2008; and *Oršuš and Others v. Croatia*, no. 15766/03, ECHR R March 16, 2010. Race discrimination in housing allocation: *Bagdonavichus v. Russia*, no. 19841/06, ECHR (pending). Forced sterilization of Roma women: *I.G., M.K. and R.H. v. Slovakia*, no. 15966/04, ECHR September 22, 2009 (admissibility), and *V.C. v. Slovakia*, no. 18968/07, ECHR February 8, 2012.

7. This exclusion arises where asylum applicants are disqualified as nationals of states seeking EU membership. Roma citizens deported from EU member states to countries of origin where they lack legal status and access to basic minimum social and economic rights (education, housing, emergency health care, protection from violence) might qualify for protection as refugees, proving their well-founded fear to persecution because of their nationality or membership of a particular social group. But their claims for protection are ineffective, a different aspect of the politics of evidence.

8. EU laws relevant to Roma integration and participation include the Racial Equality Directive (2000/43/EC); the Employment Equality Directive (2000/78/EC); the Integrated European Platform for Roma Inclusion (2008); the EU Strategy on Roma Inclusion (March 2011); and the EU Framework for National Roma Integration Strategies up to 2020 (April 2011).

EXPERT TESTIMONY AND THE
EVIDENTIARY BURDEN OF STATELESSNESS

BENJAMIN N. LAWRANCE

> Sitting there, waiting for the bus to start moving, Asad examined the new stamp on his
> watermarked travel document. He glared at it resentfully and restrained himself from
> tearing it to shreds. It occurred to him that the document itself had probably been invented
> for the purpose of fleecing people without documents. It was something for which you
> paid one set of officials clearly; and when you presented it to another set, many hundreds
> of miles away, it announced that you were up for more fleecing. Not for the first time in the
> last few days he felt a fool, a person whose purpose on this planet was to be duped.
> —Jonny Steinberg, *A Man of Good Hope*

In 2015, the Home Office of the United Kingdom attempted to deport a Gambian woman to her birth country. "Princess" (not her real name) had lived in Austria since the age of ten, and came to the United Kingdom in 2010 to escape her father's attempt to coerce her into a marriage.[1] In 2013, she was lured back to Gambia, where she was forcibly subjected to genital cutting. Upon return to the United Kingdom she bore a child with a UK "settled person" of Tanzanian origin. Princess applied for refugee status for her daughter, based on her fear that she too would be cut if returned to the Gambia. The Home Office, however, held that the daughter was *not* eligible for refugee status because she *was* eligible to *apply* for registration as a "British national." The rejection letter stated, in the "absence of any information to the contrary, such as the rejection of your application . . . you appear to be entitled to British nationality."

Princess insisted that she could not afford the application fee of £749. Her lawyers argued that "eligibility" is not a recognized nationality status. In my expert report, I explained that the infant was a Gambian national, according to Gambian law, and that, were she returned to Gambia, the risk of cutting would be high. In early 2016, a judge of the First Tier Tribunal ruled that one either *is* or *is not* a British national; no liminal status existed in between. Princess could not afford the nationality application; her daughter is not a UK national. She was thus eligible to apply for protection, and he granted refugee status.

The confounding encounter of Princess and her daughter with immigration regulations illustrates the burden placed on individuals to document—or be seen to be actively acquiring documentation of—citizenship. The imagining, by British bureaucrats, of a contingent, pre-applicatory status, a pseudo- or protonationality, the hypothetical existence of which negates or obviates access to humanitarian and refugee protections, may surprise or shock. But it is only one of the many examples of arbitrary or outright capricious interpretations of immigration rules and regulations refugee lawyers and advocates encounter seemingly routinely, each with uniquely idiomatic and insidious impacts on the lives of society's most vulnerable.

This chapter discusses the predicament of Princess and her kinfolk and, relatedly, the experience of serving as an expert witness in citizenship disputes and statelessness claims of African migrants. Expertise pertaining to country conditions is employed with increasing frequency in refugee matters (Lawrance and Ruffer 2015). Asylum claims in particular "exist at the juncture of law, advocacy, human rights, and expert evidence" (Andrews 2015, vii), and they rely on experts to furnish data, analysis, and evidence. Seeking asylum represents a striking challenge whereby asylum seekers "demand recognition as individual rights-bearing subjects amid the bureaucratic indifference and xenophobic hostility endemic to the nation-state" (Lawrance et al. 2015, 5). As an expert witness in the United Kingdom in approximately a dozen citizenship disputes and statelessness claims by West Africans, I routinely testify to the applicability of citizenship and nationality laws, analyze documentary evidence, and evaluate personal narratives of claimants against known country conditions.

The role of expert testimony in navigating statelessness claims is an underappreciated dimension of the lived experience of citizenship in question. While thematic content and rhetorical format have emerged as areas of research, the contours of expertise in statelessness claims have not been described or analyzed in depth. British jurisprudence supports the contention that arbitrarily denying citizenship or nationality is a form of persecution and may constitute a protection basis.[2] Further, courts also have held that the role of documentation, or lack thereof, in establishing the context of persecution "is essentially a question for a fact finding Tribunal."[3]

Country conditions experts have unique capabilities to participate in assessments recognizing new persecutory harm paradigms, such as forced marriage, homophobia, or female genital cutting (Berger et al. 2015; Lawrance and Walker-Said 2016; Musalo 2015) based on broader principles of human dignity, autonomy, and consent, or on medical humanitarian concerns (Lawrance 2013, 2015). The "unique evidentiary challenges" residing at the heart of what we might call statelessness-in-question makes expertise "critical" (Musalo 2015, 93).

Expert evaluations are often crucial for statelessness determinations. These are invariably "a mixed question of fact and law" (UNHCR 2014b, ¶24). Thus, a "purely formalistic analysis of the application of nationality laws" (UNHCR 2014b, ¶24) is often insufficient. Expert testimony affects the evidentiary burdens borne by stateless migrants in complex ways. Drawing on actual statelessness claims and the growing body of critical studies of irregular migration, immigration detention, and asylum (e.g., Fuglerud 2004; Good 2007, 2015; Griffiths 2012, 2013; Hall 2012; Hertzog 1999; Le Courant 2013; Whyte 2011), I argue expert testimony is often a double-edged sword. Like the medico-legal reports examined by Didier Fassin and Estelle D'Halluin (2005), expert country conditions reports are often necessary but rarely definitive. On the one hand, depending on the expert's charge, a report can highlight paths to, and obstructions of, an individual's capacity to document his or her relationship with a state. On the other hand, the limitations on expert testimony are such that it cannot anticipate all hypothetical formulations, and it may unwittingly provide openings for denying a claim.

Statelessness affects millions of people worldwide (see Babo, Flaim, Price, and Sadiq, this volume), but for migrants seeking protection in a host country like the United Kingdom, their experiences can be particularly complex. Over several years I have observed patterns with respect to the reception of expertise. Case histories are a productive site for analyzing these patterns. The stories contained herein reveal that the extraordinary imbalance between the agency of the individual and the power of the state makes it difficult to prove statelessness. The stories also show how additional, seemingly unrelated matters, such as being convicted of a crime, can give rise to a context in which statelessness is almost unprovable. A number of migrants I have encountered have served time for criminal convictions, but their unresolved civil status extends the criminal sentence effectively to a form of banishment. The case histories discussed here review the constraints on expertise, the application for and production of documents in support of yet additional papers, and finally, the treatment of statelessness claims in practice, all of which point to important patterns.

The Trials of Boubacar

"Boubacar" was seventeen when he arrived in the United Kingdom in 2004 and applied for asylum because of political persecution in his home, the Republic of Guinea. He was convicted of robbery in the United Kingdom in 2007. After serving one year of a three-year sentence, he was further detained under the Immigration Act until July 2011. After a decade of court proceedings seeking asylum and humanitarian protection for Boubacar, his barrister argued that his client had been arbitrarily deprived of his nationality and was stateless. Statelessness, the barrister contended, was brought about by the Guinean authorities' refusal to grant him an Emergency Travel Document (ETD).

Before the First Tier Tribunal immigration judge (IJ), Boubacar's advocates described his predicament as a "state of limbo."[4] Boubacar has no documentation of his identity. He left Guinea a child. He has never seen his birth certificate and never had a Guinean government-issued ID card or a passport. He assisted with UK Home Office (UKHO) efforts to acquire an ETD, but based on his failure to conform to specific bureaucratic requirements, the UKHO has deemed him uncooperative.

My expert report—produced as a paid consultant for Boubacar and for most of the cases discussed in this chapter—stated that, while Boubacar was a Guinean citizen under Guinean law, that law places the burden of proof entirely on the individual. The Guinean embassy is under no statutory obligation to provide an opinion as to whether or not Boubacar is a national. I described Boubacar as "effectively stateless," having seemingly exhausted all lawful means and personal agency to prove his identity and establish his nationality. Lawyers for the government countered that, whereas deprivation of a right to citizenship and denial of a right to return "can amount to persecution" and constitute a basis for refugee protection, Boubacar produced no evidence that Guinean authorities deprived him of citizenship.[5]

The IJ agreed with the UKHO. He wrote, Boubacar "claims that he wishes to return to Guinea and that he has done everything he can to establish his nationality so that he can be returned," but "I have significant credibility concerns as to whether he can be believed." According to the judge, Boubacar "has been remarkably inactive in taking any further steps on his own initiative." He has "made no attempt to contact" his former college, "no attempt to get help from

Guinean nationals with whom he is in contact in the UK," and no attempt "to contact" the "birth registration authorities in Guinea"; he has "not asked for help from his solicitors," has made "no attempt to contact members of his family," and has not "approached any agency such as the Refugee Council or the Red Cross." In rejecting the statelessness claim, the judge concluded, "If the Appellant were to take reasonable steps on his own initiative to obtain proof of his identity and nationality, I have no reason to believe . . . he would be refused" an ETD. As of 2015, Boubacar is acting on the judge's suggestions and, based on their futility, appealing the decision.

Boubacar's predicament is a classic illustration of a contemporary problem encountered by asylum seekers and refugees who seek protection under national laws operationalizing the Convention on Statelessness (1954) and the 1967 Protocol, namely, how to demonstrate genuine and thorough, if not exhaustive, engagement with the responsibilities imposed by the burden of proof of identity. The United Nations High Commissioner for Refugees (UNHCR) "Handbook on Protection of Statelessness Persons" (2014b) describes the definition in Article 1(1) of the convention as requiring "proof of a negative—that an individual is not considered as a national by any State under the operation of its law." It notes, "This presents significant challenges to applicants" (UNHCR 2014b, ¶88).

The UNHCR guidance (¶89) observes that the "burden of proof" in statelessness determinations "is in principle shared, in that both the applicant and examiner must cooperate to obtain evidence and to establish the facts." Determining authorities need to "take . . . into account" the difficulties applicants face in obtaining "documentary evidence" and, "where appropriate," give "sympathetic consideration to testimonial evidence" (¶90). Stateless migrants must exhaust all processes before appealing administrative findings (UNHCR/Asylum Aid 2011, 77–79). Boubacar's statelessness claim was thus deemed premature. Insofar as the determination procedure "is a collaborative one" (¶89), the IJ extrapolated from my expert testimony that Boubacar continued to bear a burden to undertake further cooperation. Examining case histories closely contributes to the understanding of the predicament that I describe as statelessness-in-question. The limitations on expert testimony are such that it cannot answer all questions or anticipate all hypotheticals. Any number of tests, such as the litany adumbrated by the IJ, may result in pertinent information. Expert reports narrating the theoretical application of nationality law may inadvertently provide grounds for a denial of a statelessness claim, even when the expert on balance discerned a record consistent with actual statelessness.

Expertise and the Evidentiary Burdens of Statelessness

There is no formal statelessness determination procedure in the United Kingdom, as there is in other countries, only "established caselaw" on "evidentiary requirements" (UNHCR/Asylum Aid 2011, 76). In rejecting Boubacar's argument, the IJ's determination cast important light on two interrelated evidentiary burdens. First, before asserting statelessness, Boubacar must take "all reasonable steps" to obtain documentation.[6] This first evidentiary burden is anchored in British legislation domesticating the 1951 Refugee Convention, the 1954 Statelessness Convention, the 1967 Protocol, UK Immigration Rules, and related jurisprudence (see UNHCR/Asylum Aid 2011, 66–70).[7] This first burden highlights the interpretative latitude granted to government authorities. It is for the executive (the UKHO) or the judiciary, not the claimant, to decide whether means have been exhausted.

Second, as an ostensibly Guinean subject, Boubacar can reasonably be expected to observe the Guinean nationality law, which places the burden entirely on the applicant: an especially difficult task if the migrant is in immigration detention with very limited access to legal counsel. This second evidentiary burden emerged from the Statelessness Convention and relates to the role of "competent authorities." And yet the Guinean embassy in London was under no statutory obligation to assist Boubacar. This second burden draws attention to the disequilibrium between a citizen's agency to request evidence and competent authorities' capacity to deny or ignore it.

The first burden, of pursuing evidence of statelessness, resonates with the UNHCR's description of "evidence relating to the individual's personal circumstances" (UNHCR 2014b, ¶83). The UNHCR's "non-exhaustive" catalog of evidence of personal circumstances lists personal testimony (e.g., a written application or formal interview); responses from foreign authorities to inquiries; identity documents (e.g., birth certificate, civil register extracts, national ID cards, voter registration); travel documents (including expired ones); applications to acquire nationality or obtain proof of nationality; naturalization certificates; nationality renunciation certificates; previous responses by states to nationality inquiries; marriage certificates; military service record/discharge certificates; school certificates; medical certificates/records (e.g., attestations from birth hospital, vaccination booklets); identity and travel documents of parents, spouse, or children; immigration documents; residence permits; other documents pertaining to residence (e.g., employment documents, property deeds, tenancy agreements, school records, baptismal certificates); or records of sworn oral testimony of neighbors and community members.

Physical documents are generally accorded greater weight than oral testimony in the United Kingdom (Thuen 2004, 275). Melanie Griffiths's observation of UK asylum tribunals found that the UKHO and the Asylum and Immigration Tribunal (AIT) "clearly assigned greatest weight to documentary evidence, to the extent that at times documents seemed almost to be valorised" (2014, 270). Despite this, documents often give claimants a false sense of security. The UKHO may lose documents, reject them for unspecified administrative reasons, or contest specific details; "although [documentary] evidence is sometimes deemed sufficient, it is usually challenged as inadequate or false" (271), or even fraudulent. Even acquiring documentation opens the door to a basis for rejecting a claim. Griffiths observed an arrest warrant dismissed with the argument that court documents can "easily be forged" and are "readily available in the country" in question, and a party membership letter refuted on the basis that such a document is "easily obtainable" (271).

The UNHCR does not directly define the appropriate means of acquiring documents. Thus, UK practices and precedents are controlling. In 2009, the Lord Justice Elias outlined the burden an individual encumbers when disputing national origin or attempting to forestall return:

> Where the essential issue . . . is whether someone will or will not be returned, the Tribunal should in the normal case require the applicant to act *bona fide* and take all reasonably practicable steps to seek to obtain the requisite documents to enable her to return. There may be cases where it would be unreasonable to require this, such as if disclosure of identity might put the applicant at risk, or perhaps third parties, such as relatives of the applicant who may be at risk in the home state if it is known that the applicant has claimed asylum. That is not this case, however. There is no reason why the appellant should not herself visit the embassy to seek to obtain the relevant papers.[8]

When an asylum seeker or refugee claims to be stateless, he or she must, *in good faith*, take "all reasonably practicable steps," such as visiting an embassy and requesting documentation.[9]

This second evidentiary burden—following Guinean law—resonates with a second category of evidence the UNHCR describes as "concerning the laws and other circumstances in the country in question" (UNHCR 2014b, ¶83), or what is commonly referred to as Country of Origin Information (COI). This may consist of "evidence about the nationality and other relevant laws, their implementation and practices of relevant States, as well as the general legal environment in those jurisdictions in terms of respect by the executive branch for judicial decisions. It can be obtained from a variety of sources, governmental and non-governmental." The UNHCR cautions that, "to be treated as accurate," COI "needs to be obtained from reliable and unbiased sources, preferably more than one," "continuously updated," and "contemporaneous with the nationality events that are under consideration in the case in question" (¶86). And because nationality law and practice are complex, decision making "may justify recourse to expert evidence in some cases" (¶85).

The research product colloquially referred to as COI is an empirical and methodological outcome of the "hermeneutics of suspicion" (Gadamer 1984; Kessler 2005; Ricœur 1965; Stewart 1989) that characterizes asylum and refugee proceedings wherein the global application of refugee status determination increasingly uses empirical research for credibility findings (CREDO 2013; UNHCR 2013). Country conditions information may demonstrate how the law operates (or does not), and expert evidence may provide insight into the "practicability" of acquiring other evidence. But the UNHCR and Asylum Aid noted, "It is not clear whether [UK] decision-makers systematically make use of this facility [COI research] or fully understand how to assess nationality laws when identifying statelessness" (UNHCR/Asylum Aid 2011, 81).

Thus, interwoven into the two burdens to prove statelessness borne by Boubacar (exhausting British law *and* exhausting Guinean law) are expectations of expert witnessing. In Boubacar's case, the IJ required evidence of an attempt to find citizenship evidence, *and* evidence that he followed Guinean law, that is, that he had contacted all competent authorities. The Guinean embassy had provided a letter simply stating Boubacar was not a citizen, with no explanation for how he occupied the status of citizenship (and statelessness) in question. The IJ found this incomplete. The evidentiary burden is thus revealed to be remarkably specific and the criteria for evaluating the "reasonable effort" unstated.

Viewed together, these two burdens always produce extreme inequity and often mean impossibly high evidentiary requirements for the stateless. With adequate lead time and research capacity, an expert may be able to provide information about school or birth registration procedures, the capacity of the Red Cross in family contact and reunification, and a complete list of "competent authorities." It can also, qualitatively and quantitatively, document levels of government transparency, cooperation, accessibility, corruption, and accountability in providing such documents. Expert evidence can indeed engage both of Boubacar's evidentiary burdens. But the majority of migrants making such claims in the United Kingdom and elsewhere do not have legal representation, or if they do, they have trouble contacting the counselor while in detention, cannot afford application fees, and struggle with language and translation. Without good legal counsel, however, little is possible, and even this cannot extract documents from nonresponsive state agents or negotiate the ambiguities of IJ criteria and determinations.

Documentary Encounters and Statelessness in Britain

Boubacar's experience can hardly be considered exceptional. A central contention articulated in Jacqueline Stevens's introduction and Polly Price's chapter is that, what many scholars, journalists, and governments describe as exceptional is revealed, upon closer scrutiny, to be disturbingly commonplace. Three case histories from individuals whose cases I reviewed and wrote about, and who have given permission for their stories to be used pseudonymously, parallel many aspects of Boubacar's case. The experiences of "Akossiwa," "Kofi," and "Ibrahim" highlight issues of identity, documentation, citizenship, and nationality in relation to Ghana, Togo, Sierra Leone, Guinea, and Côte d'Ivoire. When read together, they demonstrate the centrality of documentation to advancing statelessness, the role of state authorities throughout the process, and the complexities arising when expertise is introduced.

AKOSSIWA

"Akossiwa" was born in Portugal to a Portuguese father and a Togolese mother. According to the countries' respective citizenship laws, she is both Togolese and Portuguese. At the age of five, she left Lisbon with her parents, traveled to Togo, and crossed into Ghana without any registration. Her mother died, and her maternal aunt raised her. Akossiwa's father left her in Ghana but returned to collect her several years later, while she was still a young child. In an interview she said he was her father, and "he showed me a photo of my mum," and so she returned to Portugal.[10] She entered the United Kingdom in 1998 as an adult with her father, on her own Portuguese passport. Her father soon left and has not been seen since. In 1999, she visited the Portuguese embassy to request a birth certificate copy to qualify for education assistance. After posing questions in Portuguese, which Akossiwa could not answer, an embassy agent seized her passport, claiming it had been tampered with. She retained counsel in London and Lisbon to investigate.

Over several years, efforts were made to ascertain her identity. In 2002, her lawyers requested she be recognized as "stateless." In 2003, she applied for a driver's license and submitted a photocopy of her seized passport. The license agency inaccurately informed the UKHO that she had submitted a fraudulent Portuguese national ID card, whereupon eight immigration officials visited her home. In the meantime, the Ghanaian embassy correctly informed her there was no way she could acquire Ghanaian citizenship. Her Lisbon lawyer could not find her birth certificate. In 2009, her lawyers informed the UK Border Agency (UKBA, now UK Visas and Immigration) that they would force a decision by judicial action under Article 6 (excessive delay) and Article 8 (private/family life) of the European Convention on Human Rights (ECHR). In 2010 UKBA rejected her statelessness claim, concluding that she either did not know her identity or knew it and was deliberately withholding information.[11] It further contended that she was working illegally and threatened to inform her employer.

Before the First Tier Tribunal in August 2010, Akossiwa's barrister argued that the delayed determination, only provoked after a threat of judicial review, undermined a right to a private life and was grounds for stopping her removal, per Article 8's protections of privacy and family life. A narrow path might qualify her for Togolese nationality, but pursuing it was effectively impossible. (Again, there existed no basis for asserting Ghanaian nationality.) The UKHO did not send a barrister to court, nor could it produce the alleged (nonexistent) Portuguese ID card. Whereas Akossiwa conceded no government would likely ever affirm her Portuguese nationality, she continued to insist she is a Portuguese and European national. The judge, however, found that she was not a Portuguese national "even though she appears to have genuinely believed that she was." After resolving that Akossiwa did not submit an ID card as part of her driver's license application, thus reinforcing her credibility, the judge determined she was "stateless" and "without nationality."[12] Her appeal was granted on the basis that her removal would breach Article 8.

KOFI

"Kofi" was born in Togo in 1962 to Togolese parents, but as with so many children in Togo then and globally now—as Amanda Flaim, Jacqueline Bhabha, Rachel Rosenbloom, and Kamal Sadiq, in this volume, show—his birth was not registered. He became involved in opposition politics and was beaten and detained. In 2000, he was tortured in Sotoboua military camp. He escaped with fifteen detainees, fled to neighboring Benin, and registered as a refugee with the UNHCR. Because of close ties between the Benin and Togo governments, Kofi remained fearful. He acquired a fake passport and a visa for unimpeded travel within the Schengen treaty zone, and flew to France. From France he arrived in the United Kingdom in 2000.

Kofi claimed asylum on the basis of political and ethnic persecution, which the UKHO denied in 2000. An IJ denied his appeal, filed without expert evidence, in 2002. Asylees frequently use fraudulent documents (or legitimate documents acquired fraudulently) to enter safe havens, but Kofi's use thereof was cited as evidence of lack of credibility. Over the next two years he filed several unsuccessful appeals. In 2005, he made a further request for indefinite leave to remain on the basis of having fathered two children with a legal UK resident. This was granted in August 2005. During this period, he remained on his own recognizance. In November 2006, Kofi was convicted of sexual assault and sentenced to four years in prison. A deportation order was served in 2008 pursuant to the UK Borders Act of 2007 requiring deportation of foreign criminals sentenced to at least twelve months. Immigration officers tried to deport him at that time but could not obtain travel documents from Togo.

Kofi served the balance of his sentence, but instead of being released, he was asked to assist in procuring documents that would allow his entry to Togo and signed papers submitted to Togo's embassy in Paris. During this time Kofi remained in immigration detention without any apparent lawful basis. Immigration agents subjected him to a language analysis and nationality test to demonstrate his Togo origins (uncooperative behavior may negatively affect credibility). He was provided a phone card and called the Togo embassy under the supervision of five immigration officers. In 2010, two years after his immigration detention began and six years after he entered prison, new lawyers filed a motion alleging illegal incarceration. A second filing provided psychiatric expertise and country conditions testimony. The submissions were refused. In January 2011, Kofi was finally released from detention. Kofi then appealed the deportation order, arguing that it was a violation of the ECHR's protection of the stateless. Accompanying this appeal was an "anonymity order," protecting his identity from disclosure, because a UK newspaper named him a pedophile in a case of mistaken identity and published his photograph and address.

Kofi's barrister argued that because the UK government had been unable to obtain travel documents, Kofi was "irremovable." He also argued that because of "his lack of documentation," Kofi would face significant difficulties.[13] The government countered that Kofi posed a "high risk" to women and that his remaining in the United Kingdom would violate the domestic law under which his deportation was first sought. In 2011, an IJ granted Kofi temporary relief and suspended deportation. Kofi was not in detention, but he had no right to work and had to remain at a registered address. His statelessness claim was dismissed. The IJ noted the government's inaction indicated a lack of "urgency," but that citizenship inquiries were "still ongoing."[14] Kofi sued for compensation and filed a fresh asylum claim; he still asserts statelessness. The suspended removal order was made indefinite in 2012, but Kofi's statelessness and citizenship remain in question.[15]

"Ibrahim" was born to a Guinean mother and Sierra Leonean father and raised in Abidjan, Côte d'Ivoire. By Guinean and Sierra Leonean law he is a citizen of both countries. He is ethnically Dioula and Muslim but has never had an Ivoirian ID card or citizenship because the country did not recognize him as a citizen. He has an Ivoirian birth certificate, as does his sister, who tried unsuccessfully to acquire an Ivoirian ID card. (For details on Ivoirian citizenship practices, see Alfred Babo, this volume.) Ibrahim has never been to Sierra Leone or Guinea. The violence and political upheaval in Côte d'Ivoire, described in Babo's chapter, also ensnared Ibrahim. Ibrahim experienced discrimination based on his ancestry, his father's occupation, and his family's support for the opposition. In 1998, when Ibrahim was sixteen and after failing to produce an ID, he was arrested. As the violence increased from 1999, he was arrested with a larger group and put in a truck. The group was dumped in the field and forced to run as soldiers fired at them. He was hit three times in his chest and legs. Upon recovery he learned that his father had been murdered and soldiers had burned his home. His mother told him to flee. He journeyed to the Netherlands by boat, arriving in January 2000. He applied for asylum but was refused in 2003. He took the Eurostar to London with a fake French passport.

In the United Kingdom, Ibrahim was found naked and walking aimlessly; he was arrested for marijuana possession in September 2009. He was convicted and immediately served with removal papers for Côte d'Ivoire. After custodial release he tried to travel to the United States to live with his sister, but he was again arrested, charged with and convicted of using a fake passport, and sentenced to one year in prison. In 2010, in immigration detention, he attempted suicide. He then began regular psychotherapy and medication. As his condition stabilized, he visited the Ivoirian, Sierra Leonean, and Guinean embassies in London to establish his identity or lack thereof.

At the Ivoirian embassy, in the presence of a barrister, Ibrahim attempted to establish Ivoirian nationality. The embassy officer required documentation. The barrister mentioned Ibrahim's birth certificate and asked if inquiries could be made with the local authorities to obtain a copy. The officer stated this would be time-consuming and likely to be unsuccessful, regardless of the birth certificate's erstwhile existence. Moreover, in a parallel to Stevens's apologues of citizenship (this volume), the official required a birth certificate before he would pursue further investigation of the existence of a birth certificate. A superior officer stated that Ibrahim was not an Ivoirian citizen "as he saw it" but possibly "a national of a different country either Sierra Leone or Guinea."[16] The officer stated that for an Ivoirian ETD, the embassy would first need to see an

Ivoirian passport or ID card. The barrister asked if there was any way to appeal to the Ivoirian Court of Justice but received no reply.

Visits to the Sierra Leonean and Guinean embassies were equally futile. Informed that Ibrahim's father was Sierra Leonean, the embassy officer stated that even though "he was not the decision maker," if he were "going to make the decision," he would state he "was not satisfied" that Ibrahim could return to Sierra Leone. According to "his understanding of Sierra Leone nationality law," Ibrahim "would not be entitled [to] citizenship." At the Guinean embassy, an officer stated "he could not decide" whether Ibrahim could reside in Guinea, but "he was sure that the Appellant was not Guinean because he does not possess any Guinean documents." Even though Ibrahim's mother was currently residing in Guinea, a consular official stated (incorrectly) that "Guinean nationality is derived through the father and not the mother."[17]

Ibrahim's ordeal in Côte d'Ivoire and his asylum claims have had a profound effect on his mental health and his capacity to access legal representation. After a series of trials and appeals, first to an IJ and then to a three-person panel of two IJs and a physician, Ibrahim was granted protection under Articles 3 and 8 of the ECHR, namely, the prohibition on torture, and the right to a family life. The suicide risk, caused by post-traumatic stress disorder stemming from political and deep-seated historical ethnic persecution, was compelling.

Nonetheless, in 2014, a British tribunal rejected Ibrahim's claim of statelessness. The tribunal held that the evidence "taken at its highest does not establish that he would not be able to return for a [statelessness] convention reason." Ibrahim as a minor could have applied for citizenship, but he did not. He was not "historically . . . deprived of nationality." The panel also stated that "it is not clear" that the officials of the three embassies were "qualified to give such advice relating to issues of nationality." It held that "we have not been presented with the best evidence."[18] If an Ivoirian birth certificate were obtained, a path to return to Côte d'Ivoire would open: "It may be difficult for him to obtain citizenship or to return to Ivory Coast, but the evidence in our view establishes that it would be reasonably likely that the Appellant would be able to return there." Ibrahim can remain in the United Kingdom, but, like the others described herein, his citizenship and statelessness remain in question.

Expert Evidence and Statelessness in Practice

Expert evidence in UK immigration courts is a "relatively recent development" (Griffiths 2014, 262). Country conditions experts may level the playing field in a manner of speaking (Kerns 2000). Judges, for example, may call upon experts when the documentary evidence is inadequate or an identity is in question (see Kam 2015). Anthony Good (2015) demonstrated how expert testimony addresses specific political, cultural, and social conditions, and the degree whereby returning a refugee or asylum seeker may cause peril. The panoply of tasks is expansive and the role "broadly defined" (Malphrus 2010, 8). A claimant's legal counsel privately contracts an expert report and conveys instructions about specific questions. Reports are addressed to a court, not a claimant. Experts supply "objective unbiased opinion," subject to established standards and regulations (see Good 2015), and unlike in the United States or elsewhere, may not advocate for specific remedies. Oral testimony and cross-examination are subject to additional tests (Good 2004a, 2008). Government-funded legal aid may be available, subject to increasingly complex and restrictive residency and means tests, as well as newer "probability of success" checks (Griffiths 2014).

Whereas experts theoretically provide specialist knowledge while remaining balanced and unbiased (Thomas 2011, 183), UK adjudicators frequently treat experts like professional liars (Good 2004a, 363). This may be because lawyers increasingly turn to experts to translate a narrative of "personal trauma into an act of political aggression" anchored to Refugee Convention articles (Shuman and Bohmer 2004, 396). Nonetheless, judges seem receptive to experts employing historical narrative or historicizing arguments (Lawrance et al. 2015, 30). And while UK judges may try to curtail the use of experts, often dismissing experts as advocates, expertise rarely has a neat linear relationship with the specific claims of migrants.

Expert evidence can raise as many questions as it answers. As Boubacar's experience demonstrates, expert testimony facilitated the rejection of his statelessness claim. The IJ's assertion that other competent authorities existed, and ought to be explored, emerged directly from my expert report. Boubacar's misfortune confirms how expert testimony interweaves the very fabric of evidentiary burdens of statelessness in complex and unpredictable ways. Expert testimony has the potential to account for the paths to, or obstruction of, an individual's capacity to document his or her relationship with a state, yet expertise is limited by its capacity to anticipate all hypotheticals. The final section of this chapter briefly reviews three content areas in statelessness—interpretation of law by judges and diplomats, analyses of documentation, and evaluation of claimants' narratives—for which expertise may be either foundational or hazardous.

Experts interpret domestic statutes, such as nationality and citizenship laws, and apply them to statelessness claims. Interpreting how law may operate is a deeply problematic component of the expert's role because it inherently involves speculation or hypothesis. The IJ described my attempts to interpret the Guinean embassy's interactions with Boubacar as speculation, noting that I am "not a lawyer and cannot be regarded as an expert in that regard."[19] Notwithstanding the risk of speculation, I often provide an extensive legal discussion and interpret how or under what conditions an individual may or may not be recognized as a citizen, scholarly evaluations of which are not obviously less reliable than those made by someone with a law degree. (Immigration judges must weigh opinions offered by one side in an adversarial setting as they see fit; but whether the witness holds an advanced law or academic degree seems less relevant than country condition and legal expertise per se.)

In Kofi's case, I evaluated Togo's 1961 and 1978 citizenship and nationality laws. Togolese nationality follows jus sanguinis, subject to Chapter II, Article 3, if one or both parents are Togolese nationals, or jus soli, subject to Article 2, if birth is in Togo. If Kofi was born in Togo, he is a Togolese national; but because his birth was not registered, any request framed along these lines would likely be subject to judicial review. Because both parents' identities and locations are unknown, and he has no record of their nationality or birth, any request may be denied. The UNHCR guidelines contemplate situations where individuals apply for passports and receive rejection notices; they do not anticipate a country having no diplomatic presence in a particular country, or being unable to travel to a third country for a passport because of a lack of papers.

For Ibrahim's lawyers, I applied the 1961 and 1972 Ivoirian nationality and citizenship laws to his predicament. Articles 6 through 8 describe *ivoirité* by birthright. In the absence of a birth certificate or passport, however, Ibrahim would have to seek a "décision de l'autorité publique." If Ibrahim were then to "prove" his citizenship, he would be subject to a "reintegration" procedure. Reintegration (governed by Chapter I, Section II, Articles 34–41, and 63–69) requires an in-country "inquest." Negative decisions may be appealed directly to the minister of justice (Art. 68), and civil courts are the sole "competent authority." Ivoirian law prohibits Ibrahim from entering the country to ascertain and reacquire his Ivoirian citizenship. It would thus be impossible for Ibrahim to be deported to Côte d'Ivoire prior to acquiring citizenship documents.

For Akossiwa I reviewed the Ghanaian laws and concluded that Ghanaian citizenship was unlikely. The Immigration Act of 2000 (Act 573) and the Citizenship Act of 2002 (Act 591) govern Ghanaian nationality. As neither parent was

Ghanaian, and Akossiwa claimed to be born in Portugal, very limited circumstances existed whereby she could apply for naturalization. She could conceivably obtain citizenship by "naturalisation," but because she could not meet the subjective qualifications of minimum period and indigenous language (i.e., other than English) competency, it remained at the discretion of the Home Office minister and the president, whose decisions "in doubtful cases" (Art. 20) are final.

DOCUMENTATION

Experts are routinely asked to evaluate claimants' documentation, a potentially perilous engagement. Experts are often the only people in court who have seen a real ID card for a particular political party, but first and foremost we are country conditions experts, not forensic document analysts, a caveat I provide before offering any testimony. Nonetheless, in appeal cases, I also inquire as to the comparative empirical information or scholarship that has been consulted—such as exemplars of real and fake ID cards—that permitted the UKHO findings of fraud.

In a second expert statement for Kofi, I reviewed a letter from Koffi Mawenya Guedze, clerk of the First Instance Tribunal of Aného's Second Chamber. Because I am familiar with the court structure and I have personally visited Aného's courts, I was able to state that nothing on the face of it suggested inauthenticity. After reviewing the contents of Guedze's report, which made clear no individual, other than Kofi, could have a birth registered by a judge, I reaffirmed my earlier interpretation. Kofi could acquire neither travel documents nor a passport in the absence of a birth certificate or nationality certificate. Kofi could not acquire a birth certificate unless he presented in person before the court; but he could not enter the country, and hence the court, without the travel document. It was hard to avoid the conclusion that Kofi was being arbitrarily deprived of nationality and thus was stateless.

As these examples reveal, documentary deprivation poses extreme risks. Akossiwa's passport was seized by the Portuguese embassy based on inaccurate inferences about her language skills. My report highlighted the dangers facing her and her children, were she returned to Togo or Ghana. Without citizenship or documentation, Ghana and Togo would provide no form of social welfare, accommodation, employment advice, or general economic support. She would be unable to open a bank account, secure credit, or rent accommodations without a loan guarantor. She could not enroll herself or her children in urgent health care or school. Without government support for pressing social and family needs, she would have become destitute, likely living on the streets like many impoverished stateless. These conclusions were fundamental to the statelessness claims under which she sought protection.

Immigration experts lack guidelines for weighting documents and their legal significance, and court rulings are not helpful. A 2015 determination for an Ivoirian individual whom the UKHO maintains is Malian is illustrative. In this case, Aliou entered the United Kingdom in 2011 with a Malian passport and claimed asylum. The Malian passport was genuine but had been obtained fraudulently. After denying Aliou's asylum claim, the UK court decided to deport him to Mali, stating: "You have submitted copies of your claimed Ivoirian identity [documents] and therefore no weight can be attached to these documents, especially considering that you have produced an original Malian passport which has been verified as genuine by the N[ational] D[ocumentary] F[orensics] U[nit]. It is reasonable to infer that you could obtain genuine documentation to attest your claimed identity."[20] The statement appears to suggest that the existence of a real passport from one country precludes the possibility of being a national of a second, which is not accurate. It also shows that our regime of asylum and citizenship laws is prone to bureaucrats and judges rewriting the very identities their jurisprudence suggests are given at birth.

As Melanie Griffiths notes, deportation policy is "a set of often incoherent, contradictory and multi-authored processes" (2014, 28). Regardless of the legitimacy of Aliou's asylum claim, the preceding narrative suggests a regime of government identification operations unable or unwilling to track biographical events, and content with fraudulent data and documents procured thereby, in this case Aliou's Malian passport. The uneven ability of countries to produce and evaluate identity documents is not a failure of bureaucratic capabilities but, as Stevens points out (in the introduction and chapter 12), a symptom of the possibilities and failures of citizenship narratives that rely on ascriptive elements, such as birth and ancestry. Such documentary conventions, without which nationality would not exist, at once secure these narratives for countries as well as individuals and also invite their undoing.

CLAIMANT NARRATIVES AND COUNTRY CONDITIONS

Less tied to notations internal to government databases and documents are the country condition reports. Stateless claims must be viewed in the context of prevailing country conditions, such as published scholarship or reports by nongovernmental organizations, interviews with people on the ground, or publicly accessible COI. Political or ethnic violence, the availability and accessibility of documentary production, and the history of discriminatory application of nationality law are but three of innumerable country conditions issues pertinent to the consideration of statelessness claims.

The complex Ivoirian struggle over Ivoirian identity, as narrated in Babo's chapter, anchored Ibrahim's statelessness. My report contextualized Ibrahim's documentary problems accordingly. Ethnic discrimination operates at every level of Ivoirian society and affects social and economic relations. Scholarship demonstrates how the roots of ethnic conflict are tied to the prejudicial land tenancy arrangements emerging after colonialism that marginalized northern minorities and Islamic communities, depriving them of economic wealth and social mobility (Bassett 2004; Romani 2003; Woods 2003).

Kofi's experiences of political persecution changed him into someone unable to document his identity. Country conditions matter, including the events that occurred in the United Kingdom, as he struggled to verify his statelessness. Although his 2002 asylum application did not introduce expert evidence, my reports explained his predicament as a consequence of this ordeal. Furthermore, Kofi was convicted and served his sentence; neither British criminal law nor deportation law prescribes statelessness as the penalty.

And for Boubacar, as one possible path to Guinean citizenship included accessing his birth certificate in Guinea, COI data contextualize the hurdles. Birth registration in Guinea is managed locally and monitored nationally. In the event Boubacar is unable to find his original birth certificate, he could visit the site of initial registration.[21] He claimed birth in Conakry, which increased the likelihood that records existed. But if there were no traceable certification, he would lack the critical documentation to vindicate his nationality, exposing him to considerable dangers.

Conclusion

Compared with Kofi, Ibrahim, and Akossiwa, it might appear that Boubacar was rightly denied affirmation of his claim for statelessness because he neglected the full extent of his evidentiary burdens under both UK law *and* Guinean law. But broadly speaking, are such evidentiary requirements rational, or even possible, in a climate so suspicious and hostile to migration? The stories narrated here demonstrate that statelessness appears as difficult to prove as citizenship. For these individuals and countless others, the documentary burdens must seem endless, even capricious.

Stateless individuals outside their countries of origin have a difficult enough time maintaining possession of their limited documentation, let alone acquiring new documents. Is it reasonable to expect them to navigate the domestic particularities of statelessness determination procedures alone, often from prison or immigration detention? All too few of them seek legal advice to assist with their claims. Few have funding for legal counsel. And yet fewer still are able to source expert reports, and these may inadvertently open doors to new burdens and new tests.

Griffiths (2014, 30) observes that the UK asylum system operates as if identity were "innate and fixed," a framework that is a legal fiction convenient for adjudicators and a legal attack on those for whom this means statelessness. The fiction of a fixed and self-evident legal identity provides adjudicators with a "relatively straightforward" (31) mechanism by which to allege fraud and mendacity and deny applications. Adjudicators demand new forms of evidence in the routine exercise of administrative duties. The devised tests and burdens of proof may appear to follow UNHCR guidance, but this is quite permissive, and closer scrutiny reveals that in so doing they are largely creating self-serving domestic techniques. The Philippines adopted the UNHCR's suggestion of "established to a reasonable degree."[22] Hungarian law stipulates individuals shall "prove or substantiate."[23]

All states permit the consideration of expert testimony, but granting asylum is entirely discretionary. Expert evidence is advisory and may be relegated to only another possible explanation. In this light, expert testimony is only another data point, on a par with other state agents who insert themselves into the adjudicatory process, such as the Guinean embassy officer who incorrectly applied the law, or the Sierra Leonean who became a de facto decision maker. Ought there not to be clear boundaries to these tests and burdens, and clear rules about expert evidence? As Boubacar's case illustrates, the evidentiary burdens borne by stateless individuals may seemingly follow UNHCR guidance in statelessness determination. But, importantly, domestic precedent provides expansive agency to adjudicators to set parameters and create new tests.

A 2015 ruling by the Hungarian Constitutional Court offers some hope that evidentiary burdens borne by stateless individuals may yet be contained. The court overturned a 2007 procedure, one that stipulated that only "lawfully" present persons may claim statelessness, as contrary to the Fundamental Law.[24] The ruling also enhanced the UNHCR's role, all too often marginalized as advisory or mere guidance. Paragraph 18 asserted an expanded function, declaring that "while the Guidelines belong to the so-called non-binding international instruments, it is nevertheless indisputable that the UNHCR is the most authentic entity to interpret international legal questions and practice related to the Statelessness Convention."[25] Perhaps emboldened by this ruling, the UNHCR will issue unequivocal guidance on evidentiary burdens, documentation, and expert evidence for statelessness.

I thank Jacqueline Stevens, Arzoo Osanloo, Melanie Griffiths, Dan Kanstroom, Rogers Smith, and the anonymous reviewers for their time, comments, and suggestions.

1. To protect the identities of the individuals, all names are pseudonyms, and other details have been changed.

2. See *Lazarevic v. SSHD* [1997] EWCA Civ 1007; [1997] Imm AR 251, Hutchison LJ at page 1126E.

3. *EB v. SSHD* [2007] EWCA Civ 809, at ¶59.

4. Appeal No. DA/01045/2014 [February 3, 2015] ¶12.

5. *MA [Ethiopia] v. Secretary of State for the Home Department* ([2009] EWCA Civ 289, [2010] INLR 1).

6. Appeal No. DA/01045/2014 [February 3, 2015] ¶23, compared with [2009] EWCA Civ 289 ¶50.

7. Key legislative instruments include the British Nationality Act (1981); the Nationality, Immigration and Asylum Act (2002); and the Immigration, Asylum and Nationality Act (2006). UK Immigration Rules Part 14 pertains to statelessness; see https://www.gov .uk/government/uploads/system/uploads/attachment_data/file/279697/Immigration _Rules_-_Part_14.pdf.

8. [2009] EWCA Civ 289, [2010] INLR 1 at ¶50.

9. In rejecting Boubacar's claim, the IJ misquoted Lord Justice Elias. The IJ wrote that "all reasonable steps" were required (at ¶23), and "reasonableness" was stripped of practicability constraints. See note 6 above.

10. Interview with Akossiwa, London, December 2011.

11. Akossiwa, UKBA Reasons for Refusal Letter, 2010. See *Revenko v Secretary of State for the Home Department* [2000] EWCA Civ 500; [2001] QB 601 (July 31, 2000).

12. Akossiwa, First Tribunal determination, August 2010.

13. Kofi, First Tribunal determination, September 2011.

14. Including *MS (Ivory Coast) v. Secretary of State for the Home Department* [2007] EWCA Civ 133, United Kingdom: Court of Appeal (England and Wales), February 22, 2007. In weighing the "finely balanced" gravity of the interference encumbered by deportation, the judge turned to *R (Razgar) v SSHD (2004)* UKHL 27 for guidance.

15. *S. v. Secretary of State for the Home Department [2012]* EWHC 1939 (QB) at 192, Case No: CO/10777/2010.

16. Appeal No. DA/01045/2014 [February 3, 2015] ¶22.

17. Appeal No. DA/01045/2014 [February 3, 2015] ¶¶24–25.

18. Appeal No. DA/01045/2014 [February 3, 2015] ¶¶104, 110.

19. The widespread attacks to which judges have subjected experts over the years led to a letter in the *Guardian*. See Afua Hirsch, "Asylum Tribunal Apologises for Questioning Academic's Evidence," *Guardian*, October 26, 2008, http://www.theguardian.com/education /2008/oct/27/alan-george-libel-case.

20. Aliou, RFRL, February 20, 2015, pertaining to Claim C1237402.

21. Fewer than 50 percent of Guinean children were registered at birth in the 1990s; this has since risen to two-thirds ("Birth Registration," Plan International, accessed

June 1, 2015, https://plan-international.org/birthregistration/resources/country-case
-studies/guinea). Swiss Refugee Council, *Identitätsdokumente in ausgewählten afri-
kanischen Flüchtlings-Herkunftsländern*, March 2005, http://www.refworld.org/docid
/4b30d3630.html.

22. *Department Circular No. 058: Establishing the Refugees and Stateless Status Determination Procedure*, Department of Justice, October 18, 2012, section 9.

23. *Act II of 2007 on the Admission and Right of Residence of Third-Country Nationals*,
July 1, 2007, section 79 (1).

24. A harmadik országbeli állampolgárok beutazásáról és tartózkodásáról szóló
2007. évi II. törvény 76. § (1) bekezdés "jogszerű tartózkodás" szövegrésze elleni bírói
kezdeményezés (hontalanság megállapításának feltétele), Budapest, February 23, 2015,
http://public.mkab.hu/dev/dontesek.nsf/0/28DDC0E14E5BC80BC1257D7100259
A90?OpenDocument.

25. Translation by Gábor Gyulai, a trustee and president of the European Network
on Statelessness. See Gábor Gyulai, "Hungarian Constitutional Court Declares That
Lawful Stay Requirement in Statelessness Determination Breaches International
Law," European Network on Statelessness, March 2, 2015, http://www.statelessness.eu
/blog/hungarian-constitutional-court-declares-lawful-stay-requirement-statelessness
-determination#sthash.0FaBfBtv.dpuf.

4. REPRODUCING UNCERTAINTY

DOCUMENTING CONTESTED SOVEREIGNTY AND CITIZENSHIP ACROSS THE TAIWAN STRAIT

SARA L. FRIEDMAN

Documents, so the assumption goes, constitute the evidentiary signs of citizenship, statehood, and sovereignty. Whether passports, national ID cards, travel passes, visas, or entry permits, official documents ostensibly sanctify both the identity of their bearers and the standing of the body that issued them. But what kind of work is performed by identity and travel documents in contexts where citizenship and sovereignty are contested or fragile? Instead of assuming that documents necessarily enact the qualities of recognized statehood or bestow citizenship, this chapter examines how bureaucrats and immigrants infuse documentary practices with their own aspirations and emotional investments, with the result that documents do not affirm legal recognition or sovereign claims so much as they reproduce the uncertain status of contested borders and the individuals who journey across them.

If a government's sovereign standing is not self-evident, then what does this mean for its ability to bestow and recognize citizenship? How is citizenship produced or undermined when some of its ostensibly foundational conditions—recognized borders, distinct groups of nationals and foreigners, and sovereign recognition—are uncertain at best and hotly contested at worst? How does movement across borders heighten the destabilizing features of this context, rendering national identity and legal status matters of contention and calling into question the security of state-bestowed identities, citizenship included?

This chapter addresses one small piece of this larger puzzle by examining the work that identity and travel documents do in a context of contested sovereignty. Other scholars approach documents as elements in a larger state classificatory project—a project through which states aim to recognize and make legible their own populations while simultaneously excluding outsiders from the citizen body (Caplan and Torpey 2001; Scott 1998; Torpey 2000). This chapter begins from the assumption that classifications of individuals and groups are rarely seamless or uncontested.[1] Together with chapters by Sadiq, Rosenbloom, and McKenzie, it argues that these moments of friction and even failure offer valuable insights into how both citizenship and sovereignty are produced and struggled over in diverse settings in the world today (Wang 2004; Yngvesson and Coutin 2006).

My analytic point of departure is the state of largely de facto sovereignty experienced by Taiwan (also known as the Republic of China [ROC]) and Taiwan's contested relationship with the People's Republic of China (PRC), which claims the island as a renegade province destined eventually to return to the PRC's sovereign orbit. By examining the travel documents Taiwanese and Chinese use to move between the two countries and the identity documents issued to Chinese immigrants in Taiwan, I show how these atypical documents both substantiate Taiwan's claims to sovereign standing and simultaneously undo those very claims through their ambiguous features: the documents mimic internationally recognized evidentiary standards for citizenship that legitimate cross-border mobility, but their "not quite" features also affirm Taiwan's "not quite" state of national sovereignty. In other words, the documents themselves and the actions performed on or with them reproduce, rather than resolve, the anomalous status of the border travelers cross and the uncertain standing of Taiwan as a document-issuing and document-recognizing sovereign authority. One consequence of these documentary effects is to bestow an exceptional (although legal) status on Chinese immigrants in Taiwan and to call into question their ability to realize the full promise of naturalized citizenship in their new home.

I focus here on two groups for whom the documentary bases of identity are particularly fraught: Taiwanese bureaucrats charged with regulating cross-border mobility and the largest population of permanent immigrants to Taiwan, the mainland Chinese spouses of Taiwanese citizens. Travel and identity documents animate both groups' quests for security and legitimation. Chinese spouses desire recognition as legitimate members of Taiwanese families and the Taiwanese nation, while Taiwanese bureaucrats seek international acknowledgment of their status as representatives of a sovereign state. Documents, I suggest, mediate these groups' relationship to desired states of existence—citizen inclusion and sovereign recognition—but that mediation more often than not fails to resolve the anxieties each group faces as it seeks to attain modes of belonging promised by idealized models of both citizenship and sovereignty. These failures result from documents' inability to escape the historically contingent legal and geopolitical configurations that demand they function merely as "as if" material forms of recognition, skirting the thorny questions of sovereignty and national identity that continue to plague cross-Strait relations.

Documentary Border Crossings

China's mid-twentieth-century civil war produced two regimes that claimed to represent the legitimate government of all of China: the Nationalists, who retreated in defeat to the island of Taiwan in 1949, and the Communists, who thereafter took control of the Chinese mainland. Military conflict and intense ideological battles persisted across the Taiwan Strait during the bitter Cold War decades that followed, but international responses to the two-state problem gradually shifted as Cold War tensions waned and more states recognized the PRC over the ROC.[2] This multidecade process of ROC derecognition has culminated in a situation today whereby Taiwan functions as a de facto independent state with its own democratically elected government, military, and currency, but it lacks de jure recognition from all but a mere twenty-two small countries in the world. In short, Taiwan's political status vis-à-vis China remains ambiguous.

The cross-Strait political stalemate began to thaw in 1987 and renewed ties opened up the possibility of civilian flows across the Strait. One result of this new relationship was a growing number of marriages between Chinese and Taiwanese, the vast majority of which paired a Chinese woman with a Taiwanese man, with the couple often residing in Taiwan. On the basis of their family reunification claims, mainland Chinese spouses enjoy rights to legal residence and future citizenship status in Taiwan. To regulate this contested group of immigrants and contain their impact on Taiwanese society, the ROC government has created an increasingly complex immigration regime that enacts Taiwan's sovereign aspirations while striving to assuage widespread anxieties about the country's political future.

By the late twentieth century, Taiwan had begun to grant entry to temporary labor migrants from Southeast Asia and to permanent marital immigrants from China and Southeast Asia. Despite their shared status as the spouse of a Taiwanese citizen, these two groups of marital immigrants have been slotted into different categories in Taiwan's emerging immigration regime. "Foreign spouses," primarily women from countries such as Vietnam, Indonesia, Cambodia, and the Philippines, are regulated under Taiwan's Immigration Act, which grants them residency and work rights when they first arrive in Taiwan and creates a four-year time clock to naturalized citizenship. Their entry into Taiwan and status as legal immigrants are documented through recognizable evidentiary means: they cross borders using foreign passports stamped with an entry visa and receive a laminated plastic residence card shortly after arrival that resembles in form and content Taiwanese citizens' national identification card.

Chinese spouses, by contrast, are defined as neither foreigners nor natives under Taiwanese law: to identify them with either category would be viewed by China as either asserting Taiwanese independence or acquiescing to the stance that Taiwan is merely a province under China's sovereign control. Following the reestablishment of cross-Strait ties in the late 1980s, Taiwan's legislature crafted new legislation to manage this emerging relationship and the possible arrival of mainland Chinese on Taiwanese shores. Known as the Act Governing Relations between the People of the Taiwan Area and the Mainland Area, this legislation slotted all mainland Chinese into an anomalous legal category, "people of the mainland area." The act and its subsidiary policies created a distinct immigration path for Chinese spouses, generally the only group of mainland Chinese who enjoyed rights to residence and citizenship in Taiwan. Unlike their foreign counterparts who received residency status and work rights upon first arrival in Taiwan, Chinese spouses faced a delay of several years in both respects and an initial timeline to citizenship that was twice as long (eight years in total). Some of these inequalities were redressed by reforms to the act in 2009, but to this day Chinese spouses must wait six years before being eligible for Taiwanese citizenship.

Chinese spouses, therefore, occupy an exceptional legal status in Taiwan, a sign of the anxieties produced by their origins in the mainland and the potential threats they may pose to Taiwanese sovereignty once they become naturalized citizens.[3] Despite enjoying legal immigration standing in Taiwan through marriage to a citizen, Chinese spouses are marked by this exceptional status both prior to and, in certain ways, even after becoming naturalized citizens.[4] The documents that create Chinese spouses' legal identity during their many years as immigrants in Taiwan and that they use to travel across the Taiwan Strait substantiate their exceptionalism and their contested claims to future inclusion in the national polity.

Travel between China and Taiwan is regulated by a multitude of documents, but for Chinese and Taiwanese border crossers, passports are not among them.

In fact, many Chinese spouses in Taiwan do not have a PRC passport at all. If we accept, as John Torpey (2000) and Yael Navaro-Yashin (2007) contend, that passports constitute and convey "state-ness," then it should be obvious why Chinese and Taiwanese do not use passports to move across the Strait, for to do so would require that China recognize Taiwan as a sovereign nation-state.[5] Despite this absence of passports, travel between China and Taiwan does *resemble* international travel. Chinese, Taiwanese, and foreign travelers all pass through immigration and customs at airports and sea ports, and they are required to show documentary proof of identity to border officers at points of departure and arrival. Foreign nationals use passports and visas to journey between Taiwan and China, but Taiwanese and Chinese who cross these borders carry documents that are distinct from those used for travel to a third country.

To sidestep the sovereignty question, China requires Taiwanese who seek to enter the PRC to apply for a "Taiwan compatriot pass" (*taibaozheng*), which serves as their document of record while in China. In turn, the PRC government issues Chinese citizens departing for Taiwan a "travel pass" (*tongxingzheng*) designated specifically for Taiwan. These documents are small booklets that resemble a passport in form and content: they have a rigid, colored cover and a first page with a photograph and other identifying information. Inside pages contain "visas" that are valid for a fixed period of time and permit single or multiple entry and exit.[6]

The documents' official names, printed in full on the cover, demonstrate some of the common rhetorical strategies employed by China to contain cross-Strait ties within a domestic, intranational framework. First, the two countries are identified not by their formal names but as regions or areas: Taiwan and the mainland.[7] Second, the documents are defined not as passports—using the documentary language of citizenship and sovereignty—but as travel passes, a term that suggests heightened state control over internal mobility (Torpey 2000, 165). Hence, by issuing Chinese citizens "travel passes" for travel to Taiwan, the PRC government implicitly enfolds Taiwan into its domestic space. Third, the presence of directional verbs in the full names affirms the geographic perspective of China as the dominant (i.e., issuing) authority: Taiwan residents "come to" (*laiwang*) the mainland, whereas mainland residents "go to" (*wanglai*) Taiwan. These verbs position China as the central actor managing cross-Strait flows, thereby denying Taiwan any claim to independent sovereign status.

When Chinese spouses travel to Taiwan, they depart the mainland using their travel pass; they enter Taiwan, however, on a document issued to them by Taiwan's National Immigration Agency (NIA) or, prior to the establishment of the NIA in January 2007, by the Entry/Exit Immigration Police. Unlike the booklet-type documents issued by China, this "Exit and Entry Permit" is a single sheet of paper folded in thirds to make it roughly the size of a passport. The bottom third is laid out much like the first page of a passport, with a photograph in the upper left corner and identifying information to the right. Although the permit resembles a passport, it includes information that is often contained in a visa or a port-of-entry form (such as purpose of entry and address in Taiwan). To add to the confusion, the permit acts as a passport at the moment when it (and not the PRC-issued travel pass) is stamped by a Taiwan border officer as the Chinese traveler proceeds through immigration control to enter Taiwan.

These documents manage border crossings by keeping both the status of the border and the national standing of Chinese and Taiwanese who journey across it intentionally ambiguous. The documents resemble internationally recognized passports and visas but are not exactly the same. The NIA officials themselves acknowledge that the use of travel passes and entry permits reaffirms the "strange relationship" between Taiwan and mainland China and undermines Taiwan's aspirations for a recognized "state-to-state" relationship with the PRC. Although this ambiguity keeps potential political tensions across the Strait in check, it also generates its own complexities for those who move across the border and for the officials who regulate those flows.

When ties between China and Taiwan were reinstated in 1987, travel from one country to the other was a cumbersome and time-consuming process. Despite the narrow body of water separating Taiwan from the mainland, travelers were required to transit through a third location, typically Hong Kong or Macau. At the time, Hong Kong was still a British colony, and Macau was ruled by Portugal. Even after the PRC assumed control of the territories in 1997 and 1999, respectively, it designated them as special administrative regions with quasi-independent governments and border control bureaucracies. Direct travel across the Taiwan Strait became possible only with Taiwan's election of Nationalist president Ma Ying-jeou in 2008. Ma sought to expand trade and improve ties with China by introducing direct flights between Taiwan's major airports and select cities on the mainland. Although these flights began in July 2008, the Taiwan government did not permit Chinese spouses to utilize direct travel until a year later. Hence, prior to mid-2009, all Chinese spouses traveling to Taiwan were required to transit through Hong Kong or Macau.[8]

Acquiring a Taiwan-issued entry permit was the first step in a Chinese spouse's journey to Taiwan. Her Taiwanese spouse applied on her behalf for the entry permit after the couple had legally married in China and procured all required documentation. Once that application was approved, the NIA or its predecessor unit generated two copies of the entry permit: an "original" that it mailed directly to the Hong Kong or Macau airport branch of Chung Hwa Travel Service (Taiwan's unofficial consular office), and a "copy" that was stamped by the issuing body and then sent to the Chinese spouse's guarantor in Taiwan. The guarantor (typically her Taiwanese husband) then mailed the copy of the permit to China so she could use it to apply for a travel pass from PRC authorities. With the PRC-issued travel pass and the Taiwan-issued entry permit "copy," a Chinese spouse traveled by land or air to Hong Kong or Macau and, at the airport desk of Chung Hwa Travel Service, exchanged her entry permit "copy" for the "original." Now with the "original" permit safely in hand, she could board a plane for Taiwan.

Why this elaborate system of "original" and "copy"? I initially assumed that it derived from the symbolic message of sovereign recognition conveyed by a Taiwan government agency directly mailing an official document to China. When I raised this question with Mr. Zhu, a senior Taiwanese official in the NIA section that issued entry permits, he instead emphasized the practical risks involved, dangers that revolved around Chinese propensities to "forge" documents.[9] During our interview in the summer of 2009, Mr. Zhu claimed that "in the past many people forged entry permit copies and used them to enter Hong Kong to work and earn money, not to come to Taiwan." Now, however, with direct cross-Strait flights, Chinese spouses no longer had to transit through Hong Kong or Macau (although many still did because of cheaper airfares), and the NIA had no choice but to issue the "original" entry permit directly to the Taiwan guarantor, who then mailed it to his wife in China. "Because of this," Mr. Zhu continued, "the risk we over here must take is even greater! There is no 'interview,' [we] haven't seen the person. Because, after all, many of them over there forge documents."

Mr. Zhu's concerns reflect official anxiety about the identification capacity of documents in the hands of mainland Chinese and the feared lack of correspondence between an identity document and the individual who uses it.[10] The distribution of "original" and "copy" is intended to protect the "original" from fraudulent use in a context where Taiwan is unable to confirm, independently, the identity of Chinese citizens, but where government officials *assume* that Chinese will forge documents if given the opportunity. In Mr. Zhu's narrative, both the original and the copy are susceptible to forgery, but the threat of a forged original is more powerful because of the capacities for mobility that inhere in the original: the ability to leave the geopolitical orbit of the PRC and travel to Taiwan. A Derridean reading that would show all "originals" to be simply "copies" (or "copies" to be no different from "originals") fails to get at the heart of the matter here, because officials such as Mr. Zhu experience a forged original as a direct challenge to Taiwan's sovereign authority to bestow on specific individuals the right to cross its borders. The phenomenologically original document, whether authentic or faked, empowers the bearer to fly directly to Taiwan without requiring the copy's mediating bureaucratic encounter in Hong Kong or Macau.[11] Mr. Zhu's framing of this potential risk positions "we over here" against "they over there" in an attempt to maintain a distance otherwise collapsed by direct flights across the Taiwan Strait and the government's issuance of original entry permits, a distance that bureaucrats such as Mr. Zhu see as vital to Taiwan's fragile sovereignty claims.

The multiplicity of documents employed in cross-Strait travel underscores the ambiguous status of the border itself and, subsequently, of the individuals who cross it—groups who fail to fit into recognized categories of foreigners, citizens, or even nationals returning from far-flung homes in the diaspora. Much like the ostensibly suspect birth certificates that the U.S. State Department deems insufficient evidence for jus soli citizenship claims (Rosenbloom, this volume), the travel documents used by Chinese spouses are infused with suspicions that those documents may not bear a unique referential relation to their bearer. These suspicions persist even after Chinese spouses enter Taiwan and embark on the path to residency and citizenship, and they justify the exceptional documents that substantiate Chinese spouses' anomalous status in Taiwan. These documentary effects reverberate on multiple scales: on the one hand, exceptionalism undermines Chinese spouses' efforts to create a sense of belonging in Taiwan as members of Taiwanese families and as future citizens; on the other hand, exceptionalism calls into question the coherence of ostensibly recognizable categories such as citizens and foreigners with their internationally sanctioned identity and travel documents.

Documentary Acts

The documentary exceptionalism that defines cross-Strait border crossings permeates the everyday experiences of Chinese spouses once they enter Taiwan and begin life in a society where most of them lack the two most widely recognized forms of identification: a national ID card that connotes Taiwanese citizenship or a foreign passport. Burdened with a multitude of documents issued by different authorities, Chinese spouses are often unsure which document to use where or when—their entry permit (now converted to a reunion permit after passing a border interview at their port of entry) or the travel pass issued by the Chinese government. Some resort to Taiwan's widely recognized

National Health Insurance card that they receive after their first four months of residence in Taiwan. Nor are Taiwanese bureaucrats or average citizens always certain which form of identification different contexts require, even in official encounters where a premium is placed on accurate identification. The practices that emerge around identity documents, what I term here "documentary acts," affirm Veena Das and Deborah Poole's (2004b, 24) insight that state-issued identity documents "acquire a different kind of life" as they are manipulated for diverse ends by state actors, ordinary citizens, and, as the following cases suggest, immigrants from various backgrounds. These documentary acts not only undermine state projects to make populations legible but also potentially call into question the very foundations of citizenship and sovereignty on which such projects rest.

ADJUDICATING IDENTITIES

Meng Hua's experience in a Taipei district courtroom in the winter of 2008 underscored the challenges of confirming immigrants' identities through an array of documents issued by different governing bodies. A fifty-three-year-old woman from Jiangxi Province in China's interior, Meng Hua had married for the third time in 2005 to Mr. Li, an elderly veteran who had lived in Taiwan since 1949, when he fled there with the Nationalist army. From the beginning, however, Taiwanese authorities had refused to recognize the couple's marriage because Meng had previously married another Taiwanese man but had never legally divorced him in Taiwan. It took Meng several years to obtain a formal divorce, and in the confusion of that process, Meng and Li ended up divorcing in China and then remarrying twice. Only in 2007 did Meng finally receive permission to enter Taiwan as Li's legally recognized spouse.

The couple's travails did not end with Meng's arrival in Taiwan, however. Li's bad temper had fostered a habit of litigiousness, and after Meng was ostensibly mistreated at a city hospital following a hand injury, Li decided to sue the hospital. Not only did his suit fail, but the case brought the couple's marital complexities to the attention of the public prosecutor, who, so he claimed, was obligated by law to bring a case against Meng for bigamy (in reference to her 2005 marriage to Li when she had not yet divorced her previous Taiwanese husband). It was on the occasion of this court hearing that I accompanied Meng and Li to the Taipei District Criminal Court on the outskirts of the city's bustling Ximending shopping area.

Meng and Li were sitting on the wooden benches outside the courtroom when I arrived. Short and plump, with her long hair twisted carefully into a bun, Meng perched nervously on the edge of her seat, while Li, in his seventies, contained his impatience in a stiff posture honed through years of military service. The reporting clerk came bustling down the hallway and ushered us into the courtroom, asking immediately for Meng's documentation as the defendant. Meng first handed him her entry permit, but the clerk shook his head and said that he needed her "passport," stating the term in English (which neither Meng nor Li spoke) and then repeating it in Chinese (*huzhao*). "Oh, my passport [*huzhao*]," Meng replied, and handed over her travel pass issued by the PRC government. The clerk accepted the travel pass without comment and entered the necessary information into his roster.

In this exchange Meng first assumed, not without reason, that the court required an identity document issued by Taiwanese authorities, but instead the clerk privileged the PRC travel pass as the document of record. Neither commented on the confusion of terms in their encounter or the use of the travel pass as a replacement for a foreign passport. This confusion continued after the court session began, when one of the court recorders asked Meng whether she had a Taiwan national ID, to which Meng replied matter-of-factly, "No, only a passport," meaning once again her travel pass and not an official PRC passport, which she did not possess.

As the presiding judge initiated the court proceedings, she looked over both Meng's and Li's identification documents, reading their numbers aloud for the court recorder. In the midst of examining Meng's travel pass, she paused and said to Meng, "This [travel pass] is from the mainland. Didn't Taiwan give you an entry permit?" Meng quickly handed over her entry permit, and the proceedings continued, with the judge fingering both documents throughout her questioning.

Even in a formal legal setting such as a courtroom, expectations for identification documents fluctuate among individuals and over the course of the hearing itself. The ease with which both Meng and the various officials moved seamlessly between different kinds of documents issued by different authorities attests to the mediating power of documents and their ability to integrate diverse legal regimes as if they were equivalent (e.g., travel passes that stand in for passports) (Hull 2012, 253). But that presumed equivalence also raises questions about the authority of the document's issuing body and the state's capacity to produce citizenship and sovereignty by authenticating and classifying individuals under its purview. The courtroom encounter did not resolve these questions but simply suspended them in the name of legal efficiency. By demanding that a Taiwan government document be added to the mix, the presiding judge intimated that the PRC-issued travel pass failed to stand as a document of record for the purposes of definitive identification in Taiwan, but she did so without acknowledging the implicit claim to sovereign recognition that underlay the court's demand for an officially Taiwanese form of documentary identification.

The identification capacities of different kinds of documents require mutual recognition from multiple actors who make decisions about rights to mobility and resources based on the presumed power of such documents to validate an individual's identity. Atypical documents that do not fit easily within an international evidentiary regime may undermine bearers' efforts to realize their rights as citizens and documented immigrants, or they may simply make explicit potentialities that exist in recognized forms of documentation, as Sadiq, Rosenbloom, and McKenzie show in their chapters. Chinese spouses in Taiwan quickly discovered that their exceptional documents constrained their ability to move across borders, especially when their desired journeys involved travel to a third country. At stake were the various circulation effects produced by different forms of documentation: how well identity and travel documents constituted Chinese spouses as desirable travelers and how widely those documents enabled them to move. Whereas recognized documents typically (although not always) facilitate mobility within national spaces as well as across borders, atypical documents may fail to bestow the same circulation effects on their bearers, a consequence of the contested status of both the traveler and the issuing body.

In addition to creating practical obstacles for Chinese spouses who sought to travel beyond the cross-Strait orbit, identity documents also became sources of emotional investment for their bearers, in both positive and negative senses. Taiwan-issued papers "transmit an affect of tentativeness" (Navaro-Yashin 2007, 86), not only in the sense of being ephemeral (easily destroyed) or bestowing limited circulation effects but also because they affirm the uncertain sovereignty of Taiwan as the issuing body and Chinese spouses' own sense of never quite belonging in Taiwan. Chinese spouses' exceptionalism is reproduced through the ephemeral aura of the documents they carry and through the inability of those documents to constitute recognized identities and to enable desired forms of mobility—literally, across all borders, but also figuratively, in the sense of marital decisions and life circumstances in Taiwan that do not always live up to their imagined potential.

Chinese spouses' emotional investments in their documents were intertwined with the material form of the documents themselves; they were generated by and responded to documents' physical qualities and presumed effects (Hull 2012; Riles 2006; see also Sadiq, this volume). As merely "a piece of paper," the reunion permit that many of the Chinese spouses I knew received upon first arrival was frequently singled out for its lack of substance.[12] In contrast to the booklet form of a residence permit, travel pass, or passport or the laminated national ID card that connoted citizenship in both Taiwan and China, this single sheet of paper was viewed by many as insubstantial and even humiliating, its flimsiness a symbol of Chinese spouses' tentative status in Taiwan. Even Taiwanese husbands took umbrage at paper documents and associated them with officials' demeaning attitudes toward mainland Chinese. In 2003, I interviewed a Taiwanese academic who had married a Chinese woman who held a masters' degree from Beijing University, China's premier academic institution. On his wife's second visit to Taiwan in 1997, border officers at the airport seized all her documents, including her PRC passport. In his retelling of his wife's border-crossing experience, the husband described how the officer had looked at her "as if she was the same as all those other mainlanders," despite the fact that she had told him she was a teacher at an elite Beijing university. Eyeing her with suspicion, the officer had tossed a pile of papers in her direction and brusquely instructed her to fill them out. Adding insult to injury was the flimsy document she received in exchange for her other papers, a temporary ID that, in her husband's words, was merely "a very thin, very thin piece of paper."

Progressing from the insecurities of temporary reunion status to the first residency stage available to Chinese spouses was an experience marked not only by greater rights (the ability of some to work legally, for instance) but also by more substantial documents. With changes to the immigration sequence in 2004, Chinese spouses became eligible for residency following two years of marriage or the birth of a child, and they looked forward to residency status as a sign of recognized standing in Taiwan. Many articulated the transition through reference to the physical form of their new identity document. Unlike the sheet of paper that certified reunion status, residency was documented by a passport-like booklet with a light-blue cover. The weight and substance of the document defined how Chinese spouses related to their new status: they referred to it as the "booklet" or the "blue booklet" and frequently mentioned that it had multiple pages. In contrast to the lack and humiliation experienced by holders of reunion permits, the residency booklet inspired a sense of pride among its bearers because of its material substantiality.

Chinese spouses' attachment to the residency permit also derived from assumptions about the greater circulation effects of that document as opposed to the reunion permit. Luo Jing, a stylish young Chinese woman married to a Taiwanese computer entrepreneur, was eager to pick up her new residency permit on the fall day in 2007 when I accompanied her to NIA headquarters in downtown Taipei. She had checked the status of her application online that morning and had e-mailed me to arrange a time for us to meet at the bus stop near her apartment. Our bus ride took us from the upscale neighborhoods of northeastern Taipei to the mixed business and working-class streets of the older, western part of the city. We arrived at the NIA in the early afternoon and proceeded down the escalator to the cavernous hall dedicated to mainland Chinese. Fortunately, there was no line to pick up processed applications, and Luo confidently approached the woman seated at the desk. The clerk's attitude was brusque and businesslike, and upon discovering that Luo had forgotten to bring her receipt, the woman asked in an exasperated voice whether she had any identification. Luo retrieved her National Health Insurance card from her purse and handed it to the clerk, who, appeased by the familiar card, flipped through her file drawer and pulled out Luo's new document.

As we walked away from the desk, the blue booklet in hand, Luo Jing turned to me and asked whether now she could leave Taiwan without additional paperwork. In search of a definitive answer, we returned to the desk, where Luo asked whether the booklet enabled her "to come and go freely." Before departing the country, she needed an exit stamp, the woman replied, and she turned the pages to show Luo the stamp that came with her new document, but which expired in six months. We sat down on a bench in the large hall and Luo leafed carefully through the booklet. The first page of Luo's document looked very much like a passport and included her photograph and identifying information, such as date and place of birth, reason for entry, and her husband's name. There was a line stating that she was required to submit to fingerprinting on her first entry, along with a notation indicating that she had done so. The remaining interior pages were blank except for the one exit stamp and another stamp with the document's expiration date.

Luo had high hopes that this new identity document would facilitate greater mobility beyond Taiwan and China, but she would soon learn that her residency permit did not enable unfettered movement across borders. Not long after obtaining residency status, she sought to join a tour group to South Korea with her mother-in-law. But the tour was unable to accommodate Luo's anomalous documents, including the combination of her residency permit with a PRC passport newly acquired just prior to Luo's first trip to Taiwan in 2005. Because Luo had never traveled anywhere outside of China other than Taiwan, her passport contained no travel stamps to prove that she had legally departed China. In other words, although Luo was no longer physically in the mainland, her official travel document as a Chinese citizen did not provide evidence of a legal departure, entry elsewhere, or a return, all of which would constitute her as a desirable traveler who conformed to designated travel routes and permitted lengths of stay. Instead, her cross-Strait journey was documented by her travel pass and entry permit alone. For Chinese spouses in Taiwan, therefore, their passports do not reflect their cross-border movement, precisely because the Taiwan-China border is constituted as not quite international by the anomalous documents used to manage travel across the Strait. Cross-Strait mobility renders Chinese spouses out of place, located elsewhere to the routes tracked (or not) in their passports, further undermining their efforts to use valued passports and residency permits to travel beyond Taiwan and China.

Sovereign Stamps

Chinese spouses are not the only individuals in Taiwan who express affective investments in certain kinds of documents and the resources they may provide. Taiwanese immigration officials and bureaucrats, too, manage feelings of ambivalence about Taiwan's sovereignty struggles through their material engagement with identity documents. At stake here is what border officials do with these documents, especially the highly contested act of officially stamping a document issued by another government. After a series of interviews with senior NIA officials in the summer of 2009, I came to realize that as the number of Chinese travelers to Taiwan increased, the act of stamping took on heightened significance for those who staffed Taiwan's immigration posts and managed border flows.

When Chinese citizens enter Taiwan—whether they come as a spouse, to visit other relatives, as a tourist, or for business—they do not receive an immigration stamp in their PRC-issued travel pass. Instead, Taiwanese border officers stamp the entry permit provided to them by the Taiwan government. At one point in my conversation with NIA section head Zhu, I asked him to describe his own documentary journey when traveling to China. When passing through immigration into China, Zhu explained, border officers stamp his PRC-issued Taiwan compatriot pass. They might look at his Taiwan passport to confirm his identity (and he always brings it with him), but they would never stamp it. Similarly, he continued, although some Chinese citizens visiting Taiwan will carry a PRC passport, they must have an entry permit issued by the Taiwanese government to enter the country. "Taiwan authorities will not stamp the PRC passport," Mr. Zhu noted. "They will only stamp the entry permit." Mr. Zhu chuckled and paused before speaking again, this time his voice quivering with excitement: "We want very much to stamp [the PRC passport]! But at present, we still don't know what subtle effect this stamp might have on cross-Strait relations."

Mr. Zhu tempered his strong desire to imprint a Taiwan stamp on a PRC-issued document by conceding that such a simple act came weighted with significant import for relations across the Strait. His portrayal of his own border crossings shows how the very act of stamping an identity or travel document affirms the sovereign status of the stamping authority while it also recognizes the legitimacy of the government that issued the document in the first place (Wang 2004).[13] Moreover, in his expressed desire to stamp a PRC passport, Mr. Zhu acknowledged that bureaucrats' everyday documentary acts were, in fact, anything but mundane: they performed powerful political claims and bids for recognition as a sovereign authority.

Mr. Zhu was by no means the only NIA official attuned to the power of stamps. Other NIA officials brought this up on numerous occasions, both during conversations at the border and in interviews I conducted at NIA offices scattered across Taiwan. In June 2009, I traveled to Taiwan's main international airport to interview Mr. Lu, then second in command of the NIA Border Affairs Corps, about recent changes to the process for interviewing the Chinese spouses of Taiwanese citizens. In the midst of this discussion Mr. Lu, too, raised the topic of stamping a PRC travel document: "Of course, I've always thought that the immigration stamp [*zhangchuo*] is a symbol of sovereignty. Each country is the same. How do we make a breakthrough here, how do we issue that stamp in their [Chinese citizens'] passports? That is very difficult right now. . . . I *need* to stamp a 'Taiwan' here in your passport, a 'Republic of China' right here. The symbolic and practical meaning of that [act] must be stronger than the interview. This is what I firmly believe, I don't know if it is right or wrong." Like Mr. Zhu, Mr. Lu described the stamping of a PRC passport as a powerful assertion of Taiwanese sovereignty. For him, the physical presence of the stamped words "Taiwan" or "Republic of China," inked permanently onto a PRC-issued document, would produce both symbolic and practical effects. Official stamps indexically "trace a network of relations on the page" (Hetherington 2011, 194), but they also enact those relations in a specific form, in this case through the desired framework of sovereign recognition. Although Mr. Lu's "need" to imprint those characters in a Chinese passport reaffirmed his commitment to Taiwanese sovereignty, he was too savvy an official to rashly proclaim his desire to act on this impulse. Instead, he softened his "firm belief" with a final disclaimer, "I don't know if it is right or wrong."

Both men's emotional investment in the act of official stamping supports a recent shift in bureaucratic studies away from a Weberian emphasis on bureaucratic rationality and the "iron cage" of ossified rules and procedures. Bureaucracies also produce and regulate sentiments, including, as several anthropological studies have shown, the affective investments of civil servants themselves (Das and Poole 2004a; Feldman 2008; Graham 2002; Navaro-Yashin 2006, 2012; Stoler 2004). In the examples I discuss here, those affective investments are expressed through bureaucratic acts performed on documents that offer the potential to generate sovereignty effects (Friedman 2010). Although both men ultimately temper their desire with an acknowledgment of impossibility, that tempering should not be viewed simply as an example of rationality dominating emotion. Instead, their comments show how affective registers permeate the ostensibly rational lives of official documents, embedding document bearers, issuers, and handlers in shared webs of desire that weave together personal aspirations, state legibility projects, and sovereign claims.[14]

Conclusion

This chapter has shown how official documents often fail to perform as intended, despite the heartfelt investments of those who generate them, evaluate their authenticity, and use them to assert identities, claim recognition, and facilitate mobility. For Chinese spouses and Taiwanese bureaucrats, identity and travel documents are fraught sources of both anxiety and aspiration, condensing individual and national desires for recognized status and the security of belonging. Because the documents that facilitate cross-Strait travel are approximations of internationally sanctioned identity and travel documents— mere "as if" passports, visas, or identity cards—they also reproduce Taiwan's contested sovereignty and its not quite state-to-state relationship with China. For Chinese spouses, this documentary approximation has the added consequence of affirming their exceptional status as neither foreigners nor natives in Taiwan. The anomalous qualities of Chinese spouses' papers further widen the gap between them and all other foreign spouses of Taiwanese citizens. As Chinese spouses move between China and Taiwan and through Taiwanese society, their documents set them apart from other travelers and immigrants while they simultaneously reenact cross-Strait contestations over Taiwanese sovereignty.

Affective investments on the part of both Chinese spouses and Taiwanese bureaucrats affirm the powerful role of documents in creating identities and statuses necessary for both personal and national recognition. But these shared investments also expose the contested underbelly of documentary acts, the always present possibility that documents may fail to produce desired identities, facilitate cross-border mobility, or enable sovereign recognition. By turning our attention to the materiality of identity documents, we can better understand how documents engage in a form of signifying work that extends beyond specific documentary encounters: in other words, documents serve as "vehicles of imagination" (Hull 2012, 260) that generate new social and political possibilities even as they foreclose others (Riles 2006). The examples discussed in this chapter show how documents reproduce a powerful sense of uncertainty that reverberates across multiple scales of individuals, immigrant communities, state actors, and the nation-state itself.

As the lives of documents develop along unpredictable paths that extend into the future, their mediating power brings together often incommensurable domains, such that immigrants' aspirations for national inclusion and belonging become wedded to state desires for sovereign recognition. These linked projects may advance efforts to produce sovereign legitimacy in the face of categorical ambiguity, but they may be just as likely to undermine the very armature of citizenship and sovereign recognition used to contain and manage cross-border mobility.

NOTES

An earlier version of this chapter first appeared in *Exceptional States: Chinese Immigrants and Taiwanese Sovereignty* (University of California Press, 2015). I thank Benjamin Lawrance and Jacqueline Stevens for inviting me to participate in the "Citizenship-in-Question" symposium and for providing valuable feedback on earlier drafts. I am indebted to the many Chinese immigrants and Taiwanese bureaucrats and officials who shared their views and experiences with me and who taught me to appreciate the challenges of life on the margins of citizenship and sovereignty.

1. For instance, the identities produced by documents may be taken up by subjects in ways that undermine the very goals of state recognition that motivated the turn to documentary practices in the first place (Coutin 2007; Gordillo 2006; Navaro-Yashin 2007; Yngvesson and Coutin 2006).

2. In 1971, China's United Nations seat was transferred from the Nationalist regime on Taiwan to the PRC, and the United States switched its diplomatic recognition to the PRC in 1979. The "one China principle" upheld by the PRC prevents states from officially recognizing both governments.

3. Taiwanese bureaucrats, for instance, frequently mention that the total number of Chinese spouses in Taiwan is rapidly approaching the size of Taiwan's fourth-largest city. This statement is intended to suggest that former mainland Chinese could become a powerful voting bloc in Taiwan that could alter the country's political future.

4. Chinese who acquire Taiwanese citizenship are treated differently from other citizens (both birthright and naturalized) in that they are denied certain rights to civil service participation or to sponsoring kin for family reunification.

5. In his history of the passport in Western Europe, John Torpey argues that "the emergence of passport and related controls on movement is an essential aspect of the 'state-ness' of states" (2000, 3). Torpey builds on Max Weber's theory of state legitimacy

to suggest that monopolizing "the legitimate means of movement" was a critical dimension of state building in the modern period. Anthropologist Yael Navaro-Yashin extends Torpey's insight to illegal states such as the Turkish Republic of Northern Cyprus, which, she contends, must engage in documentary practices as part of asserting their own claims to "state-ness" (2007, 84).

6. In 2015 China began to issue ID-card-style Taiwan compatriot passes in place of the booklet form and removed visa requirements for pass holders.

7. The full name of the Taiwan compatriot pass is "Travel Pass for Taiwan Residents Coming to the Mainland." For mainland Chinese departing for Taiwan, their document is called a "Travel Pass for Mainland Residents Going to Taiwan." By juxtaposing Taiwan with the mainland, the PRC government implicitly denies legitimacy to Taiwanese independence supporters who argue that the name Taiwan may be used to represent a sovereign state.

8. Beginning in 2001, select categories of travelers from both countries were permitted to journey by boat between China's Fujian Province and Taiwan's offshore islands of Jinmen and Mazu. When direct flights across the Strait were introduced in 2008, the Taiwan government designated two "international" and two "domestic" airports as destinations, with one of the domestic airports (Taipei Songshan) later upgraded to international status. The existence of direct flights from both kinds of airports reaffirms the ambiguous status of cross-Strait travel as neither clearly international nor clearly domestic.

9. In a longer version of this chapter, I discuss how the presumed propensity of Chinese to forge documents undermines the value of the Taiwan passport as well because of the ease with which it may be falsified by Chinese smugglers. All personal names used in this chapter are pseudonyms.

10. Caplan and Torpey describe this core tension in the presumption that an identity document captures a unique individuality as a conflict between the "uniqueness" of an identity document and its need to serve as "an element in a classifying series that reduces individuality to a unit in a series, and that is thus simultaneously deindividualizing" (2001, 8). This tension between a unique individuality and a shared classification scheme creates the possibility that others might manipulate modes of classification to serve different ends.

11. I am indebted here to Navaro-Yashin's argument that for individuals who are the subjects of these documents (or, I might add, who handle them in their professional capacities), the difference between originals and copies is "experientially very real" (Navaro-Yashin 2003, 88). As an anthropologist invested in the study of personal experience, I pay close attention to how individuals experience documents and how such experiences might produce very different forms of subjective investment.

12. For those who first arrived between March 2004 and August 2009, the reunion permit was typically their first identity document issued in Taiwan. Policy reforms implemented in August 2009 eliminated the reunion stage and granted Chinese spouses residency rights upon first arrival.

13. The sovereignty effect of official stamping is seen in the multitude of examples worldwide where stamps are not made in the documents issued by certain countries or

where documents stamped by certain countries are not recognized by others. In the realm of cross-Strait relations, many third countries refuse to stamp the Taiwan passport out of concern that such an act would connote sovereign recognition and therefore anger Chinese authorities.

14. I borrow the phrase "life of documents" from Veena Das (2004, 240), who coins it to describe how the business of producing official documents moves between registers of legality and illegality without ultimately undermining state legitimacy.

5. WHAT IS A "REAL" AUSTRALIAN CITIZEN?
INSIGHTS FROM PAPUA NEW GUINEA
AND MR. AMOS AME

KIM RUBENSTEIN WITH JACQUELINE FIELD

This chapter highlights the way citizenship can be thrown into question by territorial transformations and the vestiges of colonialism. Drawing upon the case of *Re Minister for Immigration and Multicultural and Indigenous Affairs; Ex parte Ame* (2005) 222 CLR 439 ("Ame's Case") to respond to the question "What does it mean to be an authentic Australian citizen?" we examine how the High Court of Australia ("High Court") was called upon to recognize citizenship as a result of changes in Australia's territorial relationship with Papua New Guinea.

One of the authors of this chapter was pro bono counsel to Mr. Ame, an individual born an Australian citizen but stripped of that citizenship in 1975. Kim Rubenstein argued on his behalf that the deprivation of citizenship was unconstitutional. However, the High Court upheld the removal of Mr. Ame's citizenship, finding that his Australian citizenship as it existed before 1975 was not "real."

In Ame's Case, the High Court determined that Papuan Australians who formally held the legal status of citizen under the Australian Citizenship Act of 1948 (Commonwealth of Australia ["Cth"], henceforth "Citizenship Act"), from the Citizenship Act's inception until 1975, could have that status stripped from them by regulations. The court's decision was based on the proposition that Mr. Ame's Australian citizenship was a "technical" status, "largely nominal," and "not in fact or law full or real citizenship." The court also called Mr. Ame's prior status a "veneer of Australian citizenship," a "flawed citizenship" of a "fragile and strictly limited character," and more like "shadows ... appearances and mere titles" than an "enforceable reality."[1]

As revealed throughout this collection, evidentiary challenges may bring into question not only an individual's right to her citizenship but the very concept of citizenship itself. The borders of all countries create templates for citizenship, but the connection between these and citizenship at the level of the individual often seems abstract and vague. The details of how colonial borders become operationalized as the criteria for "real" or "authentic" Australian citizenship manifest in judicial decisions. Courts' reliance on the government's sovereign definitions of territories within territories can serve to materialize national fantasies, as opposed to passively reflecting empirical facts. The High Court in Ame's Case devalued the citizenship of Papuans based on characterizations informed by colonial standards. The court found that Papuan Australian citizens "had no right (still less a duty) to vote in Australian elections and referenda"; "could perform no jury or other civic service in Australia"; and lacked the right to enter or reside in the mainland of Australia. Thus, the court concluded, Papuan Australian citizens were "treated as ... foreigner[s]."[2] This effective disjuncture between rights and status, resulting primarily from tensions among concepts of race, Australian identity, and membership at the turn of the century, enabled the court to affirm that as a matter of law someone could hold the legal status of citizen absent an underlying right to that status.

Such a reading is a symptom of how contemporary prejudices freeze some old legal biases in place but not others. Imagine telling Australian women that since at one point they had been denied all the rights denied Papuan Australian men, their past diminished citizenship rights implied they too could have their rights violated by new laws. Mr. Ame's plight reveals how past fantasies of empire and colonization effect a precarious if not effaced citizenship for Papuan Australians today. By doing so, the High Court judgment illuminates our understanding of the nature of authentic Australian citizenship. This is a story that resonates with other colonial experiences and will be developed further in this chapter. The susceptibility of Australian citizenship to legislative interventions, at least for some populations, suggests the potential for further unfair treatment, say of recent immigrants, dual citizens, or naturalized Australians. The time is ripe for clarification of the concept of Australian citizenship in the founding document of nationhood, to define Australian citizenship in a way that is not infused by its racial foundations and better protect those who possess it.[3]

Amos Bode Ame was born in Papua on May 20, 1967, a time when Australia administered Papua as a possession of the Crown. For the purposes of the Citizenship Act, Papua was part of Australia, and those born in Papua after the Citizenship Act came into force on January 26, 1949, automatically acquired the status of Australian citizen at birth. In 1975, Papua New Guinea gained independence.[4] Mr. Ame was then eight years old. At that time, the governor-general of Australia had promulgated regulations, pursuant to Section 6 of the Papua New Guinea Independence Act 1975 (Cth), which provided that persons who became citizens of the Independent State of Papua New Guinea on independence ceased to be Australian citizens.

Mr. Ame had not entered mainland Australia before 1975, nor did he apply to become an Australian citizen by naturalization or by registration. He entered mainland Australia in 1999 and remained several years beyond the term of his visa. In 2005 the Australian government sought to remove Mr. Ame from Australia pursuant to its powers under the Migration Act 1958 (Cth) ("Migration Act").

Mr. Ame challenged his detention and removal from Australia as an unlawful noncitizen. He argued to the High Court that the relevant provisions of the Migration Act did not apply to him. The cessation of Australia's sovereignty over Papua did not erase his own Australian citizenship, he claimed. Thus he was not an alien and not subject to Australia's immigration laws. The minister for immigration and multicultural and indigenous affairs argued that the intention of the drafters of the Papua New Guinea Constitution was that people with Papuan heritage and who were born there would become citizens exclusively of the new nation. Thus, the minister argued, Mr. Ame's Australian citizenship at birth did not give him a right to enter and reside in Australia. The Papua New Guinea Constitution, and the Australian regulations operationalizing it, meant that the Commonwealth could treat him as an "alien" and thus deport him under Australia's immigration laws.[5]

The Papua New Guinea Story
COLONIAL HISTORY

Crucial to the High Court's affirmation of the minister's position in Ame's Case is Australian citizenship's historical context. Papua New Guinea's relationship with Australia is part of a colonial story that began well before Australia was a commonwealth. It is part of a broader colonial story within the British Empire, where citizenship was fluid, had several meanings, and conferred more rights on some subjects than on others.[6] The schematic story of colonization told here illustrates how the arbitrary writing of country borders creates contrivances of modern citizenship that appear based on birth and family, and how these conventions come into question when liminal cases call attention to these boundaries.

In the 1860s, the Australian colony of Queensland, motivated largely by the desire to secure Melanesian labor for Queensland's sugar plantations, became interested in the southern coast of the island of New Guinea (Waiko 1993). At the same time, the German government sought sovereignty over the country's northeastern section. By 1884 the northeast had been declared a German protectorate, and the southeast section a British protectorate, originally named British New Guinea and, later, Papua. As John Waiko writes, "The fact that the people of present day Papua New Guinea became part of the British and German colonial empires . . . was an accident of European history over which they had no control" (1993, 26). Of course all boundaries are, for better or worse, accidents to those born inside them (infants do not choose their location of birth or their parents). This particular accident led to a legal framework of administratively and politically separate territories in the first period and, later, territories that were administered together, but which maintained their politically separate legal identities.

After the establishment of the Australian Federation in 1901, British New Guinea was "placed under the authority of the Commonwealth of Australia by Letters Patent dated March 16, 1902, and was accepted by the Commonwealth as the Territory of Papua by s 5 of the *Papua Act 1905* (Cth)" (Ame's Case, 446–47).[7] Papuans, under the legislative authority of Australia, automatically became British subjects and pledged allegiance to the Crown. Edward Wolfers writes that the story of the colony's administration from the time it became a formal territory of the Commonwealth of Australia until World War II was the "already familiar one of a continued Australian lack of interest and neglect. Policy was made . . . and supervised by a single man (Sir Hubert Murray) and throughout the period 'the Murray system' became known as Australian policy" (1975, 28). Wolfers characterizes the policies as those of "unilateral intervention in village affairs, the protection of the Papuans and the preservation of European interests, standards and society" (29). In sum, Papuans were British subjects and objects of European paternalism.

From 1942, owing to World War II, civil administration was suspended in Papua. For three years, until October 1945, the Australian army through the Australian New Guinea Administrative Unit was the effective government in Papua and that part of New Guinea not under Japanese control. Indeed, "by the end of 1944 when perhaps 55,000 Papuan New Guineans were serving the

Allied cause" (Wolfers 1975, 111), the burden of war was more heavily shouldered by the indigenous people of the territories than by other Australian citizens.

FROM SUBJECTHOOD TO CITIZENSHIP

When the Citizenship Act came into force in 1949, Papuan British subjects became Australian citizens. So too did indigenous Australians become Australian citizens at that date, as did all British subjects who satisfied certain legislative requirements.[8]

People who resided in the territory of New Guinea, however, did not. Instead, they became "protected persons" (see Rubenstein 2002, 82). A 1920 mandate of the League of Nations placed the former German possession of New Guinea under Australian administration as a separate territory of New Guinea, a mandate codified in Australia under the New Guinea Act 1920 (Cth). When Australian citizenship was created in 1949, only those in Papua were identified as Australian citizens.[9]

Crucial for this chapter is that between 1949 and Papua New Guinea's independence in 1975, those born in Papua were Australian citizens by birth. However, that status had little value to Papuans—as will be discussed later in this chapter. Indeed, the most striking aspect of this story, which resonates with indigenous Australians' experience (see Chesterman and Galligan 1997) and that of certain classes of British subjects throughout the empire (see Gorman 2006), is the disjuncture between citizenship "status" and the substantive "rights" that status instantiated.

PAPUAN AUSTRALIAN CITIZENSHIP AND "REAL" CITIZENSHIP

The disjuncture between status and rights for Papuan-born Australian citizens influenced the Papua New Guinea Constitution's definitions of citizenship. Citizenship matters had become a matter of attention in the late 1950s, when Asians residing in the territory (only a small number had entered Papua) were allowed to apply for naturalization as Australian citizens (Wolfers 1975, 133). In 1962, people with mixed racial origins were allowed to apply for citizenship, although the government seemed reluctant to accede to their request.

By 1975, just before Papuan independence, Wolfers writes,

> Papuans are Australian citizens although they cannot exercise their "right" to live in Australia (unless they are married to a white or mixed race Australian). Chinese and mixed race people who have been granted Australian citizenship can.... And to press home the point as to the difference between the white Australians and the non white almost-

Australian, till 1968 Papuans and New Guineans had to apply to a District Officer for a "Permit for a Native to Leave or to be Removed from a Territory" before they went abroad. In 1967 the Migration Ordinance was amended by the House of Assembly so that a female Papua New Guinean with an expatriate spouse could be spared the embarrassment of having to apply for permission to be "removed" by her husband and with the coming into force of the new ordinance in 1968, all indigenes had only to apply to any authorized officer for a "Permit to leave the Territory." (1975, 134)

These exclusions and diminished rights affected the Papua New Guinea Constitution's definition of citizenship. Mindful of being assigned a second-class form of citizenship in Australia, the Papua New Guinea Constitutional Committee wanted to be sure that Papua New Guinea citizenship was not a mere formality for those who had the "real" or full citizenship of some other country prior to independence. To that end, Section 64 of the Papua New Guinea Constitution was drafted to state: "No person who has a real foreign citizenship may be or become a citizen."

"Real foreign citizenship" was defined as follows in Section 64(4):

For the purposes of this section, a person who:

(a) was immediately before Independence Day, an Australian citizen or an Australian Protected Person by virtue of:
  (i) birth in the former Territory of Papua, or
  (ii) birth in the former Territory of New Guinea and registration under section 11 of the Australian Citizenship Act 1948–1975 of Australia; and

(b) was never granted a right (whether revocable or not) to permanent residence in Australia, has no real foreign citizenship.

The *Final Report of the Constitutional Planning Committee* (Constitutional Planning Committee 1974) inserted the terminology of "real" foreign citizenship to exclude Australians from citizenship of Papua New Guinea. This terminology, created and inserted by Papua New Guinea itself, became the basis for the High Court to affirm that the Australian citizenship held by Papuans prior to 1975 was not "real" and to infer from this that Ame was not an Australian citizen (Ame's Case, 449).

Although the High Court inferred from these past lower rights the complete absence of citizenship status for those born prior to Papua's independence, the colonial legacy could be interpreted quite differently. According to

Graham Hassall, "Because status in the colonial era was defined by race and ethnicity, the articulation of laws of citizenship for the Independent State of Papua New Guinea was inevitably viewed by many as an opportunity to redress past imbalances" (2001, 255). Instead of reinforcing discriminatory policies, the Australian High Court might have followed the impulse to continue compensation for this. Concerned that those who already had wealth and power might overwhelm the emerging citizenry of Papua New Guinea, the drafters were attempting to protect the interests of indigenous Papua New Guineans while at the same time recognizing the historical relationship with its neighbors. The reference to "real" citizenship in the Papua New Guinea Constitution was a way of emphasizing that their status of citizenship *should* be of significance (Goldring 1978, 204), not to preclude from residence in Australia those who had been born citizens in the colonized territory.

From Citizenship to Alienage

Mr. Ame argued his citizenship was a right protected under the Australian Constitution, and thus that Australian regulations in 1975 could not strip him of this status. If citizenship were to have any legal significance or meaning (as it was a legal, statutory term), it could be argued he had a "right," indeed a valid constitutional claim, to live in Australia back in the 1970s even if that had not been asserted at the time. While the Migration Act may have been formally in force, it was not constitutionally valid. Mr. Ame argued that because he was a citizen of Australia at birth, he had a right to live anywhere in the country and could not be removed pursuant to the Migration Act for overstaying his visa.[10]

Ame argued that he was a "real Australian" at birth and did not lose this status or become a citizen of Papua in 1975. The High Court disagreed, pointing out that, while Mr. Ame had been born in "Australia" for the purposes of the Citizenship Act, the definition in the Migration Act did not include external territories such as Papua: "Whilst Papuans in the Territory of Papua before Independence Day enjoyed, by Australian law, a form of Australian citizenship it was not, in fact or law, full or real citizenship" (Ame's Case, 471). The form of citizenship held by Papuans did not confer a right to permanent residence in the states and internal territories of Australia. Justice Kirby referred to the intention of the lawmakers enacting the 1948 act:

> The Minister responsible for the Citizenship Act was specifically asked in the Parliament whether a "native of Papua" was, under the legislation

entitled to come to Australia and enjoy the right to vote in Australia. He replied, accurately:

"We do not even give them the right to come to Australia. An Englishman who came to this country and complied with our electoral laws could exercise restricted rights as a British subject, whereas a native of Papua would be an Australian citizen but would not be capable of exercising rights of citizenship."

The Minister's statement to the Federal Parliament, and the repeated references to ethnicity and race in the parliamentary debates, reflected a concern, very much alive at the time of the enactment of the Citizenship Act, to preserve to the Commonwealth the power to exclude from entry into the Australian mainland foreign nationals and even British subjects who were "ethnologically of Asiatic origin" or other "pigmentation or ethnic origin." (Ame's Case, 468, citations omitted)

The court concluded that the removal of Mr. Ame's citizenship in 1975 was authorized by Section 51(xix) of the Australian Constitution because people like Mr. Ame who were legally "Australians" but who were about to become foreign nationals could be treated as "aliens," including taking away their Australian citizenship.

The Australian Constitution references distinctions of status between "aliens" and "non-aliens" in Australia and authorizes the Parliament to make laws on "naturalisation and aliens." It was on this basis that the Parliament first legislated the naturalization of British subjects in Australia and, since 1948, has passed legislation on Australian citizenship as well as immigration and deportation laws.[11]

In Ame's Case, the High Court held that there is no limitation inherent in the "naturalisation and aliens" power that prevents using it to remove someone's citizenship (Ame's Case, 458): "The legal status of alienage has as its defining characteristic the owing of allegiance to a foreign sovereign power" (458). According to the court, "The view that concepts of alienage and citizenship describe a bilateral relationship which is a status, alteration of which requires an act on the part of the person whose status is in issue" (459), had in previous judgments been rejected.[12]

Thus, people born in the Australian territory of Papua between 1948 and 1975 were Australian citizens afforded limited rights. After September 16, 1975, these former citizens became "aliens" by operation of Australian legislation and the Papua New Guinea Constitution, and Mr. Ame could be deported.

Ame's Case makes it clear that possession of the legal status of "Australian citizen," and even the holding of an Australian passport as evidence of this status, does not necessarily entitle the holder to "real" or constitutionally protected citizenship of Australia.[13] Moreover, the case emphasizes the contingency of borders and the recognition of certain populations or territories as themselves creations of a state's identity. While in most of the cases in this book the documentary challenges are what counts as the integrity of an individual's identity, here in Ame's Case and as can also be seen in Sara Friedman's chapter in this collection, what ultimately determines citizenship is a country's sovereign determination of this status, often based on borders or other postcolonial jurisprudence.

Similar issues arise, for instance, in American Samoa, which has been a part of the United States for more than a century. Nonetheless, current federal law classifies persons born in American Samoa as "noncitizen nationals"—the only Americans so classified—thus denying American Samoans constitutional citizenship otherwise guaranteed by the citizenship clause of the Fourteenth Amendment of the U.S. Constitution.[14] How a country defines itself influences a court's legal conception of membership.

For Mr. Ame, and those like him born in Australian territory, the legal status they received at birth, as Australian citizens, was significant and meant something to them. The fact that they were ultimately not identified as Australian by constitutional authorities meant their status had no legal impact on their rights of membership and they were powerless. As discussed earlier, before 1975 Papuan Australian citizens, although Australian citizens, had to apply for a permit to enter or remain in mainland Australia. Holding the legal status of "Australian citizen" did not represent "authentic" citizenship for Papuans. The legal status was a device for international relations—Papuans could use an Australian passport to travel *outside* of Papua but not as a claim or right to travel to Australia, their country of citizenship.

Australia never created a uniform Australian citizen.[15] Citizens held different rights depending on the legal route through which that citizenship was obtained. The Papuan Australian citizens felt the legacy of that profoundly—so much so that, in creating a new Papua New Guinea state, there was an overt desire to distinguish itself from Australia to ensure a full and equal Papua New Guinean status of citizen. After the experience of the shallow, formal status of the statutory version of their Australian citizenship, the framers saw a need to bestow upon the Papua New Guinea citizenship a status of constitutional value. There was a commitment to give citizenship "real" meaning. Connected with this, in Papua New Guinea, was a belief that citizenship had to be singular. If a person was a Papua New Guinean citizen then he or she could not also be an Australian citizen—dual citizenship was constitutionally prohibited. Thus, those holding "real citizenship" of a foreign country were excluded from citizenship of Papua New Guinea at independence.

The creation of the legal term of art "real citizenship" in the Papua New Guinea Constitution became one of the key reasons for the High Court to deny Mr. Ame and those like him constitutional protections of their rights to and from citizenship. Under the Papua New Guinea Constitution, "real citizenship" of Australia was evidenced by a right to permanent residence in Australia. The High Court found that Mr. Ame "had no real foreign citizenship . . . unless he was a person who had been granted a right to permanent residence in Australia. No such right was ever granted to [Mr. Ame]" (Ame's Case, 451). The court went on to conclude that Mr. Ame became a citizen of Papua New Guinea upon independence and that an Australian regulation to deprive individuals who became citizens of Papua New Guinea of their Australian citizenship validly applied to him.

Nonetheless, Justice Kirby stated Ame's case set no precedent for the deprivation of citizenship from "other Australians":

> The change in the applicant's status as a citizen, as an incident to the achievement of the independence and national sovereignty of a former Territory of the Commonwealth, affords no precedent for any deprivation of constitutional nationality of other Australian citizens whose claim on such nationality is stronger in law and fact than that of the applicant.... having regard to the particular historical circumstances of this case and the fragile and strictly limited character of the "citizenship" of Australia which the applicant previously enjoyed, no requirement was implicit in the Australian Constitution that afforded the applicant rights of due process that might arise in another case in other circumstances of local nationality having firmer foundations. (Ame's Case, 483)

The fact that the Australian Parliament denied Papuans the political rights normally linked to citizenship—such as voting, jury service, and freedom of movement in and out of the mainland—meant that the High Court could determine they did not hold a "real citizenship."

For Mr. Ame and those like him, any sense of connection to Australia from birth in Australian territory and an identity from growing up in Australian territory were constitutionally irrelevant. As discussed in the introduction to this book, citizenship is a matter of matching one's own records with the records the government deems necessary, even when the conditions and list of documents change post hoc. Those Papuans born in Australian territory, with Australian birth certificates, had a feeling of citizenship that was not fully recognized by the state. This was so even though the state had put out legal markers such as legal status and other attributes of citizenship, including the provision of a passport to those traveling internationally, to assist in creating that feeling and sense of connection. Ultimately, the state's sovereign power to determine nationality enabled Mr. Ame's legal status to be tied to racist laws that would not be tolerated in any other context in contemporary Australia. The result reveals a country's commitment to an oddly crafted, backward-looking view of citizenship status.

"The Global Color Line" and "Authentic" Citizenship

As Marilyn Lake and Henry Reynolds have written in their groundbreaking book, "The imagined community of white men was transnational in its reach, but nationalist in its outcome" (2008, 4). Australia's experience mirrored the experience throughout the empire: "In dividing the world into white and not-white it helped render the imperial non-racial status of British subjects increasingly irrelevant and provided a direct challenge to the imperial assertion that the Empire recognized no distinction on the basis of color or race, that all subjects were alike subjects of the Crown" (5). This racialized distinction played out well into the 1970s, persisting through the status shift from British subject to Australian citizen. By creating a subcategory of Australians, who did not have a right to enter and reside in the mainland country of their citizenship, to vote, or to carry out jury service, the Australian government was able to create a class of Papuan Australian citizens whose diminished citizenship could be removed by the executive making a regulation.

This domestic or national example mirrored the practice throughout empires and also the practice in the United States. Indeed, Justice Kirby, in his separate judgment in Ame's Case, supporting the decision, drew comfort from the international practice around these issues, identifying the "countless instances in legislation designed to terminate colonial and like status, including in territories formerly part of the dominions of the Crown, involved laws of the United Kingdom Parliament relevantly similar to those made in Australia in the present instance" (Ame's Case, 486). Together with this statement he lists twenty-eight acts that followed a similar practice.[16]

The terms by which Mr. Ame and others acquired and also lost citizenship provide evidence of citizenship's malleability: citizens may be distinguished and citizenship denied on the basis of rights conferred by a changing Parliament, by changing boundaries, and subject to shifting policy contexts and political motivations.[17] Moreover, this chapter affirms the point made throughout the collection. Classifications of individuals and groups follow from close readings of laws and legal status, not experiences or civil rights, much less a feeling of political membership. Like Sara Friedman's chapter, together with chapters by Kamal Sadiq, Rachel Rosenbloom, and Beatrice McKenzie, Ame's Case strengthens the argument that these moments of friction and failure offer valuable insights into how both citizenship and sovereignty are produced and struggled over in diverse arenas around the globe. From the inception of the Australian Citizenship Act of 1948 (Cth), to the regulations allowing Mr. Ame to be stripped of his citizenship up to the current formulation (from 2007), citizenship's status and rights in Australia remain precarious and thus raise questions about whether citizenship is the bedrock of other rights or a quicksand on whose uncertain ground we notice other contingencies of rights as well.[18]

Conclusion

Before Papua New Guinea became independent in 1975, race was essential to Australia's creation of and understanding of "authentic" citizenship. Papuan Australian citizens had no claims to citizenship "rights" such as voting or residence within Australia. Such overt discrimination influenced the drafters of the Papua New Guinea Constitution to commit to a more sincere citizenship and to imbue the legal status in Papua New Guinea with authenticity.

This discrimination, and the drafting of the Papua New Guinea Constitution, contributed to the High Court's decision in Ame's Case that Papuan Australian citizens' citizenship was not "real" and could be unilaterally removed from them. The decision highlights the contested nature of Australian citizenship as a legal status; citizens could be denied rights, and their citizenship, at the discretion of the state. Thus, similar to other findings in this collection, documents may be used to question citizenship, even those that had at one point conferred it. Australian citizenship is not, we know after Ame's Case, evidenced by the possession of a passport or a legal status. The invocation of lesser substantive rights from the colonial era is not a logical truism about the nature of Australian citizenship's dependence on political rights from a previous era as much as it is an elevation of sovereign determinism over the values of the rule of law for Australian citizens.

The High Court did not consider factors such as the civic value of a persistent citizenship status, or the individual and his or her identity and community, nor did it question the need for postcolonial reckoning with past discrimination. Ultimately, in Australia and elsewhere, the sovereign determines its citizens by scripts of the state's own design. The nature and security of Australian citizenship is left floating, adrift on the waves of political persuasion and, in cases like Mr. Ame's, the tides of prejudice.

NOTES

Kim Rubenstein presented the original version of this chapter at the Boston College Center for Human Rights and International Justice workshop that was held April 19–21, 2011. Jacqueline Field worked with Rubenstein to develop the chapter for this book.

1. See Ame's Case 449 (per Gleeson CJ, McHugh, Gummow, Hayne, Callinan, Heydon JJ); 470, 471, 474, 483 (per Kirby J).

2. See Ame's Case 449, 470, 481.

3. Since the writing of this chapter, the Citizenship Act has been amended to provide for three new avenues for stripping dual citizens of their Australian citizenship, in light of the government's stated commitment to respond to threats of terrorism by Australian citizens. See Sections 35, 35AA, and 35A, introduced by the Australian Citizenship Amendment (Allegiance to Australia) Act 2015 (Cth). This is the most recent example of the susceptibility of Australian citizenship to legislative interventions, and an enduring conceptualization of different classes of Australian citizen.

4. The former Possession of British New Guinea was placed under the authority of the Commonwealth of Australia by letters patent dated March 18, 1902, and was accepted by the Commonwealth, as the Territory of Papua, by Section 5 of the Papua Act 1905 (Cth). The former German possession of New Guinea was placed under Australian administration by a mandate of the League of Nations in 1920. After 1945, Papua and New Guinea were administered jointly under legislation of the Commonwealth, both keeping their separate identities. Papua remained "a possession of the Crown." New Guinea was a "trust territory" administered by Australia under an agreement approved by the United Nations. People born in Papua were Australian citizens by birth under the Australian Citizenship Act 1948 (Cth) and also were British subjects; people born in New Guinea were "protected persons."

5. Mr. Ame has not been alone in seeking to claim Australian citizenship. For example, a series of appeals have been made to the Administrative Appeals Tribunal by Papuans seeking to resume the Australian citizenship they lost at Papuan independence under Sections 23A, 23AA, 23AB, and 23B of the Australian Citizenship Act 1948 (Cth) and its successor, Section 29 of the Citizenship Act. The tribunal has consistently confirmed that those Papuans were not Australian permanent residents and are not eligible to resume their Australian citizenship under these provisions; see, for example, *Re Gaigo and Minister for Immigration and Citizenship* [2008] AATA 590; *Re Brian and Minister for Immigration and Citizenship* (2008) 105 ALD 213; *Yamuna v. Minister for Immigration and*

Citizenship [2012] AATA 383. Section 21(7) of the Citizenship Act does provide a limited avenue for Papuans with parents who were Australian citizens born in mainland Australia to apply for citizenship. However, these statutory avenues were not relevant to Mr. Ame's claim to constitutional citizenship.

6. Daniel Gorman (2006, 20) discusses the conceptualization of citizenship in Britain's empire. He points out the stark divide in citizenship status between British subjects in the United Kingdom and white-settlement colonies, on the one hand, and the dependent empire, on the other, with those subjects born in the dependencies having fewer rights.

7. Indeed, the queen of England is also the queen of Australia, and there are still steps to be taken for Australia to become a republic and fully independent from the United Kingdom.

8. Like all Australian citizens at the time, Papuans also retained the status of British subject and indeed were both British subjects and Australian citizens until 1975. Other Australian citizens maintained the status of British subject with their Australian citizen status until 1987. See Rubenstein 2002, 88.

9. Papua New Guinea Provisional Administration Act 1945 (Cth), Papua and New Guinea Act 1949 (Cth), and Papua and New Guinea Act 1963 (Cth).

10. See *Re MIMIA; Ex parte Ame* [2005] HCATrans 66 (March 3, 2005).

11. The High Court also found that the removal of Papuans' Australian citizenship was supported by the Commonwealth's power to make laws with respect to its territories in Section 122 of the Australian Constitution. See Naturalisation Act 1903 (Cth); Nationality Act 1920 (Cth); Australian Citizenship Act 1948 (Cth); Australian Citizenship Act 2007 (Cth).

12. See *Singh v. The Commonwealth* (2004) 222 CLR 322. The Australian Parliament's power over citizenship legislation is consistent with a similar scope of authority recognized by the U.S. Supreme Court regarding Congress's power over immigration and citizenship. That said, the Fourteenth Amendment guarantees against potential legislative or executive actions citizenship rights to those born in the United States. The U.S. Supreme Court also has created more parity of rights for naturalized and natural-born U.S. citizens and generally, as a matter of statutory law, either relies on the law in place at the date of birth for assigning citizenship or provides citizenship at birth retroactively as an operation of law. See, for instance, 8 USC 1402 through 8 USC 1409, for statutes providing retroactive citizenship to those in U.S. territories or Puerto Rico; for recent immigration court decisions on this question, see Stevens 2015b.

13. This point links to the key theme that emerges from this collection of the problematic nature of relying on documents (or the lack thereof) as evidence of an individual's citizenship. See, in particular, chapters 4–8, chapter 10, and chapter 12.

14. For a comprehensive overview of the situation in the United States, see Leibowitz 1989. See also Villazor 2008, 2015.

15. Another example of citizens being afforded different rights based on racial divisions is the inferior citizenship of indigenous Australians (see Chesterman and Galligan 1997).

16. The acts he lists include Aden, Perim and Kuria Muria Islands Act 1967 (UK), Sec. 2(1) and Sch; Bahamas Independence Act 1973 (UK), Sec. 2; Barbados Independence Act 1966 (UK), Sec. 2; Botswana Independence Act 1966 (UK), Sec. 3; Cyprus

Act 1960 (UK), Sec. 4, and British Nationality (Cyprus) Order 1960 [No. 2215]; Fiji Independence Act 1970 (UK), Sec. 2; Gambia Independence Act 1964 (UK), Sec. 2; Ghana Independence Act 1957 (UK), Sec. 2; Guyana Independence Act 1966 (UK), Sec. 2; Jamaica Independence Act 1962 (UK), Sec. 2; Kenya Independence Act 1963 (UK), Sec. 2; Lesotho Independence Act 1966 (UK), Sec. 3; Malawi Independence Act 1964 (UK), Sec. 2; Malaysia Act 1963 (UK), Sec. 2; Malta Independence Act 1964 (UK), Sec. 2; Mauritius Independence Act 1968 (UK), Sec. 2; Nigeria Independence Act 1960 (UK), Sec. 2; Seychelles Act 1976 (UK), Sec. 3; Sierra Leone Independence Act 1961 (UK), Sec. 2; Swaziland Independence Act 1968 (UK), Sec. 3; Tanganyika Independence Act 1961 (UK), Sec. 2; Trinidad and Tobago Independence Act 1962 (UK), Sec. 2; Uganda Independence Act 1962 (UK), Sec. 2; West Indies Act 1967 (UK), Sec. 12 and Sch 3; Zambia Independence Act 1964 (UK), Sec. 3; Zanzibar Act 1963 (UK), Sec. 2. See also Bangladesh Citizenship (Temporary Provisions) Order 1972 (Bangl), para. 2.

17. The difficulty of defining citizenship by reference to voting rights was recognized in 1897–98 by the framers of the Australian Constitution, as women (as well as infants and "lunatics") would still be considered "citizens" but were not entitled to vote. See, for example, *Convention Debates* (1897, 1793–94).

18. See Rubenstein (2002, 24–46) for a more detailed discussion of the need for constitutional articulation of the nature of Australian citizenship.

PART II. OFFICIAL OR ADMINISTRATIVE ACTS

6. TO KNOW A CITIZEN

BIRTHRIGHT CITIZENSHIP DOCUMENTS REGIMES IN U.S. HISTORY

BEATRICE MCKENZIE

In the early 1990s I worked as a vice consul in the U.S. embassy in Kampala, Uganda. One of my duties was to issue visas to tourists and businesspeople planning to visit the United States. One day a white woman from the United States came to the embassy holding her two biracial children by the hand. She needed to apply for a visa, she explained, to return home to her parents' care because she was very ill and likely to die in the coming months. She also needed to bring her children, who had U.S. passports, home so her parents could raise them after her death, for their father had recently died. I was surprised by her request and asked why she didn't travel using the American passport that I assumed she held. She explained that she had renounced her citizenship two years earlier and was now a Ugandan citizen. She had done so because in an argument with the children's father, he had threatened to divorce her and have her deported without her children. The woman was in a terrible position: as a terminally ill Ugandan, she would not qualify for a U.S. visa, except perhaps under "humanitarian visa" criteria, and these were applied quite stringently. The children were also a concern. Ugandan orphanages were having trouble providing basic needs to the growing population of orphans due to the AIDS crisis. Fortunately, a way out presented itself. Because she had expatriated herself under duress, she was eligible to reverse the expatriation. She resumed her U.S. citizenship and presumably returned to the United States with the children.

This contemporary case shares important elements of successful citizenship claims through the twentieth century: a person who, from race, gender, and class status, conforms to stereotypes of a U.S. citizen, is found to be one. As is evident from U.S. birthright citizenship claims over time, individual bureaucrats judged citizens' claims, whether at the U.S. border or at embassies abroad, based on more than policies or documents. They required applicants to establish credibility as a citizen, a sometimes delicate, sometimes clumsy process. Citizenship is not an arbitrary status bestowed upon individuals in government offices stateside or abroad. Nor is it one that is self-evident or inferred from documents alone. It is, however, more easily defended by some individuals than others.

In addition to policies, affective responses to documents and the individuals behind them influence outcomes in specific cases (see also Friedman, Sadiq, and Babo, this volume). Throughout U.S. history, government bureaucrats at U.S. borders, in passport agencies, or in U.S. consulates or embassies abroad have often used racial or ethnic stereotyping to verify, challenge, or reject a claimant's case.[1] Race has played out in applicants' citizenship claims cases in particular ways, leading Kristin Collins (2011) to note that "the history of U.S. citizenship law cannot be understood without due recognition of racism's central role in shaping the entire regulatory field."[2] The applicant's gender has also affected outcomes. An element that added credibility and urgency to the case in Uganda was the applicant's status as the mother of American citizen children in danger. Class status, especially as it relates to racialized groups such as Chinese Americans, also has been significant. This chapter furthers our understanding of the development and uses of documents regimes and explains how decisions made on the ground, today mainly in cases of citizenship acquired by meeting certain criteria of family ties and descent, reflect biases based on an applicant's race and gender.

Birthright citizenship claims may be based on jus soli, the birth of a child on U.S. soil, or may be acquired upon birth abroad to a U.S. citizen parent, also known as jus sanguinis. Two components of establishing birthright citizenship are proof of eligibility for citizenship and proof of identity. How to prove eligibility and identity has changed through U.S. history. Craig Robertson (2010) recently argued that World War I provides a critical divide, before which documentary evidence was less important to proving a claim to citizenship. Robertson suggests the increase in the size of the population challenged local forms of validation. However, the treatment of U.S. citizens of Chinese descent poses a problem to Robertson's chronology. Decades before World War I, immigration agents used document protocols to disprove their citizenship claims. The regime lasted decades longer than Robertson acknowledges. It was so enduring one sees the same forms and documents in claimants' immigration files between the 1880s and the 1940s. The similarity in protocols allows an examination of this documents regime across generations of the same family. A review of these reveals a racialized documents regime complicated by class status and gender.

Wong Kim Ark's Right to Enter (1898): Birthright Citizenship and Race

The Wong Kim Ark case is a precedential case in the jurisprudence of U.S. citizenship. In 1870, Wong Kim Ark was born in an apartment over a storefront in San Francisco's Chinatown. While Wong's parents were Chinese nationals, his birth on U.S. soil made him a U.S. citizen. When Wong was quite young, his parents took him to their ancestral village in China, Ong Sing, in Taishan Province, where he attended school for three years. He returned to the United States at age eleven, entering with a "native born affidavit," and worked as a cook's apprentice in a Sierra Nevada mining camp. At age nineteen Wong returned to China and married Yee Shee. In keeping with the custom at the time, Wong traveled back and forth across the Pacific in adulthood to visit his wife and young children, who remained in the home village. Examining the documents Wong and his sons used to claim U.S. birthright citizenship offers a case study in the changing use of documents to match officials' changing presumptions of fraud between 1881 and 1947.[3] Chinese American challenges to racial exclusion led to a particular documents regime that relied on lengthy investigative interviews and the use of photographs and notarized affidavits.

Birthright citizenship policy was distinctly racialized from its first use in the British colonies through the passage of the Fourteenth Amendment and beyond. Adapted from English common law, citizenship by jus soli applied to the children of white immigrants, those "free white persons" deemed naturalizable by the Naturalization Act of 1790 (Haney-Lopez 2006; Kettner 1978; Schuck and Smith 1985; Smith 1997). Children of color, including the children of white fathers and enslaved African American mothers, were excluded from the jus soli regime by civil law (Finkelman 1997, 2006). Children of Native Americans born "in tribal relations" were mainly excluded by an interpretation of international law suggesting that the tribes were separate nations (Maltz 2001; Stock, this volume). Ineligibility for jus soli citizenship might appear to be lodged in the body of the person of color, but the real problem was the way skin color and ancestry triggered affective responses toward the documentary signifiers. These readings of the documents imputed alienage, an official response quite different from that triggered by whites, whose use of the evidence affirmed their U.S. citizenship. After Congress passed the Fourteenth Amendment to ensure the citizenship of African Americans, two groups whose status might be affected were Native Americans and Chinese Americans. In the era of Chinese exclusion from immigration, the U.S. Immigration Bureau sought to reject the citizenship status of Chinese born in the United States (Lee 2003; Ngai 2005).

Racial exclusion invoked an ostensible expertise in reading the body and recognizing eligibility; immigration officials excluding Chinese laborers from the United States marked a difference in border policy. With other groups, immigration officials looked for indications of inadmissibility among a largely admissible group. Immigration laws barred those who were "morally, mentally and physically deficient." For those of Chinese descent on the West Coast, however, government officials looked for admissible individuals within a largely excludable group (Robertson 2010, 172). This was also a class-based system: admissible Chinese immigrants were merchants, students, and clergy members, mainly from elite society; laborers were excluded. Laborers were identifiable by their clothing, their class of travel, and their bearing. Immigration inspectors came to believe in their ability to know citizens, too, inferring status based on appearance and speech. All citizens had to do to be recognized, according to commissioner of immigration in New York, William Williams, in 1912 was "state with accuracy their place of birth."[4] Agents' expertise could now be used to challenge individual claims of citizenship. A delicate dance between government agent and citizen claimant led to the creation of thick files of documents on tens of thousands of citizen claimants, including the files of Wong Kim Ark and his descendants.

Though Wong Kim Ark was carrying an affidavit of his status as a U.S. citizen, his claim to citizenship was first challenged when he attempted to reenter the United States in 1890. To assist him in proving his claim, Chinese consul F. E. Bee took personal statements from two witnesses who had been in California and known Wong's family for more than twenty years. Both witnesses professed that they knew "Wong Kim Ock [sic]" to have been born in the United States. One was a white lawyer named Frederick Berna; the other was a Chinese merchant named Hoo Sue. Berna explained that he had come to know the family when he was a deputy tax assessor and that, although he had not been present at the birth, he was confident the young man had been born in San Francisco because Wong's parents had lived in the same place for six or seven years prior to 1875. Hoo Sue swore that he knew Wong Kim Ark's father well and that he knew his son was born in San Francisco. It is clear in the immigration file that while theoretically the same documents regime legally applied to U.S. citizens of Chinese descent as to other claimants, extra scrutiny of Chinese Americans created problems for Wong. An unnamed Bureau of Immigration official investigated the truth of Wong's claim to birth in the United States by refuting Berna's credibility. He found the lawyer at the address indicated on the affidavit (42 Montgomery), but he noted that "nobody there seems to know if he has any employment." The investigator also observed that "although last time they did not recognize" Wong Kim Ark's photograph, "this time the firm knows the photograph." In concluding his investigation, he wrote, "I believe this [case] is fraudulent."[5] That judgment, preserved in Wong's immigration file on an unsigned piece of paper, affected his entry four years later.

Wong again faced difficulty landing in 1894, though once again he carried an affidavit of citizenship drawn up before his departure. The notarized statement of citizenship (see later discussion) may have attested to his birthplace, but it did not guarantee his citizenship. In the time since Wong's entry in 1890, scrutiny of those of Chinese descent had increased. Border officials often ignored the Fourteenth Amendment's guarantee of citizenship for those born in the United States. These officials scrutinized Chinese immigrants more closely for signs of membership in the laboring classes, the main group excluded by legislation and a status that might now, for putative U.S. citizens, supersede birth in operational significance (Lee 2003, 103; Robertson 2010, 171–77). Though the affidavit stated that "Wong Kim Ark is well known to us" and was "born in the United States," he was also a laborer, a man with three years of education who had worked as a cook since age eleven (Wong Kim Ark INS file, National Archives and Record Administration [NARA], San Bruno). His file also contained the incriminating statement by the U.S. Treasury inspector ("Investigation of Truth of Claim to Birth in the United States," 1894, NARA, San Bruno). District Attorney Henry Foote claimed that Wong's "education and political affiliation" overcame his claim to citizenship, that his claim to citizenship was based on a mere "accident of birth" in the United States (Lee 2003), overlooking the fact that everyone's birth in the United States is equally an accident.

Held on board the steamship *Coptic* in San Francisco's harbor for three months while he fought against a shifting documents regime to reenter his home country, Wong hired a prominent attorney, who filed a habeas corpus petition. The attorney argued that Wong was a U.S. citizen by birth, so immigration laws should not apply to him. A judge in the Northern District Court of California agreed that Wong's birth in the United States made him a citizen, per the Fourteenth Amendment. Immigration authorities freed him from custody in January 1896. Even so, the U.S. government appealed the case on its merits: Was the child of Chinese subjects born in the United States a citizen? Two years later a lengthy decision in the Supreme Court affirmed that the Fourteenth Amendment, "in clear words and in manifest intent, includes the children born within the territory of the United States, or all other persons, of whatever race or color, domiciled within the United States."[6]

The clarity of the language about race in the Wong Kim Ark decision settled citizenship for Americans of Chinese descent born on U.S. soil, but not if they were born abroad and otherwise might claim citizenship by descent. Immigration authorities continued to prevent Chinese—and Asians more generally—from entering. Immigration authorities challenged Wong's ability to transmit citizenship to his children born abroad, a sturdy right enjoyed by American men from 1790 to 1934. Wong himself faced further scrutiny by U.S. immigration officials in El Paso, Texas (Deportations of Chinese Immigrants, NARA, Fort Worth), just eighteen months after the Supreme Court decided his case.

The documents regime evident in Wong Kim Ark's file demonstrates how flexible the Immigration Bureau's documents requirements could be in the face of concerns about fraud. As documents like the affidavit of a respectable person who knew of a claimant's birth in the United States became suspect, the Immigration Bureau and State Department extended technologies established for Americans of Chinese descent to other groups. The entry and inspection process saw an overhaul during World War I that constituted a new documents regime. Beyond swearing an oath before a notary, an applicant now needed to present a birth certificate or, as Wong Kim Ark had been required to do in 1890 and 1895, an affidavit that proved birth on U.S. soil. Additionally, as Wong Kim Ark did in 1890, applicants had to bring a "good witness," perhaps a reputable professional or businessman, to identify them to the officer. The technologies developed for Chinese Americans were available for bureaucrats to use or ignore at their pleasure.

In spite of increased reliance on documents, bureaucrats at the border, in the passport office, and overseas were convinced that they, ultimately, could judge the veracity of a person's claims by evaluating his or her demeanor. In 1916, the State Department announced that taking an oath of allegiance with the "penetrating eye of the clerk upon him" could ensure the legitimacy of a case. Interestingly, the U.S. embassy in Warsaw reported success in verifying citizenship claims by using intensive questioning of applicants and identifying witnesses (Robertson 2010, 206). And officials continued to rely on reading personal appearance at the border. A Labor Department official testified in Congress that his staff would recognize citizens as they entered the United States whether or not they had passports because "an American's manner of speech, his appearance, and bearing" identified him as a citizen (Robertson 2010, 209). Evidence for a World War I regime is mixed; although the State Department announced a new documents regime, bureaucrats continued to use discretion based on their evaluations of people's appearance, class, and behavior. Just as the "accidental" citizenship that seems to question Wong's status reveals the contingency of citizenship more generally, the ad hoc contextual findings reveal the influence of American myths in these determinations.

Wong Kim Ark's descendants provide a full case study of how the presumption of fraud affected the reception of Chinese Americans' children as citizens. The documents for all four of Wong's sons (see, e.g., "In the Matter of Wong Yook Thue," Immigration File 29438/5-23, NARA, San Bruno) were remarkably similar. All four immigrated using an affidavit that stated, "I claim his admission to the U.S. on the ground of his being a son of a citizen of the United States" (Wong Yoke Fun [*sic*], 1910, NARA, San Bruno). The sons' immigration files are replete with documents that illustrate a claimant's attempt to prove and immigration authorities' attempts to disprove the relationship.

James Wong's Claims (1926 and 1947): Acquired Citizenship (Jus Sanguinis) and Race

From 1790, children born abroad to U.S. citizen parents could claim U.S. citizenship by descent. In 1855, Congress clarified that the right was limited to the children of U.S. citizen fathers, not mothers. Chinese exclusion and a finding of the birthright citizenship of U.S.-born children led to the development of the phenomenon of Chinese paper sons, in which a visit back to China provided an opportunity to sell a place to another family who wished to immigrate (Chin 2000; Ngai 2005). Immigration and Customs Bureau officials came to presume fraud in the case of every individual who attempted to enter the United States from China, leading to an especially harsh documents regime for such U.S. citizens.

Agents settled on the use of long interviews to challenge the documentary evidence of a father-son relationship. In 1910, an official questioned Wong Kim Ark's eldest son, Wong Yok Fun, at the newly opened Angel Island immigration facility in San Francisco Bay. The interview involved hundreds of questions and included a diagram of Ong Sing village in China and descriptions of the inhabitants of every one of the thirty-five houses in the village. After the interview, Chinese inspector Heitmann wrote to the chief Chinese inspector at Angel Island, suggesting they pose similar questions to Wong Kim Ark and ask him to draw a diagram of the village (Letter to Commissioner Immigration San Francisco,

1910, NARA, San Bruno). The interview occurred in El Paso, Texas, four days later, and a witness corroborated Wong's testimony.[7] The inspector noted in his report that the nativity and "essential trip of alleged father" were established, but that numerous discrepancies existed between the father's and son's testimonies, of which just ten discrepancies (among hundreds of responses) were noted. Four were found to be material: the age of the child when his grandmother died, whether Yok Fun was working after he quit school, the number of houses between their house and their uncle's house in the village, and the denomination of currency that Wong Kim Ark sent to his wife in China when the son was six years old. On the basis of those discrepancies, the application to land was denied in December. In January 1911, Wong's eldest son was returned to China.

Wong's three other sons immigrated successfully between 1924 and 1926, showing that the family developed expertise facing this harsh documents regime. In the interview of the third son, Wong Yok Thue (Wong Yok Thue file, NARA, San Bruno), his father and his brother acted as "friend" and "testifying relative." Thus the father was the upstanding citizen, and the brother could attest to his younger brother's birth in China. Immigration agents asked Wong Kim Ark 56 questions, his second son 91 questions, and the intending immigrant, Wong's third son, 150 questions. In nearly 300 questions, there was a single discrepancy. Wong Yok Thue entered the United States as a citizen, and the family immediately sent the youngest son to join him.

Immigration Bureau agents seemed to ease up in their scrutiny of Wong's youngest son, Wong Yok Jim. Wong Yok Jim entered the United States on July 23, after a shorter interview than those conducted with his elder brothers ("Heading for Testimony," U.S. Department of Labor, Immigration Service, July 23, 1926, NARA, San Bruno). Wong Kim Ark, now fifty-seven, was interviewed first and showed documentary proof that his son had been born in China in 1914. In the course of his interview Wong promised to send the boy to an American school, a statement that carried weight in the outcome. The applicant himself was eleven years old, but that did not prevent immigration agents from directing dozens of questions his way. He identified himself as Wong Kim Ark's son, but since his mother would have been forty-six when he was born, it is possible that he was Wong Kim Ark's grandson, a son of the son whose entry had been refused in 1910. Moreover, in the interview Wong Yok Jim identified a nephew his own age living in his house in China, along with his mother, his grandmother, his eldest brother, and his brother's four children, sons aged fifteen, eleven, and nine and a daughter aged three. Because no sister-in-law is mentioned, and his brother's children are the same ages his siblings would be,

Wong Yok Jim may have been the son and not the brother of Wong Kim Ark's eldest son, Wong Yok Fun.

The documents regime that the Wong family challenged successfully in the 1920s remained in place through World War II. Decades later, Yok Jim's son faced his own interview with the Immigration Bureau. Like his father and brothers, Yok Jim had gone back to China and married. His immigration file noted that when Yok Jim was returning to the United States in 1931, his wife in China was four months pregnant. His son was born the following year. In 1947, Wong Yok Jim, now a U.S. Navy veteran known as James Y. Wong, applied for his "blood son," Wong Hee Ngew, to enter as a citizen. The latter file included a notarized affidavit (Wong Hee Ngew file, NARA, San Bruno) from James Wong that "due to the lack of vital statistics records in China, there is no birth or baptismal record covering the birth of his said son."[8]

The interview of the fifteen-year-old boy shows that the same documents regime remained in place, but the presumption of fraud no longer was in effect.[9] The child's mother had died in November 1946 at Ong Sing village, in China. His grandmother (Wong Kim Ark's wife), aged seventy-five, was still alive in the village, the only living relative the boy had in China. There was no questioning of the father and son separately. The son had no idea whether his father had ever been in China. He knew none of his father's brothers or nephews or nieces and did not mention the death of his presumed grandfather, Wong's eldest son. He did not know where anyone had gone to school or their occupations. When asked what evidence he had to show that he was the son of James Wong, he replied, "Only my testimony" ("Statement of Applicant and Relative of Applicant for Entry," 1947, NARA, San Bruno). His testimony was quite powerful, and in two questions one gets the sense that the interviewer had already recognized him as a citizen. When asked why his mother died, the boy said, "When my father was in the Navy, my mother worried a lot. She was always crying. She got sick and she finally died." Asked whether the family had had enough to eat during the war, he replied that they had not. "Mostly we had soup. The soup was made of what vegetable we could get and some salt." The interview was immediately concluded after that, and the child was admitted as a citizen.

The recognition and acceptance of James Wong's son just after World War II contrasts with cases of other children of American veterans born in Asia in the ensuing decades, presented later in the chapter. I am struck, however, by the similarity of the case to that of the mother who was stranded in Uganda. Both cases dealt with children of "deserving" American citizen parents, she by her race, gender, and class position, he by his recent service in World War II.[10] In both cases children's lives were in peril, hers because the children might be left in an impoverished orphanage in Uganda, his because the child had lost his mother and had recently been very hungry. It is true that many children had been held at Angel Island in the preceding decades who must have looked quite pitiable to immigration officials. In this case, however, the boy looked pitiable and deserving.

One last difference between the recognition of Wong Hee Ngew as a citizen and other children who have tried to claim citizenship: his parents of the same "race" were legally married. Race, marital status, and gender have mattered in birthright citizenship policies, as is evident from the documents regime that developed for U.S.-born women who married foreign men early in the twentieth century.

Ethel Mackenzie's Citizenship (1915): Jus Soli and Gender

In the second half of the nineteenth century, U.S. policies favored a single family nationality (Bredbenner 1998; Collins 2011; Cott 2000). After 1855, foreign-born women who married American men were automatically granted citizenship. In that same period, a single passport could be used for a man, his wife, and children. A married woman could apply for her own passport, but she had to show a need to travel separately from her husband. And starting at the height of "new immigration" in 1907 and lasting until between 1922 and 1952, Congress deprived U.S. citizen women of their citizenship if they married foreigners.

This was the documents regime Ethel Coope faced in 1912 when she tried to register as a newly enfranchised California voter. Coope was born in Redwood City, California, in 1885. She first became politically active as a member of a group of progressive Republican women who formed an "insurgent movement" in Santa Cruz to pass woman suffrage legislation in California. When she moved to San Francisco, she continued her activism there and joined the Club Women's Franchise League of California (Salomons 1915). At age nineteen, Coope married her music teacher, a Scottish balladeer twice her age, Peter Gordon Mackenzie. Like Coope's recently deceased father, Gordon Mackenzie was a British citizen, a longtime resident who had not naturalized.[11] Journalists from the *San Francisco Examiner* and the *San Francisco Call* followed closely the saga of the young suffragist who married the older, flamboyant local celebrity. After women won the right to vote in California in 1911, Ethel Mackenzie applied to register to vote for the 1912 election "with the rest of her sisters." Registrar J. H. Zemansky refused her application on the grounds that she had lost her citizenship when she married a foreigner.[12]

Mackenzie's case exposes the fragility of documents regimes and the way the requirement to prove citizenship was available for political manipulation. There is no mention of a request to provide her marriage certificate, and the document would have been unnecessary, since she was widely known to be married to the Scotsman. In 1912, evidence used to prove citizenship for voting purposes varied across districts based upon the presence of party challengers and the requirements of the local election judge. Evidence could include physical appearance, collective memory of an applicant or group of applicants (Robertson 2010), or the applicant's word (*Lynch v. Clark* 1844). In this case a local official appropriated a national law and applied it beyond its original intent. Congress had passed the legislation in 1907, at the height of the wave of "new immigration" from southern and eastern Europe (Nicolosi 2000; Volpp 2005). The law, subtitled "An Act in Reference to the Expatriation of Citizens and Their Protection Abroad," was intended to apply to women who married and moved abroad permanently with their foreign husbands. By the time it stopped Ethel Mackenzie from voting, the law was being applied at home for local political reasons.

The way Mackenzie responded (*San Francisco Call*, February 4, 1913) called into question the law's authority to divest citizenship and drew on her own claim of respectability as proof against a public charge of being a false citizen. "Pickpockets, murderers, embezzlers and ex-convicts of all kinds are deprived of the right of suffrage," she complained, "but I have done nothing criminal unless it be a crime to marry a foreigner." Mackenzie then exclaimed, "If (marriage to a foreigner) constitutes a crime in America, I am perfectly willing to have my Bartillion [*sic*] measurements placed in every rogues' gallery in the world." In citing Bertillon, Mackenzie made a direct reference to a new technique being employed at the State Department in passport applications. A Frenchman named Bertillon had invented an anthropometric system for classifying criminals by physical descriptions and photographs (Kuluszynski 2001). The technique was first used to assess criminal fraud in Chinese immigration and citizenship cases (Lee 2003). Mackenzie clearly believed that unlike criminals and fraudulent claimants, she deserved U.S. citizenship and the right of suffrage. She sued on a writ of mandamus, asking the court to direct the Election Commission to register her. In *Mackenzie v. Hare* (1915), the Supreme Court rejected her citizenship claim.

Marriage has served as both a citizenship-enacting and a citizenship-divesting institution, and the marriage certificate has been used alone to document citizenship claims (Volpp 2005). A woman's marriage certificate has at times proved citizenship, but in the case of U.S. citizen women who married foreigners, it proved expatriation. Ethel Coope Mackenzie finally regained her citizenship in January 1921 when her husband renounced his allegiance to Great Britain and naturalized as a U.S. citizen. Her husband alerted the press (*San Francisco Examiner,* December 9, 1915) that he intended to give Ethel "a Christmas gift that the Supreme Court of the United States could not give her: the gift of citizenship." One of the first acts of enfranchised women was to reverse this law, though it took decades longer for the reversal to apply to American women who married citizens of Asian nations.[13]

American women gained the right to transmit citizenship in 1934 (Bredbenner 1998; McKenzie 2011). Just six years later, in 1940, Congress passed legislation that created a new documents regime for the children born abroad of unmarried American men that endured with minor changes through World War II and the Cold War, and that remains in place today. Among the estimated hundreds of thousands of possible birthright citizenship claimants was the son of a U.S. citizen born in Vietnam.

Conclusion

Documentary regimes have existed with various historical designs and purposes, but in general they have upheld the racial state. Throughout the twentieth century and into the twenty-first, on the front lines of U.S. birthright citizenship policy, whether in U.S. embassies or consulates abroad, at the border, in the war zone, or at the local polling place, establishing credibility as a citizen has been more difficult for citizens of color. The documents regime that developed for Wong Kim Ark and his descendants evidenced a complicated racialized regime with a classist element. Every case was assumed fraudulent, and immigration officials challenged the validity of documents that proved citizenship. They even tried to claim people born in the United States of Chinese descent should not be citizens at birth. That officials used the documents regime to deny the right to transmit citizenship to children born to U.S. citizen fathers in China challenged men's gendered right to transmit citizenship. Only after military service in World War II did Immigration Bureau officials view the son of a Chinese American claimant, born abroad, as deserving.

Gender has also been a significant factor in citizenship claims, a factor complicated by claimants' race(s). The marriage certificate has been used as evidence of citizenship and of expatriation in U.S. history. After Congress passed legislation seeking to expatriate U.S.-born women who married foreign men and moved abroad with their husbands, the San Francisco elections registrar determined that a suffragist who married a foreign man but stayed in the United States had expatriated herself. The case evidences how easily local officials applied national immigration laws to disenfranchise citizens. It also underscores the importance of being found deserving of citizenship. Ethel Mackenzie's protests focused on her loss of respectability for being called a false citizen. Even when, in 1922, many U.S. women regained the right to retain their native citizenship upon marriage to a foreigner, a husband's race prevented U.S.-born women who married Chinese or Japanese nationals from retaining their citizenship for up to three decades longer.

Children born outside of marriage to U.S. servicemen and foreign mothers have had difficulty proving their claims; consular officers are encouraged to scrutinize the foreign mother in order to determine whether the child deserves citizenship. The son of an American military contractor and veteran, Tuan Anh Nguyen claimed citizenship as protection against deportation in 1997. That Nguyen's father recognized his son from birth and raised him, or that the U.S. government recognized the relationship when it airlifted the child to the United States made no difference. A Supreme Court decision in 2001 rejected the son's claim to citizenship and defended the differential documentary requirements in place to prove citizenship for the children born abroad of male and female citizens. State Department instructions confirm its continued reliance on consular officers' judgments—of foreign mothers and of putative U.S. citizen fathers and children's racial compatibility—in jus sanguinis citizenship cases. Outcomes of citizenship claims in these cases rely both on documents and on what a consular officer "knows" about the case.

Citizenship claims are most often about exercising rights. Individuals have claimed citizenship to inherit an estate, to secure freedom from slavery, to vote, and to enter into and to resist deportation from the United States. In court cases the government often, though not always, appears on the opposite side of the case from the claimant, arguing against the individual's citizenship. Individuals offer their good reputations, their bodies, affidavits sworn by respectable witnesses, and eventually birth certificates, while the government challenges claims based on illegality and presumption of fraud. In rarer cases the claimant seeks to refuse U.S. citizenship to avoid one responsibility or another, often military service or taxes. In every case the initial judgment is made by an individual government bureaucrat who relies both on an examination of documents and on her or his own perception of the credibility of the applicant. The official's decision reflects moral and political judgments related to the claimant's race, gender, and social class. Local prejudices, such as the one that stopped Ethel Mackenzie from voting in California in 1912, can be magnified into federal policy that affects many others.

NOTES

I thank Torrie Hester, Debra Majeed, Linda Sturtz, and Russ Read for their comments and suggestions that helped improve this chapter. Any errors are, of course, my own.

1. Documents have become central to proof of status, causing some immigrants of color to feel the need to acquire as many as possible. See Chang 2011.

2. Race in U.S. citizenship cases is well explored in Carbado 2005; Haney-Lopez 1996; Lee 2003; Ngai 2005; and Volpp 2005.

3. These dates refer to the date Wong Kim Ark entered the United States without documentation (1881) and the date his grandson Wong Hee Ngeu entered the United States (1947).

4. Congress passed Chinese exclusion legislation in 1882, extended it in 1892, and made it permanent in 1902. Other Asian groups were added to the exclusion between 1907 and 1924. Asian exclusion ended between 1943 and 1952. Immigration laws from *Reports of the Department of Commerce and Labor*, 1907, 136; William Williams quote from "Notice Concerning Manifesting of United States Citizens and Inspection of Cabin Passengers," April 11, 1912, RG 85, quoted in Robertson 2010, 180.

5. Statement of Frederick Berna to F. A. Bee, consul, July 16, 1890; Statement of Hoo Sue, merchant, in United States since 1852, July 18, 1890. See "Investigation of Truth of Claim to Birth in the United States," by "J.S. Treasury Department," Wong Kim Ark file, NARA, San Bruno.

6. *U.S. v. Wong Kim Ark*, 169 U.S. 649 (1898), 694.

7. Letter from F. W. Berkshire, supervising inspector (El Paso), to Commissioner Immigration San Francisco, December 10, 1910, Wong Yok Fun INS file, NARA, San Bruno. The second son, Wong Yok Sue, was initially refused, but he was accepted on review.

8. Fifty-one questions were asked of the applicant, and fifty-three of the father. The form looked similar to earlier question forms. The questions were similar to questions in previous interviews, but there were follow-up questions with spaces left blank. "Statement of Applicant and Relative of Applicant for Entry," File No. 1300-04770, November 18, 1947, Wong Hee Ngeu, aka Wong Nee Ngen, NARA, San Bruno.

9. Although the G.I. Fiancées Act, 1946, allowed servicemen to bring fiancées and their children to the United States for a limited period after the war, this case shows the same documents regime was in place. The law expired December 31, 1948 (Ling 1998, 114).

10. In a letter from his lawyer, Jackie Bing, Wong is referred to as "Citizen-veteran, ex ss 'Gen. Gordon.'" Letter from Chow and Bing to district director of the Immigration Service, November 1, 1947, NARA, San Bruno.

11. The 1900 census shows that Ethel's father, John Coope, had been born in England, was a "vinyardist," and had been in the United States for nineteen years without naturalizing.

12. "Mackenzie Gordon Will Claim Bride Today: Wedding of Singer and Miss Coope to Be Simple Affair," *The Call*, August 13, 1909. Mackenzie changed his name legally in 1917 to Mackenzie Gordon. "Gordon Mackenzie Asks Name Reversal," *San Francisco Examiner*, April 12, 1917. Note that this person is of no relation to the author. *Morning Call* endorsed woman suffrage in August 1911 (Solomons 1912, 29). See Chapter IV, California, in Harper 1922, 36–45; Freeman 2008; "Mrs. Gordon to Rescue of Voteless Women: Native Daughter to See Whether She's Alien Because Wife of Englishman," *San Francisco Call*, January 23, 1913.

13. The 1922 Cable Act ended the practice of automatic citizenship for foreign women and loss of citizenship for white native-born women. Women born in the United States and married to Japanese and Chinese nationals continued to be expatriated until the end of Asian exclusion laws. Other disabilities remained, highlighting for feminists the importance of seeking a broad equal rights amendment (McKenzie 2011, 131); "Mackenzie Is to Be Citizen to Aid Wife: Singer and Clubman to Renounce Allegiance to Britain to Enfranchise Wife in the U.S.," *San Francisco Examiner*, December 9, 1915; "Long Fight of S.F. Woman for Suffrage Ends: Mrs. Peter Gordon Mackenzie Once More Is Citizen of United States," *San Francisco Chronicle*, January 7, 1921. The discussion of women's suffrage in California in *The History of Woman Suffrage* refers to the *San Francisco Chronicle* as a most "relentless opponent" (Harper 1922, 46).

7. FROM THE OUTSIDE LOOKING IN

U.S. PASSPORTS IN THE BORDERLANDS

RACHEL E. ROSENBLOOM

Juan Aranda has a birth certificate documenting his birth in 1970 in Weslaco, Texas, a small city located a few miles from the U.S.-Mexico border (Jordan 2008). He has baptism records from a Weslaco church dated two weeks later. Weslaco school records list him as a student from kindergarten through high school. He is a registered voter and has voted in U.S. federal elections. However, when he submitted his birth certificate as proof of citizenship for a passport application in 2007, the U.S. Department of State requested further information to substantiate his birth within the United States, including his mother's prenatal care records, a newspaper announcement of his birth, and his parents' U.S. school records. Aranda responded by sending in his own school and baptism records, with a note explaining that the other requested documents did not exist. (His mother had come to Texas from Mexico when she was three months' pregnant, following the death of her husband. She could not afford any prenatal care and had never attended school in the United States or placed a birth announcement in the paper.) To further support the passport application, Aranda's mother dug up a document attesting to a ten-dollar loan that she took out shortly after her son's birth, along with his immunization records and pictures from his years in the local elementary school. The response from the State Department informed Aranda that he had not "fully complied with the request for additional information." It advised him to learn about "procedures for your possible naturalization as a U.S. citizen" and informed him, "Once you obtain U.S. citizenship, you may execute another application for a U.S. passport."

The experiences of Juan Aranda and many others in the U.S.-Mexico borderlands cast a new light on U.S. passports, revealing how they function to draw lines of belonging and exclusion not only at international borders but also within the United States. This chapter describes the recent imposition of new passport requirements for U.S. citizens at the U.S.-Mexico border and the wide-scale denial of passport applications from Mexican Americans born in the borderlands of South Texas. Drawing on the work of John Torpey and others on state identification processes and the evolution of the passport, this chapter argues that the U.S. passport, although often described as a document aimed exclusively at foreign governments, has in fact come to resemble an internal passport in the areas close to the southern U.S. border. The current situation in the borderlands can be viewed as one chapter within a much longer history of the domestic use of U.S. passports by those on the margins of U.S. citizenship, and of racialized presumptions of fraud within the adjudication of passport applications. The fluctuations of evidentiary criteria reveal the racialized character of citizenship's operations and also suggest the vagaries of citizenship's core meanings. (See chapters by Flaim, Lawrance, Babo, and McKenzie, this volume, for discussions of demands for documents directed toward those encountered as members of ethnic or racial communities targeted by political elites or government officials.)

The Changing Border and Emerging Conflicts over Passports

The Fourteenth Amendment to the U.S. Constitution accords jus soli citizenship to individuals born in the United States. Thus, a birth certificate issued by a city, county, or state authority is, in theory, sufficient proof of citizenship to obtain a U.S. passport. However, as Beatrice McKenzie details in this volume, race has played a role in the adjudication of citizenship claims throughout the history of the United States. In recent years, one particular group of applicants has encountered high levels of scrutiny: Mexican Americans born in noninstitutional settings—private homes or small clinics—in areas close to the U.S.-Mexico border. In particular, residents of the Rio Grande Valley in South Texas have experienced a surge in passport denials.

For much of the twentieth century, *parteras* (lay midwives) played a key role in the provision of maternal health care in the Rio Grande Valley, which is home to one of the largest concentrations of farmworkers in the United States and is served by few hospitals (Ogolla 2008, 2). The four counties that make up the region range from 87.2 to 95.7 percent Latino, and per capita income, which ranges from $10,800 to $13,695, is among the lowest in the United States (U.S. Department of Commerce, Census Bureau, 2012). Many residents of the valley live in small *colonias* consisting of just a few houses. One study of midwives in the region has observed that "in addition to a shortage of primary care providers, Colonia residents' difficulty in accessing health care is compounded by having to travel long distances to health care facilities, fear of losing wages for time spent away from work, inconvenient health care facility hours, lack of awareness of available health care programs and no health insurance" (Ogolla 2008, 2–3).

A State Department spokesperson, Cy Ferenchak, has explained that while a birth certificate generally suffices as proof of citizenship for a passport application, "because of a history of fraudulently filed reports on the Southwest border, we don't have much faith in the [midwife-granted] document" (Sieff 2008a). The State Department has viewed midwife-signed birth certificates with heightened suspicion for several decades, but denials of passports have reached a critical mass since 2008 due to changes in federal law and a resulting surge in passport applications from residents of the borderlands. Passengers arriving in the United States by air or sea generally must present a U.S. passport to establish citizenship, but for many decades documentation requirements were more relaxed for U.S. citizens entering at land border crossings or arriving by air or sea from Mexico, Canada, or the Caribbean. In those settings— and particularly at land border crossings, where people often cross the border for just a few hours to run errands or socialize—it was common until recently for U.S. citizens returning home to use a variety of documents, such as birth certificates and driver's licenses, in lieu of passports. This changed in 2009 with the advent of the Western Hemisphere Travel Initiative (WHTI). Under the WHTI, U.S. citizens returning to the United States at a land border crossing must now present a U.S. passport or other designated identification.[1] In the lead-up to the implementation of the WHTI, many residents of the borderlands rushed to apply for passports in order to comply with the new requirements (Vogel 2008).

Over the past few years, a number of applicants who have been denied passports have brought suit in federal court. Juan Aranda was a plaintiff in one of these suits, *Castelano v. Clinton*, a class action filed in 2008 (*Castelano v. Clinton* 2008a). The class of plaintiffs was defined as individuals of Mexican descent who were born in southwestern border states and were delivered by midwives or birth attendants in private homes or local clinics rather than in hospitals.

The complaint alleged that the State Department applied heightened scrutiny to the plaintiffs' passport applications; subjected them to burdensome, unreasonable, and excessive demands for documentation of their birth that went far beyond what other applicants were required to submit; and deemed their applications to be "filed without further action" (i.e., put on hold) or abandoned rather than issuing a formal denial that could be appealed. Other lawsuits have challenged immigration enforcement actions at the border against U.S. citizens of Mexican descent. For example, Laura Nancy Castro brought suit for a declaratory judgment of citizenship after border officers detained her, along with her mother and sister, for ten hours, coerced from them a false confession that the birth certificates belonging to Castro and her sister had been falsified, confiscated her passport, and denied her entry to the United States (Ulloa 2010).

At the center of the conflict over passport adjudications is a list of "suspect birth attendants" known as the SBA List (U.S. Department of State 2009, 137–38). Although the list has never been publicly released, the State Department produced an undated copy in response to discovery requests made by passport applicants in the course of litigation. That version of the SBA List includes the names of 249 midwives who practiced in South Texas between 1961 and 1996 (*Castelano v. Clinton* 2008b; Ulloa 2010). It also includes dates that appear to refer to convictions for birth certificate fraud for 49 of the midwives, mostly from the 1980s and 1990s. There are notations next to thirteen other names that appear to refer to (undated) convictions, confessions, or indictments, as well as one notation referring to a revoked license. The remaining names on the list have no such notations but have been described as being midwives suspected of fraud by agency officials (Ulloa 2010; U.S. Department of State 2009, 137–38).

Like Juan Aranda, many Latino passport applicants born in the region and delivered by midwives in noninstitutional settings have been asked to produce extensive additional evidence, such as prenatal records, newspaper announcements of their birth, and records relating to their parents' presence in the United States at the time of their birth (Jordan 2008). Many of the births in question took place decades ago, and thus midwives and other possible witnesses, as well as documentary evidence, may no longer be available (Vogel 2008). Those who cannot produce the requested evidence have had their applications denied or put on indefinite hold (Jordan 2008).

As indicated by the SBA List, a number of midwives in South Texas were convicted of falsifying birth certificates during a wave of such prosecutions in the 1980s and 1990s. Yet the connection between "suspect" birth attendants and the authenticity of particular birth certificates that bear their signatures is tenuous at best. The majority of midwives on the SBA List have never admitted to or been convicted of falsifying birth certificates. Moreover, it is undisputed that all the midwives on the list, including those who have been convicted of falsifying birth certificates, delivered many babies inside the United States, all of whom presumably have birth certificates bearing their signature. As one news report has put it, "No one was asked which records they had been paid to forge and which were authentic, making it nearly impossible to determine which children had been delivered in the United States and which had not" (Ulloa 2010). Even the most expansive estimate of falsified birth certificates puts the total at fifteen thousand for the entire period between 1960 and the early 1990s, fewer than the number of babies delivered by midwives in the region in any given year (Hsu 2008). The use of the SBA List to deny passports has thus thrown a wide net that has prevented many people born in the United States from being able to obtain proof of citizenship.

The most insistent claims of fraud have been directed at applicants whose births were registered on both sides of the border. For example, Amalia Castelano, the lead plaintiff in the *Castelano* case, was born in Weslaco, Texas, in 1968 to Mexican parents who resided across the border in Reynosa, Mexico, but had border-crossing cards and frequently spent time in Texas (*Castelano v. Clinton* 2008a, 26). Castelano's mother went into labor while visiting family members in Weslaco and gave birth there attended by a midwife. The birth was registered in Texas on the same day, and Castelano was baptized in Weslaco two months later. Yet her parents also registered her birth across the border in Reynosa, Mexico, in 1972. She thus ended up with two separate birth records, evidencing two different births in two different countries. The State Department and the Department of Homeland Security now routinely conduct searches of Mexican birth records when investigating U.S. citizenship claims in contexts such as passport applications, removal proceedings, and applications for certificates of citizenship. The existence of a Mexican birth certificate is frequently cited as a cause for a denial of such a claim (*Garcia v. Clinton* 2011; *Rivera v. Albright* 2000).

Agency officials appear to be jumping to the conclusion that dual birth registrations are a sign of migration-related fraud. Yet a closer look at these cases and their historical context suggests a very different narrative. For most of the twentieth century, Mexican citizenship law placed families in a bind if they returned to Mexico with U.S.-born children. Mexican law did not recognize dual nationality claims, deeming any acquisition of foreign citizenship, by birth or naturalization, to result in an automatic loss of all Mexican citizenship rights

(Fitzgerald 2005, 176–77; Gutierrez 1997, 1003–5). Even Mexican naturalization laws, which included preferential treatment for immigrants from Latin American countries, provided no such accommodations for the U.S.-born children of Mexican citizens until 1974 (Fitzgerald 2005, 180–81). In 1998, the law was finally amended to recognize Mexican nationality claims of those born in Mexico who have naturalized abroad and those born abroad to at least one Mexican parent (183–86).

Faced with the disjuncture between Mexican citizenship law on the one hand and the realities of circular migration and cross-border communities on the other, many Mexicans with U.S.-born children chose a straightforward solution: reregistering their children's births in Mexico. This phenomenon is widely known in the region. As Joe Rivera, the county clerk of Cameron County, Texas, has explained:

> It is common practice in Cameron County and other border counties that the parents of children born in Texas also register their children as having been born in Mexico. This is particularly true where the parents are living in Mexico, and intend to raise the child in Mexico. There are many reasons that this occurs. Some parents do it for purely cultural reasons. Others do so in order that their children may have the benefit of Mexican Citizenship, such as attending public school, or obtaining medical services, in Mexico. I have seen many cases where parents registered their children as having been born in Mexico, when in fact they were born in the United States, regardless of whether they were born with a midwife or in a hospital. (*Trevino v. Clinton* 2007)

Amalia Castelano's story bears this out: her parents registered her birth in Reynosa so that she could access medical care (*Castelano v. Clinton* 2008a, 26). Yet the paradigm of migration-related fraud is so powerful that it has entirely obscured, for agency adjudicators, this likely explanation for many cases in which passport applicants have dual birth certificates.

Aranda and the other plaintiffs in *Castelano v. Clinton* reached a settlement with the government in 2009. The State Department agreed to readjudicate the passport applications of class members (*Castelano v. Clinton* 2009, 16–18); to apply a standard of proof that is easier for an applicant to meet ("preponderance of the evidence" rather than "substantial evidence") (13); and to issue approvals or denials rather than putting applications on hold (14–15). Under the terms of the settlement, the State Department will continue to maintain a list of midwives who have been convicted of birth certificate fraud and/or who the Department has a reasonable suspicion of having engaged in birth certificate fraud, based on: a) a conviction or plea agreement involving a crime of document fraud; b) an admission, confession, or statement of implication made by the birth attendant, a client, or a witness pertaining to birth certificate fraud by the birth attendant; c) information received from a law enforcement agency regarding the birth attendant and his/her involvement in birth certificate fraud; d) documents or other information supporting a reasonable suspicion that the birth attendant has engaged in birth certificate fraud; or e) disciplinary action taken by the Texas Midwifery Board or other state licensing agency for falsely registering births or falsely filing birth records. (10)

The settlement does not include any provision for public release of the list, but the State Department agreed that a name will be included on the list only where "there is an articulable and reasonable basis for the belief that an individual has engaged in birth certificate fraud" and that "mere guesses or hunches are insufficient" (11). It also agreed not to deny an application solely because a birth certificate was signed by someone whose name appears on the list (18). Where further information is requested of the applicant, the case will be handled by a senior-level adjudicator designated as an "SBA officer" (26). If that adjudicator determines that the application should be denied, the decision will be reviewed by an "SBA panel" made up of three SBA adjudicators (10, 21–22). The agency also agreed to provide training for its adjudicators (25–26) and to engage in outreach efforts to Texas border communities (26–27).

In the wake of the *Castelano* settlement, the State Department has taken steps that appear aimed at signaling a standardized (if still onerous) approach to adjudicating applications by those born in a noninstitutional setting. A new application form requires applicants seeking to establish citizenship on the basis of an out-of-hospital birth to provide information about every residence they had up to age eighteen and every school they attended, as well as the citizenship status and place and date of birth of relatives, including siblings, children, parents, and stepparents, living or deceased (U.S. Department of State 2013). The form asks about the parents' residences and places of employment during the year preceding the applicant's birth; the dates of each prenatal visit the mother had; and the names of individuals present at the birth. For those with noncitizen parents, the form requires information about what form of documentation, if any, the parents used to enter the country (2–3).

Contested citizenship claims reveal the inherent instability of the citizen/alien line. As I have discussed elsewhere, this instability was once widely acknowledged with the U.S. legal system (Rosenbloom 2013). A century ago, immigration officials adjudicating Chinese American citizenship claims frequently fell back on racialized assumptions in resolving cases where the evidentiary record of birth in the United States was unclear. While some federal judges were content to uphold the validity of such adjudications, others expressed distress at their own inability to distinguish "true" from "false" citizens. As one judge complained, "It is impossible in this class of cases to know what the truth is" (*U.S. v. Leu Jin* 581).

Such a confession by a judge would be remarkable in the present-day United States, where birth registration has been nearly universal for several decades and jus soli citizenship is treated as a clear-cut question to resolve. Yet the forensic contingency of citizenship, and its malleability in the hands of the state, persist. Other chapters in this volume draw our attention to the ascriptive aspects of citizenship in settings where identity documents are lacking. The passport cases serve as a reminder that the processes through which identity documents are evaluated may themselves serve as a site of such ascription.

Identity documents are a hallmark of the modern state, serving to create "legible people" (Caplan & Torpey 2001; Lyon 2009; Scott 1998; Torpey 2000). They provide access to rights and benefits (Sadiq 2008), and at the same time they subject individuals to government surveillance and control (Lyon 2009). Their function is at once inclusionary and exclusionary; John Torpey has described identification practices as a means for states, "at once sheltering and domineering," to "embrace" some citizens and exclude others (2000, 7–13).

Depending on place and circumstance, a variety of official documents may serve as proof of identity and status, including birth certificates, national ID cards, and passports. While these documents may have overlapping functions, however, they often carry widely divergent connotations. As David Lyon has noted, documentation of identity "may be carried with pride, indifference, reluctance or even fear, depending on the political conditions and the history of using such documents in the country in question" (2009, 3), a government of affective ties to which Sara Friedman and Kamal Sadiq both allude in their chapters in this volume.

Context can transform the valence of any document. Yet at the same time, it is possible to make some broad generalizations about the connotations of various types of documents. At one end of the spectrum, possession of a birth certificate carries associations that are almost entirely positive. International law proclaims birth registration to be a fundamental right (Todres 2003). A 2002 UNICEF report identified the failure of governments to register an estimated fifty million births every year as a global crisis, noting that those who are unregistered "in legal terms, do not exist" and that registration "is the official and positive recognition of a new member of society, who is entitled to all the rights and responsibilities of a valued citizen" (UNICEF Innocenti Research Centre 2002, 1). Birth registration has been the subject of vigorous campaigns by both governmental and nongovernmental agencies, with one such campaign adopting the slogan "Write me down, make me real" (Caplan 2005, 195).[2]

In contrast, national ID cards have at times generated significant opposition and critique (Lyon 2009, 10; Redman 2008, 914–15; Steinbock 2004). No form of ID card is as tainted as the internal passport, most closely associated in the twentieth century with Stalinist Russia, Nazi Germany, and apartheid-era South Africa (Garcelon 2001; Lyon 2009, 25–27). As Torpey has commented, "Where pronounced state controls on movement operate within a state today, especially when these are to the detriment of particular 'negatively privileged' status groups, we can reliably expect to find an authoritarian state (or worse)" (2000, 9). One might extend the genealogy of internal passports back further to slave passes in the antebellum United States (Lyon 2009, 27–28) and a variety of internal controls on movement in early modern Europe (Torpey 2000) and in European colonies (Lyon 2009, 28–30).

The international, or external, passport occupies a more complex position on this spectrum. On the one hand, the passport embodies the liberal ideal of freedom of movement; the text inside a U.S. passport declares, "The Secretary of State of the United States of America hereby requests all whom it may concern to permit the citizen/national of the United States named herein to pass without delay or hindrance and in case of need to give all lawful aid and protection." On the other hand, the passport also serves as a reminder of international borders and global restrictions on movement. This dual nature of the passport—simultaneously signifying both mobility and restrictions on mobility—has been widely noted. While internal passports "may be a state's principal means for discriminating among its subjects in terms of rights and privileges . . . [and] may be used to regulate the movements of certain groups of subjects, to restrict their entry into certain areas, and to deny them the freedom to depart their places of residence," external passports "serve both to facilitate the rights of an issuer state's citizens abroad, and to secure state control of movement across international boundaries" (Garcelon 2001, 83).

The recent spate of passport litigation in South Texas reveals another sort of duality embodied in the international passport, or at least in the U.S. passport as it functions in the U.S.-Mexico borderlands: although ostensibly directed at foreign governments, a passport sometimes serves its most important purpose in mediating the relationship between citizens and their own government. Many—perhaps most—of those who have sought passports since 2008 in South Texas have been motivated to do so not by the requirements of Mexico or any other foreign state but rather by the need to protect their rights at home.

This domestic aspect of the passport is often obscured. The U.S. Supreme Court, for example, has described the passport as a document "which from its nature and object is addressed to foreign powers; purporting only to be a request that the bearer of it may pass safely and freely" (*Urtetiqui v. D'Arcy* 1835). Scholarship often echoes this assumption. Adam McKeown has written that "the modern passport is addressed to a global audience; other documents can establish the link between nation and individual for domestic purposes" (2008, 1). David Lyon has contrasted the passport to the national ID card, arguing that "passports, by definition, are for travellers who wish to cross national borders . . . [while the] intent of most national ID schemes is eventually to cover entire populations" (2009, 21).

As a formal matter, it is certainly true that possessing a U.S. passport is optional, even after the imposition of passport requirements under the WHTI. Yet this perspective overlooks the extent to which the borderlands have always functioned as one region rather than two. The current U.S.-Mexico border, which came into being in its present state in 1853, did not begin to resemble a meaningful international boundary until the early twentieth century. Referring to one particular stretch of the border in 1899, a newspaper article described the two towns of Nogales—one in Arizona, the other in Mexico—"as one, for they really are such, being divided by an imaginary line only, which passes along the center of the international strip, or more properly speaking street" (Tinker Salas 1996, 89). Mexican immigrants encountered increasing scrutiny at the border beginning in the 1920s (Ettinger 2009) and were subject, along with their U.S.-born children, to mass deportations in the 1930s and 1950s (Johnson 2005). Yet Mexicans were exempt from numerical caps on immigrant visas until 1965, and unauthorized migration from Mexico was frequently overlooked by federal immigration officials, reflecting the powerful interests of agricultural employers. As one analysis put it, "The early twentieth century official practices at the border reflected a social construction of Mexico and [the] U.S. having mutual interests in cross-border or transnational communities" (Valencia-Webber and Sedillo Lopez 2010, 268). The controversy over "suspect" birth attendants is itself an indication of the degree to which border crossing has been an integral part of life in the area: a number of the midwives on the SBA List are under suspicion in part because they regularly delivered babies in both the United States and Mexico. Trinidad Saldivar, for example, has been described as having been "one of the most sought-out parteras along both sides of the Texas-Mexico border" for many years (Ulloa 2010).

Over the last few decades, the border has been radically transformed. Federal spending on border enforcement increased twenty-one-fold from 1980 to 2003 (Congressional Research Service 2008, 5). It has continued its steady rise since then, with the construction of a border fence and increases in border patrol officers. The growing emphasis on border enforcement has wrought changes not only in the lives of would-be migrants but also in the lives of U.S. citizens residing in the borderlands, who now find their own status frequently called into question (del Bosque 2012).

Even with the increasing militarization of the border, international travel is not a luxury but rather a routine part of life for many residents of the Rio Grande Valley. Laura Nancy Castro, asked to describe her trip from Brownsville, Texas, to Matamoros, Mexico, to visit her mother—the trip that resulted in her passport being confiscated on suspicion of fraud—responded, "It was just so routine," noting that it is a drive she is accustomed to making practically every weekend (Ulloa 2010). Pre-WHTI policies at the border reflected this reality. The imposition of passport requirements under the WHTI and the denials of passport applications submitted by Mexican Americans born in South Texas disrupted these long-standing cross-border communities. This disruption, in turn, has transformed the meaning of identity documents for U.S. citizens of Mexican descent in the region.

Birth certificates long assumed to be authentic have suddenly become suspect. The plaintiffs in *Castelano v. Clinton*, for example, functioned as U.S. citizens for many years before being told that their proof of citizenship was insufficient to obtain a passport. They regularly crossed the border and returned home without incident. Amalia Castelano, the lead plaintiff in the case, obtained an immigrant visa for her Mexican husband through a provision of the immigration laws granting visas to immediate relatives of U.S. citizens (*Castelano v. Clinton* 2008a, 27). Arturo Garcia, another plaintiff, has five Mexican-born children who, at the time of his passport denial, had already been issued certificates of U.S. citizenship based on their father's birth in the United States (30). Juan Luis Flores brought his father to the United States as the parent of a U.S. citizen; his Mexico-born daughter obtained a certificate of citizenship on the basis of her father's birth in the United States (36).

Although birth registration is often considered to be the foundation for rights, a birth certificate only has the power that it is accorded by the state. Further gatekeeping procedures lay bare the distance that can separate a birth record from the rights it is presumed to convey. Recent adjudications of U.S. passport applications serve as a stark reminder of the gap between birth registration and its attendant rights.

Along with this shift in the meaning of birth registration has come a shift in the meaning of the passport itself. Citizens of the United States have generally been far less likely to acquire passports than citizens of Canada and many European countries (Avon 2011). But a U.S. passport is increasingly becoming a necessary part of daily life along the border. When viewed through the lens of South Texas, the U.S. passport begins to look less like an international passport and more like an internal one. People long accustomed to traveling within the region have suddenly been required to obtain new identity documentation from the State Department in order to do so. And, crucially, as in the case of internal passports in other countries (Lyon 2009, 25–30; Torpey 2000, 9), the process that has unfolded has been one not of simply documenting status but of producing status (or lack thereof), largely along racial lines.

The requirements imposed by the WHTI are new, but this is not the first time that domestic uses of a U.S. passport have come to the fore. In the early years of the twentieth century, before the imposition of passport requirements for entry into the United States, Chinese Americans sought passports because they hoped (in vain, as it turned out) that carrying the document would spare them from the lengthy interrogations and other indignities to which Chinese immigrants were subjected during the years of the Chinese exclusion laws (Robertson 2010, 178–79). California state representative Martha Escutia has described her memories of her grandfather, a naturalized U.S. citizen born in Mexico, who would never leave his own house in Los Angeles without his U.S. passport in his pocket for fear that he would be wrongly deported (Johnson 2005, 8). Escutia, testifying before the California legislature on the enduring effects of the forced repatriation of Mexicans and Mexican Americans in the 1930s, noted that her grandfather's passport was so important to him that she buried him with the document in his pocket (8).

In ways that parallel these earlier examples, the recent conflicts over passport adjudications primarily involve attempts to access full citizenship rights within the United States rather than the privileges that a U.S. passport may carry abroad. A number of scholars have used the term "alien citizenship" to describe the tenuous hold on citizenship that these circumstances suggest. In the words of historian Mae Ngai, "The alien citizen is an American citizen by virtue of her birth in the United States but whose citizenship is suspect, if not denied, on account of the racialized identity of her immigrant ancestry. In this construction, the foreignness of non-European peoples is deemed unalterable, making nationality a kind of racial trait. Alienage, then, becomes a permanent condition, passed from generation to generation, adhering even to the native-born citizen" (2007, 2521).

Those on the margins of citizenship, who have sought passports to secure their citizenship rights, are precisely the applicants who have tended to be viewed with particular suspicion by the State Department. The heightened fraud precautions at issue in *Castelano v. Clinton* echo a long history of racialized presumptions of fraud in adjudicating U.S. passport applications. For example, one of the earliest measures to combat passport fraud was directed at Japanese Americans in Hawaii. Passports, which were required for the first time as a temporary measure during World War I, became a permanent fixture in 1926. In his history of the U.S. passport, Craig Robertson recounts the difficulties that Americans faced in applying for passports in an era in which few had documentation of their birth (states did not begin to mandate birth registration until the early years of the twentieth century, and as late as 1942, an estimated 40 percent of Americans lacked birth certificates) (2010, 105). The State Department responded to these difficulties by creating protocols to issue passports based on affidavits from those who had witnessed a birth or, if such witnesses had died or were otherwise unavailable, the sworn statement of a "respectable" person who "knew" the applicant to be a citizen (105). However, the State Department took the position that alternative evidence of birth on U.S. soil would not be accepted from Hawaii, based on the following calculus:

> The substitute evidence which we will take in the cases of persons born in this country to white fathers and mothers is appropriate when the circumstances warrant our taking such action, for we may do so with reasonable safety; but when it comes to extending the same practice to members of the Japanese race, with their well-known racial tendency to equivocate and their racial similarity of physical appearance, we cannot do so without danger of being imposed upon, both in the matter of the identity of the applicant and in the matter of his alleged birth on the soil of the United States. (107)

Like the heightened fraud precautions directed at those born in Hawaii in the 1920s, the State Department's current approach to fraud prevention suggests a narrative in which Mexican migrants are especially likely to commit fraud, and births claimed to have taken place near the border are especially suspect. Home births have been on the rise nationally over the past two decades among white women, who are now three to five times as likely to have a home birth as women of any other racial or ethnic group (Centers for Disease Control 2012, 1). In 2009, the highest rates of home births occurred in Oregon and Montana (1). Yet the State Department's scrutiny of applicants born in noninstitutional settings appears to have been confined to Latinos born near the southwestern border; no reports of passport denials or onerous document requests have emerged from other communities (Sieff 2008b). A 2009 report by the State Department's Office of the Inspector General is revealing:

> The term "suspect birth attendants" refers to a sub-set of licensed midwives or other medical practitioners who deliver children born to alien parents either at home or at an institution other than a hospital.... Unscrupulous SBAs are known to have prepared fraudulent birth documentation to show that children actually born abroad were allegedly born in the United States. In some cases, those children have subsequently applied for and been granted U.S. passports. In other cases, the children repeatedly enter the United States on their fraudulently obtained birth certificates. The vast majority of SBA cases involve children born to Mexican parents. (U.S. Department of State 2009, 137)

This language suggests that simply delivering babies who have noncitizen (and, in particular, Mexican) parents might be enough to make a midwife "suspect."

In *The Invention of the Passport* (2000), John Torpey argues that that "in the course of the past few centuries, states have successfully usurped from rival claimants such as churches and private enterprises the 'monopoly of the legitimate means of movement'" (1–2), and that this monopolization has been a crucial element of state building. "Procedures and mechanisms for identifying persons are essential to this process" because "in order to be implemented in practice, the notion of national communities must be codified in documents rather than merely 'imagined'" (6). Torpey chronicles the unfolding of this process in Western Europe and the United States since the French Revolution.

Recent developments in the use of passports at the U.S.-Mexico border reveal some additional nuances to the state monopoly on movement. Although the U.S. government has long monopolized the right to authorize and regulate movement over the U.S.-Mexico border, the ways in which it has done so have changed significantly over the years. In the borderlands, the pre-WHTI era was characterized by a multiplicity of forms of documentation—birth certificates, driver's licenses, and so forth—and diffuse authority on the part of frontline officers to determine what was acceptable. The WHTI has replaced this system with a new, centralized one in which proof of citizenship is tightly controlled by one federal agency. In the process, documents previously deemed proof of citizenship have been rendered invalid, and new lines of belonging and exclusion have been drawn.

NOTES

Many thanks to all of the other conference participants for their feedback and ideas and to Benjamin Lawrance and Jacqueline Stevens for comments on earlier drafts. I am indebted to attorneys Jaime Diez and Lisa Brodyaga for sharing their insights regarding the litigation of the passport cases and other contested citizenship claims.

1. Other acceptable forms of identification include a U.S. Passport Card, which is also issued by the Department of State; enhanced driver's licenses, which some states have begun issuing under the requirements imposed by the REAL ID Act of 2005; and the Trusted Traveler Program Card, issued by the Department of Homeland Security (U.S. Department of Homeland Security, Customs and Border Protection, 2012).

2. The failures of citizenship regimes that rely on birth registration are discussed in this volume, especially in the chapters by Polly Price, Benjamin Lawrance, and Jacqueline Bhabha.

8. PROBLEMS OF EVIDENCE, EVIDENCE OF PROBLEMS

EXPANDING CITIZENSHIP AND REPRODUCING STATELESSNESS AMONG HIGHLANDERS IN NORTHERN THAILAND

AMANDA FLAIM

> I *must* believe them. If I do not believe them,
> or if there is a problem, I ask for [more evidence].
> —The lead district official explains his decisions
> in adjudicating citizenship, 2010

> Everyone in my family is a citizen. My mother, my father, my grandparents,
> my brothers, my sisters. Everyone. The officials do not believe me. I gave them pictures.
> I showed them my household registration. I took a DNA test with my father,
> and it shows that I am his son. But still I am not a citizen. [The district official]
> asked me, "If you are a child of citizens, where is your proof?"
> —Aqcha, aged twenty, describes applying for citizenship in Thailand,
> the country of his birth, January 2011

In the discourse of the Global North, actual experiences notwithstanding, statelessness receives attention as an anomaly (see Price and Rosenbloom, this volume). But across the Global South, Aqcha's story resonates (see Sadiq, this volume). In Nepal, the Dominican Republic, Myanmar, Thailand, and beyond, millions of people cannot acquire recognition of citizenship despite sometimes generations of residence in the country of their birth (Berkeley 2009; Türk 2014; chapters by Sadiq, Lawrance, and Price, this volume). Lacking citizenship, they also lack the rights ostensibly afforded to citizens in any country in the world. In Thailand alone, hundreds of thousands of highlanders—popularly known as "hill tribes"—collectively represent one of the largest stateless populations in the world.

How do we come to understand the case of protracted statelessness among people like Aqcha? Generally acknowledged causes of statelessness in the Global South, such as state succession and state failure, do not apply to Thailand. Other causes of statelessness, like legal loopholes (Phuntip 2006; Van Waas 2008; Manly and Van Waas 2010) and discrimination by Thais against highlanders (Thongchai 1994, 2000a, 2000b; Renard 2000; Pinkaew 2003; Toyota 2005; Chutima 2006, 2010; Jonsson 2006; Mukdawan 2009) explain in part why highlanders like Aqcha have been disproportionately denied citizenship status relative to other minorities in Thailand. Yet these theories fail to explain why hundreds of thousands of highlanders have successfully acquired citizenship while he and so many others in their communities lack it, despite possessing legal claims. Nor can these theories explain why conferral rates vary widely across and within regions, ethnic groups, and even households like Aqcha's (see Flaim 2015). Drawing on intensive ethnography and extensive survey research in highland communities, I argue in this chapter that protracted statelessness among highlanders persists, paradoxically, as a result of the bureaucratic practices and procedures that have been enacted to address it. Specifically, my research reveals that the ostensibly rational evidentiary procedures deployed to register and recognize highlanders reproduce contingencies and discrimination in the application of otherwise progressive nationality law. This chapter reveals that much of the problem lies in the forensic or evidence criteria used for assessing claims to belonging—a self-referential cycle of call-and-response (see introduction and Stevens, chapter 12, this volume) upon which the state's claim to sovereignty is ultimately founded. Seen in this light, "problems of evidence" that arise in the citizenship adjudication process reflect a critical gap between the fictions of rule by the state and an applicant's subversive history or ethnic identity. As the district official asserts and Aqcha himself laments, no matter how strong the "evidence" to a citizenship claim may be, citizenship conferral ultimately requires the conferral of belief. As a consequence, citizenship adjudication—a process that has been devised to resolve cases of statelessness like Aqcha's—funnels through individual-level determinations the accretion of political biases that ultimately reproduces and reinforces the condition of statelessness.

A Note on Data and Methods

Arguments in this chapter draw on mixed-methods research conducted during two years of fieldwork in Thailand (2009–11). Unless otherwise noted, stories and quotes derive from intensive ethnographic research among kin networks of highlanders (mostly Akha), highlander advocacy groups, Thai government officials, and staff at various agencies of the United Nations. Statistics reported in this chapter derive from analysis of the 2010 UNESCO Highland Peoples' Survey II (hereafter referred to as the HPS), a survey of 292 villages located along Thailand's northern and northwestern international border. The survey includes more than fifteen thousand households comprising more than seventy thousand people who collectively represent more than twenty ethnicities. While neither survey nor ethnographic data are representative of all highlanders' experiences in Thailand, the survey and ethnographic findings presented are emblematic of the barriers to citizenship that highlanders and other noncitizens in Thailand continue to face (see Flaim 2015).

Background

The highlands of northern Thailand are a part of the foothills of the Himalayas, a zone stretching across South Asia, mainland Southeast Asia, and southern China. The vast numbers of cultural minorities who reside in the highlands constitute one of the most ethnolinguistically diverse populations in the world (Scott 2009). Until the early twentieth century, highlanders largely evaded incorporation into lowland kingdoms and polities to varying degrees (Jonsson 2006; Scott 2009), but they have been increasingly incorporated into, and participate in, the nation-states in which they have resided since World War II (Safman 2007; Scott 2009). States' practices of including highland minorities as citizens have varied considerably across both time and context, yet only in Thailand have highlanders been systematically excluded from citizenship in their own country of birth and residence (Safman 2007).

The dynamic sociocultural and historical context of exclusion of highland minorities in Thailand is well documented (see, e.g., Thongchai 1994; Jonsson 2006). An extended discussion of this history lies beyond the purview of this chapter, but a few explanations for Thailand's unique situation warrant mention here. First, although the first Nationality Act granted citizenship through jus soli, highlanders were not included in early state cadastral surveys. Consistent with pre-nation-state cosmological views of power and the polity, the early state existed in the lowlands, where paddy rice cultivation long required a relatively stable and taxable population (Wolters 1982; Scott 1998, 2009). Highland spaces—and, by extension, highland peoples—remained peripheral from the perspective of early administrators in Bangkok (Wolters 1982; Thongchai 1994; Vandergeest and Peluso 1995; Scott 2009).

Not only did the state from its inception fail to recognize highlanders as citizens, but over the course of the twentieth century, the imagined identity of Thai nationality grew increasingly exclusive as well. Through the early twentieth century, rising tides of xenophobia directed initially at urban Chinese crystallized a belief in "Thainess" (*kwambpenthai*), an identity limited to Thai-speaking Buddhists who were loyal to the king (Thongchai 1994; Renard 2000; Pinkaew 2003). By definition, "Thainess" did not apply to highlanders.

For decades, effective statelessness among highland villagers posed few problems for their day-to-day lives (Feingold 2002; Scott 2009). After World War II, however, growing state concerns over perceived threats of communist insurgency in the region and mounting international pressures to eradicate the country's opium economy (of which some highland groups were key suppliers) propelled the state apparatus to its remote borders and brought the question of citizenship for highlanders to the fore. In the charged context of the Cold War, highlanders, who had been effectively deemed non-Thai under the narrow definition of "Thainess," were increasingly seen as anti-Thai (Renard 2000; Pinkaew 2003). During the 1960s, the state initially attempted to register highlanders, but as tensions in the region grew in the 1970s, "hill tribes" (*chaokhao*), including Lua, Karen, Lahu, Hmong, Akha, Khamu, and Lisu, were scapegoated for issues ranging from communist insurgency to drug trafficking to deforestation (Renard 2000; Pinkaew 2003). Derogatory narratives of highlanders were regularly invoked to justify their exclusion from citizenship, as well as to justify a range of "development" interventions in the highlands that all but decimated local livelihoods by the 1990s (see McKinnon and Vienne 1989; Chupinit 1994; McCaskill and Kampe 1998; Pinkaew 2003; Ahlquist 2015). The process embodies the characteristics of citizenship apologues described by Stevens (this volume): the national narrative constituted some groups as legitimate members and not others, pursuant to which government officials dutifully interpellated and excluded from the Thai political community individuals based on their kinship narratives of ethnic lineage and not individual-level characteristics. That this is a matter of ascription, or official writing, is evident by its operationalization as described later.

By the 1990s, the political context had shifted dramatically, and effective statelessness presented serious problems for highlander families and communities. With diminished livelihoods in the village, growing numbers of highlanders left home to find work in Thailand's booming economy (Feingold 2000, 2003). Facing pervasive social discrimination and lacking advantages of education and social networks within cities, many highlanders were able to find work only in the most exploitable conditions, however (Feingold 2000). Moreover, because the state increased restrictions on the internal movement of noncitizens throughout the country in the 1990s, highland minority women and girls who lacked documentation of citizenship became particularly vulnerable to trafficking by smugglers, employers, and authorities at internal checkpoints (Feingold 2000, 2002; Chutima 2006, 2010). In this particular context, acquisition of the national identity card (*baht bprachaachon*) for citizens became a vital priority for highlanders seeking to secure their livelihoods and futures (see Sadiq, this volume). In 1999 and 2000, leaders of a burgeoning pan-highland movement mobilized thousands of villagers of all ethnicities to march in the northern city of Chiang Mai and demand recognition of their citizenship (McKinnon 2005; Chutima 2010).

Despite initial resistance by the state, the movement has proved successful in several ways. In immediate response to local pressure, the government decentralized citizenship adjudication to the local level. And, in 2008, the government expanded the law to include noncitizens who could prove that they were born in the country prior to February 26, 1992. In addition to extending the boundaries of citizenship, the state has also expanded the rights of noncitizens. Noncitizen residents were variously included in the country's health care program (Harris 2013; Koning 2014), and in 2005, the Ministry of Education extended compulsory schooling rights to noncitizen children. As recently as 2011, Thailand removed its Reservation on Article 7 of the Convention of the Rights of the Child, and it now guarantees birth registration to all children born in the country. The clearest result of these progressive changes can be seen, however, in citizenship conferral rates, which jumped in the first few years of the millennium (Flaim 2015). Yet, while the majority of highlanders surveyed in the HPS had acquired recognition of their citizenship by 2010, thousands of stories like Aqcha's raise questions about whether bureaucratic reforms can ever resolve persistent effective statelessness in Thailand, or indeed elsewhere (Flaim 2015).

Expanded Citizenship, Persistent Effective Statelessness

Today, hundreds of thousands of highlanders have overcome past effective statelessness and are now newly recognized citizens of Thailand. But rates of conferral and prevalence vary considerably across and within ethnic groups, districts, and even households like Aqcha's (Flaim 2015). Whereas some districts report high rates of citizenship among residents, others report extremely low rates of citizenship. One might conclude that residents of districts with low rates of citizenship are simply ineligible to be recognized as citizens. To be sure, Thailand has experienced waves of undocumented immigration from neighboring states for decades, yet migration alone does not account for variation in rates across districts and ethnic groups (see Flaim 2015). As the rest of this chapter reveals, much of the variation in citizenship conferral is attributable to variations and contingencies in civil registration practices that have unequally shaped the state's access to and interpretations of highlanders, as well as highlanders' access to and interpretations of the state.

Evidence of Problems
UNEVEN TERRITORIALIZATION OF THE HIGHLANDS AND HIGHLANDERS

Throughout the past fifty years, highlanders in Thailand have been targeted by, caught up in, and caught between the state's various attempts to identify those who "really belong" and to exclude those who do not—that is, to create and re-create congruency between territory and nation through the identification, monitoring, and enforcement of identity among peoples at the margins. This, as Keyes (2002, 1194) argues, is the ongoing work of the nation-state (see also Vandergeest and Peluso 1995). Asserting congruency between identity and territory in the highlands is not only a highly political activity but also an extremely complex administrative undertaking (Vandergeest and Peluso 1995). First and foremost is the challenge of asserting a territorially and culturally bounded identity onto a population that is famous among anthropologists for being historically mobile and ethnolinguistically diverse (Leach 1964; Keyes 2002; see also Scott 1998, 2009; Jonsson 2006). Following Leach (1964), many anthropologists of highland peoples argue that conceptions of bounded identities are incongruent to many highlanders' views of themselves and others. Scott (1998, 2009) has furthered this work to argue that their diverse political systems and historically mobile practices of swidden agriculture historically rendered them difficult to integrate and transform into permanently settled, countable and accountable, taxable citizens of the modern nation-state. Reflecting both the historical mobility of many highlanders and the state's project to permanently settle highland villages, more than 60 percent of villages surveyed in the HPS reported dates of first permanent settlement after 1960.

Barriers to accessing highlanders have also been exacerbated by the mountainous jungles in which they reside: "Beyond the last [lowland] village [the roads] end in some bushy field where the hills rise steeply. At this point the main trails take over, serving only man and his pack animals. . . . Beyond the main trails lie secondary ones where the grade is too steep or the clearing of jungle too haphazard to risk going even with a sure-footed mule" (Hanks, Sharp, and Hanks, 1964, 8–9). The preceding sentiment reflects the precariousness of travel during early stages of state expansion in the highlands as recently as the mid-1960s.

Today, an extensive network of roads into and throughout the highlands renders the area generally accessible by car or motorcycle. Nonetheless, highland villages located off the main roads remain difficult to access, particularly in the rainy season. In 2010, just over half the villages surveyed were accessible by paved roads, and 14 percent were entirely inaccessible during the rainy season. In short, conditions of travel in the highlands remain prohibitively difficult and time-consuming for many highlanders. Some must travel for as many as six hours to apply for citizenship papers. Complicating matters, Thailand operates a vast network of internal checkpoints to surveil noncitizen residents. All noncitizens are prohibited from crossing district borders without permission. As a result, even if highlanders are traveling to government offices to apply for citizenship papers, they risk detention, extortion, or arbitrary deportation by border police.

COMPLEXITY OF THE PROCESS

In Thai nationality law, no distinctions are made with regard to the presumed functioning of evidentiary procedure. Each person is assumed to undergo the same application process regardless of one's ethnic background or one's district of residence. Nevertheless, data from the HPS reveal considerable variation in application experiences across individuals and households by district (Flaim 2015).

Variations in application experience are widespread at the individual level. Among the 4,806 effective noncitizens in the survey who had applied for Thai citizenship, 71 percent were still waiting for determinations, 22 percent had been rejected, and 7 percent did not know what had happened to their application. Among 1,812 household respondents who lacked citizenship, 72 percent had applied more than once, and 15 percent had submitted applications more than five times. On average, they had been waiting for resolution to their cases for 4.5 years, but 15 percent of respondents had been waiting between 10 and 44 years for resolution. Data from the HPS also reveal that registration has not been a uniform experience for successful applicants either. Similar to the experiences of noncitizen applicants, more than 74 percent of the 2,723 respondents who acquired citizenship through application reported applying more than twice, with 30 percent applying between three and six times. Additionally, they reported waiting an average of 4 years before citizenship was conferred, with 30 percent waiting between 4 and 35 years.

VARIATIONS IN STATE-HIGHLAND RELATIONSHIPS

Rates of application and application experiences are also significantly associated with ethnic identity (see also Flaim 2015). Specifically, Karen, Hmong, and Khamu applicants reported significantly longer waiting times than Lahu, Lisu, and Akha applicants. Detected differences by ethnicity do not suggest that claims to citizenship by Lahu applicants are stronger than those of Hmong or Karen people, however. Rather, these differences reflect divergent historical relationships with Thai state authorities (see also Renard 2000), differential rates of literacy and education (indices of social capital), and variations in leadership across ethnic groups. Indeed, a few of the most outspoken leaders in the highland citizenship movement are Akha, a group that has close historical, cultural, and geographic ties with Lahu and Lisu people (see Feingold 2002; McKinnon 2005).

Reported variations in application experiences also reflect significant differences in the profiles of applicants by ethnic group. Whereas the majorities of Akha, Lahu, and Lisu noncitizens had applied for citizenship at the time of the HPS, the Karen or Hmong citizenship applicant is relatively unique among his or her ethnic group: only 14 percent of Karen and 24 percent of Hmong noncitizens reported ever applying for citizenship despite reporting the highest rates of citizenship among all minority groups in the HPS. This is not to suggest that Karen and Hmong people do not apply for citizenship. Rather, these findings likely reflect the varying circumstances under which different groups have actually acquired Thai citizenship. Specifically, because Karen historically lived closer to lowland Thais and have been more integrated into lowland life, it is likely that fewer Karen in the northernmost provinces ever needed to apply for citizenship than did ethnic Akha, Lisu, or Lahu—groups that had relatively fewer historical and cultural ties to lowland society (McKinnon and Wanat 1983). By extension, Karen applicants for citizenship do not reflect the more general experience of Thailand-born Karen who were registered as citizens in civil registration campaigns, and thus never had to formally apply.

A similar logic may be applied to understand the high rates of citizenship among the Hmong relative to other groups. However, unlike Karen people, Hmong people were scapegoated by the state and media as sources of communism and drug smuggling, and because of this, the Thai government targeted Hmong villages in particular for programs that would ensure both legibility and loyalty to the state—programs such as permanent settlement, military training, and citizenship conferral (McKinnon and Vienne 1989). State initiatives to trade citizenship for loyalty and legibility date as far back as the 1930s, with the powerful urban Chinese in Bangkok (Skinner 1957), and the 1970s, when Haw Chinese nationalists pledged to disarm in exchange for citizenship and settlement in the highlands (Thin 1986).

The point is not to confuse or belabor the issue of variation in application procedure and experience but rather to illuminate the highly divergent situation of citizenship conferral to diverse groups that were nonetheless uniformly categorized in nationality law and registration policy as "hill tribes."

At the same time, the current situation of uneven citizenship in the highlands is also indicative of the contingent and uneven civil registration process. Surveys, household registrations, and birth registrations play an important role in citizenship outcomes, as these events produce the requisite evidence of residence, blood, and birth upon which identity cards are issued and status determinations are ultimately made. As the subsequent sections of this chapter reveal, political intuitions of agents crystallize gaps, inconsistencies, and flaws in evidence into determinations and documentation of citizenship.

CONTINGENCIES IN EVIDENTIARY PROCEDURE

Stories of complexity, confusion, and inequalities associated with registration procedures and experiences provide only a surface picture of the problems associated with uneven inclusion in the highlands. Contingencies associated with the leadership in one's village and district of residence and even ethnic identity are also significantly associated with registration experiences (Flaim 2015). Specifically, the prescribed path to citizenship—from registering residence, to acquiring permissions from village leaders, to submitting papers at the district office—is not contingent; yet the capabilities, personal proclivities, and priorities of the various headmen, district office staff, and district officials who must participate in the application process, vary considerably. At the village level, the personal priorities, standards of integrity, and leadership capabilities of village headmen and assistant village headmen make a significant difference for the rates and success of villagers' applications (Mukdawan 2009; Chutima 2010; Flaim 2015). Because the structure of evidentiary procedure elevates the authority of village headman in individual applications for citizenship, the process is replete with opportunity for corruption and extortion, of which there are many stories (Feingold 2002; Sturgeon 2005; Mukdawan 2009; Chutima 2010).

During my fieldwork, I never encountered the levels of corruption that are well documented in other studies, yet I regularly encountered ineffective village leaders. Examples include one headman who simply disregarded his responsibilities and was rarely in the village at all. In the words of the villagers, "He does not take to heart the needs of the villagers at all." Another albeit well-intentioned headman unwittingly allowed con men posing as state survey registrants to survey his village at the price of several hundred baht per person. When villagers attempted to file copies of their "official surveys" as proof of residence at the district office, they were accused of attempting fraud. On the other side of the same coin, however, effective leaders can make an enormous difference in the application process by taking the initiative to be well-informed of the process, to inform villagers of their rights to register, to advocate for applicants at the district office, and to assist villagers throughout the application process by translating documents and conversations, and even driving them to and from the office.

The influence of village headmen on the experiences and outcomes of applying for citizenship is ultimately limited, however, by the capabilities and attitudes of staff and officials at the district office. At the district level, the extent to which staff and officials prioritize highlanders, or understand the challenges of the particular highland context, varies considerably. The following two quotes by two different officials reflect extreme differences in attitudes toward highlanders among officials unto whom the power of adjudicating citizenship rests.

District Official 1: Chiang Rai Province, 2011

The situation is very complicated [in the hills]. This is an issue of national security. It is my responsibility to make sure that people do not cheat the system. The law requires it. Even DNA cannot always be trusted. I can only really trust DNA tests with a person's mother. Why? Because you are born from your mother. We are not born of fathers. When someone submits a DNA test with their father without other proof, how can I know this is not the bastard child of a Burmese prostitute?

District Official 2: Chiang Rai Province, 2010

I want to issue citizenship as much as possible before I leave this district. If the [official who succeeds me] has no experience with the hill tribes, there will be a lot of confusion [when I leave my post]. For instance, each villager must submit documents to the district office, but this takes time. My staff are collecting all of the necessary documents in each village [in my district] so that I can go to a single village and certify applications for all of the applicants in one day. We are trying to visit three villages per day when we go up the mountains. . . . [Resolving citizenship problems for highland minority people] is my responsibility. I do this work for the king. If the case is clear and accurate according to the law, and it is a case that I can address, I will do it.

The statements reflect starkly contrasting perspectives from officials who are tasked with the same responsibilities of conducting status determinations within their respective jurisdictions. Despite clear differences between the two officials, neither perspective is particularly unique among the number of officials who rotate on appointed bases through highland districts (see also Chutima 2006, 2010; Mukdawan 2009).

Attitudes toward highlanders range from extremely discriminatory and distrustful to open and sympathetic, and various practices initiated by district officials to resolve citizenship in their jurisdictions range from exploitative and corrupt (see Mukdawan 2009), to those that are closed and opaque (e.g., official 1), to those that are inclusive and relatively transparent (e.g., official 2). Some officials welcome the support of nongovernmental organizations as a measure of enhancing productivity, as well as insurance against potential corruption charges.

Given the discrepancies between these two officials in terms of their attitudes toward highland minority peoples, it is clear that one's place of residence can significantly affect the application experience and the outcome of a citizenship application. For instance, although DNA testing has been initiated by the state to resolve questions of parentage for cases in which birth certificates are lacking, district officials who discriminate against highlanders will weigh such evidence differently than officials who are more sympathetic to, or even patronizing of, highland minority peoples. In declaring his intention to resolve as many cases as possible prior to reassignment, the second official indicates his keen awareness both of variation in officials' attitudes and practices and of the consequences of such variation for the lives of people who are excluded as a result.

Problems of Evidence

In addition to navigating evidentiary procedure through village and district levels, applicants must present evidence of a link to the territory of Thailand through birth, blood, and/or residence. Such evidence of the link must be considered by officials to be both sufficient and reliable. However, the criteria for these indices are vague and, most important, depend on applicants' participation in, and interpretations of, previous events of registration and documentation. For example, the quantity of evidence refers to a range of documents used for substantiating claims by birth, legal residence, and family relationships. Two of the most important documents are the birth certificate and the household registration that specifies family relationships of household members. The quality of evidence refers to, for instance, the legibility of handwriting on registration forms or the clarity of photos taken during household registrations. The deeply subjective experience of adjudicating citizenship in a context of widespread evidence gaps is readily apparent in the words of the district official who was quoted at the beginning of the chapter:

> I am someone who studied law, and I think this nationality law is hard. I have read the procedures 100 times, but I had to start using these procedures in real situations to understand it. . . . In actuality, the law in Thailand is quite open. If a birth certificate is available, there is no question. The applicant is a citizen. But the biggest problem in the highlands is that highlanders do not have birth certificates. [Sighs]. Then I have to ask for other evidence. . . . [In addition to checking other documents], I compare old and recent pictures and compare these pictures to the real person, who must be present when I sign the documents for citizenship. I look at their eyebrows, nose, mouth . . . their face structure. Sometimes their pictures are not similar. In those cases, I ask the village headman, "is this person really the same person in the photograph?" I must believe them. If I do not believe them, or if there is a problem, I ask for a DNA test.

As the official indicates, when presented with an unclear case, he requests more evidence until he finds the case to be sufficiently and reliably defensible according to the standards of the Ministry of Interior. In a broad sense, this approach to citizenship adjudication is a process whereby a person's biography gains legal significance based on the subjective view of an arbitrarily appointed official. This official, in turn, is establishing applicants' bona fides as potential citizens when they, or their children, encounter similar inquiries later. (Applicants I interviewed received no actual DNA reports; it is not clear whether Thai officials withhold reports that are inconsistent with their beliefs.) As the following sections reveal, the mere availability or clarity of surveys, photos, and even birth certificates depends upon events that were variably experienced and interpreted by both highlanders and government staff in the production of highly variable evidence. In other words, these are literary events that generate other literary events.

Since the late 1960s, the Thai government has undertaken several waves of registrations of the highlands in order to count and account for the total population, and to attempt to understand which villagers "arrived" when. The documents used and produced during these registration campaigns thus provide a baseline of evidence of "being there" against which stateless highlanders can prove their claims to citizenship. The 1969 and 1990 hill tribe surveys carry the most weight in status determinations. In the first survey, the state registered 119,591 people over the course of two years, but it issued only about 65,000 mementos to highlanders to keep as proof (Chutima 2010, 15). Over the course of the following two decades, the government conducted various surveys of immigrant and refugee groups, some of whom are of a highland ethnicity, and issued identity cards that indicate tenuous claims to residency and rights (Toyota 2005; Pinkaew 2013). In 1990 and again in 1999, the government attempted censuses of "hill tribes," during which people were issued "blue" and "green/red" cards, respectively, both of which grant cardholders semi-permanent residency but do not denote citizenship (Toyota 2005; UNESCO 2008; Chutima 2010; Pinkaew 2013). For applicants who lack proof of birth prior to February 26, 1992, and whose parents are not citizens, documented proof of participation in the 1990 or 1999 hill tribe survey (or an earlier survey) can provide crucial evidence of residence.

Prior to undertaking registrations, the state produced aerial photographs of the region. Despite attempts to "see" every village prior to the surveys, however, scholars and advocates have long noted the incompleteness of highland surveys due to budgetary, time, or capacity constraints of implementing agencies (Mukdawan 2009; Chutima 2010). The following statement by Khun Sathorn, a former registration official, about conducting a highland survey points to a stark disjuncture between the claims of the state to complete knowledge of and access to highlanders, on the one hand, and the difficulties that officials faced in attempting to reproduce and uphold that claim through surveys of the hills, on the other:

> We rode an elephant to the Karen village. The rainy season had started and there were no roads to the hill tribe villages at the time. We packed all of the surveys in bags and strapped them to the elephant's back. Each team knew where to go based on aerial pictures taken by the Thai military, and we were each assigned several villages to survey. Sometimes we came across villages that were not on the map, though. Then we had to survey those villages too.

As Khun Sathorn's experience reveals, early registrations of highlanders were carried out in a context in which the state did not possess universal knowledge of, or easy access to, highlanders. While relying on maps that ostensibly documented every village in the highlands, his teams nevertheless encountered villages that they did not know existed. The number of villages that were never found or registered cannot be estimated, but the consequences of these gaps in official knowledge resonate today: excluded villagers lack evidence of residence, which renders their claims to citizenship, and those of their descendants, dubious in the eyes of officials. The risk of being missed or counted was not random, however. As noted previously, proximity to district centers, degrees of integration into lowland society, and the relative strategic importance of a village or ethnic group could influence the likelihood of being counted in order for one's "being" to count.

The messy implementation of civil registration in the highlands is not the only reason for current gaps in evidence. Several noncitizen villagers reported that they had missed opportunities to be counted because of the delayed process of data collection over time as well. Indeed, several surveys were implemented over the course of one or several years (see Mukdawan 2009). Buqyeuhr, an older Akha woman who was stateless until 2003, recalls the pivotal moment of her initial exclusion as follows:

> When I got married . . . I left home and walked for two days across the mountain to live with my new family—with my husband and his parents. A few days after I left, some men arrived in my birth village and surveyed the households there. My parents did not include my name in their household register because I had already moved away to my husband's village. But the survey team had already interviewed my husband's village before I arrived there. His parents didn't include me in their household registration because I was not a "household resident" at the time of that survey. I was born in Thailand, and my villages were registered. But I was never included in the [1969] survey.

Buqyeuhr was eventually able to acquire recognition of her citizenship, but this required persistence, and even then she was only "naturalized." In the end, she was denied recognition of her status as a full citizen by both jus soli and jus sanguinis. Her status as a naturalized citizen remains a powerful reminder that highlanders are still perceived as outsiders or migrants whose belonging in the polity depends precariously upon recognition and belief from Thai state officials.

Buqyeuhr's story reveals that direct exclusion from state registrations undermines claims to legal status for highlanders and their children. But inclusion in state registrations has not guaranteed citizenship either. Stories abound of various misunderstandings, misrepresentations, and mistakes during village surveys that consequently generated gaps and inconsistent information about highlanders and their families. Both highlanders and officials remember the frustration and confusion that permeated interactions between survey teams and villagers, and many recall the misunderstandings and mistakes that produced problematic documents. The following statements from a stateless Akha woman and a former survey official are emblematic of these experiences:

> I was working in the fields when a man came to my village to run a survey. He was drunk and he demanded food and whiskey when he would visit the houses. He interviewed my young daughter and my elderly mother-in-law about everyone in the house. When I came home from the field, I saw a piece of paper, but I couldn't read it and I didn't know what it was. My mother-in-law and my child did not understand what it was either. Then I let my children play with the paper, but they tore it up. (Miqbahr, Akha villager, stateless)

> I remember clearly the day I first arrived in a Karen village. None of the villagers could understand us, and we couldn't understand them. We met with the village leaders . . . and tried to explain through translators and gestures what we needed to do. It was extremely difficult to communicate. We needed to identify . . . everyone in each house, collect accurate information about each person, and fill out a registration form for each household. We had to learn a few words in the local language to ask these questions, and we needed to collect the information fast. One day it was pouring rain, and some of the survey forms were soaked, making the ink run. My team did a great job, though. We dried the surveys by heating them in a frying pan over a fire. A few documents were ruined, but we saved most of them. In the end, my team finished the village survey faster than any other registration team. (Khun Jerun, former survey staff)

Reading these narratives back-to-back provides a crucial understanding of how complicated interactions between villagers and survey staff during twentieth-century registration campaigns can contribute to the delay or denial of citizenship in the twenty-first century. Both groups regularly reported feeling confusion, frustration, and anxiety during these registrations, and several reported mistakes that have generated dire consequences for highlanders and their children. Given the backdrop of discrimination, armed conflict, and militarization in the hills in which many of these campaigns were implemented, two other survey staff discussed tactics of building alliances with villages during registration campaigns as they felt that their safety was often at risk in the field. Reflecting similar fears and distrust of state officials, several villagers related stories of deliberately refusing to participate in the surveys by hiding in the forest during registrations.

NEW OPPORTUNITIES FOR (MIS)RECOGNITION

Given the significant challenges for thousands of highlanders to produce sufficient or reliable evidence of residence from early civil registration campaigns, the clearest route to resolving a citizenship claim is with documented proof of birth in the country prior to February 26, 1992. This evidence is a birth certificate or delivery certificate, which was the official record of birth issued to noncitizen families prior to 2011. According to law, births must be registered at the district office within fifteen days after delivery. The child's name is then added to the household registry, and a birth certificate is issued (UNESCO 2008). Yet there are considerable challenges associated with proving place of birth in Thailand even today. Specifically, although the proportion of all children born at home is dropping to fewer than 40 percent in the youngest age cohorts, more than 80 percent of noncitizens were born at home by 2010. And, while nearly 90 percent of highland children under the age of eleven have birth certificates, only 14 percent of noncitizen youth possess these documents (Flaim 2015).

Although every family with which I spoke understood the importance of acquiring a birth certificate for their children, mothers in particular noted their reticence to travel to the district office on a motorcycle only a few weeks postpartum, even to conduct such important business. When mothers are single or in particularly difficult circumstances, they may not receive the necessary support and assistance required to travel for birth registration. When Aqcha was born, his father was working elsewhere, and no one could accompany his mother to register him at the district center. Given that his family members are all citizens of Thailand, his lack of a birth certificate was enough to render his assertion of Thai citizenship "unbelievable" to the officials who have adjudicated his case over the years, even though a nonhighlander Thai citizen would have faced no similar challenge.[1]

Conclusion

In this chapter, I interrogate key moments and practices in civil registration to understand the reasons for uneven outcomes in legal status among highland minority people in Thailand, one of the largest stateless populations in the world. Rather than focus on the "plight of the stateless," as is the general practice in studies of protracted, widespread statelessness, this chapter examines the historical and current interactions between government staff and highlanders that generate the requisite evidence (*lakthaan*) of birth, blood, and residence for substantiating, conferring, or denying a claim to citizenship in Thailand. Rather than decontextualizing nationality laws and policies from the historical conditions and social practices that produce and enforce them, this approach considers the dynamic and particular ways that laws and policies are understood and interpreted in determinations of legal status. My analysis of civil registration in northern Thailand reveals a rationalized bureaucracy that is founded on and reproduces contingency, arbitrariness, and discrimination in the application of otherwise progressive nationality law to the perpetual exclusion of thousands of people like Aqcha. Effective statelessness is partly produced and reinforced through the very registration mechanisms that have been deployed to resolve it.

In the global system of sovereign nation-states, recognition of citizenship derives from assumed links to territory by way of birth (jus soli), descent (jus sanguinis), and/or residence. This chapter shows that highlanders' claims to citizenship in Thailand are often only as strong as the evidence they are able to marshal to prove the validity of their claims. Yet my analysis demonstrates that key moments of evidence production and interpretation during regularized civil registration procedures were problematically and variably implemented and interpreted by the state and also were inconsistently accessed and understood by highlanders themselves. As a result, these fraught moments of evidence production have generated—and continue to generate—inconsistent, flawed, and incomplete documentation of birth, blood, and residence. Yet it is this very "evidence" that nevertheless constitutes the standard against which highlanders must prove their claims to belong. In the end, the stories presented in this chapter reveal that no evidence, whether documents, data, or even DNA, can ever guarantee a place in the polity. In the case of citizenship conferral, even the smallest gap between (hi)story and evidence thereof must ultimately be bridged by the beliefs and thus the internalized national fantasies of the officials making these determinations.

All names have been changed to protect the identities of participants, and exact dates are not given because they may reveal identities of officials who wished to remain anonymous.

1. This practice resembles that described by Rachel E. Rosenbloom (this volume), who points out that most home births in the United States are to families in the interior, a population whose evidence of citizenship is not interrogated, unlike that of births to Mexican Americans near the Mexican border.

9. LIMITS OF LEGAL CITIZENSHIP

NARRATIVES FROM SOUTH AND SOUTHEAST ASIA

KAMAL SADIQ

Legal principles such as jus soli and jus sanguinis are sources that define and protect the boundaries of citizenship. Such citizenship principles confirm rights and
make visible the eligible politico-body of the state. They are the foundation for
the institutional and artifactual enactment and expansion of membership that
has marked the West. The struggles of new subjects—slaves, women, racialized
minorities, refugees, immigrants—and the institutional expansion of representation of these marginalized groups characterize liberal citizenship. Modern citizenship regimes have introduced new institutional and documentary statuses:
the worker visa, the permanent resident, the sponsored spouse, the naturalized
citizen, and the frequently traveling dual citizen. These emerging institutional
categories and statuses capture the continuing expansion of the Western liberal
rights regime beyond national boundaries.

While citizenship studies of the Global North have a long lineage, we know
relatively little about citizenship in developing states. What are the citizenship
protocols, practices, and experiences of most of the population in most of the
world? Legal institutions and forensic documentation (what I call "jus charta"
and "jus tabulae") designed to produce citizenship matter more in the Global
South than legal principles (jus soli and jus sanguinis). *Administrative citizenship*, actualized through documentation, is what people engage in daily across
regimes, as we have seen in other chapters in this collection. In so doing, they

become standard citizens, affirmed as such through juridical inquiries, such as immigration court hearings and inquiries described by Benjamin Lawrance and Kim Rubenstein (this volume). How did administrative citizenship expand throughout developing states over the last half century? Finally, what are the effects of this legal citizenship?

This chapter will trace the evolution of an administrative citizenship, torn between the expansion and regulation of rights, to produce a standardized citizen, fit for administrative manipulation. As administrative citizenship transmits a fixed, certain, stable, and final notion of citizenship, citizenship laws, institutions, and proofs can be contingent, partial, and incomplete. A variety of marginalized groups (immigrants, minorities, homeless, the poor) experience a gap between formalized institutional citizenship and their actual lived reality. Sometimes, administrative citizenship is a hurdle to those who otherwise are eligible by birth and descent. In our rush to strengthen rights and build legal citizenship, we neglect the exclusionary impact of its institutions and documents. In South and Southeast Asia, a highly regulated and formalized administrative citizenship not subject to timely judicial review produces an especially oppressive and exclusionary citizenship.

Expanding Rights or Order

Western citizenship scholarship has celebrated the "Marshallian" expansion of civil and political rights and the drive to equalize social classes and expand the modern welfare state (Marshall 1992). The growth of welfare rights and services narrowed the inequalities that liberal capitalism generated. National health, food grains, and kerosene are some of the rationed but affordable goods and services provided by the welfare state in India and Malaysia. Countering the inequalities of capitalism required enhancing the health, housing, food, and employment rights of the poorest. Bureaucracy's autonomous role in the expansion of such rights provided by the modern state has been evaluated since Max Weber (1978). In response to the rise of the welfare state, scholars led by Michel Foucault (2003b [1975–76]) have pointed to the emergence of another feature of the state—its desire to order and govern populations.

Foucault's theory of governmentality suggests an all-pervasive power that orders our society through prisons, hospitals, and policing—standardizing us as homogeneous, disciplined, and regulated objects of a surveillance state (Dandeker 1994; Lyon 2009). Recent historical scholarship by Edward Higgs (2004) points to the insatiable thirst for information that undergirds institutional development of a surveillance state. To deliver or order rights, states have to first "know" their populations through, for instance, health, food, housing, and employment needs. The transition from paper files to databases corresponds to the growth of such knowledge in Europe and North America. States deliver rights through knowledge-bearing service institutions, but in doing so they regulate and order people. Do developing states follow a similar trajectory of bureaucratic rationalization (Weber 1978), surveillance (Lyon 2009), information gathering (Higgs 2004), and governmentality (Foucault 2003) to create an infrastructure of citizenship (Sadiq 2009) that delivers rights to citizens? What welfare institutions and documents do these states deploy, and how do people negotiate access to citizenship services? What does citizenship mean as a lived reality?

On the basis of findings about European state building Higgs (2004) argues that information gathering by statelike entities is an old tradition. Contrary to recent scholarship, his work shows persuasively that information gathering in Europe was *not* an outcome of the Enlightenment or the Industrial Revolution era but preceded these events. By the nineteenth century, centralization of information became a key feature of the state. The standardized citizens were made and remade by the information gathering and centralization of the state. However now, unlike then, they also are reconfigured by a multiplicity of artifacts associated with that standardization such as health cards, electoral cards, national identity cards, and their corresponding state institutions. Citizenship both as an official category and as a lived reality cannot be explained by the subjects of the state alone (illegal immigrants, border patrol agents, green card holders); it must also be studied as state artifacts. The state itself exists in these objects and is not producing them as a separate material entity. These state papers, documents, and formats tell us more about membership, nationality, belonging, and identity than formal rules alone. In this instance, state artifacts materialize social and political relations. The document manifests society.

Scholars of developing countries trace modern conceptions of information gathering and citizenship to colonial imperatives of governance from afar, providing minimal service to "half-cooked" peoples (Scott 2009). After decolonization, developing states faced hungry, neglected, and expectant masses, so the immediate delivery of welfare to address rights claims was critical. Over time, the provision of subsidized and accessible health care, basic food, kerosene, housing, and employment meant a statewide distribution of ration cards in India and national identity cards in Indonesia (KTP) and Malaysia (MyKad). Documents with appropriately formatted individual biographical information gave access and meaning to rights. Those without such documents were without rights.

Ironically, the programs designed to ensure order created sites of instability. A tension marks the building of rights and order. As developing states systematically began distributing public goods to meet claims for rights among newly liberated populations, a tension arose between their need to expand their welfare and public services and their need to meaningfully regulate welfare's availability. The first is the source of a state's legitimacy, while the second imposes constraints on its capacity. Drawing boundaries around welfare services underlines a state's ability to order populations through rules and regulations. At the heart of the state's relationship to its citizen is an assemblage of legally sourced administrative devices, both institutions and artifacts such as ration cards. To govern populations, institutions and artifacts must order them. Postcolonial scholarship largely ignores the evolution of institutional, administrative citizenship in independent India or Malaysia. While Foucault has shown us how populations are objects of power, we are left to unravel the practices and mechanisms by which power is received and responded to. The micro-negotiations between rights-delivering institutions and artifact-bearing peoples effect citizenship, generalities and theories notwithstanding.

A Standard Citizen

The standardized, legal citizen cannot be understood only as an abstract subject of the state but must also be examined through state artifacts. These artifacts, specifically citizenship documentation, function as tools of the state and have a range of characteristics that extend beyond those placed there by design. In particular, the artifacts have affective attributes (the object instills emotive qualities) of loyalty, belonging, membership, and identity.[1] State artifacts and documentation also enable agency, which complicates and problematizes the efficacy of the tool. For example, an artifact like a passport both weakens a regime's authority over citizenship, by its inherent amenability to forgery or fraudulent acquisition, and nonetheless strengthens it, by performing the state's monopoly over its legitimate production. A ration card for subsidized grains may produce higher loan eligibility (informal or formal), property rights, local respectability, legitimacy, and power. Possessors of ration cards enjoy greater rights than those without them. Here, the state artifact determines the identity, action, and life chances of an individual. Once an individual's biographical and socioeconomic characteristics are captured in standardized information, they are targets for a normalized practice of citizenship. Information and artifacts generate the standard citizen, a citizen the state engages and prefers.

The standard citizen of the "new" India or Malaysia is a product of institutions creating laws and gathering information, and artifacts supposedly representing individuals. In order for Indian and Malaysian institution-building to reach its citizens, an administrative citizenship must generate a "standardized" citizen who will fit into the categories for delivery of services. As the state delivers more welfare, to efficiently do so requires leveling across the classes and hierarchies prevalent in developing states. Administrative citizenship appears through the breakdown of society into rational, autonomous, and stable individuals. Information allows identification of rights that equalize groups marked for interventions.

Administrative citizenship along the lines described produces outcomes that are at odds with the Marshallian concept of citizenship. Citizenship rights, including rights to welfare, fail to be effective among broad swaths of populations in India and Malaysia. This is not happening at the margins, as in the Global North, where significant but small percentages of the population are denied effective citizenship (see, e.g., Lawrance, Rosenbloom, Rubenstein, and Stevens, this volume). For the majority receiving welfare benefits of some kind, their failed administrative citizenship defines their citizenship more generally. To understand citizenship in most of the world, we have to recognize the limits of administrative citizenship and the multiple failures entailed by its search for inclusiveness through standardization.

In India, the ration card emblematizes and performs a leveling of caste. The ration card identifies the poor by categories, those below the poverty line (BPL) and above the poverty line (APL), among others. However, all poor, regardless of their caste (untouchable or backward), religion (Hindu, Muslim, Christian, Buddhist), or regional differences, were eligible. The scheme sought to bypass the constraints of feudal and hierarchical preferences in poverty alleviation. A ration card was for *all* poor Indians, institutionally identified. Similarly, in Malaysia, leveling norms in welfare required balancing between Malays, Chinese, and Indians, while removing regional disparities between advanced (Selangor) and backward (Sabah) states. Initial antipoverty schemes targeted rural Malay, indigenous Orang Asli, Kadazandusun, and Dayak communities among others institutionally identified. Leveling hierarchies was an old developmentalist goal. Yet generating an administrative match of individuals and official documents for the standard citizen became contested and political. Instituting standard norms and behavior among people located in communities of caste, religion, and regional cultures requires huge welfare capabilities. People had to be dependent on such a state for rights and protections to be socialized into such constitutional equality, a statist equality.

Standardization requires bureaucratic categories, classifications, and paperwork. The more a state seeks to intervene on welfare, the more it seeks to know. The more it knows, the more it can secure. Residents give more and more information to the state, hoping for increasing recognition of their rights and delivery of programs. In short, surveillance and citizenship go together in developing countries. This points to a fundamental impulse in both: What is sought to be standardized? Information about the survival needs of an individual is standardized in exchange for meeting those needs, for example, food delivery, health access, shelters, and electoral and property rights. Only a "standard citizen" can gain these rights, someone whose artifact—the identity card— embodies all the appropriate numerals based on common interdepartmental, interoperable norms with appropriate restrictions to others like him or her. The trifocal interaction over rights among individuals, standardizing institutions, and artifacts creates the standard citizen. Such standardization also requires a fixed territory. So, spatially, these rights have to be available to the standard citizen through institutions and artifacts equally in all corners of the state.

In developing countries, the institutions and artifacts critical to administrative citizenship have expanded immensely. For example, to deliver social rights in India, the Ministry of Food Supplies and Ministry of Health communicate through a range of state artifacts, for example, the ration cards circulating among 500 million individuals (Supreme Court Commissioners 2009, 25). Election procedures also imbue identity artifacts with new meanings. The enhancement of civil rights, the right to elect representatives or be elected, saw the rise of the election commission in India. As its budget expanded, its role in conducting government affairs grew. Its increased number of personnel spread the use and control of electoral rolls and the voter ID across India. Today, all these rights are being ordered into a central database, a national identity number scheme known as Aadhaar. Aadhaar is busy counting Indians. About 560 million Indians are in the database, leaving more than 600 million more to be numbered and tagged (Government of India, Press Information Bureau 2014).

In Malaysia, the identity card was an instrument of order, first issued in British colonial times through the Emergency Ordinance of 1948 and later reintroduced in 1960 when the Federation of Malaya launched the identity card under federal laws and established the National Registration Department (Government of Malaysia, Ministry of Home Affairs 2014). Its latest incarnation—the MyKad—was launched in 2002. This reveals objectives of rights delivery and creating order. It enhances order by compiling biographical information from the national identity card, passport, and driver's license even as it enables delivery of public needs and services—automatic toll road pass ("Touch n Go") and banking (ATM and credit functions), among others (Loo, Yeow, and Chong 2009, 362). Both India and Malaysia rely on a standard citizen constantly emitting information and receiving commands as he or she follows appropriate instructions to participate in democracy and welfare. And yet, the orderly rise of citizenship through welfare ignores specific poor.

Outsiders, Vagrants, and Bastards: Survey Shortfalls and Their Consequences

"From having no nation, I now feel I belong to this country," exclaimed Jeyaraj when he received a national identity card and citizenship in 2007 after living in Malaysia without citizenship for twenty-five years (Ramachandran 2007). Statelessness, a condition one associates with refugees and illegal immigrants, marks the experiences of actual (i.e., de jure) citizens as well. In June 2010, the Malaysian state set up a special task force to tackle statelessness among the Malaysian Indian community. By February 2011, a total of 14,882 Malaysians of Indian descent had submitted appropriate citizenship information in standardized format, while an estimated 10,000 more had collected the forms but not returned them (Government of Malaysia, Prime Minister's Department 2010). This directs us to a puzzle. How can natives of India and Malaysia, born in their respective countries (jus soli), of native parentage (jus sanguinis), live in effective statelessness? What institutional structures lead states not to recognize their citizenship?

Lack of Citizenship by Documents	
Birth certificate	3,546
Identification cards	2,569
Citizenship	7,486
Others	1,281
Total:	14,882

Administrative citizenship can be very exclusionary. In the preceding example, the absence of birth certificates led to the denial of rights to 3,546 native Malaysians. More than 14,000 Malaysian Indians were deprived of their rights, due to the demand for state documents the state itself failed to produce or provide, along the lines of the citizen-as-apologue described by Jacqueline Stevens (this volume). It took the combined efforts of several citizenship institutions to bring locally born Indians into citizenship—Ministry of Home, National Registration Department, a Special Implementation Task Force, and the personal initiative of the prime minister (Government of Malaysia, Prime Minister's

Department 2010)—while the number of those eligible but not provided evidence remains unknowable. The Malaysian task force pointed to several social relationships and practices that did not fit the standardized norms of the state. Both taboo and traditional practices on birth, marriage, health, and death pose a challenge to standardization. States recognize legal and registered marriages only. The birth of a child from a marriage unrecognized and unauthorized by the state produces an illegitimate, outlaw child, disowned socially and also administratively. Birth out of wedlock leads to a child without a birth certificate and citizenship rights because of the "shame" involved. Children of polygamous marriages, of marriages to illegal immigrants, and of marriages across religions that may be socially and politically discouraged have similar fates. Informal marriages produce offspring who first as children and then as adults are unaccepted by the community and unrecognized by the state.

Similarly, a large pool of outsiders (rural-urban migrants), legally pursued as "vagrants" and "beggars," are confounding the Indian state. Physically kept on the margins of rural and urban life, they are analytically swept under broad categories such as homeless, pavement dweller, street child, orphan, and beggar. The census, unable to count and gather information, renders them invisible. More than 40 percent of India's population are children, and yet large surveys and national reports reiterate the low coverage of minors and those who are destitute and thus especially in need of care and protection (Government of India, Ministry of Women and Child Development 2006, 58–59). The failure of the state to notice them means a range of rights formally secured by citizenship are not enjoyed by destitute children, a form of effective statelessness. The large Indian state, legally committed to delivering to the poor for decades, is simply not living up to its formal obligations. For example, nongovernmental organizations (NGOs) estimate the homeless population in Delhi at around 100,000 (Manch and Liye 2011). Such organizations are somewhat more successful than the Indian government in counting the homeless because they conduct their surveys at night as well, when the homeless return to their regular places on the pavement. Unsafe and thus insecure, many hide under blankets to conceal their identities. Counting, identifying, or tagging a biographical profile is difficult.

Homeless women and orphaned children also may not show up in NGO surveys because of their vulnerability at night; they simply vanish into hidden crevices and corners to avoid being sexually and physically battered. In contrast, the state census, confined to regular administrative daylight working hours, chose to ignore such populations. Recognizing the invisibility of such populations is rare among state institutions. So, when the Election Commission of India distributed 7,249 voter IDs to the homeless in Delhi, it was a transformative moment for many, providing respect, dignity, and identity. Julka Khatoon, a homeless recipient, said, "With this identity, we can seek work with dignity" (Pandit 2013).[2]

It took the combined efforts of several state institutions collaborating with state-recognized NGOs to bring many such native-born Indians into citizenship—the Ministry of Home's National Population Register, the Municipal Corporation of Delhi, leading NGOs such as Aashray Adhikar Abhiyan, the Supreme Court of India, the Delhi High Court, the government of Delhi's special task force known as "Mission Convergence," and the personal initiative of the chief minister of Delhi. Only such a convergence of state and social power could begin the process of constituting the homeless as standard citizens.

This collective effort led to a 2010 survey which revealed that 96.7 percent of the homeless possess no Indian identity card, including welfare cards they are eligible for, resulting in deprivation of their right to food grains and health facilities, and even their right to sleep on pavements (Government of Delhi 2010). Lacking toilet facilities, 44.9 percent defecated in the open, and 47.9 percent slept on the pavement (Government of Delhi 2010, 30). The most vulnerable populations are those most in need of state services, yet these individuals are unable to practice their rights due to a lack of appropriate documentation.

Another survey of India's homeless in the national capital of New Delhi found that 71.16 percent of those interviewed did not possess identity cards such as a ration card (for subsidized grains), a voter ID card (to vote in elections), a bank passbook (to open bank accounts or receive financial assistance), or any other type of rights card issued by a government organization (Indo-Global Social Service Society 2012, 100). Without the proper state artifacts, these individuals are unable to claim rights from the state, and they remain hidden from state welfare specifically designed to assist them.

In a recent registration drive targeting these hard-to-reach citizens, Sudhir Prajapat, a homeless man in his forties, received a voter ID and said, "I am often subjected to police brutality. . . . They question my whereabouts during night patrolling. I did not have an identity proof to quell their suspicions about me. But now I can produce my voter ID to prove that I am a resident of Delhi. It justifies my existence" (Sikdar 2013). Born in India (jus soli), of Indian parents (jus sanguinis) but without documents, the homeless and poor like Sudhir are constantly harassed by the police and cannot open bank accounts, vote, or access welfare and rights. Denied citizenship rights, many less fortunate than Sudhir die unidentified. According to data acquired through the Right to Information

Act, the Delhi police had identified 6,800 unclaimed bodies between 2007 and 2011, many of them homeless (Pandit 2012).

Some scholars have tried to explain the exclusions of citizenship through ethnic, caste, racial, and religious prejudices of the state (e.g., Oommen 1997; Nyamnjoh 2006). The Malaysian state dominated by Malay Muslims will exclude Hindus, while the Hindu-dominated Indian state will exclude Muslims and caste minorities. This does not explain the variations and why many but not most Indians live in statelessness. Generalized, ethnicized explanations only skim the surface, diverting us from disaggregating the standardizing impulse of the state, and the exclusions inherent in the process.

Other scholars assert that over time, one's presence on a territory will generate claims of citizenship. However, as Mamdani (2002) points out, long-term immigrants (settlers) are denied citizenship in Africa because of a regional politics of nativity. New arrivals, often immigrants and travelers, cannot instantly claim citizenship. Just as the changing territorial boundaries Rubenstein (this volume) references as changing the citizenship of those whose residence was persistent, for Indians and Chinese immigrants who arrived before the formation of Malaysia, acquiring citizenship can prove elusive or a decades-long process. Fong Chuen Kuen arrived in Malay in 1959, before the formation of Malaysia (*New Straits Times* 2010). After a wait of forty-seven years and six children, he received his citizenship certificate at the age of sixty-one in 2010. Gouri Dasi Malakar came to Malaysia before its formation in 1956 (*New Straits Times* 2011). On receiving her citizenship at the age of eighty, she exclaimed happily, "Finally, I got my citizenship. This has been my country for a long time. With this documentation, it means the country has accepted me. I will be able to die in peace" (*New Straits Times* 2011). One can feel like a native, and spend more than half a century on state territory, and yet without the representation of artifacts and institutions, citizenship is empty.

Time spent in a nation-state may appear to overcome exclusions of administrative citizenship. But we know that *undocumented natives* are commonplace in developing countries (Sadiq 2009). An individual's mere presence or absence on a territory for an extended period of time does not correspond to citizenship. If presence on a territory is cataloged, documented, and recorded in the administrative apparatus, such that information about an individual can be traced, the individual moves closer to citizenship. Residence alone without the recording of proof of identity and location by state institutions renders it meaningless, which is why, despite being eighty years old, Gouri Dasi Malakar was overjoyed to receive her citizenship document.

Arriving before the formation of the state and fitting into preexisting cultures (Indian and Chinese) did not effect citizenship for either Fong Chuen Kuen or Gouri Dasi Malakar. Birth on the territory did not confer citizenship for Sudhir or Jeyaraj. And even being born to citizens did not effect citizenship for Athinagappan Arulappan (Aruna 2011). In India, when Nasreen, a sex worker and migrant to Delhi, was given a state ID at age thirty-four, she said, "I finally have an identity as an Indian. Now I can send my child to school without facing harassment. Life will change; my destiny will change" (Sengupta 2009). For thirty-four years this native of India had lived in statelessness. Like Sudhir and Jeyaraj, a document brought her citizenship. Here we have natives who are meeting the cultural, birth, descent, and temporal criteria of citizenship, and yet they remain stateless. The exclusion that occurs in such a highly regulated regime happens because citizenship is based on rigid artifacts and grids of information. It is based on the exclusions generated by demands for the state-produced paper and plastic the state itself does not disseminate in the first place. Such populations are excluded from the flow of information between artifacts and institutions.

Both the highly regulated Malaysian state and a more diffuse Indian state are unable to cope with the lived reality of their populations. Institutions and artifacts demand stable and regular information that the poor, the homeless, and the mobile do not emit. These individuals neither are beneficiaries of welfare, nor can be regulated. State registrars cannot capture children of illegitimate marriages, mobile individuals, the homeless, the uprooted landless immigrant to cities, the nomad, the runaway, the drug addict, and the vagrant. In each case, their illegitimacy in society, their rootlessness, and their mobility keep them away from the state; their biographical information is not in state records, and their "regular" address is missing. Unable to meet standardized norms, they become stateless in their own state. This shows how dependent populations are on the state for giving individuals their claim to rights. Our cases show that it is very hard to presume citizenship and then demand its recognition. Jus soli (being born on the territory) combined with jus sanguinis (of native parentage) should have been enough to confer citizenship, but without jus charta/tabulae—the state artifact—it was rendered empty.

Citizenship's operationalization here undoes its own theoretical latticework. As a principle, the state recognizes individuals as bearers of rights, yet the state seems to have tied its own hands. The government has laws that, when implemented, result in excluding marginal sections of society from citizenship. The regime of administrative citizenship, enforced through citizenship artifacts, is thus producing an effective statelessness.

As noted in the introduction to this volume, the tension between the expansion of rights and the simultaneous desire for order is the hallmark of a "citizenship in question." Questioning the contours of citizenship (and the exclusionary power that it rests on) reveals citizenship to be an ongoing process made real through state artifacts such as national identity cards. Driven by the desire for a standard citizen, citizenship comes into question precisely when it misses the mark, when the individuals who have complex lives not responsive to the state's information requests fall through the cracks of administrative and legal control.

Our cases reveal that many citizens are deprived of citizenship for long periods of time because legal principles (jus soli, jus sanguinis) are meaningless without the institutions and artifacts in which they are embedded. We now have three categories of citizenship, jus soli, jus sanguinis, and jus charta/tabulae—the artifact, proofs that arise out of the cataloging and archiving of records on individuals. At the very moment liberal societies are expanding rights for de jure citizens, they are creating implicit categories of jus chartae, the laws for what is charted. Those denied recognition by, or wiped off, the legal administrative grid, so to speak, are unknowable to the state. Because administrative citizenship relies on housing status, ancestral origins, or legitimacy status and not de jure criteria, it produces effective statelessness among millions of legal citizens.

NOTES

I thank the Institute of Ethnic Studies (KITA, Universiti Kebangsaan Malaysia, Malaysia) for hosting me as a visiting fellow in 2009 and 2010. Special thanks to Shamsul A. B. (director, KITA) and Denison Jayasooria (senior fellow, KITA) for their encouragement and support.

1. For a related analysis, see Sara Friedman, this volume, in particular her discussion of Taiwanese officials' responses to passports.

2. Original in Hindi: ". . . ab is pehchaan se hum izzat se kaam mang saktey hain." Author's translation.

PART III. LEGISLATURES AND COURT DISPUTES

10. AMERICAN BIRTHRIGHT CITIZENSHIP RULES AND THE EXCLUSION OF "OUTSIDERS" FROM THE POLITICAL COMMUNITY

MARGARET D. STOCK

The United States has recently experienced vigorous and emotional debates over its immigration and citizenship policies, and among these debates, the possibility of changing America's famous "birthright citizenship" rule has been a recurring theme. A proposed statute to redefine American citizenship at birth does so in an attempt to exclude persons perceived as "outsiders"—and yet it would pose significant practical problems for state governments and for residents of the United States and would inherently exclude many "insiders" from citizenship as well. This chapter explains the historical background of this proposal and the hurdles to defining and affirming citizenship that arise from the terms—such as "allegiance"—used in the proposal, and then discusses the potential, unanticipated consequences of changing America's long-standing constitutional birthright citizenship rule. Those unanticipated consequences will include a rise in statelessness, as Polly Price discusses in chapter 1, but they will also inevitably exclude many more people from American citizenship than their proponents understand or anticipate.

The following is an excerpt from a 2012 radio interview:

RUSSELL LEWIS: Barack Obama is a Christian not a Muslim. It's an issue that came up four years ago when he ran for president. And it's not the only topic that made a return appearance last night.

John Gentile of Crossville, Tennessee, still doesn't believe Mr. Obama is allowed to be president because his father was born in Kenya.

JOHN GENTILE: I just don't like the directions that he's headed in, and personally, I don't think he qualifies to be president and a natural born citizen. And the Constitution states that you have to have two parents that were born in the United States. So there's no alternative allegiance by any member of the family.

LEWIS: The Constitution actually doesn't say that . . .

The quotation from a National Public Radio (NPR) reporter's interview with John Gentile, a Tennessee voter, is remarkable in a number of ways, but in the birthright citizenship debate in America, Gentile's statement about the U.S. Constitution reflects a fundamental, underlying truth: many Americans are unfamiliar with the constitutional reality of American citizenship or are reading new meanings into the Constitution's references to "citizen." These new meanings are being debated, discussed, and repackaged as "true" interpretations of the Constitution—at least when necessary to exclude certain persons from participation in the political community. As discussed later in this chapter, some have even sought a new statute—the Interstate Birth Certificate Compact—to correct what they believe is a long-standing incorrect interpretation of a bedrock amendment to the U.S. Constitution.

As Gentile's comments indicate, these new interpretations are not being applied in any principled way—instead, they are nearly always aimed at excluding persons who are perceived as "outsiders" while overlooking similarly situated persons thought to be "insiders." Gentile, for example, excludes Barack Obama from eligibility for the presidency on the basis that his father was born in Kenya. He says nothing, however, about the presidential eligibility of Mitt Romney (whose father was born in Mexico), Ted Cruz (whose father was born in Cuba), or Rick Santorum (whose father was born in Italy). In fact, from the context of the NPR interview, it is clear that Gentile is a Republican voter who plans to vote for a Republican candidate whose father was not born in the United States. Gentile's "principled" reason for excluding Barack Obama from eligibility for the presidency is therefore not principled at all.

Moreover, in the interview excerpted here, Gentile is incorrect about the Constitution: as stated by the journalist in response, the original text of the Constitution says that a person must be a "natural born citizen" to be president of the United States. But the document gives no definition of "natural born citizen," and says nothing about the status of one's parents or the issue of "allegiance." In fact, the original Constitution gives no definition of "citizen" at all—although it refs to a "citizen" or "citizens" some eleven times, and it distinguishes "citizens" from "persons" at several points.

The Historical Record: Exclusion of "Outsiders" from Citizenship

The first U.S. Constitutional definition of "citizen" came, of course, at the end of the Civil War, with the ratification of the Fourteenth Amendment. At the time of the Founding, the new United States encouraged immigration and also encouraged qualified foreigners to become Americans. In 1787, the United States recognized three different ways that a person could obtain American citizenship: First, a person could be born a foreigner and later apply to become a U.S. citizen through the naturalization process; this avenue was governed by Article I, Section 8, of the U.S. Constitution, which established Congress's power to create a "uniform rule of naturalization." Second, following the international law rule, a person might inherit citizenship from his or her citizen parents; this method of obtaining American citizenship—termed the "jus sanguinis," or the citizenship by blood or descent rule—was within Congress's power to legislate and was first recognized in U.S. law when Congress passed the Naturalization Act of 1790, according "natural born citizen" status to the foreign-born children of certain U.S. citizens if the child's father had resided in the United States.[1] Finally, the United States also adopted the British common-law rule of jus soli (law of the soil) for persons born within the territorial jurisdiction of the United States whose parents were subject to U.S. civil and criminal laws. This common-law birthright citizenship rule was most famously described in the New York state court case of *Lynch v. Clarke* (1844), in which Judge Lewis Sandford opined that he could "entertain no doubt, but that by the law of the United States, every person born within the dominions and allegiance of the United States, whatever were the situation of his parents, is a natural born citizen. The entire silence of the constitution in regard to it, furnishes a strong confirmation, not only that the existing law of the states was entirely uniform, but that there was no intention to abrogate or change it."

In 1857, however, in the case of *Scott v. Sandford* (commonly termed the *Dred Scott* case), the U.S. Supreme Court determined, as a matter of constitutional law, that the original political community in America had not consented to the inclusion of Africans or their descendants as full members of the American community.[2] Using its power of judicial review, the Supreme Court reinterpreted the common-law birthright citizenship rule to exclude persons of African descent. According to the majority opinion written by Chief Justice Roger Taney, Africans and their descendants born in America were not included within the common law's concept of birthright citizenship and thus were forever barred from being U.S. citizens. In reaching its decision, the Supreme Court held that mere birth on U.S. soil was not enough to confer U.S. citizenship; one also had to show that the American political community had consented to one's presence. Notably, this is the same argument that modern proponents of a change to the Fourteenth Amendment make, except that they argue that the American political community has not consented to the presence of unauthorized immigrants on American soil, and so their children should not be considered to be U.S. citizens at birth (Eastman 2004).

After the Civil War, the *Dred Scott* decision was explicitly reversed and repudiated by the Fourteenth Amendment's citizenship clause. The ratifiers of the Fourteenth Amendment chose to amend the Constitution so as to ensure that the U.S. Supreme Court would not have the power to decide which people would be U.S. citizens at birth; instead, the birthright citizenship rule would be made into an explicit constitutional right. During debates leading up to passage of the Fourteenth Amendment, there was vigorous discussion over the fact that the citizenship clause would apply to the children of foreigners, even if those foreigners were in the United States in violation of various laws. Senator Edgar Cowan of Pennsylvania, for example, expressed concern that the citizenship clause would expand the number of Chinese and Gypsies in America by granting birthright citizenship to their children, although the parents owed no "allegiance" to the United States and were committing "trespass" by being in the United States (Wydra 2011). Arguing against him, supporters of the citizenship clause defended the right of these children to be U.S. citizens at birth. Both sides in the debate agreed that the clause would extend U.S. birthright citizenship to the children born in the United States to all foreigners who were subject to U.S. civil and criminal laws—thus excluding only the children of foreign diplomats, invading armies, and sovereign Native American tribes.

Following ratification of the Fourteenth Amendment, the U.S. Supreme Court consistently followed this interpretation of the citizenship clause (there was a passing comment in the *Slaughterhouse Cases* [1873] that has caused some to argue otherwise, but *Slaughterhouse* was not a birthright citizenship or immigration case). As conflicts over Asian immigration arose in the western United States in the late 1800s, however, some government officials began to deny the rights of U.S. citizenship to U.S.-born children of Chinese descent. Thus, in 1898, the U.S. Supreme Court had occasion, in the *Wong Kim Ark* decision, to confirm unequivocally that birthright citizenship belonged to any child born within the territorial jurisdiction of the United States, as long as the child—at the time of his or her birth on U.S. soil—was subject to U.S. civil and criminal laws. The Court held that an American-born child of Chinese immi-grants was entitled to citizenship because the "Fourteenth Amendment affirms the ancient and fundamental rule of citizenship by birth within the territory, in the allegiance and under the protection of the country, including all children here born of resident aliens, with the exceptions or qualifications (as old as the rule itself) of children of foreign sovereigns or their ministers, or born on for-eign public ships, or of enemies within and during a hostile occupation of part of our territory, and with the single additional exception of children of mem-bers of the Indian tribes owing direct allegiance to their several tribes." The dis-senting view—which is the view espoused by modern proponents of a change to the citizenship clause—was resoundingly rejected by the Court's majority.

The net result, then, was that following passage of the Fourteenth Amend-ment, the U.S. government recognized all nondiplomatic persons born within the territorial jurisdiction to be Americans, regardless of the status of their par-ents. Congress also passed a number of statutes recognizing the extension of birthright citizenship to persons born within newly acquired U.S. territories, in-cluding Alaska, Hawaii, Guam, Puerto Rico, and the U.S. Virgin Islands. More recently, in the case of *Plyler v. Doe* (1982), the U.S. Supreme Court confirmed this view in an explicit statement that the Fourteenth Amendment extends to anyone "who is subject to the laws of a state," including the U.S.-born children of unauthorized immigrants. Similarly, in the case of *INS v. Rios-Pineda* (1985), the Court stated that a child born on U.S. soil to an unauthorized immigrant parent is a U.S. citizen from birth.

For modern-day proponents of a change to the meaning of the Fourteenth Amendment, however, the gloss of history appears to be irrelevant. They sug-gest that a change to the meaning of the Fourteenth Amendment should be made and can be made quite easily (Eastman 2004). First, some have argued that the U.S. Supreme Court can change the citizenship clause by reversing or reinterpreting its decision in the *Wong Kim Ark* case that all children born in the United States are U.S. citizens at birth unless they are immune from U.S. civil and criminal laws—such as the children of diplomats or children born in cer-tain sovereign Native American tribes. It is possible that a modern Supreme Court could reverse this decision and instead adopt the opinion of the *Wong Kim Ark* dissenting justices, reinstating the discredited theory of "consent" that resulted in the *Dred Scott* decision. But this is not likely to happen. The Court has had the opportunity to do so, as recently as 2006, and declined to take up the invitation. In an amicus brief filed with the U.S. Supreme Court in the *Yaser Hamdi* case, Professor John Eastman of Chapman University School of Law argued that a change in the Supreme Court's interpretation of "subject to the jurisdiction" language of the citizenship clause could retroactively take away the U.S. citizenship of Yaser Hamdi, a U.S.-born citizen who was captured fighting against American forces on the battlefield in Afghanistan; Eastman (2004) argued that the Court could punish Hamdi by reinterpreting the citizenship clause to take away Hamdi's birthright citizenship because Hamdi was born in the United States to parents who held temporary work visas at the time of his birth. Eastman's proposed new interpretation, however, if it had been adopted by the U.S. Supreme Court, would have taken away not only the U.S. citizenship of Yaser Hamdi but also the citizenship of millions of other Americans born under similar circumstances (including some of the U.S. military personnel who captured Hamdi). Unsurprisingly, the U.S. Supreme Court ignored Eastman's invitation.

In the *Hamdi* case, Eastman urged a new U.S. Supreme Court interpretation as a means of changing the citizenship clause, but others have urged congressional and state legislative approaches instead. Some have proposed congressional legislation, and some have introduced state legislation to bring back the concept of "state citizenship" so as to create a two-tier system that would deny U.S. citizenship to some babies born in the United States. Others have suggested a constitutional amendment for this purpose.

In line with the first approach, some have argued that changing the citizenship clause requires no constitutional amendment. Congress can change the Fourteenth Amendment's meaning by passing a statute that "clarifies" that "subject to the jurisdiction" means "subject to the complete or full jurisdiction." They point to Section 5 of the Fourteenth Amendment: "The Congress shall have power to enforce, by appropriate legislation, the provisions of this article." It is unlikely, however, that Congress can use its Section 5 power to reinterpret the meaning of the citizenship clause, any more than Congress can use its Article I, Section 1, powers to "reinterpret" the First or Second Amendment. Section 5 of the Fourteenth Amendment merely answers critics of the draft Fourteenth Amendment who said that the original text of the Constitution contained no language giving Congress any enumerated power to enforce the Fourteenth Amendment; Section 5 was not a grant of legislative power to change the meaning of the amendment. Section 5 also allows Congress to define the geographic jurisdiction of the United States, thereby allowing the Fourteenth Amendment to apply in acquired states and territories; it does not allow Congress to limit the application of the Fourteenth Amendment by changing the plain meaning of the text. Furthermore, Congress has already acted to enforce the citizenship clause by enacting numerous statutes reaffirming the "traditional" meaning of the clause.[3] Even if it were possible to legislate a "new interpretation" of a constitutional amendment, these existing statutes would have to be repealed before any new "interpretation" could take effect.

Attempts at such a reinterpretation are aimed at depriving newborns of U.S. citizenship if their parents do not hold certain specified lawful immigration statuses. The theory is that those parents are not subject to the "complete" jurisdiction of the United States because they hold allegiance to a foreign country. Representative Steve King (R-IA) and Senator David Vitter (R-LA) have repeatedly introduced legislation to "reinterpret" the Fourteenth Amendment in a way that would exclude more people born in the United States from American citizenship. The latest version of their proposal, the Birthright Citizenship Act of 2015, would restrict citizenship under the citizenship clause to a child at least one of whose parents is a citizen, is a lawful permanent resident, or is on active duty in the armed forces. It is unclear what effect, if any, the courts would give such a statutory reinterpretation of the Fourteenth Amendment, but if enacted, the law would immediately throw into confusion the citizenship of thousands of babies.

State Legislators for Legal Immigration (SLLI), a coalition of immigration restrictionist legislators from forty states, has proposed state legislation that would resurrect the notion of state citizenship and restrict it so as to create a two-tier caste system. The plan relies on the fact that states are the entities that issue birth certificates. Although its proposal has not yet been enacted in any state, the SLLI suggests an interstate compact strategy under which states would agree to "make a distinction in the birth certificates" of native-born persons so that Fourteenth Amendment citizenship would be denied to children born to parents who owe allegiance to any foreign sovereignty. The interstate compact would be subject to the consent of Congress under Article I, Section 10, of the Constitution. This approach would change the meaning of the citizenship clause without having to secure the approval of the president or a veto override. A significant problem with this approach—which would be expensive to implement—is it cannot obligate the U.S. State Department to recognize distinctions in the birth certificates. Some state constitutions also prohibit such discriminatory state legislation.

Assume for the sake of argument that one believes that the Fourteenth Amendment has been erroneously applied for more than a hundred years. Under the changes sought by modern-day revisionists, who would be excluded from American citizenship? What groups are targeted by modern revisionists for exclusion from the modern American political community? From the news accounts of the debate, one would think that the targeted groups include the children of "birth tourists" (Gonzalez 2011) or the children of unauthorized immigrants. In fact, however, the changes proposed to the Fourteenth

Amendment would exclude extremely large numbers of Americans—including several past U.S. presidents and many leading modern American politicians.

Why is this so? This wide-ranging exclusion of large numbers of Americans comes about because those who call for changes to the meaning of the Fourteenth Amendment's citizenship clause focus on the language "subject to the jurisdiction" and attempt to read it broadly to exclude the children of persons who (1) have no permanent immigration status in the United States or (2) hold "allegiance" to countries other than the United States (Eastman 2004). This group potentially includes millions of Americans, including several prominent American politicians who have run for or are currently running for the office of president of the United States.

If one looks up the term "allegiance" in *Black's Law Dictionary*, one finds more than five definitions. The term is defined first as "[a] citizen's obligation of fidelity and obedience to the government or sovereign in return for the benefits of the protection of the state." The definition then states, "Allegiance may be either an absolute and permanent obligation or a qualified and temporary one" (*Black's Law Dictionary* 1999). Black's then lists five types of allegiance: (1) "acquired allegiance," defined as "the allegiance owed by a naturalized citizen"; (2) "actual allegiance," defined as "the obedience owed by one who resides temporarily in a foreign country to that country's government. Foreign sovereigns, their representatives, and military personnel are typically excepted from this requirement"; (3) "natural allegiance," defined as "the allegiance that native-born citizens or subjects owe to their nation"; (4) "permanent allegiance," defined as "the lasting allegiance owed to a state by citizens or subjects"; and (5) "temporary allegiance," defined as "the impermanent allegiance owed to a state by a resident alien during the period of residence." Those who write and speak about "allegiance" as a requirement of Fourteenth Amendment citizenship do not typically indicate which type of allegiance they mean.[4] Furthermore, *Black's Law Dictionary* says nothing about allegiance requiring lawful residence in its second or last definition, both of which could apply to unauthorized immigrants—and if an unauthorized immigrant owes "allegiance" to the United States, then under some proposed changes to the Fourteenth Amendment's meaning, the immigrant's children could be U.S. citizens.

The problems in changing the Fourteenth Amendment's meaning by invoking the concept of "allegiance" are clear if one examines a model Interstate Birth Certificate Compact that was drafted and proposed by the Immigration Reform Law Institute (IRLI; State Legislators for Legal Immigration 2011). The institute's proposed "model" state law and Interstate Birth Certificate Compact read as follows:

Bill

(a) A person is a citizen of the state of [insert name of state] if:

    (1) the person is born in the United States and subject to the jurisdiction thereof, and

    (2) the person is a resident of the state of [insert name of state], as defined by [state code § xyz],

(b) For the purposes of this statute, subject to the jurisdiction of the United States has the meaning that it bears in Section 1 of the Fourteenth Amendment to the United States Constitution, namely that *the person is a child of at least one parent who owes no allegiance to any foreign sovereignty*, or a child without citizenship or nationality in any foreign country. For the purposes of this statute, *a person who owes no allegiance to any foreign sovereignty is a United States citizen or national, or an immigrant accorded the privilege of residing permanently in the United States, or a person without citizenship or nationality in any foreign country.*

(c) In addition to the criteria of citizenship described under sections (a) and (b), a person is a citizen of the state of [insert name of the state] if:

    (1) the person is naturalized in the United States, and

    (2) the person is a resident of the state of [insert the name of the state], as defined by [state code § xyz],

(d) Citizenship of the state of [insert name of the state] shall not confer upon the holder thereof any right, privilege, immunity, or benefit under law.

State Compact

(a) The signatories to this compact shall make a distinction in the birth certificates, certifications of live birth, or other birth records issued in the signatory states, between persons born in the signatory state who are born subject to the jurisdiction of the United States and persons who are not born subject to the jurisdiction of the United States. Persons born subject to the jurisdiction of the United States shall be designated as natural-born United States Citizens.

(b) Subject to the jurisdiction of the United States has the meaning that it bears in Section 1 of the Fourteenth Amendment to the United States Constitution, namely that the person is a child of at least one parent who owes no allegiance to any foreign sovereignty, or a child without citizenship or nationality in any foreign country. For the purposes of this compact, a person who owes no allegiance to any foreign sovereignty is a United States citizen or national, or an immigrant accorded the privilege of residing permanently in the United States, or a person without citizenship or nationality in any foreign country.

(c) This compact shall not take effect until Congress has given its consent, pursuant to Article I, Section 10, Clause 3 of the United States Constitution.

The IRLI is an organization affiliated with Kansas secretary of state Kris W. Kobach (State Legislators for Legal Immigration 2011),[5] a prominent immigration restrictionist. The IRLI also identifies itself as a "supporting organization" of the Federation for American Immigration Reform (2012), and has had a hand in much of the immigration restrictionist state and local legislation that has been enacted in recent years. Its lawyers, however, have little apparent practical experience with immigration and citizenship laws. Drafting flaws mean the measure will have unintended consequences and not accomplish its purported purpose—to stop the children of unauthorized immigrants from being recognized as U.S. citizens at birth.

The model Interstate Birth Certificate Compact uses the phrase "subject to the jurisdiction," language that appears in the Fourteenth Amendment's citizenship clause. As discussed earlier, the language "subject to the jurisdiction" has long been understood by the U.S. Supreme Court and the executive branch of the federal government to refer to persons who are subject to U.S. civil and criminal law, excluding only those persons who are immune from U.S. civil and criminal law, such as immunized diplomats, invading foreign armies, and members of sovereign Indian tribes. Yet the proposed compact seeks to alter that language to mean that "the person is a child of at least one parent who *owes no allegiance* to any foreign sovereignty, or a child without citizenship or nationality in any foreign country."

The model bill provides that signatory states will create a system for issuing two types of birth certificates, requiring signatory states to set up new procedures. One type of certificate, which will demonstrate citizenship in the state, may be issued only to newborns who meet certain strict requirements. Interestingly, the model legislation says nothing about whether a parent is an unauthorized immigrant. Instead, under the compact, to be a citizen of the state at birth, a baby must (1) have at least one parent "who owes no allegiance to any foreign sovereignty" or (2) has no "citizenship or nationality in any foreign country." The child of an unauthorized immigrant can easily fall within these two definitions. An unauthorized immigrant might have renounced his or her foreign citizenship, or may have lost it through some expatriating act, which might include a long absence from the country of citizenship.[6] An unauthorized immigrant may have taken an oath of allegiance to the United States upon being drafted or enlisting in the U.S. military.[7] Such an unauthorized immigrant could fall within the definition of a parent "who owes no allegiance to any foreign sovereignty."

An unauthorized immigrant could also take steps to ensure that his or her child has no "citizenship or nationality in any foreign country." Thus, a parent could intentionally fail to file the necessary paperwork with a foreign government to seek formal recognition of a U.S.-born child's foreign citizenship; if the parent failed to do so, the child would be a child without "citizenship or nationality in any foreign country."

The model bill then goes on to say that "for the purposes of this statute, a person who owes no allegiance to any foreign sovereignty is a United States citizen or national, or an immigrant accorded the privilege of residing permanently in the United States, or a person without citizenship or nationality in any foreign country." This language may be meant to allow dual citizens to be included within the law's ambit, but this section also uses the word "allegiance"—again undefined. In addition, this section includes unauthorized immigrants who are stateless. Moreover, this bill references immigrants "accorded the privilege of residing permanently in the United States," a phrase that is also undefined.[8] If the drafters meant this language to include only lawful permanent residents, then they have failed to recognize that lawful permanent residents do not owe "permanent allegiance" to the United States; instead, they owe permanent allegiance to their foreign country of citizenship, unless or until they renounce or lose that foreign citizenship through expatriation. Moreover, a lawful permanent resident typically performs no "oath of allegiance" to the United States until he or she naturalizes as a U.S. citizen.

The language of the model bill and compact also fails to explain whether dual citizens of the United States and other countries are deemed to fall within the compact's parameters; such dual citizens hold allegiance to both the United States and the foreign country in which they hold dual citizenship or nationality.[9] They cannot be said to hold "no allegiance" to a foreign country.

To illustrate the complexity and confusion that will result from attempts to apply the compact's "allegiance" rule, it is helpful to consider a famous example, Willard Mitt Romney. Mitt Romney was born in Michigan in 1947 (Reitwiesner 2012). Mitt's mother, Lenore, was a birthright U.S. citizen who was born in Utah, but she likely also held British citizenship because her father was born in England;[10] there is no evidence that she or her father ever renounced British citizenship.[11] Mitt's father, George Romney, was born in

Mexico in 1907.[12] He apparently was a birthright Mexican citizen.[13] In addition, he was a "derivative" foreign-born U.S. citizen under U.S. citizenship statutes in effect at the time of his birth.[14]

At the time of Mitt's birth, the Fourteenth Amendment's current interpretation regarding birthright citizenship was in effect, so Mitt's parents merely registered the fact of Mitt's birth in the state of Michigan, and Mitt was issued a standard Michigan birth certificate, making him a "natural born citizen" of the United States.[15] Had the proposed state compact been in effect at the time, however, Michigan would not have issued a birth certificate to Mitt without inquiring as to his parents' "allegiance" to any foreign country and his parents' citizenship. Both of his parents were likely dual citizens of the United States and other countries—Mitt's mother was apparently a dual citizen of Britain and the United States, and his father was a dual citizen of Mexico and the United States[16]—so Mitt Romney might have been unable to qualify as a state citizen under the first prong of the interstate compact as a child who has at least one parent "who owes no allegiance to any foreign sovereignty," if both of his parents "owed allegiance" to foreign countries. If Mitt could not pass the first prong of the test, the state of Michigan would have to look to the second clause of the compact, which would require his parents to show that Mitt would have no "citizenship or nationality in any foreign country."

Here, of course, the state would be presented with a complicated legal and factual dilemma: if George Romney, having been born in Mexico, chose to seek a certificate of Mexican nationality for his son Mitt, then Mexican law would allow him to obtain such a certificate because Mexican law has long granted Mexican nationality to the U.S.-born children of Mexican men who were born in Mexico (Gutierrez 1997; U.S. Office of Personnel Management 2001). But what if George Romney chose not to bother to claim Mexican nationality for his newborn son? Would the state of Michigan have the expertise to determine—based on reading Mexican law books or hiring a Mexican lawyer—that Mitt actually held Mexican nationality? Would the state simply take George Romney's word for it that his son held no "citizenship or nationality in any foreign country"? Would the state ask Mexico for its opinion on the matter? Would the state hire an expert lawyer to make the determination about the baby's eligibility for citizenship in Michigan? What if the foreign country changed its laws over time and made them retroactive—would the state readjudicate the issuance of a certain type of birth certificate when the foreign law changed, or would a child's status be frozen at the moment of birth? The state would presumably have to answer these questions before determining what type of birth certificate to issue to the newborn baby under the terms of the proposed interstate compact.

The preceding example illustrates that interpreting and implementing changes to the Fourteenth Amendment's citizenship clause would be quite cumbersome. Even implementing complex new bureaucratic rules is costly (Stock 2012). At a minimum, a state attempting to apply the new rules would have to add more questions to its questionnaire for issuing birth certificates and presumably would have to ascertain the truth of the answers to those questions and their legal significance. The state would have to determine whether it would rely on parents' representations about their citizenship and nationality, or whether the state's birth registry officials would be required to verify a child's status with foreign law sources or experts. The state would have to determine what to do if the parents' claims were false or doubtful. If parents refused to apply for proof of a foreign citizenship or nationality for their U.S.-born offspring, would the state categorize the child as a person with no citizenship or nationality in any foreign country? What if a parent, upon learning of the state's rules, chose to renounce a foreign citizenship or failed to file papers by a foreign law deadline so as to render the newborn stateless? The decision to claim state citizenship could be controlled by the parents' choice—and unauthorized immigrant parents could ensure American citizenship for a child merely by failing to register the child's birth with the appropriate foreign country or renouncing their own or their child's foreign citizenship.

The drafters of the model Interstate Birth Certificate Compact were apparently unaware that citizenship and nationality in a particular foreign country are a matter controlled by that country's domestic law and not by international law or the laws of the United States. Because the drafters failed to understand this basic principle, their Interstate Birth Certificate Compact cedes authority to foreign governments to determine who will be a state citizen. If a foreign country passes a law stating that U.S.-born children of its nationals are not citizens of that foreign country, then under the interstate compact, the foreign country could guarantee that those children could claim state citizenship in the United States because the children would be legally stateless. Mexico, for example, could ensure Mitt Romney's Michigan state citizenship—under the example given earlier—simply by changing its nationality laws so that a Michigan-born child of a male Mexican citizen would not be considered a Mexican national. Mexico could also "have it both ways" by passing a law allowing a child like Mitt Romney to claim Mexican citizenship when he reaches the age of majority or at some other convenient point after his birth.

The plain language of the interstate compact allows foreign governments to decide who will or who will not be a state citizen of the United States. The compact thus allows foreign governments to deprive thousands of U.S.-born children of state citizenship simply by passing laws granting those children citizenship or nationality in those foreign countries. Conversely, the compact also allows foreign countries to force states to grant state citizenship to U.S.-born children of foreign country nationals; the foreign country can ensure this result simply by enacting laws depriving U.S.-born children of citizenship in those foreign countries. To a large extent, then, the state compact cedes state citizenship determinations to foreign countries—and, in doing so, does little to achieve its desired purpose of denying citizenship to the children of unauthorized immigrants. In fact, the compact likely denies state citizenship only to children whose parents—both citizen and noncitizen, authorized and unauthorized—are inclined (or perhaps foolish enough) to apply for foreign citizenship documents for their children.

Moreover, unless the federal government joined in the interstate compact, the compact would not be binding on the executive branch of the federal government. Bound by the Supreme Court and executive branch understandings of the citizenship clause, the U.S. Department of State would not recognize any distinction in the birth certificates. A U.S.-born child who is given a "lesser" birth certificate could use that birth certificate to obtain a U.S. passport. Armed with federally issued presumptive proof of citizenship in the United States, the child could then turn around and demand a new birth certificate; if one is not granted, the child could sue the state for discrimination. Under federal law, the child would also have a cause of action for declaratory relief and could also seek damages against the state for the state's discriminatory treatment and failure to recognize the child's citizenship.

Some state constitutions also prohibit state legislation that discriminates on the basis of citizenship. Accordingly, a state may find that its enactment of the Interstate Birth Certificate Compact is unconstitutional under its own state constitution. Arizona may be one such state.[17]

Arizona legislators failed to pass the proposed Interstate Birth Certificate Compact, and for now, the question is moot. In early 2011, Arizona state senator Russell Pearce and nine other Arizona state senators introduced Senate Bill 1308, the Arizona Interstate Birth Certificate Compact. This bill adopted the main language of the model interstate compact that appears earlier in this chapter; it also added some further provisions, such as a "Findings and Declaration of Policy" section that states, "It is the purpose of this Compact through the joint and cooperative action among the party states to make a distinction in the birth certificates, certifications of live birth or other birth records issued in the party states between a person born in the party state who is born subject to the jurisdiction of the United States and a person who is not born subject to the jurisdiction of the United States. A person who is born subject to the jurisdiction of the United

States is a natural born United States citizen."[18] The bill made it out of committee on a vote of eight to five but then failed to pass in the Arizona Senate; it has not been resurrected (Arizona Legislature 2011; *AZ Central* 2011).

During testimony about the bill and its proposed effects, it became clear that the Arizona proponents of the bill did not understand their own proposal: "'I want to know what allegiance means,'" said Republican representative Adam Driggs of Phoenix, Arizona, a conservative Republican who "expressed skepticism about how the proposal would be carried out by state government" (ABC15 .com 2011). Similar bills were introduced in 2011 in Indiana, Mississippi, Texas, Oklahoma, and South Dakota, but after Arizona failed to pass its bill, no other state passed one.

Unprincipled Principles of "Allegiance"

Perhaps the most startling aspect of the modern calls to change the meaning of the Fourteenth Amendment's citizenship clause is the large number of persons who potentially would be affected by such a change. Presumably, any such change would not be retroactive, but many modern proponents of a change have argued that the change should be retroactive because the Fourteenth Amendment has been "misinterpreted" for more than a hundred years, and their new, revisionist interpretation is the correct one (Eastman 2004).

Take, for example, the arguments made by Professor John Eastman in the amicus brief discussed earlier in this chapter. In that case, Eastman argued that under the Fourteenth Amendment, "mere birth on U.S. soil was insufficient to confer citizenship as a matter of constitutional right. Rather, birth, together with being a person subject to the complete and exclusive jurisdiction of the United States (i.e., not owing allegiance to another sovereign) was the constitutional mandate, a floor for citizenship below which Congress cannot go in the exercise of its Article I power over naturalization." Eastman's argument was obviously intended to create a retroactive change. He filed the amicus brief for the purpose of arguing that Yasser Hamdi, an American born in Louisiana in 1980, should not be recognized as a U.S. citizen, his current status as such notwithstanding, because Hamdi's parents were in the United States temporarily on work visas when Hamdi was born.

Eastman has stated on many occasions that his interest in the case was driven by the fact that Hamdi was a member of a group fighting against the United States in Afghanistan; Eastman felt that the benefits of birthright U.S. citizenship should not be accorded to someone whose parents were on temporary work visas at the time of his birth, and who later turned out to be a terrorist.

TABLE 10.1. Prominent U.S. Politicians with "Allegiance" Issues

Name	Political Party	Birthplace and Date of Birth	Citizenship/Parentage	Outcome under New Fourteenth Amendment Rules Requiring "Allegiance" Solely to the United States
Chester Arthur	Republican	Fairfield, Vermont, USA, October 5, 1829 [Disputed]	Father was Irish and/or Canadian; Chester Arthur himself may have been born in Canada*	Owed allegiance to Ireland, Canada, United Kingdom
John F. Kennedy	Democrat	Brookline, Massachusetts, USA, May 29, 1917	Dual American-Irish citizen (Irish law grants Irish citizenship to persons with at least one Irish-born grandparent)	Owed "allegiance" to Ireland
Donald John Trump	Republican	New York, New York, USA, June 14, 1946	Father was dual citizen of Germany and the United States, mother was dual citizen of the United States and the United Kingdom	Parents owed "allegiance" to Germany and to the United Kingdom
Willard "Mitt" Romney	Republican	Detroit, Michigan, USA, March 12, 1947	Father was born in Mexico; mother was British American	Parents owe "allegiance" to Mexico, United Kingdom
Richard "Rick" Santorum	Republican	Winchester, Virginia, USA, May 10, 1958	Father was born in Italy	Father owed "allegiance" to Italy
Robert Menendez	Democrat	New York, New York, USA, January 1, 1954	Parents both held Cuban citizenship at the time of his birth	Parents both owed "allegiance" to Cuba

* The exact location of Chester Arthur's birth is disputed. According to John Curran (2009), "Nearly 123 years after his death, doubts about his US citizenship linger, thanks to lack of documentation and a political foe's assertion that Arthur was really born in Canada—and was therefore ineligible for the White House, where he served from 1881 to 1885."

Name	Political Party	Birthplace and Date of Birth	Citizenship/Parentage	Outcome under New Fourteenth Amendment Rules Requiring "Allegiance" Solely to the United States
Barack Obama	Democrat	Honolulu, Hawaii, USA, August 4, 1961	Father was born in Kenya and held student visa status in the United States when Barack Obama was born	Father owed "allegiance" to the United Kingdom and/ or Kenya
Marco Antonio Rubio	Republican	Miami, Florida, USA, May 28, 1971	Parents were both Cuban citizens at the time of his birth; they naturalized as U.S. citizens in 1975	Parents owed "allegiance" to Cuba; also, under Cuban law, Rubio himself "owes allegiance" to Cuba
Piyush "Bobby" Jindal	Republican	June 10, 1971, Baton Rouge, Louisiana, USA	Parents were both Indian citizens at the time of his birth	Parents owed "allegiance" to India
Nimrata Nikki Haley	Republican	Bamberg, South Carolina, USA, January 20, 1972	Parents were both Indian citizens at the time of her birth	Parents owed "allegiance" to India
Ludmya "Mia" Bourdeau Love	Republican	Brooklyn, New York, USA, December 6, 1975	Parents were both Haitian citizens who were in the United States in tourist status or as tourist visa overstays at the time of her birth	Parents owed "allegiance" to Haiti

But Eastman has not felt compelled to challenge the eligibility for high office of other persons whose parents were also in the United States on temporary visas at the time of their birth. He has not challenged, for example, the eligibility for high office of Republican candidate Mia Love of Utah, whose Haitian parents were in the United States in tourist status (or perhaps as unauthorized immigrants) at the time of her birth (Anderson 2012). Nor has he challenged the eligibility of Bobby Jindal to be governor of Louisiana or run for president of the United States, although Jindal's parents owed "allegiance" to India at the time of Jindal's birth.

For the sake of exploring Eastman's arguments, however, let us look at a number of U.S. politicians from the post–Fourteenth Amendment period and consider how they would fare under Eastman's interpretation of the Fourteenth Amendment and the modern-day demand that U.S. birthright citizenship be conferred only on persons whose parents do not owe "allegiance" to another sovereign. Table 10.1 lists the names, party affiliations, birthplaces, and parental citizenship status of the named politicians, along with an analysis of the "outcome" under Eastman's citizenship rules. As one can see from the table, all ten of these politicians would be excluded from complete membership in the American political community: under the new interpretation of the Fourteenth Amendment that Eastman espouses, none of these famous politicians would be U.S. citizens at birth. Some of them would also end up becoming stateless and deportable if the Fourteenth Amendment were reinterpreted in the way that Eastman urges.

In all the literature written by proponents of a "new interpretation" of the Fourteenth Amendment, the authors have used only examples of those whose politics they oppose and have not explained how their interpretation would apply to groups whom they disfavor, while not being applied to groups whom they favor. Eastman has never explained how his "allegiance" rule would be applied to Hamdi but not to Nikki Haley, Bobby Jindal, Mia Love, or Marco Rubio or to past presidents.

Proponents of a change to the American birthright citizenship rule fail to explain how their new interpretation or new rule would be implemented, and they never admit what should be obvious at this point: their new proposed rule would likely exclude more "insiders" than "outsiders" from American citizenship. The rule would not be easy to implement and would have unanticipated side effects. Of course, their proposals have not made much headway, which may underscore a fundamental theme of this volume: there is value in rules that make it relatively easy to identify the citizens of one's country, and Americans may fundamentally value a simple, more inclusive rule more than a complex, less inclusive one.

Postscript: The 2012 Egyptian Elections

As Alfred Babo explains in chapter 11, Americans have not been alone in contemplating changes to their constitutional citizenship definitions to exclude certain perceived outsiders from full participation in the political community. The Egyptian Constitution, due to recent amendment, now apparently requires that all presidential candidates—and their parents and spouses—hold only Egyptian citizenship (Fadel 2012). The new amendment had been intended to exclude Mohamed ElBaradei, the famous diplomat and Egyptian Nobel laureate, from running for the Egyptian presidency. However, the media reported that this constitutional amendment had inadvertently snared ultraconservative Egyptian politician Hazem Abu Ismail, who then faced controversy over his eligibility for the Egyptian presidency because his mother had naturalized as a U.S. citizen. Like Americans seeking to change the Fourteenth Amendment to exclude certain disfavored groups, Egyptians who supported the Egyptian constitutional amendment suddenly discovered that the constitutional citizenship exclusion net had caught many more Egyptians than originally intended.

NOTES

1. The Naturalization Act of 1790 (March 26, 1790) stated: "And the children of citizens of the United States, that may be born beyond sea, or out of the limits of the United States, shall be considered as natural born citizens: Provided, That the right of citizenship shall not descend to persons whose fathers have never been resident in the United States."

2. The U.S. Supreme Court was wrong on this point—several states had recognized persons of African descent as citizens. Abraham Lincoln famously criticized Chief Justice Taney's underlying assumptions: "Chief Justice Taney, in delivering the opinion of the majority of the Court, insists at great length that Negroes were no part of the people who made, or for whom was made, the Declaration of Independence, or the Constitution of the United States. [In several of the original States], free Negroes were voters, and, in proportion to their numbers, had the same part in making the Constitution that the white people had" (Basler 1953, 403).

3. See, for example, 8 USC 1401 ("a person born in the United States, and subject to the jurisdiction thereof" is a United States citizen); 8 USC 1402 ("All persons born in Puerto Rico on or after January 13, 1941, and subject to the jurisdiction of the United States, are citizens of the United States at birth").

4. For example, in the quoted passage at the beginning of this chapter, Tennessee voter John Gentile mentions his belief that Barack Obama's parents were required to have "allegiance" to the United States, and this apparent failure of both Obama parents to hold "allegiance" to the United States is, Gentile believes, a fatal flaw in Obama's presidential eligibility.

5. Kris W. Kobach is of counsel to the IRLI (Immigration Reform Law Institute 2012).

6. For example, a person who is Argentinian might lose Argentinian citizenship by accepting "employment or honors from a foreign government without permission"; an Armenian citizen can lose Armenian citizenship merely by living abroad for seven years and failing to register at the Armenian consulate; a Paraguayan can lose citizenship for an "unjustified absence from the country for more than three years" (U.S. Office of Personnel Management 2001, 19).

7. Unauthorized male immigrants are required to register for Selective Service and may be drafted into the U.S. armed forces, if there is a draft (Stock 2009). Everyone who enlists in or is commissioned into the U.S. military takes an oath of allegiance to the U.S. Constitution. Although unauthorized immigrants are currently not permitted to enlist voluntarily in the U.S. military, some Republican lawmakers have suggested that they should be permitted to do so (Cornyn 2011). Some unauthorized immigrants have also managed to enlist, against service policies, and have taken the oath of allegiance as a result (Jordan 2011).

8. The drafters may have meant this phrase to refer to lawful permanent residents, or they may have meant to include persons whom immigration lawyers commonly call "PRUCOL"—persons "permanently residing under color of law." Many of these persons are unauthorized immigrants (New York Department of Health 2004).

9. The U.S. Supreme Court has stated that dual citizenship is "a status long recognized in the law" and that "a person may have and exercise rights of nationality in two countries and be subject to the responsibilities of both. The mere fact that he asserts the rights of one citizenship does not without more mean that he renounces the other" (*Kawakita v. United States*, 343 U.S. 717, 723–24 (1952)). U.S. law also does not require U.S. citizens who are born with dual citizenship or acquire another citizenship after birth to choose one or the other when they reach adulthood. See *Mandeli v. Acheson*, 344 U.S. 133 (1952); *Kennedy v. Mendoza-Martinez*, 372 U.S. 144 (1963) (discussing the case of a dual Mexican-American citizen who was obligated to obey U.S. military draft laws).

10. Britain, like many countries, has long accorded citizenship to children born overseas to birthright British citizens. See U.S. Office of Personnel Management 2001, 209.

11. Naturalization as a U.S. citizen is not an act that causes a person to lose British citizenship under long-standing British law. It is not clear that Lenore Romney's father ever naturalized as a U.S. citizen, but even if he did, the British government would have considered him a British citizen unless he completed the formal process to renounce his British citizenship—and his renunciation was approved by the government of the United Kingdom.

12. According to Rosenbaum (1995), "George Wilcken Romney was born in 1907 in a Mormon colony in Chihuahua, Mexico. His parents were American citizens and monogamists, but they had moved to Mexico along with many other Mormons when Congress outlawed polygamy in the 1800's."

13. Mexico had birthright citizenship at the time of George Romney's birth, according to historical records, and accorded birthright citizenship to the Mexican-born children of Mormon settlers in Mexico. Mexico also allowed U.S.-born Mormon settlers to naturalize as Mexican citizens. Some did not, which allowed their Mexican-born sons to avoid Mexican military service (Romney 1938, 233). ("I remembered with a deep sense of gratitude to my father's memory that he refused to become citizenized lest revolution should again raise its head and his sons would be conscripted to fight side by side with

the down-trodden peon"; Romney 1938, 236, describing how Mexican-born Mormon men were Mexican citizens under Mexican law.) Many Romney cousins who remain in Mexico today hold dual U.S. and Mexican citizenship (Miroff 2011). "Many are eligible to cast absentee ballots in U.S. elections, having acquired U.S. citizenship through their parents" (MSNBC 2012).

14. George Romney's father, Gaskell (Mitt Romney's grandfather), had been born in the United States in 1871, but Gaskell Romney left the United States as a teenager in 1885; he accompanied a large group of Mormons who planned to settle in Mexico to avoid prosecution by federal authorities for polygamy (Romney 1938, 51). Gaskell Romney lived in Mexico with an intent to remain permanently and married Anna Amelia Pratt in Mexico in 1895; she was a birthright U.S. citizen due to her birth in Utah in 1876. During the Mexican Revolution, the couple fled back to the United States in 1912, taking five-year-old George with them. At the time of his birth, George Romney would have derived U.S. citizenship automatically from his father if the family had been able to prove that Gaskell Romney had resided in the United States prior to George's birth (Levy and Roth 2011). No one checked the Romneys' citizenship papers at the border when they returned to the United States, but George Romney's claim to American citizenship went unchallenged. The law of derivative U.S. citizenship is different today (and has changed repeatedly over the decades, largely because citizenship by descent laws have been statutory, not constitutional).

15. Because Mitt Romney was born in the United States, and subject to U.S. civil and criminal laws at the time of his birth (his parents did not hold diplomatic immunity from U.S. law), Mitt Romney is also a "natural born" American citizen and is eligible to be elected to the office of president of the United States (Pryor 1988). There is some dispute as to whether Mitt's father, George Romney, was so eligible (Gordon 1968).

16. Mitt's father's Mexican citizenship status may have been quite complicated to determine, depending on the point in time when the analysis was done, because Mexico has changed its laws—and sometimes made them retroactive—many times over the past hundred years (Gutierrez 1997).

17. Article II, Section 13, of the Arizona Constitution provides that "no law shall be enacted granting to any citizen, class of citizens, or corporation other than municipal, privileges or immunities which, upon the same terms, shall not equally belong to all citizens or corporations." While the matter has not been litigated—because the Interstate Birth Certificate Compact failed to pass in Arizona—this provision may render the Interstate Birth Certificate Compact unconstitutional under Arizona state law.

18. The "natural born" language in the bill upset some who believed that it was purposefully put into the bill to allow Barack Obama to be placed on the Arizona presidential ballot, although these persons question Obama's eligibility for presidential office because he is a dual citizen of the United States and Kenya (Donofrio 2011). (Donofrio writes: "Apparently, the US citizenship of anchor babies is being sacrificed to protect Obama from competing eligibility legislation—such as Arizona HB2544—which does, in fact, require Presidential candidates to prove they have never owed allegiance to a foreign nation.")

11. *IVOIRITÉ* AND CITIZENSHIP IN IVORY COAST

THE CONTROVERSIAL POLICY OF AUTHENTICITY

ALFRED BABO

International perceptions of the West African nation Ivory Coast are usually shaped by its number one world ranking for cocoa bean export or the violence of its recent civil war, which ended in 2011. For scholars of identity and political trends, however, the country is distinguished by its understanding of nationality and citizenship, and particularly its implementation of a controversial policy of national "authenticity." Known colloquially as *ivoirité*, the legislative acts that created the policy and its attendant administrative policies used documentary protocols to remove or preclude from citizenship certain Ivorian-born or naturalized individuals.

President Konan Bédié, who took power in 1993, created this concept of ivoirité to eliminate political rivals he considered non-Ivorian. In 1995, at the height of nationalist propaganda surrounding the controversy of ivoirité, President Bédié declared that his political opponent Alassane Ouattara, the former prime minister (1990–93), was not an Ivorian citizen and thus should not be permitted to run in the presidential election. Ouattara was declared a "foreigner," and his nationality was identified as that of the northern neighboring country, Burkina Faso. Under the new ivoirité statutes, he was disqualified from office, excluded from the presidential competitions of 1995 and 2000, and indicted for alleged identity fraud. In 2010, Bédié, the founder of ivoirité, reversed himself and appealed to his supporters to vote for Alassane Ouattara, who was henceforth permitted to run for election after a long battle over his nationality and citizenship issues. Bédié had done an about-face on the issue of the citizenship status and eligibility of Alassane Ouattara, who was adulated, rehabilitated, and subsequently elected president of the Republic of Ivory Coast in 2010 with the decisive support of his former detractors. How is it possible to reconcile these two narratives?

The policy of ivoirité affected the entire Ivorian society and was a main factor in the outbreak of rebellion in 2002, and subsequently the civil war of 2011. Aside from the well-known case of Alassane Ouattara, many individuals, particularly from northern Ivory Coast, were identified as "foreigners." Hundreds of thousands of Ivorian nationals have families and ancestry in neighboring countries such as Burkina Faso, Mali, and Guinea, and many were subjected to close scrutiny about their identity.[1] Like Ouattara, many faced challenges to their identity and have been victims of discrimination in the last two decades. Indeed, in some regards, Bédié's policies only cemented existing prejudices about perceived national allegiance by southern Ivorians about their northern kinsmen. The ivoirité laws permitted government agents—particularly military, police, and judges—to consolidate their doubts about the veracity of identity documents; for example, Ivorians from the north were often suspected of being "foreigners," and Malians were frequently viewed as "false" Ivorians.

The Ouattara experience was not anomalous but rather emblematic of the experience of an enormous sector of Ivorian society, but understanding what really motivated the policy of "authenticity" requires attention to competition for access to and control of political power in Ivory Coast. This chapter explores the concept of ivoirité, particularly how the implementation of regulations pertaining to documentation and proof of identity created expansive and long-lasting problems about citizenship in the life of Ivorian people and the Ivorian nation.

Before moving forward, let us question first the concept of citizenship itself as it became central in so many societies, including Africa. At some point, it is interesting to see how state institutions were instrumentalized through a political (re)construction of the concept. Accordingly, questioning the concept of citizenship means working beyond challenges individuals face when they are asked to prove their identity. Indeed, categories such as autochthony, language, and village have served to tighten the concept with birth, ethnicity, and territory. Primordialist discourses have inspired theorists of founding tribes that appeared to be relevant in the search for an identity that should be rooted in birth, kinship, language, territory, and customs (Geertz 1963; Shils 1957). This approach, instead of defining nation as *lieu de mémoire* (Schnapper 1991), challenged the constructivist theory of both nation and citizenship. For constructivists such as Benedict Anderson (1983) and Karl Deutsch (1969), the sovereignty idea has nothing to do with nature—as at birth—only because nation is a social and historical phenomenon built up by diverse social groups (insiders and outsiders). In this theoretical perspective, state institutions endorse the historical and symbolic conception of nation as a way to build citizenship.

In the Ivorian case, however, the misconstruction of the concept by scholars gathering within the "Cellule Universitaire de Réflexion et de Diffusion des Idées du Président Bédié" (CURDIPHE), a political think tank, has significantly doomed legal rethinking of Ivorian citizenship. When these scholars constructed the concept of ivoirité, they actually brought up a primordialist approach to citizenship by pointing out the necessity of keeping the nation's ethnic composition and filtering "true" from "false" citizens, and also by ignoring the historical construction of the Ivorian nation. However, tightening citizenship to belonging to an autochthonous ethnic group, or to a small territory such as a village in a country known for its long tradition of migration appeared unrealistic. In addition, laying citizenship on documented proofs in a country characterized by lack of état-civil (birth registration), with numerous children growing up without birth certificates and many uneducated people, was a challenge for both the state and the population.

The situation in Ivory Coast put citizenship in question by increasing requirements of documented proof of identity and selective enforcement of citizenship and migration policies, especially for purposes of naturalization through marriage, as well as ad hoc interpretations of ethnicity and descent. Moreover, new laws and claims of political leaders for ivoirité ignored the ascription understood as historical efforts of millions of people settled in Ivory Coast in the early 1900s to join the Ivorian political community. These laws and the theories that inspired them have thrown legitimate identity documents into doubt; have denied citizenship to people from the north who are not recognized as Ivorian; and have produced widespread statelessness. These laws empowered frontline bureaucrats similar to those described by Kamal Sadiq and Amanda Flaim (this volume), while the political debate overshadowing these changes, especially the presidential campaigns of the 1990s, resembles the U.S. debate about the validity of Barack Obama's citizenship and whether he was an authentic American or a Muslim foreigner committing fraud (see Stock, this volume).

I discuss the relevant laws of ivoirité to explain how this policy was implemented; how it challenged the prevailing electoral, nationality, land, and labor laws; and how it affected the Ivorian society. I investigate how ordinary citizens navigated laws, ultimately directed at specific political elites by political rivals, by focusing on the evidence Ivorian residents were requested to produce to demonstrate their ivoirité.

Generally, identity documents such as birth certificates, nationality certificates, passports, and national identity cards were at the heart of the problem because they were systemically viewed as false or fraudulent for a particular class of citizens. By presenting cases of individuals (both leaders and ordinary citizens), I demonstrate how, among whom, and where identity challenges took place.

Origins of the Return to Authenticity in Ivory Coast

"Authenticity" in Ivory Coast was developed and used instrumentally by those in quest of political power. Its invocations seem to occur as certain political groups reject heterogeneous, polymorphous populations within aspiring liberal political and economic communities (Comaroff and Comaroff 2003), though this is only a partial explanation. Cultural nationalism in Africa is often expressed at a political level. In Zaïre, for example, the policy of authenticity was actually a rhetorical strategy to justify the 1965 coup d'état and to institutionalize one-man rule (White 2008, 72). Opponents of the Mobutu regime were disqualified because they were represented as nonauthentic people; they were not rooted to the country by territory (jus solis) or by birth (jus sanguinis). Authenticity has also been used as an instrument of political regulation in other countries, such as Zambia (Nzongola-Ntalaja 2004, 403), Peru (Nagano 2007), and even the United States (see Stock, this volume).

Powers of Documentation within a Controversial Authenticity Policy

This chapter shows how documents such as residence permits, national identity cards, nationality certificates, and birth certificates were powerful tools operationalizing the Ivorian authenticity called ivoirité. The establishment of new citizenship and documentation laws enrobed in ivoirité played an important role in constructing an authentic Ivorian as the sole individual to whom employment, land, and political power would be accessible. The determination by some political elites to establish a new national consciousness around ivoirité created a two-tiered citizenship regime: "fake Ivorians" and "pure-blooded Ivorians." The emergence of the notion of "pure blood" in the political vernacular marks a drift to ethnonationalism subsequently codified in legislative and judicial reforms. As a result of these policies, millions of Ivorians lost their citizenship and are effectively stateless.

Moreover, many administrative documents, such as national identity cards, passports, nationality certificates, and driver's licenses, have been subsequently deemed to be unreliable and insecure due to the concomitant expansion of fraud (a point made by McKenzie in this volume). To address the perceived problem of fraudulence, in 2002 the government tried to use public hearings to confirm the citizenship status of individuals, but this operation foundered when it turned out that petitioners would have to go to their "village of origin" to enroll for a hearing. This concept of "village" in Ivorian society revealed the logic of ivoirité that was hidden behind the project. The village highlighted an ideal embedded in the imagined authentic Ivorian, insofar as he is revealed to be an individual who can substantiate deep ancestral ties with the territory through his or her roots in an autochthonous community and family. By linking citizenship with membership in a narrow community space such as a village, the government rejected the principles of an Ivorian "melting pot" and undercut existing statutes permitting naturalization and an expansive understanding of Ivorian nationhood. Indeed, because many Ivorians no longer had contact with their natal villages, and many others did not know their birth village or the villages of their parents, citizenship through these ties could not be effected. The village-based citizenship policy also overlooked the inability of naturalized citizens to indicate an Ivorian village of origin. These measures meant that West Africa foreigners, and Ivorians from the north in particular, were forcibly denied their citizenship "rights" by ivoirité laws and practices. Based on this policy, tens of thousands of Ivorians were stripped of their Ivorian citizenship and voting rights.

In these and other cases discussed later, recourse to the ideology of authenticity of blood or soil and the documents illustrating such claims were used to redefine or remake the distribution of rights between newcomers, whose parents arrived from outside present Ivory Coast boundaries, and "firstcomers," the people found in situ. Ivoirité, as an instrumental ideology, pursued precisely this logic. Ivoirité was also an invention of the 1990s, the era of democracy in African countries and the period that Comaroff and Comaroff (2009) described as the one in which nation-states elsewhere were having to come to terms with social and economic heterogeneity. In fact, this policy—understood as the reactive xenophobia that haunts heterodoxy—was in contrast to the call for capital mobility, delocalization of units of production, and mobility of labor that characterized the beginning of the 1990s. Scholarly studies have highlighted the complex identity-based roots of the crisis in Ivory Coast, and many explicitly blame the concept of ivoirité (e.g., Akindès 2004; Babo 2008; Bouquet 2003; Jolivet 2003). When a rebellion broke out in the northern part of the country against Laurent Gbagbo in September 2002, participants in the Linas-Marcoussis Agreement of 2003, which aimed at resolving the crisis, identified ivoirité as one of the major causes of the Ivorian turmoil.[2]

The complexity of this policy itself is also likely one of the reasons for the spectacular failure of the Linas-Marcoussis Agreement. According to McGovern (2011, 6), the Linas-Marcoussis approach failed because it treated a political problem as if it were a technical one to be solved by administrative action. As McGovern explains, the political and military crisis from 2002 and thereafter was not simply technical; rather, it was a complex mix of military, social, political, and economic factors.[3] With the democratic winds of 1990, a competition for political power occurred among the political parties, and subsequently among Ivorian ethnic groups. These divisions, inextricably tied to land, employment, and political power, brought identity, along with the nationality issue, to the surface (Babo 2013; Boone 2009; Crook 1997). Ivoirité emerged as a policy to regulate political conflicts on the basis of national preference. In 1994, the issue morphed into a form of nationalism when Alassane Ouattara, the leader of a dissident cohort in the ruling Democratic Party of Côte d'Ivoire / Rassemblement Démocratique Africain (PDCI/RDA), called the Rally of Republicans (RDR), indicated his intention to run for the presidency. Hailing from the north, Ouattara was accused by PDCI/RDA leaders from the center and the south of being a foreigner (specifically, a Burkinabé), even though he was born in Ivory Coast and had served as prime minister from 1990 to 1993 (Bacongo 2007). This suggests the first paradox of the citizen who is an alien, as Jacqueline Stevens has pointed out in her chapter in this volume.

Even though ivoirité was one of the root causes of the Ivory Coast crisis, advocates of the concept continue to present it in sanitized form and argue that it presents little risk to society. To former president Bédié, ivoirité is nothing more than a cultural concept, as it "constitutes first a framework of identification that places emphasis on values specific to Ivorian society. It is also a framework for integrating the first ethnic groups that gave birth to Ivory Coast with all the external contributions that came to melt into the mold of a shared destiny" (Bédié's speech at the Tenth Congress of the PDCI/RDA, August 26, 1995). Therefore, for its supporters, ivoirité is neither sectarianism nor narrow nationalism. Rather, it is the perfect synthesis of Ivory Coast's history and the affirmation of a way to be authentic. In short, it is presented as a concept identifying difference and affirming unity. Advocates of ivoirité rejected criticisms, insisting that "ivoirité is not and will not be an egotistical current that will fold in on itself, or a fertilizer for exclusion and xenophobia" (as reported in the national daily *Fraternité-Matin*, November 24, 1996).

Yet for most opponents of Bédié, notably supporters of the RDR, underneath its benign outer image, ivoirité actually hides a pernicious politics of exclusion. Indeed, from the point of view of its detractors, the political conceptualization of this ideology, in which the goal is to institutionalize discrimination between "us" and "them" or "others," opens up a political agenda vis-à-vis "the stranger" that is both restrictive and exclusionist (Jovilet 2003). According to Dozon (2000), the concept of ivoirité as understood by "scholars" within the CURDIPHE (1996), a quasi-academic center for pro-Bédié propaganda, may have seemed like harmless sentimentality. Yet its superficial definition masked pernicious seeds of division. Scrutinized through the lens of cultural nationalism, the idea of authenticity carried by the concept of ivoirité is also too easily revealed to be *akanité*, an ideology praising Bédié's Akan ethnic group's values, traditions, and systems of thought. McGovern (2011, 17) presents ivoirité as an "intellectual apparatus" that gave metaphysical and pseudo intellectual justification to an instrumentalized xenophobia whose main object was excluding Ouattara and his political adherents from Ivorian politics. This latter view is consistent with the definition of ivoirité that Bédié himself gave a few years later and that vindicates the criticisms raised by its detractors. In his 1999 book, Bédié wrote: "That which we are pursuing is clearly the affirmation of our cultural personality, the development of the Ivorian man insofar as what comprises his specificity, what we call his 'ivoirité'" (44). Thus, Ivorian people are those rooted in the southern part of the country, which he contrasts implicitly to northerners (including those from northern Ivory Coast), who are connected linguistically, religiously, and through other cultural ties to the larger societies of the West African savanna zone and Sahelian region and are "rooted" in Mali, Burkina Faso, and beyond. Bédié's terms, such as "specificity," "Ivorian man," "rooted people," and "ethnic," imbue "ivoirité" with an ideology of exclusion that is ethnic, religious, and xenophobic in form (Babo and Droz 2008). Irrespective of which version or interpretation one embraces, ivoirité as an authenticity policy or movement, via its controversial implementation at both the political and social level, was indeed one of the main causes of Ivory Coast civil war.

Implementation and Practice of Ivoirité
LAWS AND POLITICAL AND SOCIAL STAGES

Ivoirité emerged against a backdrop of political tension on the eve of the presidential elections of 1995. In this context of political competition, the concept was quickly implemented through new laws and decrees to exclude so-called foreigners from participation in national political life. Indeed, after a long campaign to highlight the distinction between "multisecular Ivorians" and "circumstantial" Ivorians, in 1994 the government of President Bédié initiated a bill and encouraged the Parliament to adopt an electoral code that limited access to the highest offices of state to those of "pure" or "original" Ivorian identity. As a result, Article 49 of Law 94-642 of December 13, 1994 stipulated, "No one may be elected President of the Republic if he is not aged at least forty years and if he is not Ivorian birth, whose father and mother themselves are Ivorian by birth. They must never have renounced their Ivorian nationality."[4]

After the 1995 general elections and after the fleeting hopes for national redemption raised by a military coup in December 1999, a movement of elites and intellectuals assuming the title of the "patriotic front" came out and endorsed ivoirité policy. Political parties, such as the Front Populaire Ivoirien, the PDCI/RDA, and the Parti Ivoirien des Travailleurs (PIT), and eventually the military junta leader Robert Guéï argued in favor of toughening the citizenship conditions for eligibility for the presidency. Thus, once again, on the eve of the presidential election of October 2000, a new constitution, including nationality requirements for candidates to the presidency that were more restrictive than those that existed previously, was adopted in July 2000. Minutes from the committee that worked on the constitutional amendments tightening the nationality requirements for a presidential candidate's parents show that members acted under the auspices of "saving Ivorian identity." Thus a new clause required candidates "never to have taken advantage of another nationality" (Article 35). In addition, a countermove to replace the stipulation that both "mother *and* father be Ivorian citizens" with the alternative that "mother *or* father be an Ivorian citizen" was defeated after several long debates in what was known at the time as the battle of "and" and "or." As a result, in the wake of the emergence of the ideological form of ivoirité, the new constitution and the electoral code of 2000 established and reinforced the jus sanguinis authenticity on the political stage insofar as both parents of any presidential candidate must "be themselves of Ivorian origin."

In Ivory Coast in 2000, the central political question thus became "Who is Ivorian?" To understand the appeal of Ivorian authenticity at the social level, we must return to the legal framework of the early independence period, combined with the long economic crisis and the attempted solutions that had raised the question of nationality. From 1960 to 1990, there was an ambiguous public policy toward foreigners that moved from jus soli to a sort of mix with jus sanguinis. First, Law 61-415 of December 14, 1961, which founded Ivorian nationality, was opened to foreigners and their children. Specific articles (6, 17 through 23, and 105) gave strength to jus soli for foreigners by focusing on two essential criteria for the attribution of nationality: their parentage and, above all, their birthplace. Thus, "all of those born in Ivory Coast are Ivorians unless both parents are foreigners."[5] In other words, to be Ivorian, an individual must have at least one Ivorian-born parent.

This article lent a less restrictive character to Ivorian citizenship due to weaknesses in the état-civil in the first years of independence. Moreover, it was also an occasion to take into account the large population of immigrants, whose naturalization would have been largely favored by this law. For example, Article 17 states, "The minor child born in Ivory Coast of foreign parents, may reclaim Ivorian nationality by declaration as conditioned in Article 57 and following, if on the date of his declaration, he has continually resided in Ivory Coast for at least 5 consecutive years and if his proof of birth results from a declaration from the civil state in the exclusion of all other means." The Ivorian legislature had thus established the processes for the acquisition of full rights to Ivorian nationality. Along with this, Article 105 prescribed, "By derogation of the provisions of Article 26, people who had their habitual residency in Ivory Coast prior to August 7, 1960, may be naturalized without condition if they formulate their request within the period of one year, beginning from the enforcement of this code. They will not be subject to the incapacities predicted by Article 43." The Ivorian nationality code thus acknowledged that historically, Ivorian society had been composed of natives and also of nonnatives, many of whom had been established in Ivory Coast for many years.

This openness was curtailed by the operational procedures that began to be imposed in the early 1970s. Law 72-852 of December 21, 1972, modified the Ivorian nationality code by introducing amendments, notably the abrogation of Articles 17 through 23 of Law 61-415. Henceforth, children born to foreign parents after 1972 no longer benefited from a simple regime of declaration, as in the past (former Article 17), to obtain Ivorian nationality. In addition, foreign parents living in Ivory Coast since colonization who did not acquire Ivorian nationality under the conditions specified by Articles 105 and 106 of the previous law of 1961 were not allowed to automatically pass Ivorian citizenship on to their children, even if the child was born in Ivory Coast.[6]

In the 1970s and 1980s, public policies toward foreigners remained less than coherent. Government employees ignored nationality requirements or implemented them with few evidentiary challenges. Numerous foreigners were present in large sections of the Ivorian economy and politics (Babo 2010) within an unclear legal and citizenship status. President Félix Houphouët-Boigny, without a clear legal foundation, hired nationals from the subregional Economic Community of West African States (ECOWAS) to serve in the Ivorian public administration and army. Furthermore, in contrast with Article 5 of the constitution, which stipulated that "only Ivorians can and should take part in voting," then president Houphouët-Boigny allowed ECOWAS nationals to vote in Ivorian elections. Finally, by declaring that the "land belongs to the one who works on it," the first president in the early 1970s provoked a gold rush for access to and proprietary ownership of land among the numerous nationals of Burkina Faso and Mali residing in the countryside who created plantations of perennial crops, principally cocoa and palm oil. Gradually, on the basis of the so-called Houphouët laws, longtime residents who were legal aliens marked their massive and durable installation in Ivory Coast (Babo 2008).

As the economic crisis became more acute in 1990, the Ivorian government passed over the supranational protocol of the ECOWAS citizenship code of May 1982 and established for the first time a temporary residency permit called *carte de séjour* for foreigners. Under Law 90-437 of May 29, 1990, all foreigners over the age of sixteen years, living in Ivory Coast more than three months (Article 6), were required to request and receive a residency permit. But in the wake of the 1995 elections, which coincided with the peak of the ethnonationalism embodied in ivoirité ideology, restrictive measures expanded for foreigners. For instance, under Law 98-448 of August 4, 1998, the cost of the annual residence permit tripled from 5,000 FCFA to 15,000 FCFA (approximately ten dollars to thirty dollars) for nationals of ECOWAS. Consequently, this measure fueled the demand for fraudulent (i.e., non-government-produced) Ivorian national identification cards. As a result of this new fraudulence problem, the ambiguities in the ID card significations meant Ivorians from the north of the country—such as Senoufo, Koyaka, Tagbana, and Malinke (often called Dioula)—were suspected of not being authentic Ivorians. In part, this was because they share many culture attributes and nomenclature with people from Burkina Faso, Mali, and Guinea. The operationalization of ID fraud detection was a means of excluding them from citizenship.

The policy of ivoirité did not end with the overthrow of Bédié in December 1999. Rather, ivoirité was expanded, exacerbating problems for Ivorians and ECOWAS nationals alike. After the 2000 elections, the administration of the new president, Laurent Gbagbo, decided to "clean up" the files of the état-civil to solve the problem of fraudulent identity documents (as reported in the national daily, *Notre Voie*, no. 1034, 2001, 5). To do so, in 2001 the government created the National Identification Office (NIO), whose mandate was to "reorganize and manage the état-civil, deliver national and foreigner identity documents to claimants, and regulate immigration and emigration of populations."[7] Ivoirité was thus expanded wholesale, when in 2002 the NIO interpreted its mandate under Law 2002-3 of January 3, 2002, as including the power to investigate, research, and confirm or otherwise the citizenship status of the general population at large.

The implementation of citizenship verification was not an isolated operation but one that emerged in tandem with other legislation. The government formulated a new rural land code 98-750 (passed on December 23, 1998) with a similar objective. Although the law aimed at regulating land rights; it also induced a nationalist agenda as it finally has been used to attempt to end foreigners' activities over the land in parts of the Ivorian agricultural sector (Bouquet 2003). In reality, the law clearly established a link between landownership and the ethnic and territorial identity of the farmer. Consequently, starting with its first article, the law restricted the ownership of rural land to persons of Ivorian nationality. Any farmer claiming ownership right over land had to prove Ivorian citizenship. Thus, far from resolving the crisis, the law brought into question the citizenship and thus other rights acquired by an entire class of allegedly nonnative farmers who had worked their lands for decades.

Additional statutes expanded the authenticity program into other sectors. Restrictions were also imposed in the labor sector. The so-called *ivoiritaire* laws, for example, sought to restrict foreign access to employment. According to the Constitution Act of 1960, only a person with Ivorian nationality could work in public service. However, Section 4 of the Decree of 1965, requiring a job applicant to provide a certificate of nationality, had been ignored under the first presidency, which led to the hiring into public administration of many "foreigners," as well as de jure Ivorians who lacked papers. But as of 1990, under the ivoirité ideology, hiring a foreigner in the public administration required exceptional authorization reflecting the government policy designed to control the presence of foreigners. Furthermore, unlike the former flexible practices, appointment of an expatriate was no longer the prerogative of only the minister but required communication to the cabinet justifying the recruitment. Authenticity also expanded from the public to the private sector. Under the new ideology of ivoirité, laws further restricted companies' ability to hire foreigners. For instance, Law 9515 of January 12, 1995, of the Labor Code (Article 95), allows aliens to occupy, on the basis of a contract, only positions that are not occupied temporarily by Ivorians.

From 2004, changes in the management of the employment of foreigners were significant in terms of both financial and administrative requirements. Documentation requirements burdened employers with visa fees of one month's gross monthly wage of the worker under consideration. For those already working in Ivory Coast, a period of six months was granted to the employer to document the status of all foreign agents. Any company that evaded the law was subject to sanctions.

Ivoirité, as stated earlier, emerged principally to target Ouattara. Once he was disqualified from competing in the elections on the grounds of his dubious citizenship status, the immediate political objective was accomplished. In this light, it is abundantly clear that the primary application of ivoirité was intimately intertwined with Ouattara's political career. He appeared for the first time in the Ivorian political sphere in 1989, at the peak of an economic crisis. President Houphouët-Boigny, cornered by the perverse effects of the economic recession, faced a wave of popular dissent. To the surprise of most, including his own party PDCI/RDA, he appointed Alassane Ouattara as prime minister in 1990. Although Ouattara was a renowned economist, familiar with the intricacies of the world economy, he was largely unknown to the Ivorian public. Notwithstanding his seeming anonymity, he had risen quickly through the ranks of the ruling party, was integrated at the center of decision making, and was effectively second in command after the president. His rapid political rise provoked his "opponents" in his own party to weaken his policies.

First among Ouattara's opponents was the former president of the National Assembly, Konan Bédié. At the political level, he advanced the rhetoric of the "Ivorian preference" or "Ivorians first" in late 1993 and applied it immediately by disqualifying all prominent politicians whose citizenship status was or might be in doubt. For Bédié, fanning the flames of Ivorian pride, already damaged by the persistent effects of the economic crisis of the late 1980s, was a strong mobilizing opportunity. In return, a large part of the Ivorians agreed with this policy.

The reliability of Ouattara's identity documentation was first questioned on the eve of the 1995 election. An administrative officer contested the identity documents, arguing that Ouattara had presented two different cards that bore two different names for his mother. On one card her name was Nabintou Cissé, whereas on the second card the name was Nabintou Ouattara. If the first could possibly be Ivorian, according to the officer, the second was certainly Burkinabé; the officer concluded, therefore, that according to the Nationality Act of 1961, Ouattara may not actually be Ivorian. At the very minimum there was reason to doubt his Ivorian nationality. Later, in 2000, when Ouattara decided to run for president, the regime emphasized his father's nationality. Ouattara's father was suspected of being Burkinabé because, although he was born in Ivory Coast, he inherited the seat of a traditional Mossi kingdom located in Sindou (Burkina Faso). When Ouattara was fifteen, he returned along with his father to Sindou and completed his schooling in Burkina Faso. When Ouattara's father died, he was buried in Sindou, further evidence that Ouattara's opponents used to claim his father was indeed a foreigner. This assumption fueled the debate around the choice of "and" or "or" in rewriting Article 35 of the Ivorian constitution, which polarized Ivorian society throughout the year 2000.

Building on these matters, another controversy appeared pertaining to a critical document, namely, the nationality certificate. Indeed, since the passage of the new constitution of July 2000 and the electoral code, all candidates are required to prove their Ivorian identity along with the birth origin of their parents. Ouattara was required to demonstrate his Ivorian nationality by providing a nationality certificate, but the executive branch interfered with a fair review. The minister of justice issued a note asking all judges to require in advance the authorization of his office before releasing any nationality certificate to Ouattara. In 1999, prior to this notice, a judge of the town of Dimbokro, where Ouattara was born, delivered a nationality certificate to him. Testimony from Epiphane Zoro, the judge who delivered the certificate, reveals the political interference:

> A few days after I delivered the document, I was summoned by the minister of justice. At this time I realized that this was not an ordinary case. All the heads of jurisdiction were present. The first person to speak was to be the chief of staff, the director of civil affairs. He said: "Mr. Zoro, sit, thank you for coming. We have here a document, it seems that it is you who have signed it, but if we look closely, it seems that there is one of the clerks who imitated your signature. Because we have the sample of your signature here and on the document the signature is slightly different, we believe that it is an imitation." I said at that time, I had issued approximately 12,000 certificates of nationality, because there were the public hearings and that by signing, it might be a slight difference. I confirmed then that it was me who had signed. They told me: "It is you who have signed up, but we are convinced that someone copied your signature. In addition, the clerk did not explain to whom these documents belong. This is probably why you have signed. These documents are those of Prime Minister Alassane Ouattara, president of the RDR. We do not tell you and you signed by error." I replied that the clerk had explained to me. I said that I had signed with informed conscience because I thought that there were no contradictory elements. Everyone was disappointed. Then, they came together, ignoring me completely. They said they will accuse a clerk, because it is easier to pursue a clerk for criminal forgery. (*Nord-Sud*, July 25, 2013)

The following day the minister of public administration announced on public television that the certificate of nationality held by Ouattara was fake. Ouattara was then indicted by the regime for identity fraud. After a long deliberation, the president of the Supreme Court announced that Ouattara was prohibited from contesting the presidential election. Specifically, he determined that Ouattara was prohibited because fraudulent documentation of Ivorian citizenship had cast doubt on his identity. What was challenged in this particular case was the credibility of both the procedure of the judge and the citizenship of the applicant, a challenge similar to that by those alleging a conspiracy to fraudulent manufacture the U.S. citizenship of President Barack Obama in the United States. The difference is that the "birther" movement came from those largely outside the government, and not those running it (see Stock, this volume).

Ouattara's experience illustrates the wider problem affecting Ivory Coast in the past several decades. Like Ouattara, many people who had been granted Ivorian nationality, as well as Ivorians from the north, were affected by this form of discrimination based on doubts about their ivoirité expressed as doubts about their documents. People from the north especially were told they were not "truly Ivorians" and therefore found themselves victims of identity conflation with nationals of Mali, Burkina Faso, and other countries of the West African subregion. Many were denied their rightful citizenship via the actions of public officers. Ivorian public officers behaved like Americans (see Stock and McKenzie, this volume). At U.S. borders or in U.S. consulates or embassies, government bureaucrats have often used racial or ethnic stereotyping to verify a claimant's case. Similarly, Ivorian officers were directed not only by the policies, but also by the sentiments and prejudices that affected their judgment on a case. One of the most widespread actions I learned of during field research concerned the behavior of police officers and soldiers at the innumerable roadblocks and checkpoints or at border crossings; identification documents (national documents for Ivorians and residence permits for foreigners), birth certificates, and nationality certificates of alleged foreigners were torn up or destroyed just because these people either bore a name that originated to the north or neighboring countries or wore traditional clothes of northern or foreign societies, a pattern that occurs in many other countries noted in this collection.

From 1994, against the backdrop of the ethnic political struggle and under the pretext of tracking and enforcing the residence permit requirement, many foreigners and northern Ivorians were victims of harassment by security forces. The experience of one personal friend, whom I identify by the pseudonym Tabsoba, illustrates the social application of ivoirité directives. "Tabsoba" is a well-known patronym from Burkina Faso. Tabsoba's father migrated to Ivory

Coast in the early 1960s and settled in the city of Bouaké (Center), where he married a local who belonged to the Baoulé ethnic group. In 1995, when Tabsoba went to the police station to procure her national identity card, an officer insulted her and rejected her claim when he learned of her name. He stated that she would instead have to apply for a residence permit. When she stated that she was Ivorian, the policeman asked her to prove it. She then said that her mother was Baoulé and explained that she spoke that language, hoping that would convince the officer. After she spoke Baoulé, the policeman insulted her mother and asserted that such women sold their Ivorian nationality to foreigners by marriage. He ejected Tabsoba from the office but demanded that she return with her mother in order that he could convey his opinion to her directly.

Many Ivorians who have one foreign parent are referred to colloquially as an "or" and suspected of being not "truly Ivorian." But this term and the attendant forms of social discrimination also apply to those who have two native parents and who originate from the northern part of the country. During my fieldwork on the issue of ivoirité in 2000, I met a judge on duty for a public census in a village in the south, in the region of the Agni ethnic group; he had encountered a very instructive case in 1999, when ivoirité policy reached its peak. He described how the principle of the public census required that all applicants for a nationality certificate establish nationality by proving kinship ties related to the territory of an Ivorian village. In his experience, the judge first heard of an applicant named Amangoua V., who gave the names of his parents as Amangou B. (father) and Badou J. (mother) and designated Arrah as his village. After considering this information and the local ethnic names, the judge quickly assumed this applicant to be without any doubt Ivorian and delivered a nationality certificate without supplemental verifications. In the course of the work, he then encountered an applicant named Sekou C., a name originating in the north and more broadly in neighboring countries. When the judge asked him where was he from, Sekou C. replied that he was born in the same village, Arrah, and that many people both in the village and in nearby areas knew him. He added that he could even speak the local Akan language, Agni. The judge then asked him for information about his parents and where they came from. When Sekou C. explained that they came from the northern Ivory Coast and had settled in Arrah more than thirty years ago, the judge stated that there was serious doubt about his nationality and refused to issue a nationality certificate. This and many similar cases illustrate how many Ivorians are the social victims of the application of ivoirité ideology.

Conclusion

The concept of ivoirité shaped the authenticity ideology that surrounded Ivorian society in the 1990s. This policy triggered documentation reviews that undermined Ivorian citizenship for millions and continue to pose problems in Ivorian society. The implementation of regulations on proving identity created a long and deep crisis about citizenship in Ivory Coast. In order to materialize the nationalist and ethnic ideology of ivoirité, laws were amended and created anew to regulate elections, nationality, land tenure, and labor. As a result, people have to present government-authorized citizenship and village documents to run for president, claim land rights, and obtain employment in administrative positions.

In practice, the new authenticity policy meant that citizenship was self-evident for a part of the population but in question for others. As a result, ordinary citizens were compelled to navigate laws originally directed at particular political elites by political rivals. The hurdles for politicians were laid down for many others, who were forced to provide specific and often impossible-to-obtain evidence to prove their ivoirité. In this process, state officials such as police officers on the street, judges during public hearings, and political elites would selectively invoke fraud, especially for citizens from the north, in failing to recognize as valid evidence of citizenship documents such as birth certificates, nationality certificates, passports, and national identity cards.

The policy of ivoirité tried to decisively alter aspects of Ivory Coast public and civic life, especially access to political office, economic activity, and citizenship. It did not bring peace to Ivorian society. Instead, it created deep divisions between populations and conflict over jobs, and land, as political power fragmented and became ever more contested over a period of twenty years. Societal fracturing occurred mainly because ivoirité erected a legal framework and enabled the application of practices by public agents against those considered "nonnative" Ivorian; identity documents and social connections were equally contested and imperiled. Despite the discriminatory patterns of this policy, this particular branding of authenticity was supported and endorsed by a large part of the population, who remain convinced by the discourse of national preference erected by different administrations since 1990.

The discourse has become so deeply rooted within the population that, even though Alassane Ouattara is currently president, during the last presidential electoral campaigns of 2010, Ouattara was portrayed as the candidate of foreigners. Many Ivorians believe that he actually received support from naturalized, or "inauthentic," Ivorians and from people who were on the electoral lists fraudulently, and that he mobilized these groups to win the election. For example, the former governor of the district of Abidjan claimed that most fraudsters were Burkinabe (20 percent) or Malians (63.88 percent), as reported in the national daily *Le Patriote*, on August 25, 2010.[8] This conviction garnered credence by the recent adoption without debate of Law 2013-653 of September 13, 2013, pertaining to nationality, land access, and statelessness. On the basis of this new legal framework, in October 2014 25,000 out of 700,000 stateless people, largely from Burkina Faso and living in the west and center of Ivory Coast, applied for Ivorian nationality. Despite Ouattara's success at the ballot box, and the new legal recognition of those previously excluded, the controversy about identity intensely increased within Ivorian society, especially on the eve of the 2015 presidential election.

NOTES

Thanks to all my students of FRN 364 of Smith College Department of French Studies–spring 2012, Professor Greg White, and Henry Heathy, who graciously read and edited this paper.

1. By foreigners I mean mainly people who are from the West African states and who are invariably considered foreigners regardless of their citizenship, documents, and Ivorian nationality.

2. See Annex III of the Linas-Marcoussis Agreement.

3. For more details on the Ivorian crisis, see Akindès 2004; Babo 2010; Blé 2005; Bouquet 2003; Dembélé 2003; McGovern 2011; Soro 2005.

4. *Official Journal of Republic of Cote d'Ivoire*, December 29, 1994.

5. Article 6, *Official Journal of Republic of Cote d'Ivoire*, December 20, 1961.

6. In fact, some restrictive measures were contained in the previous law of 1961. At that time, legislators had established a narrow dual standard—the requirement about parents' nationality and the requirement about residing in Ivorian territory. The 1961 law required that Ivory Coast be their place of birth and their place of residence for at least five consecutive years. This means that the authenticity policy can be traced all the way back to the early 1960s—the openness regime of the first president was not quite as open as some scholars have claimed. Ivorian lawmakers gave force to jus sanguinis.

7. Article 3, Decree no. 2001-103 of February 15, 2001.

8. President Ouattara came to power via a bloody civil war that he won with the strong support of ECOWAS and French military troops. Nationality code law no. 61-415 of December 14, 1961 (modified 1972, law no. 2004-662 of December 17, 2004, no. 2005-03/PR of July 15, 2005, no. 2005-09/PR of August 2005). The involvement of outside militaries in the war on Ouattara's side only confirmed, for a large number of Ivorians, that Ouattara is not truly Ivorian (Babo 2013).

12. THE ALIEN WHO IS A CITIZEN

JACQUELINE STEVENS

Apologues of Citizenship

The Prison Guard

Until his retirement the man was a Supervisor for the Bureau of Prisons. Only Citizens could work there. One day he learned he never was a Citizen. He exclaimed, "This cannot be real." When his name was removed from the register of eligible voters, he wept.

The Youth

Before the Judge stood a young man without a Lawyer. The Youth was there to demand his release from a jail for aliens. In court that morning an Attorney employed by the People, the Youth's fellow citizens, handed him a document. It had a photo of the Youth as a toddler. It stated his birth in another country. The Youth, in shock, thought it must be true. He was flown to this foreign land. Years passed. A second Attorney, also employed by the People, presented him, now a grown man, with a Passport allowing return to his native Land. The Government Agent stated that since birth he had been a Citizen. The document the Attorney showed him ten years earlier was a fraud. Years passed. A third Attorney from the People sent notice that based on encountering documents of the Government removing him decades earlier, the Government had just revoked his Passport.

The Runaway

The Runaway was caught stealing clothes. She made up a name and foreign place of birth. The Police wrote it down and secretly gave it to the employees who maintained the Government's list of Foreign Visitors allowed entry. The name the girl invented was not there. The Government flew her under her invented name to the country she had never visited. Years later, the girl's bereft family discovered her whereabouts and she returned home.

The Sincere One

The man swore he was a Citizen. The Officer signed a form saying he was Alien. The Judge said he believed the Officer and ordered the man sent away. The country of his arrival did not recognize him as their own Citizen and sent him to a third country. The third country did not recognize him as a Citizen and sent him to a fourth country. There a Diplomat procured a pass for his return home. When he reached the port of entry, the Sentry checked a register and saw the man had been deported. The Sentry ordered the man arrested and sent away.

The Boy Who Was Kidnapped

When the Father left his Wife, he took with him their Son and raised him in a foreign land. As soon as he was large enough to take care of himself, he packed a bag and found the Certificate of Birth proving he was his Mother's child and a Citizen of the same land as her own. But he had been away a long time, and no longer spoke the language. The Sentry ignored the official record in the young man's hand and refused him entrance. Hoping to find a more sympathetic Sentry the man returned another day. The second Sentry arrested him. In a court in his homeland, the Judge asked if the man could produce a document from his own country proving he was the person named on the Certificate. The man said no, he had grown up abroad. He showed the Judge a photo of himself as a child, holding a Certificate discernibly identical with the one before the Judge. The Judge said he needed a government document saying the man before him was the man named in the Certificate and deported him.

These renditions of the alien who is a citizen, all drawn from recent experiences, appear in this form to convey the apologue, the rhetorical form driving citizenship laws and operations.[1] An apologue is a form of rhetoric that is used to reaffirm the status quo. The stories we read of hardships experienced by individuals encountering state narratives at odds with their own biographical self-knowledge incite sympathy but also, in their repetition, affirm these hardships, and make them appear inevitable. The effect is to recapitulate the force of state officials and official identities.

This chapter first explores the rhetorical form of the apologue to elucidate through concepts from deconstruction how law today epistemically privileges state archives and identity papers over information gleaned from more immediate, concrete memories and relations. Second, I pursue close readings of two narratives outside the context of citizenship claims that enact the epistemic authority of written documents over other sources of information. Third, and finally, I analyze in detail paradoxes attendant three examples of U.S. citizens encountered by their government as aliens. These analyses suggest that citizenship is the materialization of sovereignty, the acts of blessing some and banishing others announcing the sovereign's eminent domain and eclipsing in importance every other political or practical contingency that follows from the status. Just as the individual's property right depends on the sovereign's enforcement and falls to the sovereign's assertion of its own prerogatives to claim title, citizenship rights must give way to the government's assertions of its own supremacy, including, paradoxically, over naming the membership body from which it is supposedly constituted.

Legal Apologues

One constant operation across the citizenship cases discussed here is the reduction of people, inherently complicated and even mysterious, to stick figures who possess just one thin and arbitrary set of characteristics of interest for the law: their own government-written documents and references to these in state registries. The use of written record keeping to constitute a citizenry is an example of what Jacques Derrida has in mind when he describes how writing forces a break from the context of any particular present, including the putatively initial one, for an apparent purpose of a moral consciousness (Derrida 1988 [1972], 18). One way to capture the meaning of this in citizenship and deportation cases is the apologue, a "moral fable, especially one having animals or inanimate objects as characters."[2] Of course one might refer to documentary stories of status and identity through other rhetorical forms, such as myths, fantasies, or legal fictions. But these other forms imply more persistent grandeur, purpose, or agency than the conventions classifying and controlling the character of the alien who is a citizen.[3] On this reading, of citizenship operations as apologue, the only intention before the law is the one created by the government's readings of its own writings.

The Reverend William Warburton, an eighteenth-century writer whose texts Derrida (1979) elsewhere examines in detail, writes: "As speech became more cultivated, [the] rude manner of speaking by action was smoothed and polished into an APOLOGUE or Fable, where the speaker to enforce his purpose by a suitable Impression, told a familiar tale of his own Invention, accompanied with such circumstances as made his design evident and persuasive" (Warburton 1837 [1742], 37). To enforce the purpose of creation and reproduction, the government tells a familiar tale of natives and foreigners accompanied with circumstances of citizenship and alienage, as well as registers and documents, that make the government's design evident and persuasive.

Rather than an instrumental response to the question, why persecute those who may or may not have documents putatively inconsistent with registration systems of citizenship and alienage, the heuristics of the apologue help us understand what this means. In addition to advancing a moral truth through stories in which the protagonists lack agency (and may not be putatively human), the apologue also sounds rote, bereft of specific detail and not just intention, as are the lives before the law of aliens who are citizens: "An apologue is a work organized as a fictional example of the truth of a formulable statement or a series of such statements" (Sacks 1964, 41). The focus on the abstract truth crowds out all else, including the singularity of the person and her emotions, desires, and other feelings. As Sacks explains, "If we become more interested in Russelas' emotional reaction to the Stoic's misery than we are in his recognition of the futility of achieving earthly happiness by the acquisition of invulnerable patience, the apologue has failed: all elements of the fiction have not been subordinated to the creation of an example of the truth of a formulaic statement" (1964, 15).[4] In the apologue and the inquiries into the alien who is a citizen, individuals lose their formal singular quality of persons before the law and appear instead as characters.

According to the *American Heritage Dictionary*, a person is a "living human," whereas a character is a "person portrayed in an artistic piece such as a drama or novel." A person at the border can demand a fair review of her singular context and insist that, as a citizen, it is not lawful to stand her before the law as an alien. But a character lacks will, intention, and responsibilities. The experiences of the animals or figures who populate apologues such as *Aesop's Fables* counsel patience, endurance, and acceptance of the status quo, regardless of its absurdity. The one-dimensional characters populating apologues destroy the susceptibility of audiences to ascribe will to fictional characters, and also foreclose affective identification. If the figure has an encounter that makes no sense, this is not told in a manner to elicit an emotional response. Apologues fail to inspire audience identification with the specific plot and characters, but this does not mean their abstract qualities lend them to generalization. Indeed, many traditional apologues offer strange, idiosyncratic lessons that convey the superior and somewhat arbitrary pessimism of the apologue's cynical author, before whom the weak are powerless.[5] These stories are inherently conservative: "Myth establishes the world. Apologue defends the world. Action investigates the world" (Crossan 1975, 42). The stories of the alien who is a citizen do not provide lessons that are helpful for others proving either alienage or citizenship but instead shore up the authority of law to enforce these distinctions.

It is tempting to imagine apologues in service of business or other material benefits. But the citizenship accounts reviewed in this chapter, and indeed many others in this volume, are based on iterations that serve no rational purpose instrumental to economic benefits, including those of White supremacists and other nativists. To the extent that the apologues advance a story of White America, this suggests the relevance of deconstruction's operations that might address the tautologies of this notion of group consciousness. The apologue exposes the paradox of the group's initial division into aliens and the guards who may be arresting their own family members. That is, there is (1) no noncircular account of how groups' putatively original borders (territorial or intergenerational) emerge, and (2) no account for the necessary participation of the alien-who-is-a-citizen guards. (Without their bilingual skills, the deportation machine in this country would grind to a halt.) Practically speaking, the inclusion of immigrants is in service of exclusion. Again, it is important to see this as characteristic of citizenship's potential and the legal tendency in the United States to reveal its citizens as aliens and vice versa, and not as the strategic individual decision to be co-opted, along the lines of the Jews who collaborated with the Nazis. The U.S. guards are working as citizens supervising and supervised by themselves, while the Jewish Kapos are employed as Jews (i.e., foreigners) by the Germans. In the case of generalized restrictions on movement across state borders, individual rationality defeats a causal explanation. In contemplating guards whose native language is Spanish, we begin to see that the absence of any persistent boundaries for the group defeats an account based on group interest and forces us to realize these are distinctions our writing imposes on ourselves reproduced as others.

The juxtaposition of the following two excerpts, from the same newspaper on the same day, reveals intuitions about the unique accuracy or proof conveyed by original written records and official sources, as well as their susceptibility to omissions, error, and correction.[6] Such an investment in a written record is crucial for the legal apologues of citizenship. Unlike other legal proceedings, especially those of criminal law, citizenship cases proceed indifferent to pain, trauma, suffering, or any other emotional facts, and they also disregard intention altogether. Examples from other contexts illustrate the simultaneous contingency and epistemic authority of written texts, those accounts gaining credibility because they exist in a medium that seems permanent, objective, and inalterable (even if also on a website and digitized).

Consider these examples from the *New York Times*:

In the absence of those half-century-old records, [Richard] Parsons's unspectacular time on the freshman team cannot be fully authenticated. Because he did not play beyond his freshman semester, he does not appear on a list of varsity lettermen. (*New York Times* 2014b, B13)

An article last Friday about the killing of two young Palestinians in clashes with Israeli security forces, using information from a hospital, misstated the name and age one of them. He was Mohammad Mahmoud Odeh Salameh, not Muhammad Odeh Abu al Daher, and he was 16, not 20. (*New York Times* 2014a, A2)

In the first instance, the journalist, who points out the University of Hawaii athletics department lacks the relevant records, has tracked down a teammate of Parsons, who confirms his team membership: "Bill Robinson, who attended Hawaii in the 1964–65 academic year, recalled playing with Parsons on the freshman team. 'I can verify that,' said Robinson, a lawyer and retired naval aviator whose name was provided by the N.B.A. 'You have my word on it.'" But for the reporter and Robinson himself, his word is not enough. The last line of the article quotes Robinson, "I don't know if you can find proof that I played, either."

Robinson's eyewitness testimony memorialized in his own mind indicates Parsons played. Likewise, the "Corrections" section on that same date, the second passage quoted, about the killing of a Palestinian, indicates basic facts about someone's name and age were incorrectly published in the *New York Times* on the basis of information conveyed from an authoritative hospital source.

These instances might be construed as evidence for trusting oral statements and doubting the accuracy of information in the written, official record. And yet in encounters with immigration files, officials, and adjudicators, as well as federal judges, citizen supplicants regularly have their personal testimony and that of their friends and relations subordinated to records containing information unverifiable save for a signature, regardless of who affixed it. The preceding passages might thus serve as context for explaining misunderstandings about the true personal histories for those who are de jure U.S.-American citizens but fail to have this status recognized de facto. However, these are not the points this chapter develops.

Instead, I want to use these examples, alongside the apologues preceding them, to suggest that the very possibility of the truth to which we ascribe not only the written record but also its possible supplements is fantastic thinking: in the name of truth, what really is at stake in U.S. citizenship cases is internal coherence and the state authority derived therefrom. Consider the case of Teresa Trinh, whom U.S. authorities denied permission to change her certificate of naturalization to reflect the date of birth on her Vietnamese birth certificate.[7] Several features are noteworthy. First, Trinh sought permission to change the naturalization certificate because its failure to match her birth certificate prompted state authorities to deny her a driver's license, and federal authorities a U.S. passport. Second, the U.S. government resisted changing her naturalization certificate, even though it found nothing wanting in the accuracy of the Vietnamese birth certificate. The government claimed that allowing any changes jeopardized the integrity and thus authority of their document regime (see McKenzie, this volume). The district court judge wrote: "USCIS [U.S. Citizenship and Immigration Services] argues that it 'has a strong interest in denying amendment requests that, if granted, would encourage naturalization applications containing untruthful information, undermine the reliability of naturalization certificates, and erode respect for the naturalization process.'"[8] Here, the government is claiming that inaccurate information on its naturalization certificates is preferable to accurate information, because changing information to match other authoritative and required government documents, in this case the Vietnamese birth certificate, would undermine the credibility of its record keeping.

Third, despite the judge ultimately ordering USCIS to amend the certificate, his narrative of the initial confusion obscures the government's responsibility for this. The judge writes, "Petitioner's parents have not explained how immigration authorities arrived at this date."[9] But how could they? The bureaucrats, not the parents, were the ones who created the official record. (Most likely a U.S. immigration agent, perhaps relying on a refugee camp doctor's estimate, produced this outcome.) The effect of the judge's observation is to leave the impression that individuals are responsible for their state records, and to elide the centrality of government records and actors to the creation of our biographies. Moreover, nothing in the order for this individual case changes the CIS policy of not making changes to its database, or the substantial and expensive burden on individuals seeking to rectify inconsistencies. Thus, it is not surprising when there are inconsistencies and when these are viewed in a light that favors the government's interpretation and not that of the citizen supplicant.

The documentary gaps, inconsistencies, potential lies, and so forth occasioning citizenship certificates' production, amendments, and removals may seem to be failures of the signifier (i.e., the naturalization certificate) to match the signified (Trinh's actual date of birth).[10] Instead, these and many other accounts reveal the triumph of official signatures that convey a putatively unique inaugural moment of a person's legal recognition over any other memory or experience of identity. If we recall Henry David Thoreau's objection to paying taxes—he did not consent to join the state that was taxing him for policies he found morally repugnant—we might note he also never agreed to be identified by a first and patronymic name entered in a state register on the basis of a calendar relying on a Christian chronology. The judge imputes intentionality to Trinh's record that the law itself renders impossible. Although the judge states that Trinh's parents did not account for the inaccurate date in her immigration file, he might also have pointed out that her parents did not account for the existence of a system of sovereign authorities and its instruments of control. The parents also did not explain how it was that the United States and Vietnam existed as authoritative as to her identity, nor how they came to rely on certain criteria for assigning and evaluating its assignations, nor how these sovereignties came to the war that rendered them homeless refugees.

Moreover, in another case with a similar fact pattern, the Ninth Circuit in 2015 denied the appeal from a petitioner who, the record states, possessed an authentic 1931 U.S. birth certificate the petitioner used to obtain a U.S. Social Security card and U.S. passport in 1953 and 2005, respectively. The fifty-nine-page en banc decision contains crisscrossing concurrences and dissents as to the standard for review for factual findings of alienage; whether such findings by the federal district court judge were factual or legal; and whether under a lower standard the federal judge's factual findings about citizenship were clearly in error, the government itself having conceded that some of his factual findings were demonstrably wrong (*Salvador Mondaca-Vega v. Loretta Lynch* 2015). Perhaps most disturbing are the opinion's analogies with the standard for reviewing facts in criminal, including death penalty, cases. These also require deference to the factual findings of lower courts, but *these facts are findings of juries*. The absence not only of any de novo review of facts in citizenship cases in which the government controls the records but also of judicial cognizance that the federal courts are effectively placing someone's citizenship in the hands of a single judge, who in this case misstated points of law and fact, is reminiscent of the protocols of the 1850 federal law authorizing the capture and return of "fugitives"— the word "slave" does not appear in the so-called Fugitive Slave Act—and challenges thereto.[11]

In pursuing further analysis of the U.S. documents regime for citizens and aliens, conveyed especially pointedly in a regulation that describes how "aliens" can prove they are "citizens" (8 CFR 1235.3, discussed later), I am relying on insights about the written record and the signature Derrida introduces in "Signature, Event, Context" (1988 [1972]). His discussion of the effect of writing has important implications for problems of assigning citizenship. Derrida points out that writing appears as a medium passively communicating information from the past, but that writing also, more insidiously "carries with it a force that breaks with its context" (9), without appearing to do so. Recalling the experience of Trinh, we see that if she wants to leave and return home (either by car or through a U.S. border checkpoint), she must go to court. She must address in the government's own idiom of documents its documentary entries, and thus endure a clear break of her present context and the government's intrusion into her web of family, work, and other relations, as well as her habits, pleasures, aversions, and aspirations.

Derrida's dense essay on the signature, event, and context reviews the relation between J. L. Austin's performatives and their written, legal contexts. Derrida's insights here, and also from "Force of Law: The 'Mystical Foundation of Authority'" (1989–90), provide metaphors and accounts central to understanding the infelicities of the U.S. citizen who appears before the law as an alien. Summarizing Derrida's work for understanding failures of police responsiveness in India, Veena Das writes: "If the written sign breaks from the context because of the contradictory aspects of its legibility and iterability, it would mean that once the state institutes forms of governance through technologies of writing, it simultaneously institutes the power of forgery, imitation, and the mimetic performances of power. This, in turn, brings the whole domain of infelicities and excuses on the part of the state into the realm of public" (2004,

227). To produce authentic pasts through technologies of writing, the state makes possible their forgeries.

Like all paradoxes, those here betray attempts at analysis through logic, and thus allow no foothold for an instrumental explanation for why the U.S. government would devote millions of dollars each year to arresting and deporting its own citizens.[12] In these cases, any explanation for one result, including racism, easily may be undermined by the possibility of its opposite, that is, civil rights laws against this passed by a majority, as well as the reliance on border patrol agents who are U.S. citizens of Mexican descent. In the case of U.S. citizens before the law as aliens, the first paradox lies in the legal texts themselves, which posit the character before the law as "an alien . . . who is a citizen," even though U.S. law also stipulates that a citizen is by definition not an alien. (Dual citizenship is largely legal, save those swearing fealty to foreign sovereigns, and does not require an admission of alienage.)[13]

The second paradox, parasitic on the first one, is that of a political community governed by laws passed by a constituency of these aliens who are citizens. We are used to thinking of exclusions by "us" (or "them") of "the other." This regulation exemplifies and concretizes an otherwise abstract idea: the alien who is a citizen makes up the political community passing legislation. Thus citizenship law not only penalizes those authorizing the law (when citizens are treated as aliens) but also is fundamentally incoherent. The alien-who-is-a-citizen is the part of us we cannot recognize as such, the foreignness from which we create ourselves as others, and through law perform our otherness. But this process, understood reciprocally, means that the foreigners we create from and as ourselves also are the ones passing these laws. Thus the laws producing aliens come from a citizenry that is alien. Such a demographic violates policies confining the franchise to citizens and prompts rethinking the real basis and significations of our membership protocols.

Finally, third, there is the paradox of those charged with reading the law actually rewriting or otherwise circumventing it. The examples from the apologues, the operations of which are described in more detail later, reveal officials and judges inventing texts they claim to be enforcing. This is not a shortcoming of policy implementation specific to citizenship laws. But because the determinations at stake are always purely those of status, and the implications raise existential questions about the political community as such, these challenges of textual interpretation, as well as document creation and destruction by states and others, expose the paradoxical fragility of laws whose enforcement depends on their rigidity and persistence.

Definition of the Alien Who Is a Citizen (Self-Contradiction)

(iv) *Review of order for claimed lawful permanent residents, refugees, asylees, or U.S. citizens.* A person whose claim to U.S. citizenship has been verified may not be ordered removed. When an alien whose status has not been verified but who is claiming under oath or under penalty of perjury to be a . . . U.S. citizen is ordered removed pursuant to section 235(b) (1) of the Act, the case will be referred to an immigration judge. . . . If the immigration judge determines that the alien was once so admitted as a lawful permanent resident or as a refugee, or was granted asylum status, *or is a U.S. citizen*, and such status has not been terminated by final administrative action, the immigration judge will terminate proceedings and vacate the expedited removal order. The Service may initiate removal proceedings against such an alien, but not against a person determined to be a U.S. citizen, in proceedings under section 240 of the Act.[14]

The regulation at the heart of this chapter defines the one who stands before the law as "an alien." Yet this definition is subject to refutation, unlike actual axioms, which may not be so refuted by empirical evidence. By contrast, most laws refer to those before them as persons or else use pronouns for those who may or may not have committed specific acts the government codifies as illegal. For instance, the law against defrauding the government concerns "*whoever*, knowingly and with intent to defraud the United States, or any agency thereof, possesses any false, altered, forged, or counterfeited writing or document" (18 USC § 1002, emphasis added), not "fraudsters" whom judges later may determine have not committed fraud.

Laws Deporting Aliens Who Are Citizens (Self-Exclusion)

The citizens brought before immigration judges typically are U.S. citizens at birth either because of the Fourteenth Amendment or under statutes conferring citizenship by descent automatically by operation of law. Citizens who have this status because of naturalization are less likely to receive, but not immune from, treatment as aliens—their records assigning citizenship are more available (Becker 2011; Stevens 2011). In cases of those born in Latin America, which, like many other postcolonial countries relies on jus soli (see Price, this volume), people may hold dual citizenship at birth. Still, as long as the criteria for U.S. citizenship are met, such persons are citizens and not aliens under U.S. citizenship law. By standing before the law as aliens those who are its citizens, the government per-forms the illegitimacy of those laws.[15] The alien who is a citizen crystallizes the paradox that shoots through U.S. citizenship's significations: Who will verify the alien who is a citizen who will verify the alien who is a citizen? Those au-thorizing these laws lack recognition for their eligibility to pass or enforce such measures, posing the infinitely regressive impossibility of verifying the identity of those eligible to verify identity. This scenario calls into question the formal legitimacy not only of citizenship laws but of all other laws as well.

The enforcement of citizenship laws shares some infelicities with other realms of law enforcement. But there are also some important differences. First, the rates of agent and guard abuse, false confessions, and erratic judicial opin-ions in the United States are higher and often have more serious consequences in deportation proceedings than in the sphere of criminal arrests and trials.[16] Second, the violation of immigration and citizenship laws is purely a status vio-lation, which means it is by its very nature a failure of one set of records and documentation to comport with the criteria deemed relevant for another set of records and documents. Although assessments of citizenship status often are based on information that is visual or oral (e.g., clothing, lack of fluency in English), and these ensuing assessments ultimately may lead to the revoca-tion of U.S. citizenship, these operations are performed via the production of written documents. Questions about intent at the time of an encounter or any other time frame, or other states of mind, are moot. If the written docu-ments verify a U.S. citizenship and agents desire another outcome, then agents may force people in their custody to affix signatures to documents announc-ing alienage, tear up birth certificates issued in the United States, or commit perjury (Johnson 2013; Stevens 2011a, 2011b). Although rarely does the gov-ernment actually come forward and announce that it values its authority over accuracy in specific cases, the rationale behind the dispute driving Trinh's court case reveals undesirable outcomes when the government advocates its own un-questioned executive authority over the databases and certificates creating our identities and status of citizenship and alienage more generally. Likewise, the Ninth Circuit decision in *Mondaca-Vega* reveals what happens when we leave the review of these decisions to a single judge and not a jury.

In several cases discussed thus far, the supplicants have been of non-European descent. Mai Ngai has introduced the concept of "alien citizenship" to refer to the "nullification of the rights of citizenship—from the right to be territorially present to the range of civil rights and liberties—without formal revocation of citizenship status" and as an example references the mass forced migration of U.S. citizens of Mexican descent in the Great Depression and the internment of citizens and residents of Japanese descent in World War II (2006/2007, 2522). The focus on racialized citizenship is crucial for pursuing questions about individual- and community-level experiences of unlawful discrimination and the specific jurisprudence of second-class citizenship that enables it. To do so, Ngai describes citizenship practices unfolding through historical and current racial hierarchies. Her work and other important work on citizens whose rights the U.S. government marginalizes, including Leti Volpp's (2006/2007) fascinating discussion of the effective statelessness of accused terrorists, occur within the confines of the historical present's distribution of affinities, trust, and power.

Studies of racialized and securitized citizenship are crucial for orienting us to important political challenges. This chapter offers something else, namely, a close reading of the inherently paradoxical scene of citizenship's reproductive phenomenology: an ontologically unstable dynamic of affirmations and othering produced by aliens differentiating within themselves through creating citizens, and by these very citizens differentiating within themselves as aliens.[17] Rather than describe the synchronic effects of a racialized history, this chapter looks at how our citizenship scenes are written and in particular considers the significations produced *by the alien*. The legal protagonist here, the alien who is a citizen, embodies in its fluidity and contingent morphologies the literal, legal, and thus political sovereign citizen subjects who are manufacturing their own self-marginalizations and copies that are disadvantaging themselves.

The persistent inability of state actors in the United States to tell a coherent narrative—that is, to characterize those introduced at one moment as bearing the same identity in later chapters of the legal story of that person or the country—typically occurs under one or more of the following conditions: (1) individual government agents lack knowledge of citizenship laws, (2) lawyers lack knowledge of citizenship laws, (3) government standards of proof are not met, (4) officials knowingly violate the law, or (5) immigration judges knowingly violate the law. Consequent to these events, the government makes interpretations of documents inconsistent with those dictated by earlier ascriptive conventions. In short, the agents fail to follow the rules that obligate them, and those who are mislabeled cannot effectively challenge these decisions or never have known the identities and statuses that were theirs under prevailing laws and the circumstances of their own family histories. It is absolutely the case that the low level of protections afforded people in these contexts reflects current domestic and global distributions of wealth and sovereign power, but it is also the case that these distributions (1) are not ontological but emerge in a manner that is cyclical, self-splitting, and also self-destructive; and (2) require attention to their specific emergences and persistence. Instead of the White race excluding Asians, for example, we start by reflecting on how Asians, Europeans, and Africans emerged from accidents of imagination that also created the maps, family genealogies, religions, and banal pathos of daily lives unable to find anything more interesting than resort to these narratives in particular to alleviate existential anxieties (see Stevens 1999, 193; 2009b, 1–26).

The following examples illustrate these five failures of coherent storytelling, what happens when the fictions of the moment deviate substantially from past stories. Before proceeding, it is important to recognize that the written record invites the possibility of fraud. Das attends to fraud because it reveals how the government's document regime is amenable to falsehoods. The analysis here recognizes this phenomenology but also stresses how these mishaps illustrate the ways in which the records are not a written past tense that freezes a moment's truth. Archives are ongoing writings that are constantly (re)creating new pasts (i.e., new stories) amid expectations that these records are persistent, self-identical, and transparent.

NO KNOWLEDGE OF THE LAW (1) AND (2)

According to the federal appellate court, Sigifredo Saldana Irachata's application for a certificate of citizenship was denied because "no decision maker has clearly applied the correct Mexican statutes to Saldana's claim of citizenship." The court goes on to note: "In both Saldana's case and other cases involving similar situations, DHS officers and the Administrative Appeals Office ('AAO') within DHS have relied on provisions of the Mexican Constitution that either never existed or do not say what DHS claims they say."[18] The court ridiculed the government's excuses: "Though the government attempted to dismiss the error as a mere 'typo,' we cannot agree. It is unclear what legal authority the BIA actually relied on in Reyes.... The BIA's mistake in citing a non-existent constitutional provision, perpetuated and uncorrected by DHS in subsequent years, prevented the agency from making the correct inquiries or possibly from applying the correct law in subsequent cases. That error has wound its way through multiple agency decisions in immigration matters, which are significant to the impacted individuals."[19] The government's position is that simple typography in one specific case misrepresented the Mexican Constitution. But the judicial panel states the government is disingenuous on this point. The court points out how the iterability of the government's invention produced the status and identities of numerous other citizens as aliens. These decisions will ripple through the offspring of those registered on the basis of the BIA's version of the Mexican Constitution.

This is an interesting natural experiment in the operation of citizenship rules applied more generally. What if a branch of government just invented a rule and relied on that one for the designation of citizenship, rather than on the statutes passed by Congress? We now know the answer: for thirty-five years it looked no different from the application of every other correct rule, regulation, and law for determining citizenship. Of course, there is no current evidence of how many other laws or constitutions are being similarly rewritten by the officials in the BIA, and even federal courts, including the Supreme Court, are adding to this their own literary creations.[20]

BURDENS OF PROOF (3)

If one asserts birth in the United States of America, then the burden of proving alienage is on the government, and the standard of evidence is "clear, unequivocal, and credible." If one concedes birth in a foreign country, say, the Republic of Mexico, the person in removal proceedings bears the burden of proving U.S. citizenship.[21]

There are numerous reasons people may lack the documents sufficient to confirm the status legally theirs at birth. These mostly derive from time and distance attenuating a foreign-born person's ties to the citizen parent(s), who possess(es) the required evidentiary documents. If charged with violating immigration laws that are part of the criminal and not civil code, the burden of proving guilt, in this case alienage, is on the government, as is the case with any other criminal charges. Numerous individuals have been found "not guilty" of illegal reentry (8 USC § 1324) or false personation of a citizen (18 USC § 911) based on evidence of their U.S. citizenship persuasive to either a jury or a U.S. attorney (who drops the charge), and yet are immediately thereafter deported by Immigration and Customs Enforcement (ICE) (Stevens 2011b).

The disparity in the standards of proof, and perhaps differences between how the guards, officials, and adjudicators employed by the deportation agencies and those outside those bureaucracies (juries and U.S. attorneys) evaluate the evidence clearly are leading to different outcomes. For instance, in 2008, a jury found Esteban Tiznado not guilty of illegal reentry (Stevens 2011–13). Jury notes and a trial transcript indicate they relied on the baptismal certificate and other evidence presented by his government-assigned attorney (not available in civil proceedings), vindicating the accuracy of his father's Arizona birth certificate and discrediting statements by an official testifying for CIS (Stevens 2011a). Since 2008, Mr. Tiznado has been repeatedly deported and inhabits that space between the criminal and civil standards of proof: a constitutional bar against trying anyone twice on the same charge (double jeopardy) means the government cannot again charge him with illegal reentry.[22] But the file, created in part by false statements coerced by a Border Patrol agent, means the U.S. government repeatedly ignores Tiznado's assertions of U.S. citizenship.[23] In other cases, prosecutors see the evidence of U.S. citizenship and drop the criminal immigration charges. In these cases the U.S. attorney may alert ICE but not the lawyers or their clients, who abruptly find themselves on the Mexican side of the border bereft of identification or funds.[24] To advance their own narratives of U.S. citizenship, those in deportation proceedings must produce documents they do not possess.

In most of these cases, the government, having itself generated the basis of these beliefs about U.S. citizenship held by those in its custody, itself possesses the most relevant evidentiary documents but does not release or, in many cases, read them. According to one U.S. citizen in ICE custody for several months: "[The ICE agent] was asking for something to prove my citizenship. I told him, 'I'm in prison. Whatever I told you is all I can give you. I gave you my social security number; my ex-wife is a permanent resident because of me. All you have to do is go to the immigration building.' I don't think anyone did nothing to find out. All they had to do is call to the [U.S.] embassy in Mexico. I really don't think he did a thing to find this out" (Stevens 2011b, 665). In this and other cases, the government produces a certain written record, fails to read it carefully if at all, and fails to make it available to those claiming to be the character the government scripted and not another.

AGENT MISCONDUCT (4)

Government agents at the border or behind a desk may intentionally destroy pieces of the person's story previously created (Stevens 2011, 656), coerce signatures to statements to create a database of life events producing an alien when the actual story is one of citizenship (Johnson 2013; Stevens 2009a); or disregard the information in their systems' records and create a new narrative, one in which the character who is a U.S. citizen is rewritten as an alien (Stevens 2011–14).

IMMIGRATION JUDGE MISCONDUCT (5)

The government appoints people to supervise the law's consistency, the apparent purpose being a responsible rendition of the country's Book of Life—that is, an accurate registry of all its members in perpetuity.[25] This is a task for God, not mortals. Frustrated by the nuances of citizenship laws and the complexities of persons' lives, immigration adjudicators take shortcuts and simply defer to the stories written by their colleagues in other government agencies, turning the hearing rooms put forward as chambers of independent analysis into another office where government attorneys dressed in black robes demonstrate their proficiency with a rubber stamp.

Jimmie Benton, a recently retired adjudicator, in response to my questions about inaccurate statements he made in the 2013 hearings for a U.S. citizen, Frank Serna, in ICE custody in 2004 and 2012–13 (Stevens 2013a), wrote the following to me in an e-mail he intended published: "Based upon the two cases you brought to my attention I was obviously flawed in my analysis of the citizenship claim. It would also be fair to say that I was weak in the area of citizenship. This was definitely something that EOIR [Executive Office of Immigration Review] should have addressed in the form of training. The substantive IJ [immigration judge] training involving active give and take, questions and learned input from colleagues has been sorely missing for several years now" (see also Stevens [2011b, 609–10, 631n86, 669]; 2010).

Analyses of Paradoxes

In a long paper prepared for a conference at Cardozo Law School, Derrida states, "For me it is always a question of differential force, especially of all the paradoxical situations in which the greatest force and the greatest weakness strangely enough exchange places" (1989–90, 929). Commentators, including Derrida himself, often have focused on the paradox of legal violence, especially as explicated in Walter Benjamin's "Critique of Violence" (1986 [1921]). Only claims of justice render actions legitimate that in real time are just violence. Benjamin stresses the object lesson provided by the present state's very emergence out of civil war or war. An equally if not more compelling figure of legal paradox is the alien who is a citizen, implying the transitive definition of the citizen who is an alien. The citizen who is an alien also embodies the paradoxical law authored by the character who signifies in law her own inability to signify.[26] Derrida's ideas about the signature help us understand how this impossible character emerges from a legal context implied by the performative effect of the signature of the alien who is a citizen: her legal testimony of her own identity instantiated, recognized, and destroyed before the law. The signature of hers, the agents, and those from previously executed certificates, orders, sworn testimonies, and other documents are the effects of a law that assumes them as their axiomatic preconditions. The legal context conjures a presignifying identity and signature that logically cannot exist without the legal infrastructure productive of the signatory identities in the first place.

This scenario is hard to follow amid concrete examples of well-known, individually motivated signatures on legal documents. It certainly is the case that John Hancock approved the Declaration of Independence, and many witnessed this in person, and thus could confirm Hancock's endorsement even without his signature. Still, the Hancock signature is not a prelegal fact of nature. The legal infrastructure of files, seals, registers, and inspectors to verify their authenticity are more than legal niceties for confirming de facto identities. Rather, the signature authorizing the government underlying the possibility of a signature indicates an identity indivisible from a status constituted by the state, one that nonetheless appears to be one's own unique prelegal persona, an effect Derrida shows is constituted by the form of writing itself, which establishes the originary moment that can be invoked to shape events at a much later time. The government-registered individual "John Hancock" makes possible this signature.

It is this scenario of a scripted apparent origin that appears at a later time, and possibly generation, as the so-called truth at the border—and all other venues that interrogate legal status—that confronts the alien who is a citizen. The records establish a reality and are most meaningfully analyzed through synchronic readings, that is, readings that view context as a snapshot of the present. Rather than look for meaning anterior to or within an individual's documentation, the documents are today's story. Once we grasp how documents are pre-forming, a-scribing scripts we perform—and not reporting on our God-given roles in life—the role of the past starts to appear more obviously as one that is historiographical, as a written medium that incites studies and interrogations of a written past that irresponsibly intrudes into the present. These reports, perhaps in the form of "alien files," can then be seen as deliberate, written iterations of continuity with a plausible, discernible, storied origin. Understood thus, the political problem with the document regime is not our failures of transcription or investigations but the discourse that legitimates inquisitions into inconsistencies and holds individuals responsible for them.[27]

While the paradoxical alien who is a citizen can be understood internal to the meanings of the law, the failure of the government to track its own laws might be best understood through the work of Franz Kafka, not least because federal judges cite him in their citizenship decisions.[28] In the same section where Derrida mentions his interest in paradox, he also references a passage from Kafka's novel *The Trial* (*Der Prozess*) (1998 [1925]), a work dramatizing how government irrationality is of a piece of, though not reducible to, those who work for and authorize it: government employees and citizens. The protagonist K's downfall is a result of the monstrosities and stupidities of the people, of whom he is himself a part, and not anything separate (e.g., a Weberian bureaucracy). The domestic spaces and activities inside K's court building (e.g., K. enters a kitchen in a judge's chamber as meals are being prepared) call into question the formal dichotomy between officialdom and our personal lives. Kafka shows us as we really are. Unlike the Weberian impersonal administrator mechanically grinding out fair if heartless memorandums, Kafka's robed people in government offices are us every bit as much as is K. Kafka narrates K's subjectivity, but this only fills out the effects of what we have wrought on ourselves. Throughout his essay referencing Kafka's work, Derrida foregrounds the impossibility of easily and definitively observing discrete moments of legitimate or just, or illegitimate or unjust, violence absent contexts created through writing and its iterations and readings over time. Kafka and Derrida both help us see how in the name of establishing law and order we are destroying ourselves and the justice on which law is founded, and creating instead paradoxes and injustice.[29]

Conclusion

The alien who is a citizen in U.S. law certainly can be understood as a more generalizable characterization of a liminal, paradoxical status that holds across regimes and countries. Readers are encouraged to note these, and also attend to features specific to an archive of the laws, registers, and identity papers reviewed by the government of the United States. All state-nations (Stevens 2009b, 134) require targeting those whose otherness "we" are ourselves creating. The deconstructive readings in this chapter are in service of delineating how we split ourselves such that some of us are citizens and others aliens. As the chapters heretofore have demonstrated, contemporary document regimes across countries share many features. Still, variations in techniques require strategies of forensic intelligence most appropriate to resistance and change in specific contexts (Stevens 2015a). The hardships and confusions of citizenship, easily noticed through the legal obstacles confronting aliens who are citizens before the law, are not due to legal failures but reveal law's dominion over our identities. These cases distill the essence of citizenship's paradoxes in the United States and also encourage us to expand on the texts that might provide similar lessons of sovereign tales told through the misery of those whose backstories are less amenable to the more obvious configurations of their citizenship status. The child born in the territory mapped as Guatemala and turned around en route to the United States by Mexican border guards, for instance, is no less a paradoxical character in citizenship fables than those with documents verifying U.S. citizenship that are eventually recognized (or rejected, or both) by the U.S. federal government. Both indulge irresponsible, tragic fantasies. Our traumas cannot be eased by better documents created to appease sovereign (national) fantasies or document regimes, but require nomos for the earth and lives of mortal citizens.

NOTES

1. The sources, in order presented, are Alvarez 2014; Stevens 2013b; Jonsson 2012; Stevens 2012; and Stevens 2011a, 659.

2. From the Greek *apologos*: *apo + logos* (*American Heritage Dictionary*).

3. Other forms of storytelling of course play a major role in America's creation. For instance, the knight chivalry tales animating the conquest and exploration of the Americans by the Spanish and English produced narratives that were violent and racialized. These stories are youthful, aspirational, and heroic (Goodman 1998). The stories of the alien who is a citizen are those of the settled nation: backward-looking to a cold-blooded register the apologues themselves create.

4. Sacks is aware that other fictions may be written to didactically convey specific moral lessons but nonetheless stresses the focus of this in the apologue, for its exclusion of everything else. Booth (1964, 187n22) emphasizes the apologue's overlap with other forms of persuasive fiction.

5. Curiously, many of these substantially reinforce the lessons of the border and other arbitrary conventions of inequality codified by law or practice. For instance, "The Dove and the Crow" is a lesson on how the restrictions of mobility turn the joy of life into its endurance. "A Dove shut up in a cage was boasting of the large number of young ones which she had hatched. A Crow hearing her, said: 'My good friend, cease from this unseasonable boasting. The larger the number of your family, the greater your cause of sorrow, in seeing them shut up in this prison-house.'" In the tradition of the parable, the story might invite those so caged to escape, or perhaps call into question the advantages of class privilege as mere appearances, and in fact a gilded cage. However, the apologues are stories of hard knocks, told only to point out that life for those who may appear well off is demeaning, not to change this. Consider as well "The Farmer and the Stork," in which the farmer, to preserve his seed, slaughters cranes. A stork caught in his net pleads for release: "I am not a Crane, I am a Stork, a bird of excellent character." The stork explains his broken leg accounts for his presence in the farmer's field, his respect for his family, and his innocence of any harm to the farmer. "Look too, at my feathers—they are not the least like those of a Crane. The Farmer laughed . . . , 'It may be all as you say, I only know this: I have taken you with these robbers, the Cranes, and you must die in their company.'" The apologue is known for the lesson "Birds of a feather flock together." But note that the farmer observes in the stork no malice of will, weakness of character, or evidence of deceit on these points. Thus, there are no possible lessons for others seeking to elude the destiny of group slaughter. In other words, birds may be found together who are of different feathers, and yet the lesson about collective guilt will prevail nonetheless.

6. This is *the* paper of record and thus a demonstration project for the truth.

7. "Petitioner and her family did not have any identification documents with them when they were forced to flee Vietnam. Consequently, Petitioner did not have any written documentation confirming her date of birth . . . at the time of her . . . refugee application." Case 14-mc-80337-MEJ, Order, May 5, 2015.

8. Case 14-mc-80337-MEJ, p. 4.

9. Case 14-mc-80337-MEJ, p. 1.

10. I rely here on Ferdinand de Saussure's formulation of the sign (a concept, e.g., the citizen) conveying the inherently conjoined signifier (the word, e.g., "citizen") and the signified (the referent, e.g., the phenomenology of a biological or ontological, factual citizen) (Saussure 1986 [1916]).

11. Arguing for the "Unconstitutionality of the Acts of Congress of 1793 and 1850," Lysander Spooner writes: "1. They authorize the delivery of the slaves without a trial by jury" (1850, 5).

12. Elsewhere I have summarized the economic literature indicating such policies are economically irrational and also fail to advance other material instrumental goals (Stevens 2009b, esp. chap. 1). See also Carens 1987, 2013.

13. 8 USC 1481 § 349(a)(1). For its interpretation by the U.S. government, see the State Department webpage "Dual Nationality," https://travel.state.gov/content/en/legal-considerations/us-citizenship-laws-policies/citizenship-and-dual-nationality/dual-nationality.html.

14. 8 CFR 1235.3, emphasis added. 8 USC 1182(a)(6)(C)(ii) contains the same language referring to "aliens" who may be admissible if they believe they have a parenting fact pattern indicating they are in fact U.S. citizens at birth.

15. One percent of those in removal proceedings have their deportation orders terminated because they are U.S. citizens (Stevens 2011b). The absolute number of those so affected may not always affect electoral outcomes, though the intergenerational effects of prior ethnic cleansing are not so infinitesimally small as to be omitted from political consideration.

16. The rate of erratic judicial opinions has been noted by numerous commentators and in biting federal court decisions, including a notorious Seventh Circuit rebuke in which Judge Richard Posner detailed the low quality of immigration court decisions: "In the year ending on the date of the argument, different panels of this court reversed Board of Immigration Appeals in whole or in part a staggering 40 percent of the 136 petitions" and pointed out that 18 percent of other civil case decisions in which the United States was the appellee were overturned. He then excerpted some comments by his colleagues on these cases, e.g., "There is a gaping hole in the reasoning of the board and the immigration judge." *Niam v. Ashcroft*, 354 F. 3d 652, 654 (7th Cir. 2003), quoted in *Benslimane v. Gonzales*, 430 F. 3d 828 (7th Cir. 2005). All of the factors identified by Wes Skogan and Tracey Meares (2004) that correlate with police misconduct are endemic to the enforcement of immigration laws. See Julia Dona (2011–12), an empirical analysis of detention custody hearings; Jennifer Lee Koh (2012), an empirical study of deportations in absentia and through coerced or fraudulently obtained waivers; Fatma Marouf, Michael Kagan, and Rebecca Gill (2014), documenting "errant deportations"; Wadhia (2014), on speed producing wrongful classifications of removability; Mark Noferi (2012), on the effects

of deportation hearings absent attorneys; and M. Isabel Medina (2012), on the problems with allowing nonlawyer legal assistance to those in deportation proceedings.

17. On this view, race emerges from the legal territories that are the touchstone for actual or observed physical characteristics associated with a geographic territory of origins. On this view, the Chinese American, Japanese American, or Asian American is the outcome of one or more countries that make up Asia, for instance (tautologically defined by reference to its component countries), while governments also navigate specific of shifting sovereign alliances that produce the racialized alien or "terrorist" (Stevens 1999, chap. 5).

18. *SI v. Eric Holder, Jr.*, U.S. Attorney General, Case 12-60087 (Fifth Circuit Panel, September 11, 2013).

19. *SI v. Eric Holder, Jr.*, U.S. Attorney General, note 3.

20. See Laura Murray-Tjan's blog, Huffingtonpost.com/.

21. For references and discussion of the relevant laws and regulations, see Stevens 2011b, 636–38.

22. Insofar as alienage is a status distinction, the government, unable to prove Tiznado's alienage "beyond a reasonable doubt," cannot retry him for subsequent reentry into the United States, and in fact has not subsequently prosecuted Tiznado on this charge on encountering him in the United States following his deportation to Mexico (Stevens 2011–13).

23. Stevens 2011b, 2011–13. Additional cases include those of Hector Trevino and Sergio Madrid, whose 1326 prosecutions were withdrawn after U.S. attorneys saw evidence of their U.S. citizenship; both are now in Juarez, Mexico.

24. Cases on file with author.

25. The Christian Bible references the "Book of Life" as God's running list of names for those allowed entry to heaven (Philippians 3:5; Revelations 4:8 and passim).

26. Bonnie Honig's (2001) point about the episodic possibility of the lawmaker requiring foreignness or alienage is another characteristic of this paradox, insofar as those theorizing if not establishing constitutions concede the moment of founding as inevitably leveraged from an Archimedean point implying externality. The foreigner as founder and the citizen who is an alien both convey the fragility of the nation's imagined unity and coherence.

27. By referring to the quest for iterations of the original signature and context as "irresponsible," I am alluding to other portions of Derrida's work in which he finds in critical legal studies an aspiration to "intervene in an efficient and responsible though always, of course, very mediated way" (1989–90, 931) in projects pursuing justice. The iterations of the signature and the state's documentations of identity, by contrast, lack any self-conscious reflexivity and are for this reason irresponsible, etymologically from the Greek "sponde, a drink-offering, hence libations being made on the occasion, a solemn truce, and its v spendein, to make a drink-offering, hence to make a treaty, and to [Hittite] sipand-, to pour a libation" (Partridge 1958, "Despond" entry, para. 3). My own engagements are less ambitious than those Derrida ascribes to his colleagues, interventions mobilized by a desire to avoid injustice.

28. See, e.g., *Sazar Dent v. Eric Holder Jr.*, 627 F.3d 365, 374; and *Miguel Noel Fierro v. Immigration and Naturalization Service*, 81 F. Supp. 2d 167 ("Imagine for the moment the agony of living one's life in exile, knowing that the decision to deport hinged, at least partially, on an error of basic arithmetic. Kafka himself would recoil at such a blunder" [168]).

29. Derrida here also explains that deconstruction and his texts in particular only "*seem*, I do say *seem*, not to foreground the theme of justice" when in fact Derrida notes that it "was normal, foreseeable, desirable that studies of deconstructive style should culminate in the problematic of law (*droit*), of law and justice. It is even the most proper place for them, if such a thing exists" (1989–90, 929).

AFTERWORD

DANIEL KANSTROOM

> I speak an open and disengaged language, dictated by no passion but that of
> humanity. . . . My country is the world, and my religion is to do good.
> —Thomas Paine, *The Rights of Man*

> I said, "They deported a citizen." He said, "They can't do that."
> —Johann "Ace" Francis

Diogenes ("the Cynic"), when asked where he came from, was said to have an-
swered, "I am a citizen of the world" (he used the term now rendered in English as "cosmopolitan") (Laertius 1979 [1925], 6:2:64). Over the centuries, of
course, much has been made of this as a theoretical matter. But, after reading this
powerful collection of observations about the theory, practice, and forensics of
modern citizenship, I thought of a different (and, so far as I am aware, a unique)
question about Diogenes's assertion: What if he had been asked to prove it?

Such a hypothetical interrogation seems facetious, if not absurd. Who,
apart perhaps from an extraterrestrial immigration agent, would ever have
asked such a thing? Why *would* anyone ask for such proof? What sort of proof
could there possibly be? The answers all reduce to the most salient point of
this book: nation-state citizenship is not only a theoretical construct about
identity, rights, membership, the "right to remain," and the like. Unlike the

claims of the aspirational cosmopolitan, in the real world it is often a *problem of proof*. And because of this it is much more accessible to some than to others and much more subject to invidious discrimination and to government manipulation than is generally understood. Heisenberg's famous indeterminacy principle produces abstract, paradoxical constraints on knowledge. But citizenship law—in virtually every modern legal system—has a very different rule: *that which cannot be known and proved does not exist*. Those who cannot prove that they are citizens fall into and inhabit the abyss of this indeterminacy: the residual, marginalized, and pejorative category of "aliens." Indeed, for them, the very idea that citizenship is part of (if not the apotheosis of) the "rule of law," with its attendant requirements of consistency, transparency, and predictability, becomes bitterly questionable. And such proof is often quite complicated and sometimes impossible. Are these cases outliers or anomalies about which it is unfair to make too much fuss? If this book proves anything, it is that the answer to that question must be no.

The forensic problem of citizenship proof is, of course, deeply entwined with questions about membership in the nation-state and rights. Our imagined interrogation of Diogenes illustrates this, too. Indeed, his namesake, Diogenes Laertius, reported that Diogenes himself did not embrace the (unprovable) cosmopolitan variant of citizenship willingly, but from exile. He was born in Greek Sinope on the south coast of the Black Sea, around 410 BC. Thus, Diogenes's citizenship was of that city. But, in a twist that is similar to some of the modern case histories recounted in this volume, Diogenes was banished from Sinope, reportedly due to allegations of debasement or adulteration of currency. As Diogenes Laertius put it, "All the curses of tragedy, he used to say, had lighted upon him. At all events he was 'A homeless exile, to his country dead. A wanderer who begs his daily bread'" (Laertius 1979 [1925], 6:2:38–39).

Thus, when he made his famous idealistic protocosmopolitan declaration, Diogenes had already been denationalized and deported. In effect, his assertion of cosmopolitan citizenship was a robust, if perhaps Quixotic, attempt to defend himself against what Hannah Arendt (1966, 295) would later describe as the "calamity" of the stateless, whom she denominated as effectively "rightless." Diogenes sought to make lemonade from the lemons he had been given by the people of Sinope.

In the modern world, however, problems of denationalization have recurred on a massive scale, with horrific consequences. "The calamity of the rightless," Arendt wrote, "is not that they are deprived of life, liberty, and the pursuit of happiness, or of equality before the law and the freedom of opinion—formulas which were designed to solve problems within given communities—but they no longer belong to any community whatsoever" (1966, 295–96). Those of us who study or practice human rights law in the context of deportation also cling to the aspirations of Diogenes and find strong versions of Arendt's formula especially problematic. Indeed, it has often been overstated and misunderstood. This is particularly true of a famous passage written by Chief Justice Earl Warren, who—implicitly channeling Arendt—once referred to citizenship as "the right to have rights." This was a formulation that worked passably well in the context in which it was written: a dissent in a case involving the involuntary deprivation of citizenship. But it raises all sorts of problems if taken seriously as a general assertion.[1] Still, it is clearly true that many powerful rights claims—especially the "right to remain"—often depend on proof of citizenship status. What is the character of citizenship rights today, amid conundrums caused by citizenship's elusiveness to proof? As Johann "Ace" Francis's address in the preface poignantly notes, lack of proof is the linchpin of absurdity and contradiction. We move from the completely understandable: "When you grow up and you think of yourself as an American, you don't really think otherwise" to the illogical and absurd: "I've been deported from the U.S. and I'm a citizen." Any lawyer who reads this latter sentence knows that it is impossible. U.S. citizens cannot be deported. The relevant statute could not be clearer. In fact, in its very first sentence, it says the word "alien" *four times*: "Any *alien* (including an *alien* crewman) shall, upon the order of the Attorney General, be removed" if the *alien* is within one or more of the following classes of deportable *aliens* (8 U.S.C. §1227). When we speak of citizenship, then, we must live with contradiction, paradox, and, sometimes, tragedy—all of which the very idea of citizenship as a provable, bounded legal category ostensibly is designed to mitigate.

The introduction to this book provocatively asks "whether the citizenship they are discussing actually exists." Of course, it does. It must. But what may seem a bright line in theory is inevitably a forensic continuum in practice, more like the boundary between energy and matter than it is like matter itself. Jacqueline Stevens, in her impossibly but truly titled chapter, "The Alien Who Is a Citizen," explains with great clarity how this is so as she highlights a series of legal, political, and interpretive paradoxes with which we must come to grips.

Interestingly enough, ambiguity and paradox about citizenship have historically run both ways. We have seen poignant examples of the fragility (and sometimes the irrelevance) of citizenship status. On February 19, 1942, President Franklin D. Roosevelt issued Executive Order 9066, authorizing the army to control *all* persons of Japanese ancestry in four western states. This is well known. What is perhaps less well known is that the subsequent "civilian exclusion orders" issued by General John DeWitt applied to a rather peculiarly defined group: "all persons of Japanese ancestry, *both alien and non-alien*."[2] This strangely inverted citizenship phrasing ("non-alien") was a clear indicator not only of how "'foreignness' was imposed on U.S.- born citizens of Asian descent" (Saito 2001, 1n44). It also demonstrated the potential fragility of citizenship status as a guarantor of rights in hard times and the inevitable relevance of such (aspirationally) irrelevant factors as race, national origin, and class.

Indeed, contrary to what most would suspect, it is not always advantageous to prove one's U.S. citizenship. Consider, for example, *Perez v. Brownell* (1958), in which Chief Justice Earl Warren channeled Hannah Arendt's assertion about citizenship being the "right to have rights." The case involved a jus soli U.S. citizen who had lived most of his life in Texas but who had voted in Mexico and also apparently stayed outside the United States to avoid military service.[3] By the time the case got to court, Mr. Perez was strenuously trying to defeat deportation by proving that Congress could not constitutionally deprive him of his birthright citizenship for his alleged offenses. But here is a little-known, interesting twist: Perez had actually previously reentered the United States *three times* as a laborer (a "Mexican alien railroad worker" pursuant to the 1942 bracero program), by falsely claiming to be a *Mexican* citizen.[4] The government highlighted this point during oral argument. In fact, Oscar H. Davis mocked Perez as saying, once he was caught but not before: "I am not really a Mexican, I am an American citizen. I want to adjust my status [*sic*]." He concluded, "And of course they began deportation proceedings."[5] But, as those who read this book now understand, there is no such thing as "really" Mexican or "really" an American citizen. We cannot escape the rigors of proof or the requirements of constitutional normativity. As Sara Friedman nicely puts it in her chapter in this volume: "Documents do not affirm legal recognition or sovereign claims so much as they reproduce the uncertain status of contested borders and the individuals who journey across them." Moreover, as Kamal Sadiq piquantly notes in this volume, "State papers, documents, and formats tell us more about membership, nationality, belonging, and identity than formal rules alone. . . . The document manifests society."

This, I think, brings us to the most important implicit leitmotif of this work. We are ultimately talking not about status but about the rights (or at least the rights claims) of the stateless. Contrary to Chief Justice Warren's implication, Arendt's position was *not* that citizenship *should be* the right to have rights. Rather, as she put it: "The Rights of Man, supposedly inalienable, proved to be *unenforceable* . . . whenever people appeared who were no longer citizens of any sovereign state" (1966, 293). Her primary concern was practical. Stateless aliens lacked any *enforceable* protections.

Of course, there is also a deeper, substantive question. As Arendt herself worried: "Recent attempts to frame a new bill of human rights, . . . seem to have demonstrated that no one seems able to define with any assurance what these general human rights, as distinguished from the rights of citizen, really are" (1966, 296–97). But *The Origins of Totalitarianism* was first published in 1951. It hardly needs to be said that—despite its evident challenges and deficiencies—the corpus of human rights protections for noncitizens is much more specific, more robust, and more widely enforced today than was the case during the times she considered. As Jacqueline Bhabha notes in this volume, we now see powerful norms of what she terms "regional citizenship" and "global citizenship."[6] There are, to be sure, still major gaps, especially regarding the rights of the deported (see Kanstroom and Chicco 2015). But the concrete difference between the rights of citizens and "the rights of others" is much less than it once was (see Benhabib 2014).

In the end, let us return to the Diogenes of Sinope and then of the world. Though perhaps most famous for being an early cosmopolitan philosopher, he also was acutely aware—as a banished stranger—of the importance of class and power. Indeed, he reportedly suggested that the word "disability" ought to be applied not to the deaf or blind, but to the poor (Laertius 1979 [1925], 6:2:34). Thus, it is undeniably true, as Beatrice McKenzie notes in this volume about today's expensive legal proceedings, that citizenship is a status "more easily defended by some individuals than others." There may be no better way to avoid the Arendtian "calamity of the rightless" than to strengthen citizenship protections and to ease its acquisition and its requirements of proof. But, as this book demonstrates, these goals are in tension with each other. Strengthening the protections of citizenship for future "non-aliens" may inevitably have two perverse consequences. First, it could render citizenship still more precious and thus ever harder to achieve and to prove. Second, it could relegate noncitizens— especially the deported—to a dangerous rightless realm. We must therefore do the harder, more basic work of defining and instantiating meaningful human rights protections for *all* people, regardless of status or location. This, in the end, is the best way to resist "the numerous small and not so small evils with which the road to hell is paved" (Arendt 1994, 271).

NOTES

1. *Perez v. Brownell*, 356 U.S. 44, 64 (1958) (Warren, C.J., dissenting).

2. See, e.g., Civilian Exclusion Order No. 34, quoted in *Korematsu v. United States*, 323 U.S. 214, 229n6 (1944) (providing that, after twelve o'clock on May 8, 1942, all

persons of Japanese ancestry, "both alien and non-alien, were to be excluded from a described portion of Military Area No. 1").

3. The 1940 law at issue had been passed largely in response to voting by American citizens in a 1935 plebiscite relating to Hitler's annexation of the Saar region. As one member of Congress put it, the legislation aimed to "relieve this country of the responsibility of those who reside in foreign lands and only claim citizenship when it serves their purposes." *Perez v. Brownell*, 356 U.S. 44, 55 (1958) (opinion of Justice Frankfurter).

4. *Perez v. Brownell,* 235 F. 2d 364 (9th Cir. 1956). The railroad bracero program was negotiated to supply U.S. railroads initially with unskilled workers for track maintenance. It eventually included other unskilled and skilled labor. See "World War II Homefront Era: 1940s: Bracero Program Establishes New Migration Patterns," Picture This, http:// museumca.org/picturethis/pictures/bracero-workers-repair-railroad-track-southern -pacific-line-oakland-california.

5. First Oral Argument, *Perez v. Brownell* (May 1, 1957; the case was reargued on October 28, 1957); http://www.oyez.org/cases/1950-1959/1956/1956_44_2 (at 36:53–37:20).

6. The former seems more citizenship-like than the latter, which requires certain categorical points to be proven.

REFERENCES

ABC15.com. 2011. "Vote on Birthright Citizenship Called Off at Last Minute." February 7. http://www.abc15.com/dpp/news/region_phoenix_metro/central_phoenix/vote-on -birthright-citizenship-called-off-at-last-minute.

Abdel-Whab v. Orthopedic Association of Dutchess. 2006. 415 F. Supp. 2d 293 (S.D. N.Y. 2006).

Agamben, Giorgio. 1998. *Homo sacer: Sovereign Power and Bare Life*. Stanford, CA: Stanford University Press.

Ahlquist, Daniel. 2015. "Losing Place in the Corn Mountains: Forest Conservation, In Situ Displacement, and Agrarian Transformation in Upland Northern Thailand." PhD diss., Cornell University.

Akindès, Francis. 2004. "The Roots of the Military-Political Crises in Côte d'Ivoire." Research Report 128. Oslo: Nordika Afrikainstitut; Dakar: Codesria.

Alienikoff, Thomas Alexander, David Martin, Hiroshi Motomura, and Maryellen Fullerton. 2012. *Immigration and Citizenship: Process and Policy*. St. Paul, MN: West.

Alvarez, Lizette. 2014. "After Forming Deep Roots in U.S., Man Discovers He Isn't a Citizen." *New York Times*, May 13, A10.

Amnesty International. 2013. *Told to Move On: Forced Evictions of Roma in France*. London: Amnesty International Publications.

Anderson, Benedict. 1983. *Imagined Communities: Reflections on the Origin and Spread of Nationalism*. London: Verso.

Anderson, Stuart. 2012. "Mia Love May Be Right about Her Family's Immigration History." *Forbes*, September 28. http://www.forbes.com/sites/stuartanderson/2012/09 /28/mia-love-may-be-right-about-her-familys-immigration-history/.

Andrews, Penelope. 2015. "Foreword." In *African Asylum at a Crossroads: Activism, Expert Testimony, and Refugee Rights*, edited by Iris Berger, Tricia Redeker Hepner, Benjamin N. Lawrance, Joanna Tague, and Meredith Terretta, vii–xi. Athens: Ohio University Press.

Appell, Annette. 2014. "Certifying Identity." *Capital University Law Review* 42:361–405.

Arcioni, Elisa. 2014. "Identity at the Edge of the Constitutional Community." In *Allegiance and Identity in a Globalised World*, edited by Fiona Jenkins, Mark Nolan, and Kim Rubenstein, 31–51. Cambridge: Cambridge University Press.

Arendt, Hannah. 1966. *The Origins of Totalitarianism*. New York: Harcourt, Brace and World.

———. 1994. *Essays in Understanding 1930–1954: Formation, Exile, and Totalitarianism.* New York: Schocken Books.

———. 2007a [1944]. "The Jew as Pariah." In *The Jewish Writings*, 275–97. New York: Schocken Books.

———. 2007b [1943]. "We Refugees." In *The Jewish Writings*, 264–74. New York: Schocken Books.

Arizona Constitution. Article II, § 13. 2012.

Arizona Legislature. 2011. Bill Status Overview: Vote Detail, Senate Bill 1308, 50th Legislature, 1st Regular Session (Arizona). http://www.azleg.gov//FormatDocument.asp?inDoc=/legtext/50leg/1r/bills/sb1308.sthird.1.asp&Session_ID=102.

Aruna, P. 2011. "80-Year-Old Finally a Malaysian—after 55 Years." *Star*, July 30. http://thestar.com.my/metro/story.asp?sec=nation&file=/2011/7/30/nation/9207749.

Asencio, Karen Mercado. 2012. "The Under-Registration of Births in Mexico: Consequences for Children, Adults, and Migrants." *Migration Information Source*. Accessed December 11, 2013. http://www.migrationpolicy.org/article/under-registration-births -mexico-consequences-children-adults-and-migrants.

Assessment of the Human Rights Situation of Roma and Sinti in Italy. Warsaw: OSCE.

Associazione per gli studi giuridici sull'immigrazione (ASGI) and E. Rozzi. 2013. *Out of Limbo: Promoting the Right of Undocumented and Stateless Roma Migrants to a Legal Status in Italy [Statement of Activities].* June 20.

Atger, Anaïs Faure. 2013. "European Citizenship Revealed: Sites, Actors and Roma Access to Justice in the EU." In *Enacting European Citizenship*, edited by Engin F. Isin and Michael Saward, 178–94. Cambridge: Cambridge University Press.

Austin, J. L. 1962. *How to Do Things with Words*. Oxford: Clarendon.

Avon, Natalie. 2011. "Why More Americans Don't Travel Abroad." CNN, February 4. http://www.cnn.com/2011/TRAVEL/02/04/americans.travel.domestically/.

AZ Central. 2011. "Arizona Birthright Citizenship Law Passed by Senate Panel." February 22. http://www.azcentral.com/news/election/azelections/articles/2011/02/22 /20110222arizona-immigration-birthright-citizenship-bill-advances.html.

Babo, Alfred. 2008. "Enjeux et jeux d'acteurs dans la crise identitaire en Côte d'Ivoire." *Kasa Bya Kasa* 13:99–121.

———. 2010a. "Conflits fonciers, ethnicité politique et guerre en Côte d'Ivoire." *Alternative Sud* 17 (2): 95–117.

———. 2010b. "La politique publique de l'étranger et la crise sociopolitique en Côte d'Ivoire." In *Côte d'Ivoire: La réinvention de soi dans la violence*, edited by Francis Akindès, 39–62. Dakar: Codesria.

———. 2013a. "The Crisis of Public Policies in Côte d'Ivoire: Land Law and the Nationality Trap in Tabou's Rural Communities." *Africa* 83:100–119.

———. 2013b. *L'étranger en Côte d'Ivoire: Crises et controverses autour d'une catégorie sociale*. Paris: l'Harmattan.

Babo, Alfred, and Yvan Droz. 2008. "Conflits fonciers, de l'ethnie à la nation: Rapports interethniques et 'ivoirité' dans le sud-ouest de la Côte d'Ivoire." *Cahiers d'Etudes Africaines* 192:741–64.

Bacongo, Cissé Ibrahim. 2007. *Alassane Dramane Ouattara, une vie singulière*. Abidjan: NEI-CEDA.

Barany, Zoltan D. 1998. "Memory and Experience: Anti-Roma Prejudice in Eastern Europe." Woodrow Wilson International Center for Scholars, Working Paper 50.

Barbin, Herculine. 1980. *Herculine Barbin: Being the recently discovered memoirs of a nineteenth-century French hermaphrodite*. New York: Pantheon Books.

Barrouquere, Brett. 2011. "Sisters Settle Suit over Social Security Cards." *CNS News*. Accessed December 11, 2013. http://cnsnews.com/news/article/sisters-settle-suit-over-social-security-cards.

Basler, Roy P., ed. 1953. *The Collected Works of Abraham Lincoln*. Vol. 2. New Brunswick, NJ: Rutgers University Press.

Bassett, Thomas J. 2004. "Containing the Donzow: The Politics of Scale in Côte d'Ivoire." *Africa Today* 50 (4): 31–49.

Becker, Andrew. 2011. "Immigration Agency Pays Army Veteran $400,000 for Wrongfully Detaining Him." *LA Times*, February 24. http://articles.latimes.com/2011/feb/24/local/la-me-citizen-sweep-20110224.

Bédié, Henri Konan. 1999. *Les chemins de ma vie*. Paris: Plon.

Benhabib, Seyla. 2007. "Twilight of Sovereignty or the Emergence of Cosmopolitan Norms: Rethinking Citizenship in Volatile Times." *Citizenship Studies* 11:19–36.

———. 2014. *The Rights of Others: Aliens, Residents, and Citizens*. Cambridge: Cambridge University Press.

Benjamin, Walter. 1986 [1921]. "A Critique of Violence." In *Reflections: Essays, Aphorisms, Autobiographical Writing*, 277–300. New York: Schocken Books.

Berger, Iris, Tricia Redeker Hepner, Benjamin N. Lawrance, Joanna Tague, and Meredith Terretta, eds. 2015. *African Asylum at a Crossroads: Activism, Expert Testimony, and Refugee Rights*. Athens: Ohio University Press.

Berkeley, Bill. 2009. "Stateless People, Violent States." *World Policy Journal* 26 (1): 3–15.

Bhabha, Jacqueline. 2009. "Arendt's Children: Do Today's Migrant Children Have a Right to Have Rights?" *Human Rights Quarterly* 31:410–51.

———, ed. 2011. *Children without a State: A Global Human Rights Challenge*. Cambridge, MA: MIT Press.

Bingham, Laura, Julia Harrington Reddy, and Sebastian Köhn. 2011. "De Jure Statelessness in the Real World: Applying the Prato Summary Conclusions." *Open Society Justice Initiative*. Accessed December 11, 2013. http://www.soros.org/sites/default/files/prato-statelessness-20110303.pdf.

Black's Law Dictionary. 1999. 7th ed. St. Paul's, MN: West Group.

Blé, Goudé Charles. 2005. *Crise Ivoirienne: Ma part de vérité*. Abidjan: Frat-mat Editions.

Blitz, Brad K., and Maureen Lynch, eds. 2009. *Statelessness and the Benefits of Citizenship: A Comparative Study*. Northampton: Edward Elgar.

Boone, Catherine. 2009. "Electoral Populism Where Property Rights Are Weak: Land Politics in Contemporary Sub-Saharan Africa." *Comparative Politics* 41:183–201.

Booth, Wayne. 1974. *Modern Dogma and the Rhetoric of Assent*. Chicago: University of Chicago Press.

Bosniak, Linda. 2000. "Citizenship Denationalized." *Indiana Journal of Global Legal Studies* 7:447–509.

———. 2007. "Being Here: Ethical Territoriality and the Rights of Immigrants." *Theoretical Inquiries in Law* 8 (2): 389–410.

Boswell, John. 1994. *Same-Sex Unions in Premodern Europe*. New York: Villard Books.

Bouquet, Christian. 2003. "Le poids des étrangers en Côte d'Ivoire." *Annales de Géographie* 630:115–45.

Bradley, Megan. 2014. "Rethinking Refugeehood: Statelessness, Repatriation, and Refugee Agency." *Review of International Studies* 40:101–23.

Bredbenner, Candice. 1998. *A Nationality of Her Own: Women, Marriage, and the Law of Citizenship*. Berkeley: University of California Press.

Bryant, Chris. 2010. "Deported Roma Return to Poverty." *Financial Times*, September 24.

Burnett, Victoria. 2012. "New Hints at Looser Rules on Travel Stir Hope in Cuba." *New York Times*, May 20, A8.

Butler, Judith. 1991. "Imitation and Gender Insubordination." In *Inside/Out: Lesbian Theories, Gay Theories*, edited by Diana Fuss, 13–31. New York: Routledge.

Çağlar, Ayşe, and Sebastian Mehling. 2013. "Sites and the Scales of Law: Third Country Nationals and EU Roma Citizens." In *Enacting European Citizenship*, edited by Engin F. Isin and Michael Saward, 155–77. Cambridge: Cambridge University Press.

Cahn, Claude, and Elspeth Guild. 2010. "Recent Migration of Roma in Europe." Organization for Security and Cooperation in Europe. 2nd ed. http://www.osce.org/hcnm /78034?download=true.

Cames R. 2013. "Government by Expulsion: The Roma Camp, Citizenship and the State." Paper presented at Resourceful Cities Research Committee, Sociology of Urban and Regional Development, International Sociological Association, Berlin, August 29–31. http://www.academia.edu/5618161/Government_by_Expulsion_The _Roma_Camp_Citizenship_and_the_State.

Canty, Rachel. 2004. "The New World of Immigration Custody Determinations after *Zadvydas v. Davis.*" *Georgetown Immigration Law Journal* 18:467–504.

Caplan, Jane. 2005. "Write Me Down, Make Me Real." *History Workshop Journal* 60:195–201.

Caplan, Jane, and John Torpey. 2001. *Documenting Individual Identity: The Development of State Practices in the Modern World*. Princeton, NJ: Princeton University Press.

Carbado, Devon. 2005. "Racial Naturalization." *American Quarterly* 57 (3): 633–58.

Carens, Joseph. 1987. "Aliens and Citizens: The Case for Open Borders." *Review of Politics* 49:251–73.

———. 2013. *The Ethics of Immigration*. Oxford: Oxford University Press.

Carrera, Sergio. 2013. "Shifting Responsibilities for EU Roma Citizens: The 2010 French Affair on Roma Evictions and Expulsions Continued." Center for European Policy Studies Paper No. 55. June.

Castelano v. Clinton. 2008a. No. 08-cv-00057 (S.D. Tx. 2008). Second Amended Complaint.

Castelano v. Clinton. 2008b. No. 08-cv-00057 (S.D. Tx. 2008). Exh. 1 to Second Amended Complaint.

Castelano v. Clinton. 2009. No. 08-cv-00057 (S.D. Tx. 2009). Stipulation and Agreement of Settlement and Release.

Castillo, Manuel Angel. 2006. "Mexico: Caught between the United States and Central America." *Migration Information Source.* Accessed December 11, 2013. http://www .migrationinformation.org/Feature/display.cfm?ID=389.

Cellule Universitaire de recherche pour la diffusion des idées du président Henri Konan Bédié (curdiphe). 1996. *L'ivoirité ou l'esprit du nouveau contrat social d'Henri Konan Bédié.* Abidjan: Presse Universitaire d'Abidjan.

Center for Migration Studies. 2012. "The Impact of Birth Registration within and across Borders." Accessed December 11, 2013. http://cmsny.org/2012/03/26/birth -registration-across-borders/.

Centers for Disease Control. 2012. *Home Births in the United States, 1990–2009.* National Center for Health Statistics. Accessed June 1, 2015. http://www.cdc.gov/nchs/data /databriefs/db84.htm.

Chang, Aurora. 2011. "Undocumented to Hyperdocumented: A Jornada of Protection, Papers, and PhD Status." *Harvard Educational Review* 81 (3): 508–21.

Chesterman, John, and Brian Galligan. 1997. *Citizens without Rights: Aborigines and Australian Citizenship.* Cambridge: Cambridge University Press.

Chin, Tun Pok. 2000. *Paper Son: One Man's Story.* Philadelphia: Temple University Press.

Chu Kheng Lim v. Minister for Immigration, Local Government and Ethnic Affairs. 1992. 176 CLR 1.

Chupinit Kesmanee. 1994. "Dubious Concepts in the Thai Highlands: The Chao Khao in Transition." *Law and Society Review* 28 (3): 673–86.

Chutima "Miju" Morlaeku. 2006. *Problems Concerning the Laxity of Legal Status within the Thai Highland Population.* Internal report. Bangkok: UNESCO.

———. 2010. *Addressing the Remaining Legal Status Question.* Internal report. Bangkok: UNESCO.

Citizenship and Immigration Canada. 2013. "Changes to Citizenship Rules as of April 2009." Accessed December 11, 2013. http://www.cic.gc.ca/english/citizenship/rules -citizenship.asp.

Clark, Colin, and Elaine Campbell. 2000. " 'Gypsy Invasion': A Critical Analysis of Newspaper Reaction to Czech and Slovak Romani Asylum-Seekers in Britain, 1997." *Romani Studies* 10 (1): 5–31.

Clark, Jane Perry. 1969. *Deportation of Aliens from the United States to Europe.* New York: Arno.

Clark v. Martinez. 2005. 543 U.S. 371.

Cohen, Andrew. 2011. "A Deeper, Darker Prejudice." *Ottawa Citizen,* June 16.

Collins, Kristin. 2011. "A Short History of Sex and Citizenship: The Historians' Amicus Brief in *Flores-Villar v. United States.*" *Boston University Law Review* 61:1485–515.

———. 2014. "Illegitimate Borders: Jus Sanguinis Citizenship and the Legal Construction of Family, Race, and Nation." *Yale Law Journal* 124:2134–235.

Comaroff, Jean, and John L. Comaroff. 2003. "Reflections on Liberalism, Policicultural-
ism, and ID-ology: Citizenship and Difference in South Africa." *Social Identities*
9:45–74.

———. 2009. *Ethnicity, Inc.* Chicago. University of Chicago Press.

Congressional Research Service. 2008. *Border Security: The Role of the U.S. Border
Patrol.* Accessed September 21, 2012. http://digital.library.unt.edu/ark:/67531
/metacrs8464/.

Constitucion de la Republica Dominica. 2010. Accessed December 12, 2013. http://pdba
.georgetown.edu/Constitutions/DomRep/vigente.html.

Constitutional Planning Committee. 1974. *Final Report of the Constitutional Planning
Committee*: Pt. 1. Port Moresby: Government Printer.

Convention between the American Republics Regarding the Status of Aliens in Their
Respective Territories. 1928. Art. 6. 46 Stat. 2753. Accessed December 11, 2013.
http://www.jstor.org/stable/2213101.

Convention Debates, Official Report of the National Australasian. 1897. First Session.
Adelaide.

Convention on the Reduction of Statelessness. 1961. Accessed December 11, 2013.
http://www.unhcr.org/3bbb286d8.html.

Convention on the Rights of the Child. 1989. Accessed December 11, 2013. http://
www.unhcr.org/50f941fe9.html.

Convention Relating to the Status of Refugees and Protocol. 1951 and 1967. UNHCR.
Accessed December 11, 2013. http://www.unhcr.org/4ec262df9.html.

Convention Relating to the Status of Stateless Persons. 1954. Accessed December 11, 2013.
http://www.unhcr.org/3bbb25729.html.

Cornyn, John. 2011. Statement of Sen. Cornyn, Ranking Member, Senate Subcom-
mittee on Immigration, Refugees and Border Security Development, Relief and
Education for Minors (DREAM) Act of 2011. *Hearing on S. 952 Before the Senate
Judiciary Subcommittee on Immigration, Refugees and Border Security.* 112th
Congress.

Cott, Nancy. 2000. *Public Vows: A History of Marriage and the Nation.* Cambridge, MA:
Harvard University Press.

Council of Europe. 2012. *Human Rights of Roma and Travellers.* Strasbourg: Council of
Europe Publishing.

———. 2013. *The Council of Europe: Protecting the Rights of Roma.* Strasbourg: Council
of Europe Publishing.

Cour Nationale du Droit d'Asile. 2011. No. 10011958. November 2.

Coutin, Susan Bibler. 2007. *Nations of Emigrants: Shifting Boundaries of Citizenship in
El Salvador and the United States.* Ithaca, NY: Cornell University Press.

———. 2013. "In the Breach: Citizenship and Its Approximations." *Indiana Journal of
Global Legal Studies* 20:109–40.

Crook, Richard C. 1997. "Winning Coalition and Ethno-regional Politics: The Failure
of the Opposition in the 1990 and 1995 Elections in Côte d'Ivoire." *African Affairs*
96:215–42.

Crossan, J. 1975. *The Dark Interval: Towards a Theology of Story.* Niles, IL: Argus.

Crumley, Bruce. 2010. "Anger as Sarkozy Targets Roma in Crime Crackdown." *Time*, July 23.

Curran, John. 2009. "Chester Arthur Rumor Still Lingers in Vermont." Associated Press, August 17.

Dandeker, Christopher. 1994. *Surveillance, Power and Modernity: Bureaucracy and Discipline from 1700 to the Present Day*. Cambridge: Polity.

Das, Veena. 2004. "The Signature of the State: The Paradox of Illegibility." In *Anthropology in the Margins of the State*, edited by Veena Das and Deborah Poole, 225–52. Santa Fe: School of American Research Press.

Das, Veena, and Deborah Poole, eds. 2004a. *Anthropology in the Margins of the State*. Santa Fe, NM: School of American Research Press.

Das, Veena, and Deborah Poole. 2004b. "State and Its Margins: Comparative Ethnographies." In *Anthropology in the Margins of the State*, edited by Veena Das and Deborah Poole, 3–33. Santa Fe, NM: School of American Research Press.

da Silva, Lurdes C. 2008. "Deportation of U.S. Citizens: It's Just the Tip of the Iceberg." *Detention Watch*. Accessed December 11, 2013. http://www.detentionwatchnetwork.org/node/1188.

del Bosque, Melissa. 2012. "Life in the Constitution-Free Zone." *Texas Observer*, February 17. http://www.texasobserver.org/lalinea/life-in-the-constitution-free-zone.

Dembélé, Ousmane. 2003. "Côte d'Ivoire: La fracture communautaire." *Politique Africaine* 89:34–48.

Dembélé, Ousmane. 2002. "La construction economique et politique de la catégorie 'Etranger' en Côte d'Ivoire." In *Côte d'Ivoire, l'Année Terrible 1999–2000*, edited by Marc Le Pape and Claudine Vidal, 123–71. Paris: Karthala–Les Afriques.

Dent v. Holder. 2010. 627 F.3d 365 (9th Cir.).

Derrida, Jacques. 1979. "Scribble (Writing Power)," translated by Cary Plotkin, *Yale French Studies* 58:117–47.

———. 1981a [1972]. *Dissemination*. Edited and translated by Barbara Johnson. Chicago: University of Chicago Press.

———. 1981b [1968]. "Plato's Pharmacy." In *Dissemination*, 95–117. Edited and translated by Barbara Johnson. Chicago: University of Chicago Press.

———. 1988 [1972]. "Signature, Event, Context." In *Limited Inc.*, 1–23. Translated by Samuel Weber and Jeffrey Mehlman. Evanston, IL: Northwestern University Press.

———. 1989–90. "Force of Law: The 'Mystical Foundation of Authority.'" *Cardozo Law Review* 11:920–1045.

Deutsch, Karl. 1969. *Nationalism and Social Communication: An Inquiry into the Foundations of Nationality*. Cambridge, MA: MIT Press.

Dillon, Nancy. 2012. "Texas Runaway Found Pregnant in Colombia after She Was Mistakenly Deported: Report." *New York Daily News*, January 5.

DiVirgilio, Lisa. 2010. "Report: Hundreds of U.S. Citizens Wrongfully Deported Every Year." *Syracuse.com*. Accessed December 11, 2013. www.syracuse.com/news/index.ssf/2010/07/report_hundreds_of_us_citizens.html.

Dolidze, Anna. 2011. "Lampedusa and Beyond: Recognition, Implementation, and Justiciability of Stateless Persons' Rights under International Law." *Interdisciplinary Journal of Human Rights Law* 6:131–32.

Domínguez, Virginia R. 1986. *White by Definition: Social Classification in Creole Louisiana.* New Brunswick, NJ: Rutgers University Press.

Donofrio, Leo. 2011. "Beware: Arizona Senate Bill 1308 Defines Dual Citizens as Natural Born Citizens." *Natural Born Citizen.* Accessed February 19, 2012. http://naturalborncitizen.wordpress.com/2011/02/23/beware-arizona-senate-bill-1308-defines-dual-citizens-to-be-natural-born-citizens/.

Dozon, Jean-Pierre. 2000. "La Côte d'Ivoire au péril de l'ivoirité." *Afrique Contemporaine* 193:13–24.

Dupree, Thomas H. 2011. "Keep Our Communities Safe Act of 2011: Hearing on H.R. 1932 before the Subcomm. on Immigration Policy & Enforcement of the H. Comm. on the Judiciary, 112th Cong." Unpublished paper.

Durand, Jorge, and Douglas S. Massey. 2010. "New World Orders: Continuities and Changes in Latin American Migration." *Annals of the American Academy of Political and Social Science* 630 (1): 20–52. Accessed December 11, 2103. http://www.ncbi.nlm.nih.gov/pmc/articles/PMC2931359/.

Durkheim, Émile. 1915. *Elementary Forms of Religious Life.* Translated by Joseph Swain. London: George Allen and Unwin.

Eastman, John. 2004. *Brief of Amicus Curiae: The Claremont Institute Center for Constitutional Jurisprudence in Support of Respondents, Yaser Esam Hamdi v. Rumsfeld.* No. 03-6696 (March 29).

Ettinger, Patrick. 2010. *Imaginary Lines: Border Enforcement and the Origins of Undocumented Immigration, 1882–1930.* Austin: University of Texas Press.

Etzioni, Amitai. 2007. "Citizenship Tests: A Comparative, Communitarian Perspective." *Political Quarterly* 78 (3): 353–63.

European Commission. 2011. "Communication from the Commission to the European Parliament, the Council, the European Economic and Social Committee and the Committee of the Regions: European Agenda for the Integration of Third-Country Nationals." *COM* 248.

———. 2013. "European Council Recommendation for Roma Inclusion." IP/13/607, Memo 13/610. Accessed May 1, 2016. http://europa.eu/rapid/press-release_IP-13-1226_en.htm.

European Roma Rights Center. 2013a. "For Consideration by the European Commission on the Transposition and Application of the Race Directive and on the Legal Issues Relevant to Roma Integration."

———. 2013b. "Written Comments Concerning Serbia for Consideration by the Committee on Economic, Social, and Cultural Rights at the 52nd Session."

European Union Agency for Fundamental Rights. 2009. "Housing Conditions of Roma and Travelers in the European Union—Comparative Report."

European Union Agency for Fundamental Rights, UNDP, and European Commission. 2012. "The Situation of Roma in 11 EU Member States: Survey Results at a Glance."

Fadel, Leila. 2012. "In Egypt, Foreign Citizenship Rule Roils Presidential Race." *Washington Post*, April 7.

Faiola, Anthony. 2010. "Italy Closes the Door on Gypsies." *Washington Post,* October 12.

Fassin, Didier, and Estelle D'Halluin. 2005. "The Truth from the Body: Medical Certificates as Ultimate Evidence for Asylum Seekers." *American Anthropologist* 107:597–608.

Fausto-Sterling, Anne. 1992. *Myths of Gender: Biological Theories about Women and Men.* 2nd ed. New York: Basic Books.

Federation for American Immigration Reform. 2012. "About FAIR." Accessed February 19, 2012. http://www.fairus.org/site/PageNavigator/about.html.

Feingold, David. 2000. "The Hell of Good Intentions: Some Preliminary Thoughts on Opium in the Political Ecology of the Trade in Girls and Women." In *Where China Meets Southeast Asia: Social and Cultural Change in the Border Regions*, edited by G. Evans, C. Hutton, and K. K. Eng. New York: St. Martin's.

———. 2002. *A Right to Belong.* Ophidian Films, Ltd. for UNESCO.

———. 2003. *Trading Women.* Ophidian Films.

Feldman, Ilana. 2008. *Governing Gaza: Bureaucracy, Authority, and the Work of Rule, 1917–1967.* Durham, NC: Duke University Press.

Ferme, Mariane. 2004. "Deterritorialized Citizenship and the Resonances of the Sierra Leonean State." In *Anthropology in the Margins of the State*, edited by Veena Das and Deborah Poole, 35–66. Santa Fe, NM: School of American Research Press, 2004.

Finkelman, Paul. 1997. *Slavery and the Law.* Madison, WI: Madison House.

———. 2006. "The Dragon St. George Could Not Slay: Tucker's Plan to End Slavery." *William and Mary Quarterly* 47:1213–43.

Fitzgerald, David. 2005. "Nationality and Migration in Modern Mexico." *Journal of Ethnic and Migration Studies* 31:171–91.

Flaim, Amanda. 2015. "No Man's Land: Sovereignty, Legal Status, and the Production of Statelessness among Highlanders in Northern Thailand." PhD diss., Cornell University.

Foucault, Michel. 1978. *History of Sexuality: An Introduction.* Vol. 1. Translated by Robert Hurley. New York: Pantheon.

———. 2003a [1974–75]. *Abnormal: Lectures at the Collège de France, 1974–1975.* Translated by Graham Burchell. New York: Verso.

———. 2003b [1975–76]. *Society Must Be Defended: Lectures at the Collège de France, 1975–1976.* New York: Picador.

Freeman, Jo. 2008. "The Rise of Political Woman in the Election of 1912." In *We Will Be Heard: Women's Struggles for Political Power in the United States*, 49–75. New York: Rowman and Littlefield.

Friedman, Sara L. 2010. "Determining 'Truth' at the Border: Immigration Interviews, Chinese Marital Migrants, and Taiwan's Sovereignty Dilemmas." *Citizenship Studies* 14:167–83.

Fuglerud, Oivind. 2004. "Constructing Exclusion: The Micro-sociology of an Immigration Department." *Social Anthropology* 12:25–40.

Fullerton, Maryellen. 2014. "The Intersection of Statelessness and Refugee Protection in U.S. Asylum Policy." *Journal on Migration and Human Security* 2:144–64.

Gadamer, Hans-Georg. 1984. "The Hermeneutics of Suspicion." In *Hermeneutics: Questions and Prospects*, edited by Gary Shapiro and Alan Sica, 54–65. Amherst: University of Massachusetts Press.

Garcelon, Marc. 2001. "Colonizing the Subject: The Genealogy and Legacy of the Soviet Internal Passport." In *Documenting Individual Identity: The Development of State Practices in the Modern World*, edited by Jane Caplan and John Torpey, 83–100. Princeton, NJ: Princeton University Press.

Garcia v. Clinton 2011. 2011. WL 2173689 (S.D. Tx 2011).

Geertz, Clifford. 1963. "The Integrative Revolution: Primordial Sentiments and Civil Politics in the New States." In *Old Societies, News States*, edited by C. Geertz, 105–57. New York: Free Press of Glencoe.

Goldring, John. 1978. *The Constitution of Papua New Guinea: A Study in Legal Nationalism*. Sydney: Law Book Company.

Gonzalez, Daniel. 2011. "'Birth Tourism' Not a Widespread Practice in U.S., Data Show." *Arizona Republic*, August 17.

Good, Anthony. 2004a. "Expert Evidence in Asylum and Human Rights Appeals: An Expert's View." *International Journal of Refugee Law* 16:358–80.

———. 2004b. "Undoubtedly an Expert? Anthropologists in British Asylum Courts." *Journal of the Royal Anthropological Institute* 10:113–33.

———. 2007. *Anthropology and Expertise in the Asylum Courts*. London: Routledge.

———. 2008. "Cultural Evidence in Courts of Law." *Journal of the Royal Anthropological Institute* 14 (April): S47–S60.

———. 2015. "Anthropological Evidence and Country of Origin Information in British Asylum Courts." In *Adjudicating Refugee and Asylum Status*, edited by B. N. Lawrance and G. B. Ruffer, 122–44. Cambridge: Cambridge University Press.

Goodman, Jennifer. 1998. *Chivalry and Exploration, 1298–1630*. Woodsbridge, England: Boydell.

Gordillo, Gastón. 2006. "The Crucible of Citizenship: ID-Paper Fetishism in the Argentinean Chaco." *American Ethnologist* 33:162–76.

Gordon, Charles. 1968. "Who Can Be President of the United States: The Unresolved Enigma." *Maryland Law Review* 28 (1): 1–32.

Gorman, Daniel. 2006. *Imperial Citizenship: Empire and the Question of Belonging*. Manchester: Manchester University Press.

Government of Delhi. 2010. *Homeless Survey 2010*. Delhi.

Government of India, Ministry of Women and Child Development. 2006. *India: Building a Protective Environment for Children*. July 22. Delhi.

Government of India, Press Information Bureau. 2014. "Unique Identification Authority of India (UIDAI) Issues 56 Crore Aadhaar Numbers." January 16.

Government of Malaysia, Ministry of Home Affairs. 2014. "National Registration Department of Malaysia: History." Accessed March 6, 2014. http://www.jpn.gov.my/en/profil/history.

Government of Malaysia, Prime Minister's Department. 2010. "Special Implementation Taskforce on Indian Community (PM Department)." June. Accessed May 7, 2011. http://taskforceindiancommunity.blogspot.com/2011/03/initial-findings-of-my-daftar-campaign.html.

Graham, Mark. 2002. "Emotional Bureaucracies: Emotions, Civil Servants, and Immigrants in the Swedish Welfare State." *Ethnos* 30:199–226.

Green, Nicole, and Todd Pierce. 2009. "Combating Statelessness: A Government Perspective." *Forced Migration Review* 32:34–35. Accessed December 11, 2013. http://www.fmreview.org/FMRpdfs/FMR32/34–35.pdf.

Griffiths, Melanie. 2012. "Anonymous Aliens? Questions of Identification in the Detention and Deportation of Failed Asylum Seekers." *Population, Space and Place* 18:715–27.

———. 2013. " 'Establishing Your True Identity': Immigration Detention and Contemporary Identification Debates." In *Identification and Registration Practices in Transnational Perspective: People, Papers and Practices*, edited by J. Brown, I. About, and G. Lonergan, 281–301. Basingstoke: Palgrave Macmillan.

———. 2014. " 'Who Is Who Now?': Truth, Trust and Identification in the British Asylum and Immigration Detention System." PhD diss., University of Oxford.

Guild, Elspeth, and Sergio Carrera. 2013. "Introduction. International Relations, Citizenship and Minority Discrimination: Setting the Scene." In *Foreigners, Refugees or Minorities? Rethinking People in the Context of Border Controls and Visas*, edited by Bigo Didier, Sergio Carrera, and Elspeth Guild, 1–20. Surrey: Ashgate.

Gutierrez, Paula. 1997. "Mexico's Dual Nationality Amendments: They Do Not Undermine U.S. Citizens' Allegiance and Loyalty or U.S. Political Sovereignty." *Loyola of Los Angeles—International and Comparative Law Review* 19:999, 1003–4.

Gyulai, Gábor, Michael Kagan, Jane Herlihy, Stuart Turner, Lilla Hárdi, and Éva Tessza Udvarhelyi. 2013. *Hungarian Helsinki Committee, Credibility Assessment in Asylum Procedures—A Multidisciplinary Training Manual*. Vol. 1. Budapest: Hungarian Helsinki Committee.

Hall, Alexandra. 2012. *Border Watch: Cultures of Immigration, Detention, and Control*. London: Pluto.

Hammarberg, Thomas. 2011. "The Romani Holocaust and Contemporary Challenges: Tackling Discrimination and Human Rights Abuse of Roma." October 21. Accessed June 1, 2015. https://wcd.coe.int/ViewDoc.jsp?p=&id=1855485&direct=true.

Hancock, Ian. 2002. *We Are the Romani People (Ame Sam E Rromane Džene)*. Hertfordshire: University of Hertfordshire Press.

Haney-Lopez, Ian. 2006. *White by Law: The Legal Construction of Race*. New York: New York University Press.

Hanks, Lucien M., Lauriston Sharp, and Jane R. Hanks. 1964. "A Report on Tribal Peoples in Chiengrai Province North of the Mae Kok River." Bennington-Cornell Anthropological Survey of Hill Tribes in Thailand. Data Paper Number 1. Bangkok: Siam Society.

Harper, Ida Husted, ed. 1922. *History of Woman Suffrage*. Vol. 6, *1900–1920*. New York: Little and Ives.

Harris, Joseph. 2013. "Uneven Inclusion: Consequences of Universal Healthcare in Thailand." *Citizenship Studies* 17:111–27.

Harvey, Alison. 2010. "Statelessness: The 'de facto' Statelessness Debate." *Immigration, Asylum and Nationality Law* 24 (3): 257–64.

Hassall, Graham. 2001. "Citizenship." In *Twenty Years of the Papua New Guinea Constitution*, edited by Anthony Regan, Woen Jessup, and Eric Kwa, 255–71. Port Moresby: University of Papua New Guinea Press.

Hayslip, Le Ly. 1993. *Child of War, Woman of Peace*. New York: Doubleday.

Hearing before the House Committee on the Judiciary, Subcommittee on Immigration Policy and Enforcement: H.R. 1932 ("Keep Our Communities Safe Act of 2011"). 2011. Accessed December 11, 2013. http://judiciary.house.gov/hearings/hear_05242011.html.

Hegel, G. W. F. 1967 [1821]. *Philosophy of Right*. Oxford: Oxford University Press.

Hertzog, Esther. 1999. *Immigrants and Bureaucrats: Ethiopians in an Israeli Absorption Center*. New York: Berghahn.

Hetherington, Kregg. 2011. *Guerilla Auditors: The Politics of Transparency in Neoliberal Paraguay*. Durham, NC: Duke University Press.

Hey, Jody. 2001. *Genes, Categories, and Species: The Evolutionary and Cognitive Causes of the Species Problem*. Oxford: Oxford University Press.

Higgs, Edward. 2004. *The Information State in England: The Central Collection of Information on Citizens since 1500*. New York: Palgrave Macmillan.

Honig, Bonnie. 2001. *Democracy and the Foreigner*. Princeton, NJ: Princeton University Press.

Houston Chronicle. 2008. "Citizenship for Midwives' Deliveries Questioned." July 21. http://www.chron.com/news/houston-texas/article/Citizenship-for-midwives -deliveries-questioned-1774064.php.

Hsu, Spencer S. 2008. "Midwife Delivery Can Lead to Passport Denial." *Washington Post*, September 9. http://www.washingtonpost.com/wp-dyn/content/article/2008/09 /08/AR2008090802623.html?wpisrc=newsletter.

Hull, Matthew S. 2012. "Documents and Bureaucracy." *Annual Review of Anthropology* 41:251–67.

Human Rights First. 2008. *2008 Hate Crime Survey*. Washington, DC: Human Rights First.

Human Rights Watch. 2014. *World Report 2014*. New York: Human Rights Watch.

Huus, Kari. 2010. "Wrongfully Deported American Home after 3 Month Fight." MSNBC. Accessed May 2, 2016. http://www.msnbc.msn.com/id/39180275/ns/us _news-immigration_a_nation_divided/t/wrongfully-deported-american-home-after -month-fight/#.UGxKf1GwVhI.

Immigration Reform Law Institute. 2012a. "Attorneys and Staff." February 19. http:// www.irli.org/about/attorneys.

———. 2012b. "Board of Directors." February 19. http://www.irli.org/about/board.

———. 2012c. "Litigation, Federal Courts, State Courts, Agencies." February 19. http:// www.irli.org/litigation.

INA § 241(a)(2), 8 U.S.C. § 1231(a)(2) (2006).

Indo-Global Social Service Society. 2012. *The Unsung CityMakers: A Study of the Homeless Residents of Delhi*. New Delhi: Indo-Global Social Service Society.

INS v. Rios-Pineda. 1985. 471 U.S. 444.

Institute on Statelessness and Inclusion. 2014. *The World's Stateless*. Oisterwijk, the Netherlands: Wolf Legal.

Irving, Helen. 2008. "Still Call Australia Home: The Constitution and the Citizen's Right of Abode." *Sydney Law Review* 30:133–53.

Isin, Engin. 2012. *Citizens without Frontiers*. New York: Continuum Books.

Al Jazeera. 2013. "Deported Roma Girl's Family Beaten in Street." October 21.

Johnson, Barbara. 1987. *A World of Difference.* Baltimore: Johns Hopkins University Press.

———. 1998. "Anthropomorphism in Lyric and Law." *Yale Journal of Law and the Humanities* 10 (2): 205–28.

Johnson, Bryan. 2013. "Once Deported and Exiled U.S. Citizen Is Officially Recognized as U.S. Citizen." Accessed May 2, 2016. http://amjolaw.com/tag/blanca-alfaro/.

Johnson, Kevin R. 2005. "The Forgotten 'Repatriation' of Persons of Mexican Ancestry and Lessons for the 'War on Terror.'" *Pace Law Review* 26 (Fall): 1–26.

Jolivet, Elen. 2003. *L'ivoirité: De la conceptualisation a la manipulation de l'identité ivoirienne.* Mémoire. Rennes: Institut d'Etudes Politiques.

Jonsson, Hjorleifur. 2006. *Mien Relations: Mountain People and State Control in Thailand.* Chiang Mai: Silkworm Books.

Jonsson, Patrik. 2012. "Mistakenly Deported US Teen Coming Home: Was She Victim or Adventurer?" *Christian Science Monitor,* January 6. http://www.csmonitor.com /USA/2012/0106/Mistakenly-deported-US-teen-coming-home.-Was-she-victim-or -adventurer.

Jordan, Miriam. 2008. "They Say They Were Born in the U.S.A. The State Department Says Prove It." *Wall Street Journal,* August 11. http://online.wsj.com/article /SB121842058533028907.html.

———. 2011. "Soldier Finds Minefield on Road to Citizenship." *Wall Street Journal,* February 10. http://online.wsj.com/article/SB10001424052748704570104576124091 336851306.html.

Kafka, Franz. 1998 [1925]. *The Trial.* New York: Schocken Books.

Kam, Noé Mahop. 2015. "Recovering the Sociological Identity of Asylum Seekers: Language Analysis for Determining National Origin in the European Union." In *Adjudicating Refugee and Asylum Status: The Role of Witness, Expert, and Testimony,* edited by Benjamin N. Lawrance and Galya Ruffer, 54–83. Cambridge: Cambridge University Press.

Kanstroom, Daniel. 2007. *Deportation Nation: Outsiders in American History.* Cambridge, MA: Harvard University Press.

Kanstroom, Daniel, and Jessica Chicco. 2015. "The Forgotten Deported: A Declaration on the Rights of Expelled and Deported Persons." NYU *Journal of International Law and Policy* 47:537–92.

Kawakita v. U.S. 1952. 343 U.S. 717, 723–24.

Kaya, Ayhan. 1999. *Sicher in Kreuzberg: Constructing Diasporas: Turkish Hip-Hop Youth in Berlin.* New Brunswick, NJ: Transaction.

Kennedy v. Mendoza-Martinez. 1963. 372 U.S. 144.

Kerber, Linda. 1998. *No Constitutional Right to Be Ladies: Women and the Constitutional Obligations of Citizenship.* New York: Hill and Wang.

Kerns, Susan K. 2000. "Country Conditions Documentation in U.S. Asylum Cases: Leveling the Evidentiary Playing Field." *Indiana Journal of Global Legal Studies* 8 (1): 197–222.

Kessler, Amalia D. 2005. "Our Inquisitorial Tradition: Equity Procedure, Due Process, and the Search for an Alternative to the Adversarial." *Cornell Law Review* 90:1181–275.

Kettner, James. 1978. *The Development of American Citizenship, 1608–1870*. Chapel Hill: University of North Carolina Press.

Keyes, Charles. 2002. Presidential Address: "'The Peoples of Asia'—Science and Politics in the Classification of Ethnic Groups in Thailand, China, and Vietnam." *Journal of Asian Studies* 61:1163–203.

Koning, Stephanie M. 2014. "Could Universal Health Care Coverage Restrict Access? The Mixed Effects of Universal Coverage on Minorities' Receipt of Obstetric Care in Northern Thailand." *Lancet Global Health* 1 (Supplement 2): S17.

Kosinski, Stacie. 2009. "State of Uncertainty: Citizenship, Statelessness and Discrimination in the Dominican Republic." *Boston College International and Comparative Law Review* 32 (2): 377–98.

Kostlán, František. 2012. "Analysis: Czech Media Baiting Romani Family Attacked by Ultra-right Arsonists." *Romea*, March 16. Accessed May 2, 2016. http://www.romea.cz/en/news/czech/analysis-czech-media-baiting-romani-family-attacked-by-ultra-right-arsonists.

Kuluszynski, Martine. 2001. "Republican Identity: Bertillonage as Government Technique." In *Documenting Individual Identity: The Development of State Practices in the Modern World*, edited by Jane Caplan and John Torpey, 123–28. Princeton, NJ: Princeton University Press.

Laertius, Diogenes. 1979 [1925]. *Lives of Eminent Philosophers*. Translated by Robert Drew Hicks. Cambridge, MA: Harvard University Press.

Lair, Meredith. 2011. *Armed with Abundance: Consumerism and Soldiering in the Vietnam War*. Chapel Hill: University of North Carolina Press.

Lake, Marilyn, and Henry Reynolds. 2008. *Drawing the Global Colour Line: White Men's Countries and the Question of Racial Equality*. Carlton: Melbourne University Press.

Lape, Susan. 2004. *Reproducing Athens: Menander's Comedy, Democratic Culture, and the Hellenistic City*. Princeton, NJ: Princeton University Press.

Lawrance, Benjamin N. 2013. "Humanitarian Claims and Expert Testimonies: Contestation over Health Care for Ghanaian Migrants in the United Kingdom." *Ghana Studies* 15–16:251–86.

———. 2015. "From 'Health Tourism' to 'Atrocious Barbarism': Contextualizing African Migrant Choice, Expertise, and Medical Humanitarian Practice." In *Adjudicating Refugee and Asylum Status: The Role of Witness, Expertise, and Testimony*, edited by Benjamin N. Lawrance and Galya Ruffer, 221–44. Cambridge: Cambridge University Press.

Lawrance, Benjamin, Iris Berger, Tricia Redeker Hepner, Joanna Tague, and Meredith Terretta. 2015. "Law, Expertise, and Protean Ideas about African Migrants." In *African Asylum at a Crossroads: Activism, Expert Testimony, and Refugee Rights*, 1–37. Athens: Ohio University Press.

Lawrance, Benjamin, and Galya Ruffer, eds. 2015. *Adjudicating Refugee and Asylum Status: The Role of Witness, Expertise, and Testimony*. Cambridge: Cambridge University Press.

Lawrance, Benjamin, and Charlotte Walker-Said. 2016. "Resisting Patriarchy, Contesting Homophobia: Expert Testimony and the Construction of African Forced Marriage Asylum Claims." In *Marriage by Force? Contestation over Consent and Coercion in*

Africa, edited by A. Bunting, B. N. Lawrance, and R. L. Roberts, 199–224. Athens: Ohio University Press.

Leach, Edmund R. 1964. *Political Systems of Highland Burma: A Study of Kachin Social Structure*. London: Athlone.

Le Courant, S. 2013. "What Can We Learn from a 'Liar' and a 'Madman'? Serendipity and Double Commitment during Fieldwork." *Social Anthropology* 21 (2): 186–98.

Lee, Erika. 2003. *At America's Gates: Chinese Immigration during the Exclusion Era, 1882–1943*. Chapel Hill: University of North Carolina Press.

Leibowitz, Arnold H. 1989. *Defining Status: A Comprehensive Analysis of United States Territorial Relations*. Dordrecht: Martinus Nijhoff.

Lemon, Don. 2010. "U.S. Citizens Deported." CNN. Accessed December 12, 2013 http://newsroom.blogs.cnn.com/2010/07/26/u-s-citizens-deported/.

Lévi-Strauss, Claude. 1969. *Elementary Structures of Kinship*. Boston: Beacon.

Levy, Daniel, and Charles Roth, eds. 2011. *U.S. Citizenship and Naturalization Handbook* 2011–2012 Edition. St. Paul, MN: Clark Boardman Callaghan.

Liégeois, Jean-Pierre. 2008. *Roma in Europe*. Strasbourg: Council of Europe Publishing.

Ling, Huping. 1998. *Surviving on Gold Mountain: A History of Chinese American Women and Their Lives*. Albany: SUNY Press.

Lok v. INS. 1977. 548 F.2d 37 (Second Circuit).

Loo, W. H., Paul H. P. Yeow, and S. C. Chong. 2009. "User Acceptance of Malaysian Government Multipurpose Smartcard Application." *Government Information Quarterly* 26:358–67.

Loraux, Nicole. 1993. *The Children of Athena: Athenian Ideas about Citizenship and the Division between the Sexes*. Translated by Caroline Levine. Princeton, NJ: Princeton University Press.

Loraux, Nicole. 2000. *Born of the Earth: Myth and Politics in Athens*. Translated by Selina Stewart. Ithaca, NY: Cornell University Press.

Lucero, Florinda, and Jill Collum. 2006. "The Roma: During and after Communism." *Human Rights and Human Welfare Topical Research Digest*: 98–106. http://www.du.edu/korbel/hrhw/researchdigest/russia/index.html.

Lynch v. Clarke. 1844. 1 Sandford 583 (New York).

Lyon, David. 2009. *Identifying Citizens: ID Cards as Surveillance*. Cambridge: Polity.

Maas, Willem. 2008–9. "Unrespected, Unequal, Hollow—Contingent Citizenship and Reversible Rights in the European Union." *Columbia Journal of International Law* 15:265–80.

Mackenzie v. Hare. 1915. 239 U.S. 299.

Malphrus, Garry. 2010. "Expert Witnesses in Immigration Proceedings." *Immigration Law Advisor* 4 (5): 1–14.

Maltz, Earl M. 2001. "The Fourteenth Amendment and Native American Citizenship." *Immigration Law and Review* 17:555–74.

Mamdani, Mahmood. 2002. *When Victims Become Killers: Colonialism, Nativism, and the Genocide in Rwanda*. Princeton, NJ: Princeton University Press.

Mandeli v. Acheson. 1952. 344 U.S. 133.

Manly, Mark, and Laura van Waas. 2010. "The Value of a Human Security Framework in Addressing Statelessness." In *Human Security and Non-citizens: Law, Policy and*

International Affairs, edited by A. Edwards and C. Ferstman, 49–81. Cambridge: Cambridge University Press.

Mapping Militant Organizations. 2012. "Revolutionary Armed Forces of Colombia—People's Army." Stanford University. Accessed December 12, 2013. http://www.stanford.edu/group/mappingmilitants/cgi-bin/groups/view/89.

Marshall, T. H. 1992 [1949]. *Citizenship and Social Class*. London: Pluto.

Martin, David A. 2001. "Graduated Application of Constitutional Protections for Aliens: The Real Meaning of *Zadvydas v. Davis*." *Supreme Court Review* 1:47–137.

Marushiakova, Elena, and Veselin Popov. 2008. *State Policies under Communism*. Strasburg: Council of Europe.

McCaskill, Don, and Ken Kampe. 1998. *Development or Domestication? Indigenous Peoples of Southeast Asia*. Chiang Mai: Silkworm Books.

McGovern, Mike. 2011. *Making War in Côte d'Ivoire*. Chicago: University of Chicago Press.

McKenzie, Beatrice. 2011. "The Power of International Positioning: The National Woman's Party, International Law, and Diplomacy, 1928–1934." *Gender and History* 23:130–46.

McKeown, Adam M. 2008. *Melancholy Order: Asian Migration and the Globalization of Borders*. New York: Columbia University Press.

McKinnon, John, and Wanat Bhruksasri. 1983. *Highlanders of Thailand*. Oxford: Oxford University Press.

McKinnon, John, and Bernard Vienne. 1989. *Hill Tribes Today: Problems in Change*. Bangkok: White Lotus-Orstom.

McKinnon, Kathryn. 2005. "(Im)Mobilization and Hegemony: 'Hill Tribe' Subjects and the 'Thai' State." *Social and Cultural Geography* 6 (1): 31–46.

Migration Act 1958 (Cth).

Miroff, Nick. 2011. "In Beseiged Mormon Colony, Mitt Romney's Mexican Roots." *Washington Post*, July 24.

Moon, Katherine H. S. 1997. *Sex among Allies: Military Prostitution in U.S.-Korean Relations*. New York: Columbia University Press.

Morawetz, Nancy. 2007a. "Citizenship and the Courts." *University of Chicago Legal Forum* 447:447–69.

———. 2007b. "The Invisible Border: Restrictions on Short-Term Travel by Noncitizens." *Georgetown Immigration Law Journal* 21:201–38.

MSNBC. 2012. "Romney's Roots: Meet Mitt Romney's Relatives in Mexico." January 9. http://video.msnbc.msn.com/rock-center/45936316.

Mukdawan Sakboon. 2009. "Citizenship and Education as the Basis for National Integration of Ethnic Minorities in North Thailand." PhD diss., Macquarie University.

Multi-American. 2011. "The Model Bill to Challenge the 14th Amendment." January 5. http://multiamerican.scpr.org/2011/01/the-model-bill-to-challenge-the-14th-amendment.

Musalo, Karen. 2015. "The Evolving Refugee Definition: How Shifting Elements of Eligibility Affect the Nature and Focus of Expert Testimony in Asylum Proceedings." In *African Asylum at a Crossroads: Activism, Expert Testimony, and Refugee Rights*, edited by Iris Berger, Tricia Redeker Hepner, Benjamin N. Lawrance, Joanna Tague, and Meredith Terretta, 75–101. Athens: Ohio University Press.

Nagano, Yuriko. 2007. "Still Wanted in Peru, Alberto Fujimori Runs for Office in Japan." *Christian Science Monitor*, July 25.

Nationality Act 1920 (Commonwealth of Australia).

Naturalisation Act 1903 (Commonwealth of Australia).

Naturalization Act of 1790 (United States of America).

Navaro-Yashin, Yael. 2003. "Legal/Illegal Counterpoints: Subjecthood and Subjectivity in an Unrecognized State." In *Human Rights in Global Perspective: Anthropological Studies of Rights, Claims and Entitlements,* edited by Richard Ashby Wilson and Jon P. Mitchell, 71–92. London: Routledge.

———. 2006. "Affect in the Civil Service: A Study of a Modern State-System." *Postcolonial Studies* 9:281–94.

———. 2007. "Make-Believe Papers, Legal Forms, and the Counterfeit: Affective Interactions between Documents and People in Britain and Cyprus." *Anthropological Theory* 7:79–96.

———. 2012. *The Make-Believe Space: Affective Geography in a Postwar Polity.* Durham, NC: Duke University Press.

Neuman, Gerald. 1987. "Book Review: Back to Dred Scott?" *San Diego Law Review* 24:485–500.

New Straits Times. 2010. "47 Years Citizenship Wait for 61-Year-Old Man." April 18. Accessed April 18, 2010. http://www.nst.com.my/Current_News/NST/articles/20100418193832/Article/index_html.

———. 2011. "Patriotism Fills the Air as 100 Become Citizens." July 29. Accessed August 7, 2011. http://www.nst.com.my/nst/articles/5hisa/Article/#ixzz1UObDZrg7.

New York Department of Health. 2004. *Documentation Guide for PRUCOL Alien Categories.* July 15.

New York Times. 2014a. "Corrections." May 23, A2.

———. 2014b. "An Old Mystery Surrounds the Clippers' Fill-In C.E.O." May 23, B13.

Ngai, Mae. 2005. *Impossible Subjects: Illegal Aliens and the Making of Modern America.* Princeton, NJ: Princeton University Press.

———. 2007. "Birthright Citizenship and the Alien Citizen." *Fordham Law Review* 75:2521–30.

Nicolosi, Ann Marie. 2000. "'We Do Not Want Our Girls to Marry Foreigners': Gender, Race and American Citizenship." *National Women's Studies Association Journal* 13:1–20.

Nietzsche, Friedrich. 1974 [1882, 1887]. *The Gay Science.* Edited by Walter Kaufmann. New York: Vintage.

Noiriel, Gérard. 2001. "The Identification of the Citizen: The Birth of Republican Civil Status in France." In *Documenting Individual Identity: The Development of State Practices in the Modern World,* edited by Jane Caplan and John Torpey, 28–48. Princeton, NJ: Princeton University Press.

Nyamnjoh, Francis. 2006. *Insiders and Outsiders: Citizenship and Xenophobia in Contemporary Southern Africa.* London: Zed Books.

Nyers, Peter. 2006. "The Accidental Citizen: Acts of Sovereignty and (Un)making Citizenship." *Economy and Society* 35:22–41.

Nzongola-Ntalaja, Georges. 2004. "Citizenship, Political Violence, and Democratization in Africa." *Global Governance* 10:403–9.

Ogolla, Chris. 2008. "Lay Midwives and Access to Healthcare in Lower Rio Grande Valley, Texas. A Clash of Two Cultures?" *Health Law Perspectives* (November):1–4. http://www.law.uh.edu/healthlaw/perspectives/2008/(CO)%20midwives.pdf.

Ong, Aihwa. 1999. *Flexible Citizenship: The Cultural Logics of Transnationality*. Durham, NC: Duke University Press.

Oommen, T. K. 1997. *Citizenship, Nationality and Ethnicity: Reconciling Competing Identities*. Cambridge: Polity.

Organization of American States. 1969. *American Convention on Human Rights*. Art. 20, § 2. 1144 U.N.T.S. 123. Accessed December 11, 2013. http://www.oas.org/juridico/english/treaties/b-32.html.

———. 2013. "Press Release: IAHCR Expresses Deep Concern over Ruling by the Constitutional Court of the Dominican Republic." Accessed December 12, 2013. http://www.oas.org/en/iachr/media_center/PReleases/2013/073.asp.

Owen, Richard. 2008. "Gypsy Shanty Towns Burn in Naples as Italian Police Swoop on Illegal Immigrants." *Times Online*, May 16.

Paine, Thomas. 1951. *The Rights of Man*. New York: Dutton.

Pandit, Ambika. 2012. "Govt's Cold Attitude Fatal for City's Homeless." *Times of India*, December 1.

———. 2013. "7,000 Homeless Get Voter IDs in Delhi." *Times of India*, October 9. Accessed March 4, 2014. http://timesofindia.indiatimes.com/home/specials/assembly-elections-2013/delhi-assembly-elections/7000-homeless-get-voter-IDs-in-Delhi/articleshow/23834874.cms.

Partridge, Eric. 1958. *Origins: A Short Etymological Dictionary of Modern English*. New York: Greenwich House.

Peschanski, Denis. 2002. "The Gypsies in the Upheaval: The Situation in France, 1939–1946." In *Roma and Sinti: Under-Studied Victims of Nazism, Symposium Proceedings*, 49–58. Washington, DC: USHMM.

Phuntip K. Saisoonthorn. 2006. "Development of Concepts of Nationality and Efforts to Reduce Statelessness in Thailand." *Refugee Survey Quarterly* 25 (3): 40–53.

Pinkaew Laungaramsri. 2003. "Ethnicity and the Politics of Ethnic Classification in Thailand." In *Ethnicity in Asia*, edited by C. Mackerras, 157–73. London: Routledge Curzon.

———. 2013. "Contested Citizenship: Cards, Colors and the Culture of Identification." In *Ethnicity, Borders, and the Grassroots Interface with the State: Studies on Southeast Asia in Honor of Charles F. Keyes*, edited by John A. Marston, 143–64. Chiang Mai: Silkworm Books.

Pitkin, Hanna. 1973. *Wittgenstein and Justice*. Berkeley: University of California Press.

Plyler v. Doe. 1982. 457 U.S. 202.

Praxis. 2008. "Legally Invisible Persons in Seven Stories: Why Should the Law on Procedure for Recognition of Persons before the Law Be Adopted." October: 4–21.

http://praxis.org.rs/images/praxis_downloads/Legally_invisible_persons_in_seven
_stories.pdf.

———. 2010. "Persons at Risk of Statelessness in Serbia: Case Studies." December: 2–53. http://www.praxis.org.rs/images/praxis_downloads/praxis-persons-at-risk-of
-statelessness-in-serbia.pdf.

Price, Polly J. 2013. "Stateless in the United States: Current Reality and a Future Prediction." *Vanderbilt Journal of Transnational Law* 46:443–514.

Pryor, Jill A. 1988. "The Natural-Born Citizen Clause and Presidential Eligibility: An Approach for Resolving Two Hundred Years of Uncertainty." *Yale Law Journal* 97:881–99.

Ramachandran, Sonia. 2007. "Finally, I Belong Here, Says Jeyaraj." *New Straits Times*, November 28.

Ramachandran, Sujata. 2015. "Capricious Citizenship: Identity, Identification, and Banglo-Indians." In *The Human Right to Citizenship: A Slippery Concept*, edited by Rhoda Howard-Hassman and Margaret Walton-Roberts, 115–29. Philadelphia: University of Pennsylvania Press.

Rawls, John. 1999. *The Law of Peoples*. Cambridge, MA: Harvard University Press.

Re Brian and Minister for Immigration and Citizenship (2008) 105 ALD 213.

Redman, Renee C. 2008. "National Identification Cards: Powerful Tools for Defining and Identifying Who Belongs in the United States." *Albany Law Review* 71:907–26.

Re Gaigo and Minister for Immigration and Citizenship [2008] AATA 590.

Reitwiesner, William Addams. 2012. "The Ancestry of Mitt Romney." William Addams Reitwiesner Genealogical Services. Accessed February 19. http://www.wargs.com
/political/romney.html.

Re MIMIA; Ex parte Ame [2005] HCATrans 66 (March 6, 2005).

Re Minister for Immigration and Multicultural and Indigenous Affairs; Ex parte Ame (2005) 222 CLR 439.

Renard, Ronald D. 2000. "The Differential Integration of Hill People into the Thai State." In *Civility and Savagery: Social Identity in Tai States*, edited by A. Turton, 63–83. Richmond, Surrey: Curzon.

Ricœur, Paul. 1965. *Freud and Philosophy: An Essay on Interpretation*. New Haven, CT: Yale University Press.

Riles, Annelise. 2006. "Introduction: In Response." In *Documents: Artifacts of Modern Knowledge*, edited by Annelise Riles, 1–40. Ann Arbor: University of Michigan Press.

Rivera v. Albright. 2000. 2000 WL 1514075 (N.D. Ill. 2000).

Roach v. Electoral Commissioner. 2007. 233 CLR 162.

Robertson, Craig. 2010. *The Passport in America: The History of a Document*. Oxford: Oxford University Press.

Romani, Mattia. 2003. "Love Thy Neighbour? Evidence from Ethnic Discrimination in Information Sharing within Villages in Côte d'Ivoire." *Journal of African Economics* 12:533–63.

Romney, Thomas Cottam. 1938. *The Mormon Colonies in Mexico*. Salt Lake City, Utah: Deseret Book Company.

Rosenbaum, David E. 1995. "George Romney Dies at 88; A Leading G.O.P. Figure." *New York Times*, July 27.

Rosenbloom, Rachel. 2013. "The Citizenship Line: Rethinking Immigration Exceptionalism." *Boston College Law Review* 54:1965–2024.

Rozzi, Elena. 2013. "Out of Limbo: Promoting the Right of Stateless Roma People to a Legal Status in Italy." November 12. *European Network on Statelessness Blog*. Accessed May 2, 2016. http://www.statelessness.eu/blog/out-limbo-promoting-right-stateless -roma-people-legal-status-italy.

Rubenstein, Kim. 2002. *Australian Citizenship Law in Context*. Sydney: Lawbook Company.

Rubin, Alissa. 2013. "Protests after France Expels 2 Immigrant Students." *New York Times,* October 17.

Sacks, Sheldon. 1964. *Fiction and the Shape of Belief: A Study of Henry Fielding, with a Glance at Swift, Johnson and Richardson*. Chicago: University of Chicago Press.

Sadiq, Kamal. 2009. *Paper Citizens: How Illegal Immigrants Acquire Citizenship in Developing Countries*. Oxford: Oxford University Press.

Safman, Rachel M. 2007. "Minorities and State-Building in Mainland Southeast Asia." In *Myanmar: State, Society, and Ethnicity*, edited by N. Ganesan and K. Y. Hlaing, 3–31. Hiroshima: Hiroshima Peace Institute.

Saito, Natsu Taylor. 2001. "Symbolism under Siege: Japanese American Redress and the 'Racing' of Arab Americans as 'Terrorists.'" *Asian Law Journal* 8:1–29.

Salvador Mondaca-Vega v. Loretta Lynch. 2015. No. 03-71369. December 15.

Sardelic, Julija. 2015. "Romani Minorities and Uneven Citizenship Access in the Post-Yugoslav Space." *Ethnopolitics* 14:159–79.

Saussure, Ferdinand de. 1986 [1916]. *Course in General Linguistics*. LaSalle, IL: Open Court.

Sayare, Scott. 2014. "France: Roma Evictions Increase." *New York Times*, January 14.

Schnapper, Dominique. 1991. *La France de l'intégration: Sociologie de la nation en 1990*. Paris: Gallimard.

Schuck, Peter, and Rogers Smith. 1985. *Citizenship without Consent: Illegal Aliens in the American Polity*. New Haven, CT: Yale University Press.

Schwartz, Eric P. 2011. "Recognizing Statelessness." *U.S. Department of State Official Blog*. Accessed December 11, 2013. http://blogs.state.gov/index.php/site/entry/recognizing _statelessness.

Scott, James C. 1998. *Seeing Like a State: How Certain Schemes to Improve the Human Condition Have Failed*. New Haven, CT: Yale University Press.

———. 2009. *The Art of Not Being Governed: An Anarchist History of Upland Southeast Asia*. New Haven, CT: Yale University Press.

Scott v. Sandford. 1857. 60 U.S. 393.

Sengupta, Ananya. 2009. "Card of Hope of a Better Future for Child." *Telegraph*, May 7. Accessed March 4, 2014. http://www.telegraphindia.com/1090507/jsp/nation/story _10928608.jsp#.

Shachar, Ayelet. 2007. "The Shifting Border of Immigration Regulation." *Stanford Journal of Civil Rights and Civil Liberties* 3:165–90.

———. 2009. *The Birthright Lottery: Citizenship and Global Inequality*. Cambridge, MA: Harvard University Press.

Shahri Adhikar Manch: Begharon Ke Liye. 2011. "Coalition for the Homeless Alarmed over Inaccurate and Biased Media Reports." Press release. July 21. New Delhi: Shahri Adhikar Manch: Begharon Ke Liye.

Shils, Edward. 1957. "Primordial, Personal, Sacred and Civilities." *British Journal of Sociology* 8:130–47.

Shore, Cris, and Susan Wright, eds. 1997. *Anthropology of Policy: Critical Perspectives on Governance and Power*. London: Routledge.

Shuman, Amy, and Carol Bohmer. 2004. "Representing Trauma: Political Asylum Narrative." *Journal of American Folklore* 117 (466): 394–414.

Sieff, Kevin. 2008a. "Harsh Reality: Faulty Midwife Practices Has the Federal Government Questioning Border Residents' Citizenship." *Brownsville Herald*, July 20. http://www.brownsvilleherald.com/news/born-88511-grande-mile.html.

———. 2008b. "Women Unite to Expose Passport Double Standard." *Brownsville Herald*, July 21. http://www.brownsvilleherald.com/news/austin-88524-one-hart.html.

Sikdar, Shubhomoy. 2013. "A Vote of Thanks from the Capital's Homeless." *The Hindu*, November 21. Accessed March 6, 2014. http://www.thehindu.com.todays-paper/tp -newdelhi/a-vote-of-thanks-from-the-capitals-homeless/article5374058.ece.

Singh v. The Commonwealth. (2004) 222 CLR 322.

Skinner, G. William. 1957. *Chinese Society in Thailand: An Analytical History*. Ithaca, NY: Cornell University Press.

Slaughterhouse Cases. 1873. 83 U.S. 36.

Smith, R. E. 1954. "Latins and the Roman Citizenship in Roman Colonies: Livy, 34, 42, 5–6." *Journal of Roman Studies* 44:18–20.

Smith, Rogers M. 1997. *Civic Ideals: Conflicting Visions of Citizenship in U.S. History*. New Haven, CT: Yale University Press.

Solomons, Selina. 1912. *How We Won the Vote in California*. San Francisco: New Woman.

Soro, Guillaume Kigbafori. 2005. *Pourquoi je suis devenu rebelle*. Paris: Seuil.

Southwick, Katherine, and M. Lynch. 2009. "Nationality Rights for All: A Progress Report and Global Survey on Statelessness." *Refugees International*. Accessed December 11, 2013. www.refintl.org/sites/default/files/RI%20Stateless%20Report_FINAL _031109.pdf.

Soysal, Yasmin. 1994. *Limits of Citizenship: Migrants and Postnational Membership in Europe*. Chicago: University of Chicago Press.

———. 2012. "Citizenship, Immigration, and the European Social Project: Rights and Obligations of Individuality." *British Journal of Sociology* 63:1–21.

Spiro, Peter. 2008. *Beyond Citizenship: American Identity after Globalization*. New York: Oxford University Press.

Spooner, Lysander. 1850. *A Defence for Fugitive Slaves, against the Acts of Congress of February 12, 1793, and September 18, 1850*. Boston: Bela Marsh.

Sretzer, Simon. 2006. "The Right of Registration: Development, Identity Registration, and Social Security—A Historical Perspective." *World Development* 35:67–86.

State Legislators for Legal Immigration. 2011. "State Lawmakers Convened in D.C. to Deliver Historic, Nationwide Correction to the 14th Amendment Misapplication." Press release. January 5.

Steinberg, Jonny. 2015. *A Man of Good Hope*. New York: Knopf.

Steinbock, Daniel J. 2004. "National Identity Cards: Fourth and Fifth Amendment Issues." *Florida Law Review* 56:697–760.

Stevens, Jacqueline. 1999. *Reproducing the State*. Princeton, NJ: Princeton University Press.

———. 2008. "Thin ICE." *Nation*, June 23.

———. 2009a. "Customs and Border Protection Destroys Birth Certificates of Mexican-American U.S.-Born Teenage Boys." Accessed May 1, 2016. http://stateswithoutnations.blogspot.com/2009/05/customs-and-border-patrol-destroys.html.

———. 2009b. *States without Nations: Citizenship for Mortals*. New York: Columbia University Press.

———. 2010. "Lawless Courts." *Nation*, November 8.

———. 2011a. "USCIS Official Jaime Yslas Testifies Falsely about Dual Citizenship." *States without Nations*. Accessed December 9, 2011. http://stateswithoutnations.blogspot.com/2011/12/uscis-official-jaime-yslas-testifies.html.

———. 2011b. "U.S. Government Unlawfully Detaining and Deporting U.S. Citizens as Aliens." *University of Virginia Journal of Social Policy and the Law* 18:606–720.

———. 2011–13. Frank Serna tag. *States without Nations*. Accessed May 1, 2016. http://stateswithoutnations.blogspot.com/search/label/Esteban%20Serna/.

———. 2011–14. Andres Robles tag. *States without Nations*. Accessed May 1, 2016. http://stateswithoutnations.blogspot.com/search/label/Andres%20Robles/.

———. 2012. "U.S. Citizen Mark Lyttle Settles Lawsuit for Deportation, Government Conducts Sham Investigation." *States without Nations*. October 12. http://stateswithoutnations.blogspot.com/2012/10/us-citizen-mark-lyttle-settles-lawsuit.html/.

———. 2013a. "Ex-Immigration Judge Jimmie Benton to U.S. Citizen: Go Tell It to the Government." *States without Nations*. Accessed November 7, 2013. http://stateswithoutnations.blogspot.com/2013/11/ex-immigration-judge-jimmie-benton-to.html.

———. 2013b. "Massachusetts Native, Deported for Ten Years, Sues for $12 Million." *States without Nations*. January. http://stateswithoutnations.blogspot.com/2013/01/massachusetts-native-deported-for-ten.html/.

———. 2015a. "The Deportation Research Clinic and Forensic Intelligence: Toward a New Paradigm." *Perspectives on Politics* 13 (September): 722–38.

———. 2015b. "Probable U.S. Citizen Robinson Martinez Returns after Deportation: Locked Up as Alien." *States without Nations*. Accessed May 1, 2016. http://stateswithoutnations.blogspot.com/2015/06/probable-us-citizen-robinson-martinez.html/.

Stewart, David. 1989. "The Hermeneutics of Suspicion." *Literature and Theology* 3:296–307.

Stock, Margaret. 2009. *Essential to the Fight: Immigrants in the Military Eight Years after 9/11*. Washington, DC: Immigration Policy Center.

———. 2012. "The Cost to Americans and America of Ending Birthright Citizenship." National Foundation for American Policy. February: 1–25. http://www.nfap.com/pdf/NFAPPolicyBrief.BirthrightCitizenship.March2012.pdf.

Stoler, Ann. 2002. *Carnal Knowledge and Imperial Power*. Berkeley: University of California Press.

———. 2004. "Affective States." In *A Companion to the Anthropology of Politics*, edited by David Nugent and Joan Vincent, 4–20. Malden, MA: Blackwell.

Sturgeon, J. 2005. *Border Landscapes: The Politics of Akha Land Use in China and Thailand*. Seattle: University of Washington Press.

Supreme Court Commissioners. 2009. *Ninth Report of the Commissioners*. CWP 196/2001. September.

Szreter, Simon. 2007. "The Right of Registration: Development, Identity Registration, and Social Security—A Historical Perspective." *World Development* 35:67–86.

Taylor, John P. 2001. "Authenticity and Sincerity in Tourism." *Annals of Tourism Research* 28:7–26.

Telegraph. 2011. "Silvio Berlusconi Attacks Italy's 'Gypsy-Loving' Left-Wing." May 23.

Thin Thai. 1986. "Order Given to Survey KMT Troops, Carry Out Final Registration." March 13. Radio broadcast in Thai. Translation available through handle.dtic.mil/100.2/ADA342412.

Thomas, Robert. 2011. *Administrative Justice and Asylum Appeals: A Study of Tribunal Adjudication*. Oxford: Hart.

Thongchai Winichakul. 1994. *Siam Mapped: A History of the Geo-Body of a Nation*. Honolulu: University of Hawai'i Press.

———. 2000a. "The Others Within: Travel and Ethno-Spatial Differentiation of Siamese Subjects: 1885–1910." In *Civility and Savagery: Social Identity in Tai States*, edited by A. Turton, 38–62. Richmond, Surrey: Curzon.

———. 2000b. "The Quest for 'Siwilai': A Geographical Discourse of Civilizational Thinking in the Late Nineteenth and Early Twentieth-Century Siam." *Journal of Asian Studies* 59:528–49.

Thuen, Trond. 2004. "Anthropological Knowledge in the Courtroom: Conflicting Paradigms." *Social Anthropology* 12:265–87.

Tinker Salas, Miguel. 1996. "Sonora: The Making of a Border Society, 1880–1910." In *U.S.-Mexico Borderlands: Historical and Contemporary Perspectives*, edited by Oscar J. Martínez, 86–97. Wilmington, DE: Rowman and Littlefield.

Todres, Jonathan. 2003. "Birth Registration: An Essential First Step toward Ensuring the Rights of All Children." *Human Rights* 10 (Spring): 32–35.

Torpey, John. 2000. *The Invention of the Passport: Surveillance, Citizenship and the State*. Cambridge: Cambridge University Press.

Toyota, Mika. 2005. "Subjects of the Nation without Citizenship: The Case of 'Hill Tribes' in Thailand." In *Multiculturalism in Asia*, edited by Will Kymlicka and Baogang He, 110–35. Oxford: Oxford University Press.

Trevino v. Clinton. 2007. No. 07-cv-00218 (S.D. Tx.). Declaration of Joe Rivera.

Türk, Volker. 2014. "Introductory Remarks by the Director of International Protection, UNHCR at the International Conference on Migration and Statelessness: Identifying Challenges and the Way Forward." June 23–24, Ashgabat, Turkmenistan.

Ulloa, Jazmine. 2010. "Born to Be Barred." *Texas Observer*, May 13. http://www.texasobserver.org/cover-story/born-to-be-barred.

UNESCO. 2008. *Capacity Building on Birth Registration and Citizenship in Thailand: Citizenship Manual.* Bangkok: UNESCO.

UN General Assembly, Convention on the Reduction of Statelessness, August 30, 1961, United Nations, Treaty Series, vol. 989:1–16.

UNHCR (Hugh Massey). 2010. Legal and Protection Policy Research Series: UNHCR and De Facto Statelessness. April. http://www.unhcr.org/4bc2ddeb9.pdf.

———. 2013. "Beyond Proof: Credibility Assessment in EU Asylum Systems." May.

———. 2014a. "Cartagena+30: Latin America and the Caribbean Adopt a Common Roadmap to Address New Displacement Trends and End Statelessness within the Next Decade." Accessed February 10, 2015. http://www.acnur.org/cartagena30/en /background-and-challenges.

———. 2014b. *Handbook on Protection of Stateless Persons.* Geneva: UNHCR.

UNHCR/Asylum Aid. 2011. "Mapping Statelessness in the United Kingdom."

UNHCR Division of International Protection. 2010. "UNHCR Action to Address Statelessness: A Strategy Note." *International Journal of Refugee Law* 22:297–98.

UNICEF. 1998. "UNICEF on Deficient Birth Registration in Developing Countries." *Population and Development Review* 24:659–64.

———. 2007. "Breaking the Cycle of Exclusion: Roma Children in South East Europe." Belgrade, Serbia: UNICEF. http://www.unicef.org/ceecis/070305-Subregional_Study _Roma_Children.pdf.

———. 2011. "The Right of Roma Children to Education: Position Paper." Geneva: UNICEF Regional Office for Central and Eastern Europe and the Commonwealth of Independent States.

UNICEF Innocenti Research Centre. 2002. Birth Registration: Right from the Start.

United States Code 8, §§ 1401–1402, 1409, 1503; 42, §§ 1983, 1988(b).

UN News Centre. 2010. "Half of Roma Children Drop Out of Primary School, UN-Backed Report Finds." September 27.

Urtetiqui v. D'Arcy. 1835. 34 U.S. 692.

U.S. Department of Commerce, Census Bureau. 2012. "State and County Quickfacts, Texas." Accessed May 2, 2016. http://www.census.gov/quickfacts/table/PST120214/48.

U.S. Department of Homeland Security, Customs and Border Protection. 2012. "Western Hemisphere Travel Initiative." Accessed May 2, 2016. http://getyouhome.gov/html /lang_eng/index.html.

U.S. Department of State. 2008a. *Bolivia Country Reports on Human Rights Practices.* Accessed December 11, 2013. http://www.state.gov/j/drl/rls/hrrpt/2008/wha/119149.htm.

———. 2008b. *Brazil Country Reports on Human Rights Practices.* Accessed December 11, 2013. http://www.state.gov/j/drl/rls/hrrpt/2008/wha/119150.htm.

———. 2008c. Ecuador Country Reports on Human Rights Practices. Accessed December 11, 2013. http://www.state.gov/j/drl/rls/hrrpt/2008/wha/119158.htm.

———. 2009. Foreign Affairs Manual: Acquisition of U.S. Citizenship by Birth in the United States. 7 FAM 1110. August 21.

———. 2010a. Costa Rica Country Reports on Human Rights Practices. Accessed December 11, 2013. http://www.state.gov/documents/organization/160159.pdf.

———. 2010b. *Peru Country Reports on Human Rights Practices*. Accessed December 11, 2013. http://www.state.gov/documents/organization/160473.pdf.

———. 2011a. *Bahamas Country Reports on Human Rights Practices*. Accessed December 11, 2013. htttp://www.state.gov/documents/organization/186698.pdf.

———. 2011b. *Bolivia Country Reports on Human Rights Practices*. Accessed December 11, 2013. http://www.state.gov/j/drl/rls/hrrpt/humanrightsreport/index.htm?dlid=186494.

———. 2011c. *Brazil Country Reports on Human Rights Practices*. Accessed December 11, 2013. http://www.state.gov/documents/organization/186707.pdf.

———. 2011d. Colombia Country Reports on Human Rights Practices. Accessed December 11, 2013. http://www.state.gov/j/drl/rls/hrrpt/humanrightsreport/index.htm?dlid=186502.

———. 2011e. Costa Rica Country Reports on Human Rights Practices. Accessed December 11, 2013. http://www.state.gov/j/drl/rls/hrrpt/humanrightsreport/index.htm?dlid=186503.

———. 2011f. Ecuador Country Reports on Human Rights Practices. Accessed December 11, 2013. http://www.state.gov/j/drl/rls/hrrpt/humanrightsreport/index.htm?dlid=186512.

———. 2011g. *Nicaragua Country Reports on Human Rights Practices*. Accessed December 11, 2013. http://www.state.gov/j/drl/rls/hrrpt/humanrightsreport/index.htm?dlid=186529.

———. 2011h. *Peru Country Reports on Human Rights Practices*. Accessed December 11, 2013. http://www.state.gov/j/drl/rls/hrrpt/humanrightsreport/index.htm?dlid=186536.

———. 2012a. *Dominican Republic Country Reports on Human Rights Practices*. Accessed December 11, 2013. http://www.state.gov/j/drl/rls/hrrpt/humanrightsreport/#wrapper.

———. 2012b. *Nicaragua Country Reports on Human Rights Practices*. Accessed April 28, 2016. http://www.refworld.org/docid/517e6dfbf.html.

———. 2013. Form DS-5513, Supplemental Questionnaire to Determine Entitlement for a U.S. Passport. Accessed April 29, 2016. http://www.state.gov/documents/organization/213293.pdf.

U.S. Department of State, Office of the Inspector General. 2009. *Report of Inspection, The Bureau of Consular Affairs, Passport Services*. http://oig.state.gov/documents/organization/128607.pdf.

U.S. House of Representatives. 2008. Problems with ICE Interrogation, Detention, and Removal Procedures: Hearing before the Subcommittee on Immigration, Citizenship, Refugees, Border Security and International Law of the H. Comm. on the Judiciary, 110th Congress. Accessed May 8, 2016. https://www.gpo.gov/fdsys/pkg/CRPT-110hrpt941/html/CRPT-110hrpt941.htm.

U.S. House of Representatives. 2011. Chairman Smith Introduces Keep Our Communities Safe Act. Committee on Judiciary. Accessed December 11, 2013. http://www.gpo.gov/fdsys/pkg/CHRG-112hhrg66539/html/CHRG-112hhrg66539.htm.

U.S. Office of Personnel Management Investigations Service. 2001. *Citizenship Laws of the World*. Accessed December 11, 2013. http://www.multiplecitizenship.com /documents/IS-01.pdf.

U.S. v. Leu Jin. 1911. 192 F. 580.

U.S. v. Wong Kim Ark. 1898. 169 U.S. 649.

Valencia-Webber, Gloria, and Antionette Sedillo Lopez. 2010. "Stories in Mexico and the United States about the Border: The Rhetoric and the Realities." *Intercultural Human Rights Law Review* 5:241–312.

Vandergeest, Peter, and Nancy Lee Peluso. 1995. "Territorialization and State Power in Thailand." *Theory and Society* 24:385–426.

Van Waas, Laura. 2008. *Nationality Matters: Statelessness under International Law.* Antwerp: Intersentia.

Villazor, Rose Cuison. 2008. "Blood Quantum Land Laws and the Race versus Political Identity Dilemma." *California Law Review* 96:801–37.

———. 2015. "Update on American Samoa Birthright Citizenship Case: *Tuaua v. United States.*" *Law Professor Blogs Network.* Accessed 5 May, 2015. http://lawprofessors .typepad.com/immigration/2015/02/update-on-american-samoa-birthright -citizenship-case.html.

VINCI Foundation and Reporters d'Espoirs. 2010. "The 'Hors la Rue' ('Off the Street') Association: 'We Must Help Solitary Romany Children.'" October.

Vogel, Chris. 2008. "Hispanics Delivered by Border Midwives Are Having Trouble Getting U.S. Passports." *Houston Chronicle*, December 17. http://www.houstonpress .com/2008-12-18/news/hispanics-delivered-by-border-midwives-are-having-trouble -getting-u-s-passports/.

Volpp, Leti. 2005. "Divesting Citizenship: On Asian American History and the Loss of Citizenship through Marriage." *UCLA Law Review* 53:405–83.

———. 2006/2007. "Citizenship Undone." *Fordham Law Review* 75:2579–86.

Waiko, John Dademo. 1993. *A Short History of Papua New Guinea.* Melbourne: Oxford University Press Australia and New Zealand.

Walsh, Nonee. 2014. "Advocates Want Law Abolished after Thousands Taken Off Electoral Roll for Being of 'Unsound Mind.'" *ABC News.* Accessed January 30, 2014. www.abc.net.au/news/2014-01-25/thousands-taken-off-electoral-roll-for-being-of -unsound-mind/5218656.

Walzer, Michael. 1983. *Spheres of Justice: A Defense of Pluralism and Equality.* New York: Basic Books.

Wang, Horng-luen. 2004. "Regulating Transnational Flows of People: An Institutional Analysis of Passports and Visas as a Regime of Mobility." *Identities: Global Studies in Culture and Power* 11:351–76.

Warburton, William. 1837 [1742]. *The Divine Legation of Moses Demonstrated.* Vol. 2. London: Thomas Tegg and Son.

Warnke, Adam. 1999. "Vagabonds, Tinkers, and Travelers: Statelessness among the East European Roma." *Indiana Journal of Global Legal Studies* 7 (1): 335–67.

Washington Post. 2001. "Md. Family Ensnared in Immigration Maze." April 24.

———. 2003. "U.S. to End Registration Program." December 2.

Washington Times. 2011. "Willard 'Mitt' Mitt Romney." December 7.

Weber, Max. 1978. *Economy and Society: An Outline of Interpretive Sociology*. 2 vols. Berkeley: University of California Press.

White, Bob. 2008. *Rumba Rules: The Politics of Dance Music in Mobutu's Zaire*. Durham, NC: Duke University Press.

Whyte, Zacha. 2011. "Enter the Myopticon: Uncertain Surveillance in the Danish Asylum System." *Anthropology Today* 27 (3): 18–21.

Wolfers, Edward P. 1975. *Race Relations and Colonial Rule in Papua New Guinea*. Sydney: Australia and New Zealand Book Company.

Wolters, Oliver. 1982. *History, Culture, and Region in Southeast Asian Perspectives*. Ithaca, NY: Southeast Asia Studies Press.

Woods, Dwayne. 2003. "The Tragedy of the Cocoa Pod: Rent-Seeking, Land and Ethnic Conflict in Ivory Coast." *Journal of Modern African Studies* 41:641–55.

Wydra, Elizabeth B. 2011. "Truths and Untruths about the Constitutional Origins of Birthright Citizenship." *Huffington Post*, August 17. http://www.huffingtonpost.com /elizabeth-b-wydra/truths-and-untruths-about_b_811880.htm.

Yamuna and Minister for Immigration and Citizenship [2012] AATA 383.

Yean and Bosico v. Dominican Republic. 2005. Judgment, Inter-Am. Ct. H.R. Accessed December 11, 2013. http://www.refworld.org/docid/44e497d94.html.

Yngvesson, Barbara, and Susan Bibler Coutin. 2006. "Backed by Papers: Undoing Persons, Histories, and Return." *American Ethnologist* 33:177–90.

Yuh, Ji-Yeon. 2002. *Beyond the Shadow of Camptown: Korean Military Brides in America*. New York: New York University Press.

Zadvydas v. Davis. 2001. 533 U.S. 678.

Zeiger, Susan. 2010. *Entangling Alliances: Foreign War Brides and American Soldiers in the 20th Century*. New York: New York University Press.

Ziff, Paul. 1967. *Semantic Analysis*. Ithaca, NY: Cornell University Press.

CONTRIBUTORS

ALFRED BABO is Assistant Professor of Anthropology and African Studies at Smith College. As Resident Scholar, he directs the Humanities Lab on "Forced Displacement, Immigration and Refugees." Babo taught at the University of Bouaké, Ivory Coast, before joining Smith College. In the fall of 2016, he will be joining Fairfield University. Babo's research focuses on sustainable development, social change, immigration, and conflict and postconflict society. He is the author of *L'étranger en Côte d'Ivoire: Crises et controverses autour d'une catégorie sociale* (2013). He is a member of CIRDIS-University of Quebec in Montreal, and the 2004 recipient of the Royal Museum for Central Africa, Belgian Development Cooperation Prize.

JACQUELINE BHABHA is a Professor of the Practice of Health and Human Rights at the Harvard School of Public Health, the Jeremiah Smith Jr. Lecturer in Law at Harvard Law School, an Adjunct Lecturer in Public Policy at the Harvard Kennedy School, and the Director of Research at the FXB Center for Health and Human Rights. A graduate of Oxford University, she practiced law in London and at the Strasbourg European Court of Human Rights, before moving to the academy in the United States. Bhabha directed the University of Chicago Human Rights Program from 1997 to 2001. She has published on transnational child migration, refugee protection, and children's rights and citizenship, including *Children without a State* (2011) and *Child Migration and Human Rights in a Global Age* (2014).

JACQUELINE FIELD is an Australian lawyer. She has been working with Kim Rubenstein in the area of citizenship law since 2012, including on the second edition of Rubenstein's book *Australian Citizenship Law in Context* (forthcoming). Jacqueline is currently based in Singapore and has previously worked with a regional nongovernmental organization that advocates for migrant worker rights.

AMANDA FLAIM (James Madison College, Michigan State University) is the former lead research consultant on statelessness to UNESCO in Thailand and to UNHCR in Nepal. Her studies, which comprise two of the largest and most comprehensive studies of statelessness conducted to date, have subsequently informed policy and legal reforms in both countries. Prior to joining the faculty at James Madison College, she served as a Postdoctoral Associate at Duke University in joint positions at the Sanford School of Public Policy, the Social Science Research Institute, and the Kenan Institute for Ethics. Her dissertation, "No Land's Man: Sovereignty, Legal Status, and the Production of Statelessness among Highlanders in Northern Thailand" (2015), is available through Cornell University Libraries.

SARA L. FRIEDMAN is Associate Professor of Anthropology and Gender Studies at Indiana University, Bloomington. She has written on intimacy and state power, gender and sexuality in Chinese societies, and citizenship and immigration. Her recent books include *Exceptional States: Chinese Immigrants and Taiwanese Sovereignty* (2015) and the coedited volume *Migrant Encounters: Intimate Labor, the State, and Mobility across Asia* (2015).

DANIEL KANSTROOM is Professor of Law, Thomas F. Carney Distinguished Scholar, and Associate Director of the Center for Human Rights and International Justice, Boston College. His research interests include immigration and refugee law, human rights law, and constitutional and administrative law. He cofounded the Post-Deportation Human Rights Project, which conceptualizes new legal theories while representing U.S. deportees. Recent books include *Constructing Immigrant "Illegality": Critiques, Experiences, and Responses* (2013), coedited with Cecilia Menjívar; *Aftermath: Deportation Law and the New American Diaspora* (2012); and *Deportation Nation: Outsiders in American History* (2007). He was a member of the Immigration Commission of the American Bar Association.

BENJAMIN N. LAWRANCE is the Hon. Barber B. Conable, Jr. Endowed Chair in International Studies and Professor of History and Anthropology at the Rochester Institute of Technology. His research interests include comparative and contemporary slavery, human trafficking, cuisine and globalization, human rights, refugee issues, and asylum policies. Among his ten books are *Amistad's Orphans: An Atlantic Story of Children, Slavery, and Smuggling* (2014) and *Adjudicating Refugee and Asylum Status: The Role of Witness, Expertise, and Testimony* (2015), with Galya Ruffer. Lawrance consults on contemporary West Africa issues and has served as expert witness in more than three hundred asylum claims.

BEATRICE MCKENZIE is Associate Professor of History at Beloit College. She studies how legal structures have shaped categories of American citizens. Before joining Beloit in 2006, she studied at the University of Oregon. She was previously a U.S. diplomat in embassies in Cape Verde, Uganda, and Hong Kong and a Peace Corps volunteer in Burkina Faso. Her dissertation on U.S. birthright citizenship law, "American at Birth: U.S. Citizenship in Nation and Empire, 1868–1934," examines the ways in which U.S. birthright citizenship law, thought exceptionally liberal and universal, has been used throughout U.S. history to create distinct categories of citizens based on the child's or parent's race and/or gender.

POLLY J. PRICE is Professor of Law and Associated Faculty, Department of History, at Emory University. An honors graduate of Harvard Law School, Price is the author of two books and numerous articles on American legal history, citizenship, immigration, property rights, and the judiciary. Her areas of expertise include immigration law, legislation and administrative law, global public health law, and Latin American legal systems. She was an invited speaker at the first Global Forum on Statelessness, held at The Hague in 2014.

RACHEL E. ROSENBLOOM is Professor of Law at Northeastern University School of Law, where she teaches courses on immigration law, refugee and asylum law, and administrative law. Prior to beginning her teaching career, she was the supervising attorney at the Post-Deportation Human Rights Project. Her recent scholarship has focused on the intersection of criminal law and immigration law, the possibilities and limits of transnational legal advocacy in advancing the rights of deportees, and the role of race and immigration enforcement in the construction of U.S. citizenship.

KIM RUBENSTEIN is Professor in the ANU College of Law at the Australian National University, where she was also the Director of the Centre for International and Public Law (2006–2015) and the Inaugural Convenor of the ANU Gender Institute (2011–2012). She is also a Public Policy Fellow at the Australian National University. She is Australia's leading expert on citizenship, and her research also covers gender and public law. She is coeditor of the Cambridge University Press series Connecting International Law with Public Law, which includes the fifth volume coedited with Fiona Jenkins and Mark Nolan, *Allegiance and Identity in a Globalised World* (2014).

KAMAL SADIQ is Associate Professor of Political Science at the University of California, Irvine, and author of *Paper Citizens: How Illegal Immigrants Acquire Citizenship in Developing Countries* (2009). He specializes in citizenship, immigration, urbanization, and law and society in developing countries. His regional expertise is in South Asia (India, Pakistan) and Southeast Asia (Malaysia, Indonesia). He was Chair of the Ethnicity, Nationalism, and Migration section of the International Studies Association (2013–15). He currently serves as Co-President of the Citizenship and Migration section of the American Political Science Association (2015–17).

JACQUELINE STEVENS is Professor in Political Science and Legal Studies at Northwestern University and founding director of the Deportation Research Clinic at the Buffett Institute for Global Studies. She teaches political and legal theory. She received a Guggenheim Fellowship for her project "200 Percent American," a work of literary nonfiction that will present contemporary experiences of deportation in the context of fictional narratives influencing the Spanish and English conquests of the Americas. Her research has been covered by the *New Yorker*, the *New York Times*, and NPR and has been the basis of successful lawsuits challenging government misconduct.

MARGARET D. STOCK, Lieutenant Colonel (retired), is an attorney with Cascadia Cross Border Law Group LLC in Anchorage and a 2013 MacArthur Foundation Fellow. She transferred to the Retired U.S. Army Reserve in 2010 after twenty-eight years as a Military Police officer. A graduate of Harvard-Radcliffe, Harvard Law School, and the Army

War College, Stock is admitted to practice law in Alaska, the U.S. District Court for the District of Alaska, and the U.S. Ninth Circuit Court of Appeals. She has also served as a member of the American Bar Association's Commission on Immigration. She authored *Immigration Law and the Military* and numerous articles and book chapters on citizenship issues.

civil conflict, 3, 32, 33, 35, 83, 233

civil war: Ivory Coast, 200, 201, 203, 204, 206, 216n8; U.S., 181, 182

class. *See* social class

Cold War, 48, 83, 128, 150

Colombia, 32–33, 39

colonialism, 13, 77, 86, 119, 140, 170, 208; in Papua New Guinea, 100–114; postcolonialism, 15, 23n6, 167–68, 227

Comaroff, Jean, and John L. Comaroff, 203, 204

common law, 119, 181–82

communicative methodology, 58

Constitution: Australia, 106–9, 113n11, 114n17; Dominican Republic, 31; Egypt, 197; Germany (Weimar), 47; Ivory Coast, 207, 208, 210, 212; Mexico, 230; Papua New Guinea, 102, 104–7, 109, 111. *See also* Fourteenth Amendment (U.S. Constitution)

consulate, 32, 38, 40, 118, 128, 198, 213. *See also* embassy

Costa Rica, 12, 32–33, 34

Couitin, Susan, 5, 20, 82, 97n1

country conditions, 61–62, 67, 70, 72, 74, 75; claimant narratives and, 76–77

Country of Origin Information (COI), 66–67, 76, 77

courts: Asylum and Immigration Tribunal (AIT), 66; Australian High Court, 13, 100–102, 105–7, 109, 111–12, 113n11; European Court of Human Rights, 48–49; immigration, 3, 11, 17, 36, 66, 166, 237n16; Inter-American Court of Human Rights, 31; and legislatures, 16–23; U.S. Supreme Court, 9, 113n12, 122, 127, 129, 141, 181–84, 188, 192, 197n2, 198n9, 231. *See also* United States court cases

criminal activities, 49, 127, 212

criminal conviction, 36, 62, 63, 70–71, 77, 135–36, 138, 216, 228

criminal law, 19, 77, 89, 181–83, 188, 199n15, 222, 225, 231–32, 277

Czech Republic, 47–48, 49, 51, 56

Das, Veena, 89, 96, 99n14, 225, 230

deconstruction, 5, 17, 22, 23n4, 44, 219, 221, 239n29

democracy, 17, 18, 30, 43, 171, 204

Dent, Sazar, 35–36. *See also* United States court cases

deportation, 5, 8, 17, 23n5, 35–38, 42n7, 48, 49–50, 54–57, 57n3, 59n7, 60, 70, 74, 76, 77, 102, 107, 117, 129, 141, 196, 219, 221, 226, 231–32, 238n22, 239n28, 241–45; of aliens who are citizens, 227–30; wrongful, ix–xiii, 14, 31, 143, 153, 237nn15–16

Derrida, Jacques, 5–6, 13, 17, 20–21, 219–20, 225, 233–35, 238n27, 239n29

descent, citizenship laws of, 8, 24n8, 31, 38–40, 46, 52, 55, 118, 120–23, 128, 134–35, 142, 163, 166, 171, 175, 181–82, 197, 199, 202, 226–29, 244. *See also* ancestry; jus sanguinis; parentage

detainment, 17, 36, 42n7, 63, 135

Deutsch, Karl, 202

developing countries, 15, 165–70, 174, 277

DeWitt, General John, 243

Diogenes, 241–43, 245

discrimination, 16, 28, 41, 43, 47–50, 55–58, 59n6, 71, 77, 111–12, 148, 151, 162–63, 173, 192, 201, 206, 213–14, 229, 241; nondiscrimination, 33, 42n2, 44, 48, 53

DNA, 2, 15, 19, 147, 156–58, 163

documentary acts, 88–89, 95, 96

documentary border crossings, 83–88

documentary life of citizenship and passports, 139–46

documents and documentation, 75–76; and birthright citizenship in U.S. history, 117–31; and contested sovereignty across the Taiwan Strait, 81–99; powers of, 203–6; and statelessness in Britain, 68–72. *See also* identity documents

Dominican Republic, 31–32, 147

dual citizen. *See* citizen: dual

Eastman, John, 182, 183–84, 186, 193, 196

Ecuador, 32, 39

education, 12, 19, 28, 46, 49, 52, 54–56, 59nn6–7, 68, 121, 151, 154, 202; school records, 46, 54, 65, 67, 132, 138

effective citizenship, 11, 17, 23n5, 53, 169

effective statelessness, 2–4, 8, 11, 13, 14, 28, 41, 50–51, 146n2, 163, 171, 172, 175–76, 229; expanded citizenship and, 151–52; Latin American examples of, 30–35; U.S. examples of, 35–38. *See also* statelessness

Hollande, President François (France), 49
homeless, 15, 51, 166, 172–75, 224, 242
Houphouët-Boigny, President Félix (Ivory Coast), 208–9, 211
Human Being Project, 20
human rights, 17, 27, 29, 30–31, 42n2, 49, 55, 61, 243, 245
human rights courts and treaties: American Convention on Human Rights, 42n2; European Convention on Human Rights, 69, 70, 72; European Court of Human Rights, 48–49; Inter-American Commission on Human Rights, 31; Inter-American Court of Human Rights, 31
Hungary, 47–48, 56, 78

"Ibrahim," 68, 71–72, 74, 77
identity, 2–7, 9–10, 13, 18, 20, 23n3, 36, 46, 53, 56, 66, 68, 69, 70, 73, 74, 76–78; adjudicating, 89–91; legal, 5, 56, 78, 84; national, 7, 20, 56, 77, 81, 83; proof of, 63–64, 65, 71, 85, 118, 139, 174, 201, 202
identity documents (IDs), 3, 6, 96, 155, 159, 173; circulation effects, 91–94; national, 18, 33, 151, 167, 170, 171, 176, 203, 214, 215. See also passports; travel documents
immigrants, 7, 32, 37, 81, 83–84, 89, 90, 96, 97, 101, 119, 130n1, 144, 159, 165, 166, 175, 187, 189, 208, 221; Chinese, 82, 120–24, 143, 174; illegal, 40, 167, 171–72; unauthorized, 182–83, 185–86, 188–89, 191–92, 196, 198nn7–8
immigration, 2, 38, 76, 83–84, 92, 120, 123–24, 126–28, 135, 152, 181–82, 209, 224; courts of, 3, 11, 17, 36, 66, 166, 237n16; detention centers, 11, 62, 65, 70, 71, 72; laws and regulations of, 52, 63, 65, 74, 84, 85, 86, 94–96, 102, 107, 120–21, 129, 142, 179, 185–88, 198n8, 228, 230. See also judges: immigration
immigration agents, 42, 68, 70, 94, 118, 120–25, 128, 139, 141, 223; erratic behavior of, 230–33, 237n16
India, 4, 14, 15, 20, 47, 166–75, 195, 196, 225
indigenous people, 32–34, 41, 75, 100, 102, 104, 106, 113n15, 169. See also Americans: Native; primordialist discourse; Thailand: Highlanders

integration, 4, 43, 54–58, 59n8, 74, 152, 154, 160, 205, 211
international conventions and treaties, 28–30, 50, 52, 69–70, 72. See also League of Nations; United Nations
international courts, 31, 48–49
Ireland, 59n3, 194
Italy, 30, 47, 49, 52, 55, 180
ivoirité, 16, 74; implementation and practice of, 206–10; and political and social practice, 211–14
Ivory Coast, Republic of, 16, 18, 72, 200–216

Jamaica, ix–xiii, 23
Japan, 103, 129, 131
Japanese, 103, 129, 131, 144, 229, 238n17, 243–44, 246n2
judges, 11, 13–14, 21, 22, 73, 75, 76, 79n19, 90, 121, 127, 139, 181, 201, 212–15, 223–26, 228, 234; immigration, 36, 63–64, 67–68, 69, 70, 72, 74, 79n9, 227, 229, 232–33
jus charta, 165, 175, 176. See also forensic analysis
jus sanguinis, 6, 31, 37, 38–40, 51, 74, 118, 129, 160, 163, 165, 171, 173, 175–76, 181, 203, 207, 216n6; and race (U.S.), 123–26. See also descent, citizenship laws of; parentage
jus soli, 6, 8, 12, 23n5, 50, 74, 88, 118, 119, 133, 139, 149, 160, 163, 165, 171, 173, 175–76, 181, 203, 207, 227, 244; and gender, 126–28; generational promise of, 38–41; and statelessness, 27–42

Kafka, Franz, 17, 21, 234–35, 239n28
Kanstroom, Daniel, 17, 241–46
kinship, 7, 24n8, 150, 201, 214. See also family
Kirby, Justice (Australia), 106, 109, 110
"Kofi," 68, 69–70, 74, 75, 77
Kosovo, 48, 55–57

labor, 34, 83, 103, 202, 204, 210, 215, 244, 246n4; U.S. Dept. of Labor, 122, 124
Laertius, Diogenes, 241
Lake, Marilyn, 110
land access and ownership, 33, 77, 202, 203, 205, 208–9, 210, 215–16
language and linguistics, 21, 50, 51, 55, 67, 70, 75, 85, 122, 149, 152, 161, 201, 206, 214; bilingual skills, 221

West Africa, 61, 200, 204, 206, 208, 213, 216n1

Western Hemisphere Travel Initiative (WHTI), 134, 141–43, 145–46

Wolfers, Edward, 103–5

Wong, James, 123–26

World War I, 118–19, 122–23, 144

World War II, 44, 48, 103, 125, 128, 149, 150, 229

xenophobia, 49, 150, 204–6

Ying-jeou, President Ma (Taiwan), 86

Yngvesson, Barbara, 20, 82

Yugoslavia, 48, 51–52

Zaïre, 203

Zambia, 203